ELECTRICITY
AND
THE ENVIRONMENT
The Reform of Legal Institutions

Report of
The Association of the Bar
of the City of New York
Special Committee on Electric
Power and the
Environment

SHELDON OLIENSIS, Chairman

Maurice Axelrad	William F. Kennedy
Dana C. Backus	Robert Lowenstein
Albert K. Butzel	Arthur W. Murphy
Theodore J. Carlson	Sheldon Raab
James B. Henry	David Sive

CHARLES A. EHREN, Jr.,
Executive Director

CLIFFORD P. CASE, III
and
DAVID SCHOENBROD
Staff Attorneys

ST. PAUL, MINN.
WEST PUBLISHING CO. –
1972

Electricity and the Environment

FOREWORD

On behalf of The Association of the Bar of the City of New York, the Special Committee on Electric Power and the Environment respectfully submits its Report on the task assigned to it: to analyze and to reconcile, to the extent possible, two important social interests—the nation's need for an adequate supply of electric energy and the need to conserve and protect our environment.

The Special Committee grew out of a joint project originated early in 1971 by four regular committees of the Association—the Committees on Administrative Law, Atomic Energy, Environmental Law, and Science and Law—dealing with electric plant-siting problems in the State of New York. Quite early, however, it became clear that no meaningful study could be limited either to plant-siting *per se* or to the problems of one state in isolation.

Thus, with a broader national study in mind, the Association formed the Special Committee, with membership reflecting the broad interests and expertise represented by the four original committees and the Section on Public Utilities of the Committee on Post-Admission Legal Education.

The Report represents almost a year of work by the Committee and its Staff, a year which included innumerable consultations with experts in many fields: industrial, administrative, environmental, technological, economic and governmental. Cognizant of the importance of public comment, the Committee, in early May of this year, issued a working draft which was widely circulated to government, industry, environmental interests and the general public. An Open Forum was held at the House of Association on May 25, at which representatives of a wide spectrum of views appeared and presented their comments to the Committee. Written comments were thereafter received from many other sources as well. The Committee expresses its gratitude to all those who devoted such substantial time and effort to assist the Committee in its task. The comments submitted aided the Committee immeasurably in the preparation of its final Report.

III

Foreword

The Committee itself included a broad diversity of viewpoints. While unanimity on a Report of this scope was not expected or felt necessary, it is gratifying that a substantial consensus was in fact achieved. It should not, of course, be assumed that all members of the Committee majority concurred on all positions taken or all views expressed, and an individual Committee member's concurrence in the Report does not necessarily mean that he endorses the Report, or the specific language used, in its entirety. Individual views of certain members of the Committee and the views of two members who dissented in major part are appended at the end of the Report. These statements, and particularly the dissents, should be read, as thoughtful and articulate expressions of viewpoints other than those adopted by the Committee majority.

The Chairman wishes to express his personal thanks to the members of the Committee and to its Staff. Behind the Report lies a long process of research, analysis, discussion, evaluation and reevaluation of positions, which exerted heavy demands on the Committee and Staff. The Committee profited from the wide diversity of views represented among its members, and it is a tribute to the spirit in which the Committee members approached their task that, while the discussion was always vigorous, the Committee and Staff, from start to finish, functioned as a team. Thanks are particularly due to The Ford Foundation, whose generous grant made the study possible, and to Edward A. Ames, of the Foundation, whose wise assistance at every stage was enormously helpful to the Committee.

It is the Committee's hope that the Report will prove of value to legal, legislative and administrative bodies concerned with the problem with which it deals, and may be helpful in assisting in resolving that problem.

Respectfully submitted,

SHELDON OLIENSIS
Chairman

August 1, 1972

COMMITTEE AND STAFF

Personal
Data

On this and the succeeding pages are listed the members of the Committee and its Staff, together with the public and professional positions held by them.

THE COMMITTEE

SHELDON OLIENSIS, CHAIRMAN · *Partner, Kaye, Scholer, Fierman, Hays & Handler, New York City; Vice Chairman, Harvard Law School Association of New York City; former Member, Executive Committee and former Chairman, Committee on State Legislation and Committee on Revision of Constitution and By-Laws, The Association of the Bar of the City of New York.*

MAURICE AXELRAD · *Secretary, Associate Counsel, and Assistant General Manager, New York State Atomic and Space Development Authority; former Counsel, New York State Office of Atomic and Space Development; former Attorney, Office of General Counsel, United States Atomic Energy Commission; former Chairman, Committee on Atomic Energy, The Association of the Bar of the City of New York.*

DANA C. BACKUS · *Partner, Kramer, Marx, Greenlee & Backus, New York City; former Trustee, Harvard Law School Association of New York City; former Chairman, Committee on Administrative Law, Committee on International Law, Municipal Court Committee, and Junior Bar Committee, The Association of the Bar of the City of New York.*

ALBERT K. BUTZEL · *Partner, Berle & Butzel, New York City; Member, Committee on Environmental Law and former Member, Committee on Administrative Law, The Association of the Bar of the City of New York.*

THEODORE J. CARLSON · *Partner, Gould & Wilkie, New York City; Member, Legal Committee, Edison Electric Institute and Committee on Public Utilities, New York State Bar Association; Chairman, Section on Public Utilities, Committee on Post-Admission Legal Education, The Association of the Bar of the City of New York.*

JAMES B. HENRY · *Vice President, General Counsel and Secretary, American Electric Power Service Corporation, New York City; Member, Legal Committee, Edison Electric Institute.*

THE STAFF

*

CONTENTS

Contents

IV. *An Overview of the Decision-Making Process* —Continued

VII. *Current Legislative Reform Approaches* —Continued

†

ELECTRICITY
AND
THE ENVIRONMENT

*

I. PROLOGUE

A. NATURE OF THE PROBLEM

Only in recent years has the nation awakened to a truly national problem—the accommodation of society's competing interests in assuring a reliable supply of electric energy and in achieving and maintaining a safe, healthful, and pleasing human environment.

Until a few years ago, no such conflict of public interests was perceived. Only anonymous engineers in utilities and regulatory commissions worried about electric reliability and only scattered conservationists talked of exhaustible energy resources and nature's limited capacity to absorb waste. Without fear of power shortages or environmental harm, national practice could promote rapid growth in the demand for electricity. This attitude reached its height with the wide acceptance in 1964 of the Federal Power Commission's first National Power Survey.[1] While paying scant attention to environmental matters,[2] that document urged that "maximum growth" in electric demand be "encouraged by reductions in rates and steady improvements in service," an approach characterized as a "far-sighted philosophy." [3]

The nation soon became aware, however, of electric reliability as a public issue and the environmental costs of generating and transmitting electricity. The year 1965 brought both the infamous "Northeast Blackout" [4] and the landmark decision in the *Scenic Hudson* case.[5] Less serious, but noteworthy interruptions in normal electric service have followed the 1965 blackout. The *Scenic Hudson* litigation has continued,[6] joined by numerous other litigative and non-litigative approaches to the environmental impact of electricity.[7]

In short, the United States has perceived limits upon those public air, water, and land resources that we call "the environment" and possible limits, as well, on our primary energy resources. But the regulatory systems that grew up during the era of electric power promotion now are not working very well in accommodating the newer perceptions.

Many reforms have been proposed for the electricity/environment problem: "one-stop" licensing to speed construction of new facilities;

3

crash research to develop potential new energy sources; and drastically curbing or even reversing growth in the demand for power. Such individual reforms vary widely in approach, but they are alike in failing to consider all significant aspects of this complex problem, and in failing to explore sufficiently the consequences of the particular solutions proposed. This report, while recognizing that lawyers' skills may contribute more to the improvement of the decision-making process than to the decisions themselves, attempts to take a broader view.

As a lawyer's study, it has focused on the structures and procedures by which the issues are addressed. It examines the sorts of agencies and procedures that determine, or ought to determine, whether, for example, the vast power development in the Four Corners area of the Southwest really is necessary and whether it is most appropriate that large portions of the power needs of the West Coast should be satisfied by generating plants located in an environment a thousand miles inland. Parallel issues exist about where generating capacity should be located to serve the City of New York, whether it should be regarded as the responsibility of the City or the State of New York or, perhaps, should be located in New England, Pennsylvania, or even farther away. This report is not a study of the particular cases just mentioned, but rather of the decision-making structures and processes through which matters such as those are, or ought to be, determined.

One important fact deserves prominent mention. That is the interrelationship between electric energy problems and general energy problems. Any examination of the former leads inexorably to the latter because electricity is a derived energy form, depending on the availability of primary energy sources such as fossil or nuclear fuel. Also, such other sources of energy are, to some degree, mutually substitutable with electric energy. This study has avoided detailed examination of overall energy problems,[8] but it does attempt to create an institutional framework which will permit electric power/environment problems to be addressed while treatment of broader energy questions begins.[9]

To lay a foundation for analysis of the agencies and laws dealing with electricity and environment, Chapter II discusses the relationship of electricity and the economy, commenting on past and present trends and power supply problems, and Chapter III summarizes the environmental effects of producing power. Chapter IV describes the present regulatory system for electric power, and Chapter V critiques that system. Chapter VI discusses the economic implications of altering the rate of growth in electric power use, and ways in which legislative decisions might be made to affect that growth rate. Chapter VII reviews various pending legislative reforms. Finally, Chapter VIII contains the Committee's recommendations for reform.

B. Principal Ideas

While Chapter VIII contains our full conclusions and recommendations, our principle ideas follow. Today's decision-making process satisfies no one. Environmentalists lack a forum to raise many important issues and feel that they receive scant attention on others. Utilities must go through repetitive reviews to clear the way for each plant or transmission line, and feel that the time thus consumed endangers electric reliability. Overall, the process does little to increase public confidence or to reduce the chasm of mistrust often separating those on either side of the electricity/environment dispute.

1. Congressional Examination of Demand

A major flaw in the current approach to the electric energy problem is the absence of any mechanism by which the growth in electric energy demand may be evaluated. As a society, we do not ask whether the resource base is sufficient. Nor do we inquire whether we can afford—or somehow, through technology, avoid—the seemingly predictable environmental costs of meeting such increased demand. It seems obvious that national policy should be predicated upon conscious determinations of those questions just as it must reflect considered judgments about the complex of questions relating to reliability and supply.

In the truest sense, however, this is a political matter. Whether and how electric demand might be shaped by national policy involves a complex of issues going to the fundamental economic organization and social well-being of the nation. Although America may be perceiving new resource and environment issues in the electric power question, query whether she is ready to modify significantly her energy-intensive practices. What, in fact, would be the effects of demand modification, and would it be possible of accomplishment?

Only Congress has the capability and standing to decide such profound questions, questions which should be examined consciously, deliberately and soon.[10]

Although taking no position on whether or when future demand growth should be limited, this report notes the advantages of responding to any future need to affect demand by beginning now to implement any new policies gradually. An annual Congressional review and evaluation is recommended. An energy tax is discussed as one possible legislative tool,[11] but one that should be used in simultaneous application to all energy forms in order to minimize dislocation and other undesirable side effects.

Policies and mechanisms designed to mold future demand should be distinguished from the methods adopted for efficiently meeting such demand as may be predictable on the basis of Congressional policy. The Committee's recommendations contemplate continued use of the best present methods for predicting future demand patterns.[12]

2. UNITARY TREATMENT OF ENERGY FORMS

Next, this Committee recommends an end to the present fragmented regulation of nuclear, hydroelectric, and fossil-fuel plants. Moreover, any commission treating electric energy matters also should be responsible for policy respecting all other energy forms. On the other hand, research and development programs should be handled by an agency separate from the commission carrying out regulatory functions.[13]

Thus, a federal research and development agency would set research and development goals and be responsible for carrying out or supervising major R&D programs. In setting goals, the agency must consider all energy potentialities and balance the national interests in fossil-fuel, nuclear, and hydroelectric power development.

The Committee then recommends the creation of a separate federal energy commission responsible for analyzing and evaluating demand and preparing an annual energy report to the Congress in aid of the yearly Congressional policy evaluation of demand.

As a separate function, the energy commission would also project, regionally and nationally, the amount of future generation and transmission capacity needed to satisfy the demand for power which the Congressional policies would produce. In carrying out this function, the commission would be expected to review neutrally the best available projections.[14] The energy commission would determine, with full NEPA analysis, in what general locations such capacity should be built. It would then assign, regionally and to the states, the responsibility for allowing such construction to take place.[15]

6

Finally, the energy commission would determine nuclear safety standards, would license all nuclear plants for safety, and would exercise a limited override responsibility with respect to state licensing, mentioned below.

3. AIR AND WATER POLLUTION CONTROL

The Committee recommendations contemplate that the Environmental Protection Agency would continue to exercise its responsibilities as at present. Similarly, they contemplate that existing state regulation pursuant to the federal regulatory scheme would continue as at present.[16]

Those recommendations are not intended as an endorsement either of state regulatory history in these areas or of the present environmental control structure. Rather, they recognize that general environmental control systems should apply to utility facilities just as they apply to all other types of facilities.

4. PLANT SITING AS A FUNCTION OF STATE LAND-USE CONTROL

A number of important determinations already will have been made before a question arises as to the exact location of a particular electric facility: the need for the construction of particular capacity in the particular state will have been determined by the federal commission, and applicable environmental standards will have been determined pursuant to the federal-state regulatory scheme essentially as presently existing, or by some successor of the present system.

Thus, the remaining questions would center, first, on land-use considerations, and, second, on type of plant and plant design.

The Committee recommends that the states be induced by Congress to establish state-wide land-use-planning programs which would, as a part of planning for all purposes, identify sites and corridors for utility facilities on a long-range basis in accordance with the capacity allocated to the state by the federal commission.[17] The state land-use-control agency would invite applications and data from utilities and others in seeking to fulfill its responsibility for licensing the quantity of electric facilities required by the overall federal plan. The land-use agency would have final authority with respect to questions of state and local law except air pollution and water pollution questions, as to which the applicant would be required to produce evidence that

7

its plan had satisfied the state air pollution and water pollution control agencies. In the case of a proposed nuclear plant, the applicant would have to make a similar showing of compliance with federal atomic safety standards.

As noted, the recommendations would provide for a possible federal override of the state decision-making process if it could be demonstrated that the state agency was attempting to impede the construction of facilities required by the long-range federal plan.

5. The Reform of Decision-Making

An important group of recommendations is directed toward reorganizing the decision-making processes ordinarily associated with "licensing proceedings." The report suggests that many issues are common to all similar licensing cases. As "generic" issues, they should be decided in a "generic" proceeding.[18]

"Generic" proceedings should be adversary in nature and, in certain situations, might be trial-type proceedings. Industry, public interest groups, and governmental bodies should be permitted to enter such proceedings, and, in appropriate cases, should be permitted rights of discovery, of submitting evidence, and of cross-examining witnesses.

At the federal level, the energy commission's determinations of future need for electric capacity and the allocation of such capacity to regions and states would be made upon a record in such generic proceedings. Similarly, nuclear safety and other environmental standards would be determined in generic proceedings. At the state level, many land-use-planning questions would be treated generically. To the extent of state authority to determine environmental standards, such standards would be determined generically as well.

To be sure, it would be necessary to provide that issues decided generically could be reopened generically in the event of sufficiently changed circumstances.[19] But, in general, it would not be open for such issues to be relitigated in individual licensing proceedings without a showing that the generic rule is improper in a particular case.[20]

6. Public Participation

The Committee recommends that all stages of the decision-making process be opened up to effective public participation.[21] That group of recommendations flows from two conclusions: first, that a more open decision-making process is more likely to arrive at sound decisions in the public interest, and, second, that the credibility of such processes cannot withstand the cynicism that inevitably flows from the exclusion of persons or interest groups who reasonably believe themselves to be affected by the results of such proceedings.

If the long-range planning in generic proceedings is to be at all effective in rationalizing decision-making processes, then public participation must be permitted and encouraged. Also, states and utility companies must be allowed to participate as parties in the federal commission proceedings to determine need and to allocate capacity.

Enhanced procedures for disclosure of internal planning and decision-making should be adopted by both governmental agencies and utilities. All parties, including public intervenors, should be granted broad prehearing discovery rights so as to sharpen the formulation of issues. Also, administrative procedure requirements, even to the extent of rules relating to the availability of trial transcripts, should be examined with a view toward modifying those that tend to impede public participation.

In short, the Committee recommends that government agencies take all steps necessary to ventilate these decision-making processes and thereby make them sounder.

7. THE NEPA BALANCING FUNCTION

This Committee's recommendations do not contemplate any compromise of the profoundly important social balancing function [22] incorporated into law by the National Environmental Policy Act.

Specifically, the Committee contemplates that a full NEPA analysis would be required at almost every stage of decision-making with respect to the issues being decided at that stage.[23] In each type of proceeding, whether generic or an *ad hoc* licensing proceeding, with only one exception, the environmental and other issues to be decided in that proceeding would be determined on the basis of a full analysis of alternatives, benefits, and detriments.

For example, it would be contemplated that the annual energy report to the Congress by the energy commission would include a complete NEPA analysis of all recommendations. Similarly, the energy commission's allocations of capacity between one region and another and one state and another would be required to conform to the NEPA analysis.

At the state level, the same would be true of the long-range selection of utility sites. The state licensing proceeding, as contemplated by these recommendations, would include the one exception to the full NEPA analysis rule. While the initial site-selection stage would be subject to the NEPA analysis, the final, design stage would not be. Since the design and operation of every generating plant would be required to conform to all applicable air pollution, water pollution, and radiological safety standards, and since the full NEPA analysis already would have been applied at all prior, generic stages, including those determining questions of generation mode and land use, it is felt that NEPA analysis would be repetitive and unnecessary at the design stage.

8. GENERAL COMMENTARY

This Committee quite advisedly has avoided characterizing its recommendations as directed toward "power plant siting." That rubric assumes the omission of most of the important stages of public decision-making—for example, evaluation of demand, projection of need, long-range planning, and allocation of capacity. Deciding on the permissible location, size, design, and operating characteristics of a particular electric facility or group of facilities is really only the final step in a long, highly complex decisional chain.

It is true, of course, that, for the most part, proceedings for the licensing of particular plans have provided the setting for controversies between environmental and reliability values.[24] The highly visible centering of reliability-versus-environment controversies in licensing proceedings, however, is only symptomatic of more basic difficulties. Those controversies arise at the licensing stage because, at the present time, there is substantially no open, public-agency decision-making at the earlier stages. There is no forum in which such issues can be addressed.

Under this Committee's recommendations, every important stage of decision-making would be subjected to public-agency determination upon the record of an open proceeding.

Moreover, that scheme of open, public agency determination of issues relates importantly to democratic opportunities for citizen input.

It is a practical reality that the extent of possible public participation in decision-making is quite dependent upon the extent to which the process is a public agency responsibility. To that extent, there can be imposed rules and regulations for such participation, there usually will be a record, and, for those and other reasons, fairness to all interested parties can be monitored. (And that would be an aim of this Committee's recommendations.)

Where decision-making is entirely an industry matter, however, it is most difficult to mandate "public participation." Consultative functions cannot be mandated very effectively by law. On the other hand, mere publication of long-range plans without an incident of public-agency decision leaves potential intervenors with information but again without a forum.

At the present time, however, the largest number of publicly important decisions in this area are either made solely by the utility industry, or are initiated by the industry and carried forward far enough before public agency review so that the decisional options of responsible public agencies are quite limited. (Examples are the projection of future national and regional construction needs, determinations of size, type, and design of facilities, and initial site-location decisions.) Either individually or through regional reliability councils and pooling arrangements, the industry presently goes quite far toward final decisions before any regulatory proceeding is formally commenced.

This Committee's recommendations would open up that process by providing that the projection of future need and the allocation of responsibility for construction shall be federal commission determinations, each of which must be made upon the record of a generic proceeding. Thus, the public agency role would no longer be limited only to reacting to industry initiatives. A publicly responsible agency would exercise a greater part in the initiating process, thereby enhancing the possibility of optimizing all public interest factors in system planning, including environmental factors.

C. THE SCOPE OF THIS STUDY

The Committee has elected, for primarily practical reasons, to omit considering a number of matters. For example, in suggesting the creation of a unitary federal energy commission to include the licensing jurisdiction of the AEC and a unitary agency to include its promotional responsibilities, this report makes no recommendation concerning the

11

disposition of present AEC military and security functions. The Committee is aware of the importance of such matters but believes that it would have little basis upon which to formulate any opinion upon military and security questions.

Also, the Committee has made no attempt to draft legislation for the implementation of any recommendations. It did not seem that any such detailed work would be appropriate. A number of considerations militated against any such detailed drafting. Such questions as the possible complexity of potential jurisdictional conflicts among existing departments, agencies, bureaus, divisions, and, perhaps, individuals bear importantly on implementation but are beyond the scope of this study.

A vitally related matter, which the Committee observes, but about which it makes no recommendation, is the multiplicity of jurisdictional interests among Congressional committees. It has been reported that eighteen committees and subcommittees of the present Congress have in some way considered the instant subject.[25] It seems worth noting that, more than once, it has been suggested to this Committee that Congress should form a joint committee on energy and the environment, or at least a unitary committee on the subject in each house, for the consideration of legislative reforms.[26]

Another centrally important matter should be mentioned, although the Committee has regarded it as beyond the scope of this study. That is the observable trend toward concentration within the energy industry.[27] The reforms suggested by this Committee depend, for their success, upon the existence of a competitive energy industry. Just as competition in the market place can help the economy, competition in administrative and political processes can improve the decisions made. If, for instance, in seeking research funds, the nuclear industry criticizes fossil plants and the coal industry criticizes atomic plants, both government and the public will receive information useful throughout the regulatory process. But, if otherwise rival trade associations have largely overlapping memberships, they will be less likely to serve their traditionally useful function of checking each other's power. While there is some such intraindustry criticism now, it may be diminished by trends toward concentration.

Such trends raise many questions beyond the scope of this Report including any impact on price, the possible efficiencies of scale, and the application and adequacy of existing antitrust law. Utility industry representatives have voiced concern over the effect these trends may have on utility fuel supplies [28] and have also suggested that they might force the uilities to assume an unfair regulatory burden as compared with the rest of the energy industry.[29] Leaving these questions unanswered, we must recognize, nevertheless, that a highly concentrated energy industry would be more difficult to regulate in the public interest and thus perhaps make inadequate the reforms here suggested. At the ultimate extreme, an energy industry dominated by a handful of companies would be unregulatable by conventional means. While the issues relating to industry structure are many and complex, considerations in any review of the situation should include the impact of concentration on the flow of information and the efficacy of governmental processes.

In general, matters omitted from this study have been avoided so as to allow the Committee to address those issues that could be examined usefully within the parameters of available time and manpower.

Finally, the Committee urges the reader to note that the instant proposals cannot be regarded as any final or ideal answer to the problems of electric power reliability and the environment. Analysis of the existing regulatory scheme should disabuse one of any such false expectation.[30]

Rather, the conclusions and recommendations should be viewed as proposing a beginning. This Committee has stated what it believes to be the important realities the Nation must consider. Where specific recommendations have been articulated, the Committee would urge that they be implemented. But they are not advanced as likely to achieve perfection. They are advanced only as likely improvements compared with present arrangements or with other current reform proposals.

Notes for Chapter I

1. *Federal Power Commission, National Power Survey, 1964* [hereinafter cited as *1964 Power Survey*].

2. For example, out of 719 pages in two volumes, only eleven pages were devoted to a discussion of "Air and Water Pollution at Thermal-Electric Generating Plants," concluding with the thought that "the nation's capacity to produce needed electrical energy will not be impaired because of those environmental considerations." *1964 Power Survey* at 137–47. *See*, also, *Id.* at 155 regarding rights-of-way, where the Survey apparently adopts an advisory committee view that public authorities should be required to "resist the pressures from minority groups and special interests to force utilities to use uneconomical locations and forms of construction."

3. *1964 Power Survey* at 35. In the same paragraph, the Commission expressly assumed that the electric industry "will recognize the advantage of selling its product at the lowest possible price in order to promote the additional demand for electric service in a growing economy." *Id.* Whether such "philosophy" can be said to reflect an affirmative Congressional policy of power promotion at the expense of environmental and resource considerations is another matter. The basic Congressional directive to the Federal Power Commission on this subject states as its purpose:

> "assuring an abundant supply of electric energy throughout the United States with the greatest possible economy and with regard to the *proper utilization and conservation of natural resources* . . . ."

Federal Power Act, § 202(a), 16 U.S.C. § 824a(a) (1970) (emphasis supplied).

4. "The Longest Night," *Newsweek*, Nov. 27, 1965, at 27.

5. Scenic Hudson Preservation Conf. v. FPC, 354 F.2d 608 (2d Cir. 1965), *cert. denied*, 384 U.S. 941 (1966).

6. Scenic Hudson Preservation Conf. v. FPC, 453 F.2d 463 (2d Cir. 1971), *cert. denied*, 40 U.S.L.W. 3599 (June 19, 1972).

7. *See*, for example, Greene County Planning Board v. FPC, 455 F.2d 412 (2d Cir. 1972); Kalur v. Resor, 335 F.Supp. 1 (D.D.C. 1971); and Calvert Cliffs' Coordinating Comm., Inc. v. AEC, 449 F.2d 1109 (D.C.Cir. 1971).

8. The Committee elected not to subscribe to the view that everything is so interrelated to everything else that reform efforts cannot feasibly begin anywhere.

9. We do not, however, believe that such a crisis is upon the Nation that immediate action must be taken by Congress at all cost. The enactment of interim licensing legislation, P.L. 92–307 (1972) should lessen the immediate danger of electric power shortages chargeable to consideration of environmental issues.

10. *See* Chapter VIII, § C(1), *infra*.

11. *See* Chapter VI, *infra*.

12. They do not recommend any deliberate limitation on plant construction as a means of limiting demand.

13. *See* Chapter VIII, § E(1), *infra*.

14. Since the Committee takes no position respecting what demand policy Congress ought to adopt, *a fortiori* it does not recommend the creation of

14

artificial limits on construction. That is not to say, however, that the Congress should blind itself and avoid examining the merits of arguments that continued expansion of capacity itself contributes to the upward pressure on demand.

15. It is suggested also that the intraregional allocations might be made by a regional agency formed by interstate compact among all the states in the region, provided that those states create a strong agency and give it teeth in accordance with a strict Congressionally mandated structure. Such state action, however, is highly problematical.

16. *See* Chapter VIII, §§ E(1) and (2), *infra.*

17. *See* Chapter VIII, § E(2), *infra.*

18. *See* Chapter VIII, § F, *infra.*

19. Changed circumstances might include a technological breakthrough in the case of nuclear safety standards or facts compelling a change in projected demand in a capacity allocation proceeding.

20. It seems likely that unforeseen events or developments, very recent changes in fact or policy, matters ordinarily handled on a generic basis, may become material to the issues in a licensing proceeding from time to time. Such incidents should be highly unusual and infrequent, however. It is not inconsistent with the generic approach to provide a procedural escape valve allowing such matters to be taken up in a licensing proceeding under very special circumstances.

21. *See* Chapter VIII, § H, *infra.*

22. The term, "social balancing function," is not intended to suggest that the subjects, values, and interests to be considered are all quantifiable or that the function is inhibited by any concepts drawn from the economist's "cost benefit analysis." Rather, that term is intended to denote a very broad and deep examination of all relevant *social* values—e. g., society's competing interests in reliable electric service and in a decent environment.

23. *See,* generally, Chapter VIII, *infra; see* also Chapter VIII, § E(3), *infra.*

24. *See* Udall v. FPC, 387 U.S. 428 (1967); and *see* cases cited in notes 5, 6, and 7, *supra.*

25. N. Y. Times, May 20, 1972, at 28, col. 1 (editorial).

26. The history of the development of the Federal Water Power Act of 1920 may be instructive, here. After decades of public discussion and conflict, that historic conservation and power measure finally was enacted only after the formation of a special Congressional committee to handle it. *See Kerwin*, Federal Water-Power Legislation, 217–263 (1926).

27. The predominant example of these trends is the acquisition by oil companies of competing fuel suppliers, coupled with existing concentration within the petroleum industry. *See Subcomm. on Special Small Business Problems of the House Select Comm. on Small Business, Concentration by Competing Raw Fuel Industries in the Energy Market and Its Impact on Small Business,* H.R. Rep.No.92–719, 92d Cong., 1st Sess. (1971); B. C. Netschert, "The Energy Company: A Monopoly Trend in the Energy Markets," 27 *Bulletin of the Atomic Scientists* 13 (Oct. 1971).

28. Address by W. Donham Crawford, "Energy Policy—The Eectric Utility Industry's View," Fortieth Annual Convention of the Edison Electric Institute, San Diego, California, June 6, 1972.

Electricity and the Environment

29. Letter from Hunton, Williams, Gay & Gibson to the Special Committee on Electric Power and the Environment, June 12, 1972.

30. Note, for example, the Federal Power Act, which was, in its day, as the Federal Water Power Act of 1920, such an important breakthrough in resource management. *See* Pinchot, "The Long Struggle for Effective Federal Water Power Legislation," 14 *George Washington Law Review* 9 (1945).

16

II. ELECTRICITY AND THE ECONOMY

Electric power is an integral, pervasive element of today's economy. Communications, industrial production, farming, and even homelife have become dependent on the use of electric power. Certainly, it is not unreasonable to conclude that "[w]ithout electricity, our twentieth century civilization—as we know it—cannot survive." [1] But there is much disagreement as to how much electricity is needed, or advisable. Factual disputes rage over the relationship of electricity and the economy and electricity and the environment. Differing value judgments lead to differences in the importance accorded to more goods and services sold in the market place as opposed to more environmental protection. Suggestions range from intentional quick cut-backs in power use to strong efforts to encourage faster growth of elecricity consumption. Chapter VI discusses these disputes in more detail, although this Committee cannot and does not reach any conclusions as to whether demand for power ought to be curbed.

Whatever the merits of a purposeful policy to accelerate or reverse growth in electricity use, in the long or short run, unintended blackouts would strike hard at the average citizen. Even if his or her home were not electrically heated, the electric thermostat would prevent the furnace from operating. But that would be only the first worry: the American home is replete with electric appliances, and the trend toward the use of more appliances by more families appears unlikely to end soon. In 1969, almost all homes in America contained televisions, refrigerators, radios, and clothes washers, and nearly half had room air conditioners. [2]

This expansion in electricity use and the resulting dependence on electricity have been made possible by the growth of the electric utilities. As the utilities expanded, and generation became more and more efficient, the unit cost of electricity steadily decreased, at least until recently. Thus, the electric utilities have been able to provide more electricity to more people at lower costs.

The growth of the nation's dependence upon electric power has its roots in the rapid increase in energy use which began during the Industrial Revolution. In the mid-nineteenth century, wind and water accounted for about two-thirds of total mechanical work output.[3] Belt-driven machinery powered by steam engines then became commonplace, but by the turn of the century the more efficient electric motor began to replace steam systems, and from 1900 to 1920, consumption of electricity grew four times as fast as total energy consumption.[4] From 1920 to 1970, electricity consumption in the United States increased almost 29 times, while total energy consumption increased just under three and one-half times and the population doubled. Thus, electricity consumption has doubled every ten years. Table I demonstrates the marked expansion of electricity use, while Table II shows how electricity has steadily become more popular than other forms of energy.

TABLE I

MEASURES OF ELECTRICITY CONSUMPTION AS COMPARED TO TOTAL ENERGY CONSUMPTION, POPULATION, AND GNP, SELECTED YEARS, 1920–1970.*

Year	Per Capita Energy Consumption (Million Btu)	Per Capita Electricity Consumption (kwh)	Energy Consumption (Thousand Btu) per $1 of GNP	Electricity Consumption (kwh) per $1 of GNP
1920	185.8	540	141.3	0.41
1930	181.1	944	121.5	0.63
1940	180.3	1,376	105.2	0.80
1950	224.3	2,564	96.1	1.10
1960	248.8	4,967	92.2	1.74
1965	276.4	5,948	87.1	1.87
1970	335.0	8,025	95.0	2.28

* Source: *Energy Research Needs*, a report to the National Science Foundation prepared by Resources for the Future, Inc., in co-operation with MIT Environmental Laboratory, at I–7, table 1 (1971). GNP expressed in 1958 dollars.

TABLE II

TOTAL U. S. ENERGY CONSUMPTION AND ELECTRICITY CONSUMPTION, SELECTED YEARS, 1920–1970.*

Year	Total Consumption (Trillion Btu)	Eectricity Consumption (Trillion Btu)	Electricity Consumption as Percentage of Total Energy Consumption
1920	19,782	196	1.0%
1930	22,288	396	1.8%
1940	23,908	621	2.6%
1950	34,154	1,332	3.9%
1960	44,960	2,896	6.4%
1965	53,785	3,949	7.3%
1970	68,810	5,624	8.2%

* Source: *Energy Research Needs*, a report to the National Science Foundation prepared by Resources for the Future, Inc., in co-operation with MIT Environmental Laboratory, at I–7, table 1 (1971).

The expansion of electricity consumption has come in the residential and industrial-commercial markets, while the transportation sector has not made any significant use of electric power. In industry and commerce, electricity purchased from utilities has steadily replaced energy produced directly on the premises, and electricity has also supplanted other forms of energy in the home, as shown in Table III.

TABLE III

UTILITY ELECTRICITY AS A PROPORTION
OF TOTAL ENERGY USED *

Year	Industry—Commerce	Residential
1950	21%	16%
1965	28%	29%
1980	40%	47%

* Source: J. Winger, J. Emerson and G. Gunning, *Outlook for Energy in the United States* at 23-24 (Chase Manhattan Bank Energy Division, 1968). The percentages for 1980 are estimates which assume the continuation of present trends.

The Federal Power Commission predicts that the growth in electricity consumption will continue: by 1990, consumption is expected to reach nearly 6 million megawatt hours, or almost four times 1970 levels.[5] To satisfy the predicted peak load demand for electricity in 1990, the Commission sees a need for the construction of one million megawatts of new generating capacity, made up of about 300 new fossil and nuclear steam plants ranging in size from 500 to 4000 megawatts each, 55 new pumped storage plants of 300 megawatts or more, and 40 new hydroelectric stations of 100 megawatts or more.[6] The 300,000 miles of overhead transmission lines presently in existence, covering almost 4 million acres (an area greater in size than the State of Connecticut), are expected to increase by over 200,000 miles, requiring 3 million additional acres by 1990, even if existing corridors are used to the greatest extent possible.[7] These figures for transmission corridor acreage may overstate the problem, since they do not reflect the fact that land under transmission lines can often be put to productive use. But they may also understate the problem, since may people consider transmission lines an intrusion far beyond the bounds of the transmission corridors themselves.

Given the significance to our economy of energy in general and electricity in particular, as well as the major environmental problems associated with generating and transmitting power, decision-makers are faced with basically two problems. First, in the long run, should

19

the present trend of growing electricity use continue, and will the possible environmental benefits of a slowed or even reversed trend in the growth of electricity consumption be worth the possible impact on the consumption of goods and services? Second, in the short run, if society will not accept either curbs on use or power shortages, how and where can plants be built to supply electricity needs reliably and with the minimum environmental impact? We turn next to the short-range reliability problems, returning to the long-range situation in Chapter VI.

A.   PROBLEMS IN MEETING DEMAND

Reliability of electricity supply probably first became a concern for most people following the blackout of November 9–10, 1965, when a faulty relay in an Ontario transmission line cut off power to 30 million people in the northeastern United States and Canada for up to 13 hours.[8] Power failures were not, of course, without precedent; between 1954 and the Northeast blackout there had been 114 significant service interruptions.[9] But the scale of this failure, and its initiation through the breakdown of such a minor piece of equipment, raised questions about the reliability of the entire United States power system.

In the blackout's aftermath, the utilities, working with federal, state and local agencies, undertook to develop emergency procedures and reliability standards to avoid a repetition of a "cascading" failure of such great magnitude. The industry formed reliability councils throughout the country to coordinate long-range planning and the construction, operation and maintenance of facilities. In April, 1971, the FPC's Bureau of Power reported that the utilities had "largely implemented"[10] the major recommendations developed by the FPC following the blackout, and the chairman of the National Electric Reliability Council has noted that since the 1967 power failure in northeastern Pennsylvania, New Jersey and the Delaware-Maryland-Virginia peninsula, there have been no "cascading outages."[11]

Although the causes of the 1965 blackout have probably been identified and effective counter measures taken, more localized power failures or shortages still present a threat, as demand for electric power has risen sharply, and existing capacity has been strained to satisfy it. Whatever the extent of the electricity supply "crisis" (some persons question its very existence),[12] certain facts are undisputed. First, in some parts of the country margins of excess capacity over predicted peak loads are smaller than is believed necessary to ensure reliability of service. Transmission capacity is also inadequate in some areas, so that even if power is available, it cannot be moved where needed. Second, inadequate capacity has forced some utilities to cut voltage or appeal for voluntary curtailment of electricity use on peak-load days. Finally, past schedules for bringing new facilities into service have in many cases proved hopelessly unrealistic.

1. CAPACITY

The FPC has warned that five "critical subregions"—New England, New York, the Virginia-Carolinas area, Florida and the northern Illinois-Wisconsin-upper Michigan area—face severe power shortages in the summer of 1972 and the following winter due to delays in plant licensing, with possible reserve margins as low as .4% in the Virginia-Carolinas area and 2% in Florida.[13]

According to a recent survey by the Power Division of the New York State Department of Public Service, New York State reserves will only reach the barely acceptable level of 21.8% for the summer of 1972 if all scheduled facilities start service on time. If, as appears likely, the Indian Point 2 nuclear plant (recently damaged by fire) and the Bowline Point 1 fossil plant are unavailable, state-wide reserves will only be 14.3%, Consolidated Edison's reserve will only be 2.4%, and Orange and Rockland Utilities' reserve will only be 2.6%. The Con Ed margin would be just 208 megawatts, so that should any of its existing equipment break down, a severe power shortage would result.[14] The situation in southeastern New York State is aggravated, according to the Power Division, by a lack of adequate transmission capacity into the area.[15]

2. CURTAILING ELECTRICITY SERVICE

Since the summer of 1970,[16] the FPC has received, through December 31, 1971, 100 reports of voltage reductions and 23 reports of appeals to the public or large individual users to curtail use.[17] Conditions during the summer of 1971 were considerably improved over conditions during the summer of 1970, probably due to cooler weather and decreased economic activity, as well as fewer equipment breakdowns.[18]

21

The most severely affected single utility has been Consolidated Edison Company of New York. In 1969, due to breakdowns of its own equipment and delays in additions to capacity by other utilities, limiting the amount of power Con Ed could purchase, the utility was forced to appeal for limitation in electricity use or to reduce voltage on eight different days. In 1970, delays in additions to Con Ed's own generating capacity and some equipment breakdowns forced appeals to the public and voltage reductions on 15 days. At one point, the utility had to cut off service entirely to 1% of its customers. Like other utilities, Con Ed avoided major difficulties in 1971 because of fewer equipment failures and no long hot spells during the summer, but through the first nine months of the year, it was still required to reduce voltage 15 times.[19]

3. DELAY

An FPC survey disclosed that almost three quarters of major steam generating plants installed from 1966 to 1970 were delayed, for periods of one to 31 months, and about one quarter of these plants were delayed for six months or more. The FPC also found that as of June 30, 1970, over 4300 miles of high voltage transmission line had been delayed, with delays of a year or longer in one quarter of the affected mileage.[20]

A survey conducted by the Edison Electric Institute of 35 large steam plants installed from 1966 to 1968 supports the FPC conclusions. EEI found that two-thirds of these plants were delayed.[21] A recent EEI review of 43 units scheduled for service in 1971 disclosed that ten of these units had been delayed over six months.[22] Such delays increase the planning time which must be allowed between a decision that new capacity is needed and the actual in-service date of this new capacity.

Most observers agree that at least until recently, environmental objections and the slowness of the regulatory process have not been significant factors in these delays. Individual delays due to litigation by environmental opponents of facilities have been very lengthy, but both the FPC and the EEI surveys demonstrate that the major past delay factors have been labor problems and equipment failures. FPC Chairman Nassikas stated in May of 1971 that "[p]resent problems are not all, or even predominantly, environmentally caused." [23]

Both the FPC and EEI are careful to point out, however, that such surveys of past difficulties are not necessarily a good indication of where future problems will lie, and in any case, these surveys do not reflect instances where plans for new plants were withdrawn or not developed by utility management because of environmental concerns.[24]   Chairman Nassikas predicts that "[e]nvironmentally caused delays are increasing and they will multiply rapidly," [25] and in a preliminary review of steam plants scheduled for service from 1971 to 1977, the FPC found that almost one quarter are already behind schedule, with 39% of the delays attributable to environmental and regulatory problems and 44% labor related.[26]   Moreover, this FPC review probably understated the future problem since it preceded three recent federal court decisions requiring much fuller environmental reviews by the three federal agencies involved in power facility licensing, the FPC, the Atomic Energy Commission and the Corps of Engineers.[27] In addition, the Sierra Club, with other groups, is seeking to force the FPC to extend its licensing jurisdiction under the Federal Power Act to steam generating plants in addition to hydroelectric projects.[28]

The costs of delay to utilities, from whatever cause, are substantial, since carrying charges must be paid whether or not a plant is in operation, and replacement power must often be bought at a price greater than what it would cost the utility to generate power itself. Replacement power can cost as much as $1.6 million weekly for certain plans, according to company estimates,[29] and delay costs generally at some plants have been set as high as $4.5 million a month.[30]   The annual cost to utilities of delays at 55 "most critically affected" plants has been fixed at between $5 and $6 billion.[31]

B.   The Structure of the Industry

The importance of the electric power industry is illustrated by its size.   It is the largest in the United States in terms of capital assets, 60% larger than its nearest rival.   It is also the largest issuer of securities, and its revenues are expected to reach $30 billion annually by 1980.[32]

There are approximately 3500 utility systems supplying electricity in the United States.   Some 400 are investor owned; their aggregate generating capacity of about 263 thousand megawatts equals 77% of the total.   Forty systems are federally owned; their aggregate

23

capacity of about 39 thousand megawatts is 11% of the total. Approximately 2000 systems are state or municipally owned; with about 34 thousand megawatts of generating capacity, they have 10% of the total. Finally, there are about 1000 cooperatively owned systems, with about 5 thousand megawatts of capacity, or less than 2% of the total.[33]

The dominant systems, in terms of both generating capacity and energy requirements, are the investor-owned utilities: in 1968, 35 of the 39 systems with the largest annual energy requirements, and 135 of the 185 systems with the largest annual energy requirements, were investor owned.[34] The 200 largest private systems own over 75% of total generating capacity and service 80% of all electricity customers.[35] 143 private utilities account for 90% of private revenues; 115 of these companies are independent and 28 are holding companies with 97 subdivisions. 35 private utilities (20 independent and 15 holding companies) represent the largest companies and control 70% of all assets.[36]

Individual plants are growing in size, along with the growth in demand for power. In the early 1950's 200-megawatt steam units were the largest built, while today units of 1000 megawatts and over are common and single sites often contain two or more of these units.[37] Moreover, by 1990, it is predicted that units of 3000 megawatts will be available.[38] In 1970, plants of 500 megawatts or more accounted for 75% of total steam generating capacity; such plants will probably account for 90% of capacity in 1980, and 97% in 1990.[39] These plants, with their associated higher capacity transmission lines, will often be of regional significance.

NOTES FOR CHAPTER II

1. Remarks by J. N. Nassikas, "Meeting Energy Demands in a Changing Society," at 1, Annual Meeting of the Association of Edison Illuminating Companies, Boca Raton, Florida, Dec. 4, 1969.

2. *Environmental Policy Division, Library of Congress, Energy—The Ultimate Resource*, A Study Submitted to the Task Force on Energy of the Subcomm. on Science, Research and Development of the House Comm. on Science and Astronautics, 92d Cong., 1st Sess., ser. J, at 114, table 8 (1971).

3. *H. Landsberg and S. Schurr, Energy in the United States* 28–29 (1968).

4. *Id.* at 62.

5. *Federal Power Commission,* 1 *The 1970 National Power Survey* I–3 to I–4 (1971); *Testimony by J. N. Nassikas in Hearings on H.R. 5277, H.R. 6970, H.R. 6971, H.R. 6972, H.R. 3838, H.R. 7045, H.R. 1079, and H.R. 1486 Before Subcomm. on Communications and Power, House Comm. on Interstate and Foreign Commerce,* 92d Cong., 1st Sess., ser. 92–31, 32, 33, pts. 1–3, Appendix A at I–2 (1971) [hereinafter cited as "Macdonald Hearings"]. The text of Chairman Nassikas' statement is in the printed hearings, but the appendices were not published and are in the files of the Subcommittee on Communications and Power. A megawatt is one thousand kilowatts, or one million watts.

6. J. N. Nassikas, *supra* note 5, Appendix A at I–4; Appendix H at 2.

7. *Id.,* Appendix A at I–14; Testimony by G. J. F. MacDonald in Macdonald Hearings at 307; *Office of Science and Technology, Energy Policy Staff, Electric Power and the Environment* 21–22 (1970).

8. Federal Power Commission, 1 *Prevention of Power Failures* 1 (1967).

9. *Id.* at 196.

10. J. N. Nassikas, *supra* note 5, Appendix N at 7.

11. Testimony by W. B. McGuire in Macdonald Hearings at 685.

12. *See, e. g.* remarks by A. J. McCollum, Manager, Advertising and Publicity, Pacific Gas & Electric Company, "Power Needs of Northern and Central California—the Role of Advertising," Cabrillo College, Mar. 2, 1971, reprinted in *Advertising and Publicity,* FYI No. 2:

> "Well, New York City is not America. Despite what you read in national news media or hear and see on network newscasts—emanating from Manhattan—there is no power shortage in most of the nation, and particularly in the West."

13. Letter from J. N. Nassikas to J. R. Schlesinger, Oct. 15, 1971 with attachment, *Bureau of Power Staff Report, Electric Generating Capacity Situation, Winter 1971–72, Summer 1972, Winter 1972–73* at 1–4.

14. *New York State Department of Public Service, Power Division, System Planning Section, The New York Power System Generation and Transmission Plans 1971–1980,* Appendix I at 3, 11 (1971).

15. *New York State Department of Public Service, Power Division, Electric System Planning in New York State* 38–39 (1971).

16. Federal Power Commission Order No. 331–1, requiring the reporting of voltage reductions and appeals for curtailment of power use, became effective June 21, 1970. FPC News Release No. 16864 (July 2, 1970).

17. FPC News Releases Nos. 17069 (Oct. 19, 1970); 17250 (Jan. 18, 1971); 17431 (April 14, 1971); 17640 (July 16, 1971); 17827 (Oct. 21, 1971); 17993 (Jan. 17, 1972).

18. FPC News Release No. 17758 (Sept. 9, 1971).

19. Statement by Consolidated Edison *In the Matter of Consolidated Edison Company of New York, Inc., (Indian Point No. 2),* AEC Docket No. 50–247, Before the Atomic Energy Commission (Oct. 19, 1971). The seriousness of the supply situation is emphasized by the plans some utilities, such as Con Ed, have had to make for shedding of loads in emergencies. Twenty-three load-shedding steps submitted by Con Ed were recently approved by the New York Public Service Commission; although most of these steps merely involve squeezing the most power possible from all generating equipment and importing all power available, some are more severe, such as 3%, 5% and 8% voltage reductions (steps 14, 17 and 20), shutting off all heat in winter in the subway system (step 21), and finally disconnecting entire areas of the Con Ed system on a rotating basis for periods of several hours at a time (step 23). More drastic steps, including cutting off power to high-rise office buildings, operation of the subways at half speed, and denying electricity to new or substantially remodelled buildings, were not approved by the Commission. Order and Opinion by New York State Public Service Commission in Case 25937 at 29–32 (1971); Dissent of Commissioner W. K. Jones at 1–16.

20. J. N. Nassikas, *supra* note 5, Appendix G.

21. Testimony by J. E. Moss in Macdonald Hearings at 375.

22. Testimony by D. B. Mansfield in Macdonald Hearings at 638.

23. J. N. Nassikas, *supra* note 5, Detailed Basic Statement at 72; Appendix G. *See also* J. E. Moss, *supra* note 21, at 375–376, and D. B. Mansfield, *supra* note 22 at 638–639, 645–647, 649.

24. Such plants would include the Breakneck Ridge plant of Central Hudson Gas & Electric Corporation (*See Central Hudson Gas & Electric Corporation, Annual Report 1969* 12), and Niagara Mohawk Power Corporation's Easton plant (*See* Findings of Hudson River Valley Commission of New York, *In the Matter of Review of Proposed 766 Megawatt Nuclear Power Generating Facility of Niagara Mohawk Power Corporation, Sponsor*). *See also* the account of William R. Gould, Senior Vice President of Southern California Edison Company, on the difficulties encountered when SCE sought to expand its Huntington Beach plant, in "Locating a Power Plant: A Case Study of Southern California Edison's Siting Problems."

25. J. N. Nassikas, *supra* note 5, Detailed Basic Statement at 72.

26. *Id.,* Appendix G.

27. The three decisions are Calvert Cliffs Coordinating Committee, Inc. v. Atomic Energy Commission, 449 F.2d 1109 (D.C.Cir. 1971), Greene County Planning Board v. FPC, 455 F.2d 412 (2d Cir. 1972); and Kalur v. Resor, 335 F.Supp. 1 (D.D.C. 1971).

28. Chemehuevi Tribe of Indians v. Arizona Public Service Co., FPC Docket No. E–7664. *See* FPC News Release No. 17856 (Nov. 4, 1971).

29. The estimates of $1.6 million weekly are for the two Zion nuclear units of Commonwealth Edison Company, and are contained in a letter from Hubert H. Nexon, Vice President of Commonwealth Edison Company, to Clifford P. Case, III, Feb. 14, 1972.

30.   The estimates of $4.5 million were made by Consumers Power Company for its Palisades nuclear plant, and are quoted in 176 *Electrical World* 15 (Dec. 15, 1971).

31.   This estimate, by Robert W. Davies of Baltimore Gas & Electric Company, is quoted in 176 *Electrical World* 15 (Dec. 15, 1971).

32.   Testimony by C. R. Ross in *Hearings on Competitive Aspects of the Energy Industry Before the Subcomm. on Antitrust and Monopoly of the Senate Comm. on the Judiciary*, 91st Cong., 2d Sess., at 620 (1970).

33.   *Federal Power Commission, supra* note 1, at I–1–10, I–1–11; J. N. Nassikas, *supra* note 5, Detailed Basic Statement at 102.

34.   *Id.* at 103.

35.   *Federal Power Commission, supra* note 1, at I–2 to I–4.

36.   C. R. Ross, *supra* note 32, at 621.

37.   Testimony by E. E. David, Jr. in Macdonald Hearings at 275.

38.   *Federal Power Commission, supra* note 1, at I–18–3.

39.   Paper by R. M. Jimeson and G. G. Adkins, "Factors in Waste Heat Disposal Associated with Power Generation," at 11, National Meeting of American Institute of Chemical Engineers, Houston, Texas, Feb. 28–Mar. 4, 1971.

III. ELECTRICITY AND THE ENVIRONMENT

Environmental opposition to power plants and transmission lines may have serious consequences, raising costs to electricity consumers and aggravating possible power shortages. In view of these consequences, and of predictions that delays due to environmental opposition are going to increase, one may well ask whether environmentalists' objections to power facilities are well founded. The answer seems to be that while concerted efforts are being made to solve many problems, serious environmental effects still result from all aspects of power production, although different kinds of facilities have relative advantages and disadvantages: fossil fuel plants do not generate nuclear wastes, for example, while atomic plants do not create air pollution. This chapter discusses the various generation and transmission modes, and the problems associated with each, recognizing that in some cases, controversy surrounds the extent and effect of the various phenomena which are described.

A. FOSSIL FUELS AND AIR POLLUTION

Fossil-fueled steam plants represented in 1970 76% of all generating capacity; by 1990, their share is predicted to fall to 44% due to the increase in nuclear steam plants, although the absolute amount of fossil steam capacity will more than double. The other users of fossil fuels, internal combustion and gas turbine units, constituted in 1970 6% of total capacity; in 1990, their share will still be 6%, although increasing in absolute terms almost four times.[1]

Together, these fossil-fuel power plants contribute major shares of three important air pollutants: about 55% of sulfur oxides discharged annually,[2] 25% of nitrogen oxides[3] and 25% of particulate matter.[4] Studies have shown that these shares may be even larger in some urban areas: in 1967, for example, power plants were responsible for 86% of the total sulfur dioxide emissions in Detroit.[5]

Unless controlled, sulfur oxide emissions from all sources may quadruple by 2000 to 126 million tons, with power generation accounting for an increasing share of the total.[6] Sulfur emissions from power plants may in 2000 even exceed natural sulfur emissions.[7] In addition, some experts have predicted that by 2000 nitrogen oxide emissions from power plants will increase by three and a half times, and fine particulate emissions from power plants will quadruple.[8] The Federal Power Commission has stated:

"Reducing air pollution from fossil fueled steam-electric plants to acceptable levels is one of the major challenges facing the electric utility industry." [8a]

The most widely studied aspect of air pollution has been its effect on human health. Studies of health effects have been particularly stimulated by widely publicized air pollution "episodes," such as those in the Meuse River Valley, Belgium in December, 1930, in Donora, Pennsylvania in October, 1948 and in London in December, 1952 and December, 1962. As a result of these episodes, it has been estimated, nearly 6000 people died and many thousands of others became ill.[8b] New York City has also suffered from several severe air pollution periods, in 1953, 1962, 1963 and 1966, with 573 estimated deaths from the last two episodes.[8c] The severity of these periods of pollution has been attributed to a combination of unfavorable meteorological conditions with sulfur oxides, particulates and fog.[9] While none of the studies of which we are aware has examined the extent to which electric power generation may have contributed to those episodes, the present annual contribution to the atmosphere of sulfur oxides and particulates by fossil-fuel power plants is a major factor, as already noted.[9a]

Recently, the view has gained acceptance that as shocking as the major air pollution incidents are, it is the minimum level of air pollution, rather than the occasional peaks, which are most significant from a public health standpoint,[10] and research has been directed toward discovering threshold levels for health effects from each type of pollutant, as well as the synergistic effect of different types acting together. Although there is often disagreement as to the concentrations of various pollutants in the air which cause particular health effects, and as to the causal relationship between some kinds of pollutants and some aspects of health,[11] most authorities now believe there is conclusive evidence of a quantitative association between air pollution and human disease and death.[12]

For example, studies of people living in areas of high air pollution have linked air pollution statistically to lung cancer, emphysema, tuberculosis, pneumonia and bronchitis, as well as a variety of other respiratory diseases, including colds and influenza.[13] Other studies have linked air pollution levels statistically to incidence of heart disease.[14] Based on laboratory experiments with animals, it has been suggested that air pollution may reduce fertility and infant survival rates and cause premature aging.[15]

Sulfur oxides, of which fossil-fueled power plants are major sources, are emitted when coal or oil containing sulfur is burned. An individual large power plant can emit as much as 1000 tons of sulfur oxides a day.[16] These emissions largely take the form of sulfur dioxide, which can convert in the atmosphere to sulfur trioxide, which in turn combines with water vapor, in the air or in the human lung, to form highly corrosive sulfuric acid.[17]

Sulfur oxides have been shown to irritate the eyes and the upper respiratory tract and to aggravate existing respiratory ailments; studies have also associated sulfur oxides statistically with respiratory and cardiac disease, and rises in death rates.[18] Sulfur oxides have been shown to damage vegetation and attack metals, masonry, stone, textiles, leather, paper and paint.[19] In sulfur-contaminated urban air, metals corrode as much as 30 times faster than in sulfur-free air.[20] Sulfur components in the atmosphere may also be transmitted to the earth in rainfall, raising acid levels in streams and lakes and on land to harmful levels, as well as injuring plants.[21]

Nitrogen oxides, a by-product of high-temperature interaction between atmospheric nitrogen and oxygen during fuel combustion, are a major constituent of photochemical smog.[22] Although the health effects of nitrogen oxides have not been the subject of as much research as have the health effects of sulfur oxides,[23] nitrogen dioxide has been associated with various diseases of the upper respiratory tract.[24] Moreover, the level of nitrogen dioxide which was found in one study to be health-related is exceeded in a high proportion of all United States cities.[25]

Photochemical oxidants, formed when nitrogen oxides interact with organic substances like hydrocarbons from unburned gasoline in sunlight, irritate the eye, and have been associated with aggravation of asthma and impairment of performance by high school athletes.[26] One of the photochemical oxidants, ozone, has been found in laboratory tests to harm the lung.[27] Nitrogen oxides and the photochemical oxidants created from them have also been implicated in damage to plants and property. Nitrogen oxides and ozone cause fabrics to deteriorate and dyes to fade; rubber is especially susceptible to ozone.[28]

Particulates can cause permanent damage to respiratory system surfaces [29] and act as reservoirs for other harmful air pollutants, carrying them further into the lung than they otherwise would reach, so that the effect of particulates and gases acting together is worse than the sum of the effects of either acting alone.[30] A study of 114 metropolitan areas in the United States linked increased levels of particulates in the air to significant rises in the death rate.[31] Particulates also soil and damage plants, masonry, metals and other materials.[32]

Attempts have been made to estimate the cost of the various types of air pollution described above, much of which is attributable to power generation. One study found that direct medical expenses and the value of earnings forgone through illness or death from air pollution total over $2 billion annually in the United States,[33] but noted that there was some evidence that the cost of air pollution health effects was as high as $29 billion.[34] Dr. Gordon J. MacDonald of the Council on Environmental Quality calculates that air pollution in 1968 cost $20 billion, and predicts that without new controls, this figure will jump to $41 billion by 1985.[35] The Environmental Protection Agency puts annual costs of air pollution at $16 billion, made up of $6 billion for health effects, $4.9 billion for materials and vegetation damage and $5.2 billion for property value losses. Intangibles like aesthetics and personal discomfort were not considered.[36] A study of the New York-New Jersey metropolitan area put the average cost of air pollution in the area at $620 per family per year, rising to a high of $850 per family per year in some parts of New York City.[37]

The costs to prevent this air pollution are also high. For example, backfitting of electrostatic precipitators to control particulate emission at three plants of the Appalachian Power Company will, according to company estimates, cost $28.8 million.[38] Various kinds of sulfur oxide control equipment will cost at least $50 per kilowatt to install at new plants; even then they may well not work effectively, and will require a great deal of power to operate.[39] Other options, such as con-

31

version to low-sulfur coal or oil, would be expensive in themselves and also require expensive modifications to existing equipment.[40] There also may not be adequate supplies of low-sulfur fuels to meet needs.[40a]

B. Fossil Fuels—Production and Wastes

Parts of the fossil-fuel cycle other than combustion also have adverse environmental effects. Other users of these fuels must share responsibility for these effects, but utilities' share of total fossil-fuel use is substantial: in 1970, power plants accounted for 57% of total U.S. coal consumption, 18% of gas consumption, and 8% of oil consumption.[41] Oil use, although comparatively small, is increasing rapidly, as utilities seek a low-sulfur substitute for coal and gas is scarce.[41a] Since effects of producing gas are small, concern centers on the effects of producing coal and oil.

About one quarter of the electric power generated in 1970 was produced by strip-mined coal.[41b] Strip mining of coal has received a great deal of attention, and will probably continue to do so in the future in view of the vast amounts of low-sulfur coal which lend themselves to surface mining in the western United States.[42] In 1970, 264 million tons of coal were surface mined, 44% of total production.[43] Of the 3 million acres which have been surface mined in the United States, only one third have been even partially reclaimed.[44] Surface mining disrupts the land, can lead to acid run-off to streams and creates vast refuse heaps.[45]

Underground mining also has problems. Of the 8 million acres of land over underground mines, 2 million have subsided;[46] 200 underground mine fires are now burning.[47] Also, underground mining, like strip mining, creates refuse and can foster acid run-off.[48] There are 23,000 acres of refuse banks now; this figure is expected to double by the year 2000.[49] Refuse banks are subject to persistent fires and can pollute streams through leaching.[50] Underground mining can also, of course, endanger those who work in the mines, through accidents or chronic disease.

Moreover, the burning of coal leaves a residue of ash. From 1958 to 1967, burning coal for power generation created 200 million tons of ash, which would occupy 2000 acres if piled forty feet high. From 1968 to 2000, it is estimated that coal-fueled power plants will produce 2 billion tons of ash, enough to cover 20,000 acres with forty-foot-high piles.[51] Uses can now be found for only a small fraction of this ash.

Use of oil, on the other hand, inevitably leads to water pollution. Sixty percent of the world's annual oil production is transported by sea.[52] Accidental spills from tankers and off-shore wells have received the most publicity: there were 92 spills of over 100 barrels each in United States waters in 1970.[53] But even if all these accidents could be prevented, only 10% of the problem would be solved, since 90% of oil discharged by man into the world's waters comes from wholly routine operations.[54]

Refining of petroleum also generates wastes which are often hard to handle in an environmentally acceptable manner, including catalysts, clays and acids. Some of these wastes are commercially valuable.[55]

C. HAZARDS FROM NUCLEAR POWER

In 1970, nuclear power plants, in which the heat from fission of uranium nuclei is used to produce steam to operate a generator, accounted for only 2% of the United States generating capacity,[56] and produced only one quarter as much energy as did the burning of wood.[57] The FPC predicts that the nuclear share in 1990 will be 38%, representing a seventy-three-fold increase in plant capacity.[58]

Dangers relating to nuclear power arise from the chances of harmful exposure to radioactive elements used as fuel in nuclear plants, to byproducts of those elements, or to materials which have been made radioactive by action of those elements during reactor operation. The debate over nuclear power centers on the question whether prevention of such exposure, during the production of nuclear fuel, routine operation of power plants, reprocessing of spent fuel and storage of wastes, as well as in the event of possible accidents, is sufficiently certain.

The nuclear fuel cycle begins with mining of uranium and thorium ore. The ores are refined and converted into various chemical forms and in most cases enriched in Uranium 235 content; the resulting compounds are made into fuel pellets and placed in metal tubes to form fuel rods. These rods are then bundled together to make up a fuel element, and hundreds of elements are positioned in a grid to form the reactor core.

In the course of the nuclear reaction which takes place in the core, heat is produced and transferred to the primary coolant which flows through the core. Steam to drive a turbine generator is then produced either directly from the primary coolant, as in the boiling-water reactor, or indirectly through heat transfer to the secondary coolant, as in the pressurized-water reactor and the high-temperature gas-cooled reactor.

When reactor fuel is spent, it is removed from the core, allowed to cool temporarily and then shipped to a reprocessing plant for recovery of valuable elements. The high-level wastes which are separated from the fuel during reprocessing, together with much less hazardous low-level wastes such as contaminated clothing, must then be carefully stored to prevent escape of dangerous radiation.[59]

Questions have been raised about several aspects of the nuclear fuel cycle outlined above. – First, some observers have contended that the routine low-level radioactive emissions from nuclear reactors and related facilities could be harmful to human health, particularly as the number of power reactors increases. Second, the effectiveness of certain reactor safety systems has been challenged. Third, the possibility that precautions during shipping and other fuel-cycle operations may be inadequate to prevent accidents or thefts has been widely mentioned. Finally, the sufficiency of present plans for high-level waste storage has been criticized.

Nuclear power reactors and processing plants routinely emit small quantities of radiation in liquid and gaseous form. Factors affecting these emissions have been stated to be:

> "(1) the level of defects in the zircaloy or stainless steel cladding of the UO_2 fuel pellets; (2) the volume of gases and liquids removed from the primary coolant system by plant operations and controlled leakage; and (3) the performance of the radioactive waste treatment equipment in containing and concentrating radioactive materials." [60]

These emissions, which are regulated by the Atomic Energy Commission, are many times lower than natural radiation levels, which range from 100 to 250 millirems per person annually in the United States,[61] or doses from diagnostic x-rays, estimated at approximately 100 millirems per person in 1970.[62] Some critics have nevertheless contended that even these low levels are not safe.[63] Much of the controversy concerning such low-level emissions has, however, abated following the recent proposal by the AEC to lower permissible emissions from power reactors. In December, 1970, the AEC announced amendments to its

34

regulations to require that radiation releases from licensed facilities be kept "as low as practicable," [64] and in June, 1971 the AEC issued notice of a proposed rulemaking to supplement the qualitative rules for new light-water-moderated reactors with numerical guides designed to limit the radiation dose to an individual on the boundary of a reactor site to 5 millirems yearly, or 5% of the average exposure from natural background radiation, and the radiation dose to sizable population groups from any plant to 1 millirem per year, or 1% of the average exposure from natural background radiation.[65] The AEC recently conducted public hearings on these proposed numerical emission guides.

Reactors in operation when these new rules come into effect will have three years in which to be brought into compliance, and the AEC will not act against a reactor unless emissions exceed four times the levels set in the rules. Moreover, since the proposed quantitative guides would only apply to present light-water reactors, not processing plants (which although many fewer in number than reactors give off higher levels of emissions per plant than reactors), gas-cooled converter reactors or breeder reactors, the debate over adequacy of emissions standards will probably continue, although with somewhat less stridency and with a somewhat more limited scope.

Debate over safety of nuclear reactors presently centers on the adequacy of emergency core cooling systems (ECCS), which are intended to prevent a reactor fuel core from overheating if it should ever lose its primary coolant due to multiple safety system failures. Overheating, if unchecked, could lead to a "melt-through" of the reactor's containment vessel, or to a steam explosion, both of which could release to the atmosphere large quantities of the reactor's "fission products inventory" —that is, highly radioactive debris.[66]

The ECCS issue first attracted public notice in May, 1971 when the Joint Committee on Atomic Energy of the Congress released an April letter from then AEC Chairman Glenn T. Seaborg to Committee Vice Chairman Senator John O. Pastore of Rhode Island. In that letter Seaborg stated that

> "The use of recently developed improved techniques for calculating fuel cladding temperatures following postulated loss-of-coolant accidents, and the results of preliminary safety research experiments, have indicated that the predicted margins of ECCS performance may not be as large as those predicted previously." [67]

Semi-scale tests in the fall of 1970 at the AEC's National Reactor Testing Station in Idaho indicated, moreover, that the emergency cooling water, instead of entering the core as planned, could instead be vaporized by the heat of the core and blown out the rupture through which the primary coolant had already escaped.[68]

In the wake of these disclosures, the AEC asked for more money from Congress to carry out further safety research and issued guidelines limiting full-power operation of certain reactors. However, a testing facility designed to confirm ECCS reliability, originally scheduled for completion in 1967, will not be finished until 1972 or 1973, and actual experiments will not yield results until 1974 or 1975.[69] One recent study summarized the ECCS controversy as follows:

"Although the evidence is not all in, judging from the AEC's actions in restricting the power level of certain operating reactors, there is at least a reasonable possibility that power reactors licensed by the AEC have been operating with a fundamental safety system (the ECCS) which was inadequate by the AEC's own standards. The fact that nuclear engineers thought they knew how ECCS would operate but that such systems had not been adequately tested is hardly an adequate excuse. As a minimum, it would seem that assurance beyond any reasonable doubt that nuclear safety systems will operate at least to AEC's own standards should have had absolute priority in the AEC's reactor development program."[70]

Hearings are presently being conducted by the AEC on the adequacy of ECCS similar to the low-level radiation emission hearings.

The rapid expansion of nuclear power which has been forecast will mean a major increase in the size and number of shipments of fuel and wastes between mines, enrichment, preparation and fabrication facilities, reactors, reprocessing facilities and waste storage sites. Can these shipments be adequately protected against accident and theft?

Although the past record in transporting radioactive materials is very good, it is clear that human error creates a finite risk of accident or at least temporary loss of radioactive material in transit. As the numbers of shipments increase, the chances of accidents will as well. According to a report by the Oak Ridge National Laboratory, the number of casks of spent fuel shipped will rise from 30 in 1970 to 9500 by the year 2000, and although the AEC strictly regulates packaging requirements according to the hazards posed by the materials to be shipped, even the sturdiest package is not proof against breakage.[71]

Increased handling of radioactive materials also raises the danger of theft, particularly of plutonium. Plutonium diversion has been discussed primarily in connection with the development of the fast breeder reactor, since the fast breeder will be fueled with, and will produce, plutonium. However, even present light-water reactors will begin using recycled plutonium for fuel fairly soon, so that a rapid rise in plutonium production and handling will soon take place whether or not the fast breeder is brought into service on schedule.[72]

Plutonium is a subject for concern because it is one of the most toxic substances known, and in addition, forms the raw material for atomic bombs. From as little as five kilograms of plutonium, a person with the requisite technical expertise can make a device capable of destroying a medium-sized city, of the type which was dropped on Nagasaki in 1945—and the civilian plutonium inventory in this country, presently 600 kilograms, is expected to rise by the year 2000 to 720,000 kilograms or more if predictions that one half our electricity needs in that year will be provided by nuclear reactors are correct.[73] Safeguarding systems can never be 100% effective, and plutonium's value might make it attractive to organized criminals as well as to political dissidents eager to blow up their opponents. Plutonium might be stolen in small quantities over a period of time from a processing plant, or a large quantity might be seized at once in a robbery. International as well as internal security might be threatened: a non-member of the nuclear club might divert plutonium given to it as reactor fuel into weapons manufacture.[74]

Outside specialists have criticized the AEC for not tightening security measures to make diversion more difficult,[75] and an AEC Commissioner has acknowledged:

> "Once special nuclear material is successfully stolen in small and possibly economically acceptable quantities, a supply-stimulated market for such illicit materials is bound to develop. And such a market can surely be expected to grow once a source of supply has been identified. As the market grows, the number and size of thefts can be expected to grow with it, and I fear such growth would be extremely rapid once it begins. Such a theft would quickly lead to serious eco-

nomic burdens to the industry and a threat to national security."[76]

Last comes the problem of waste disposal. High-level wastes resulting from reprocessing of spent fuel are very hot, very toxic and very radioactive. They contain large amounts of various long-lived dangerous radioactive isotopes with half-lives ranging from several decades to 24,000 years. Some wastes must be prevented, essentially for all time, from reaching the biosphere.[77] As nuclear power develops, moreover, the volume which must be so confined will increase rapidly. One course estimates that there will be 1300 cubic feet of solidified high-level wastes requiring storage each year by 1980, and that this figure will increase to 34,000 cubic feet each year by 2000.[78]

Until recently, the AEC planned to deal with these wastes by sealing them in a salt mine near Lyons, Kansas. The Director of the Kansas State Geological Survey has, however, likened the Lyons site to "a piece of Swiss cheese" due to oil and gas wells and old salt mines which honeycomb the site, and the AEC is apparently looking for another, more suitable, salt bed.[79] Plans have also been announced for construction of interim surface waste storage facilities, as well as more experimentation with alternative underground waste storage techniques.[79a] At this point, it seems clear that the waste disposal issue has not yet been satisfactorily resolved.[80]

D. COOLING AND ITS EFFECTS ON WATER QUALITY AND AQUATIC LIFE

A problem common to both fossil-fueled and nuclear power plants is the creation of waste heat. The average thermal efficiency of electricity generating plants in the United States in 1970 was approximately 30%;[81] in other words, 70% of the heat created was not used to generate electricity but rather had to be rejected to the environment. This waste heat from power generation would now be more than enough to heat every home in the United States.[82] The greatest attainable efficiency in a modern fossil-fueled plant is approximately 40%;[83] gas turbines achieve about 25% efficiency,[84] and the present generation of converter atomic reactor plants have efficiencies of from 31% to 32%.[85] A more advanced type of converter reactor, the high-temperature gas-cooled reactor, and the breeder reactor both show promise of attaining efficiencies equal to the best fossil plants,[86] and fossil-fueled units combining gas turbines with steam boilers may attain even higher efficiencies in the fairly near future.[87]

In a steam generating plant, nuclear or fossil, waste heat is removed from steam turbine exhaust by use of a condenser cooled by water. The predominant type of water cooling today is once-through; that is, water is removed from a source, heated by passage through the condenser, and returned to the source. Because of their lower efficiencies, and because they cannot discharge waste heat up a smokestack like fossil plants, present nuclear plants need up to 60% more cooling water and heat it to 20% higher temperatures than do fossil plants.[88]

Power plants' need for cooling water is large and getting larger. The electric industry now uses about 80% of all cooling water used by industry,[89] an amount equal to 10% of the total United States streamflow.[90] By 1980 it is predicted that cooling of generating plants will require one sixth of the total available fresh-water run-off.[91] Since short-term flood flows account for two thirds of the total run-off, the power industry will by 1980 require one half the total non-flood run-off,[92] although this demand may not be as great as it sounds, since water for cooling can be used repeatedly, once it has given off the heat it has absorbed to the atmosphere.

Many water bodies can absorb certain amounts of heat without apparent harm,[93] but excessive heat can harm water quality and aquatic life in a variety of ways. Water of higher temperature cannot contain as much oxygen as cooler water; its ability to assimilate oxygen-demanding wastes therefore decreases as it is heated.[94] Heat added to water may also suffocate living organisms, since while diminishing a water body's oxygen content, the heat increases the metabolism rate, and thus the oxygen requirements, of animals living in the water.[95] Heat can also increase organisms' sensitivity to disease or toxic substances, cause internal functional aberrations and death, interfere with critical life activities such as breeding, decrease food supplies and lead to replacement of a desirable species by one not so desirable.[96] Heated water may in addition serve as a barrier to migration.[97]

Absolute temperatures are not the only significant factors; seasonal and daily temperature variations, temperature patterns, fluctuations, extremes and averages may also be important.[98] While at some times of year a river or lake can accept large amounts of heat without damage, addition of the same amount of heat at other seasons may do great harm.[99]

Various means exist to lessen the burden of the projected heat load on waterways, by cooling heated water before it is returned to its source or using a closed cooling system. Long discharge canals can permit effluent to give off heat before returning to its source; the volume of cooling water used, and the speed of its discharge, can be manipulated to minimize heat rise.[99a] Spray and cooling ponds also permit discharge of heat to the atmosphere instead of the water source, as do cooling towers, which can be either "wet" (exposing water directly to the air to permit evaporation) or "dry" (retaining the coolant in a closed system around which air circulates). A natural-draft cooling tower relies on the chimney effect of naturally induced air currents, while forced-draft cooling towers use fans to create air flow.[99b]

There are, however, costs associated with these solutions to the heat problem. All cost more money to install and operate than simply once-through systems.[99c] There are also environmental costs: ponds require large land areas close to the generating plants, and evaporative ponds and towers use up large quantities of water, which is discharged to the atmosphere instead of being returned to its source.[99d] Under some circumstances, the water vapor emitted by evaporative cooling towers can form fog, ice or snow, and this vapor may also contain harmful chemicals.[99e] Finally, the large size of cooling towers may sometimes present aesthetic difficulties: natural-draft cooling towers can be over 300 feet in diameter at their base and over 400 feet high.[99f] These solutions to the heat discharge problem are thus not painless, and each site must be evaluated to see whether their advantages outweigh their disadvantages.[99g]

Other substances harmful to water quality and water life are often added to cooling water along with heat. Various biocides and other chemicals are routinely mixed with intake waters to prevent fouling of cooling systems and deterioration of fill in exaporative cooling towers.[100] Flushing of solids from such towers and leaching of metallic ions from all forms of heat exchange units can also be problems.[101] Studies in 1968 showed that oysters in the Patuxent River, Maryland began substantial accumulation of copper shortly after a power plant started up nearby; this accumulation spread downriver and increased with time.[102] Moreover, in addition to suffering harm from heat and chemicals added to cooling water, aquatic organisms may be physically injured or killed by being sucked into and through the cooling system itself.[103]

40

E. Energy Use and Climate

More speculative than possible harm to water quality and aquatic life is the question of the effect of heat created during energy production and use on climate, especially when combined with the carbon dioxide and particulates emitted when fossil fuels are burned. All energy eventually degrades to heat, released either at the point of production or during use. Carbon dioxide may compound the effect of such heat by acting as a one-way shield in the atmosphere, permitting sunlight to reach the earth's surface but preventing radiation of heat from the earth: the "greenhouse effect." [104] Particulates, on the other hand, may have a cooling effect because they block sunlight from reaching the earth.[105]

Worldwide, man's energy input is insignificant when compared to solar energy, and is likely to remain so for some time: it is estimated that even by 2000, man's energy use will still be much less than $\frac{1}{1000}$ of the sun's heat input.[106] Regionally, however, the effects of energy use are significant and will become more so, especially in an energy-intensive country like the United States. Manhattan now receives two and a half times more heat from combustion of fossil fuels during winter than from sunlight reaching the ground,[107] and by 2000, the release of energy in the Boston-Washington megalopolis will exceed 30% of the incident annual solar energy.[108] Measurable effects of such concentrated energy release are higher temperatures than surrounding areas (as much as 3 degrees higher in large cities during winter)[109] and greater cloudiness and precipitation (also stimulated by precipitation-inducing urban atmospheric dust).[110]

An appreciation of the magnitude of future problems may be gained from a projection of electricity consumption rates alone, leaving aside waste heat created when electricity is generated as well as all other forms of energy use. In 1970 the United States consumed 1.6 billion megawatt hours of electricity, approximately 8% of total energy use. Spread over the total U. S. land area, this electricity consumption represents an average energy release of .017 watts per square foot. Assuming consumption rates continue to double every ten years, in a century the rate of release will be 17 watts per square foot or only slightly less than the 18 to 19 watts per square foot average the United States receives from the sun.[111]

41

This projection, leaving out all forms of energy use other than electricity consumption, also leaves out possible multiplier effects of carbon dioxide emissions from burning fossil fuels. The total amount of carbon dioxide in the atmosphere has increased some 8% since 1900; [112] the amount of man-made carbon dioxide in the atmosphere is doubling every 23 years at current rates of deposition.[113] By 2000 there will be about 25% more carbon dioxide in the atmosphere than there is now.[114] The Report of the Study of Critical Environmental Problems, sponsored by the Massachusetts Institute of Technology, states:

> "Although we conclude that the probability of direct climate change in this century resulting from CO_2 [carbon dioxide] is small, we stress that the long-term potential consequences of CO_2 effects on the climate or of societal reaction to such threats are so serious that much more must be learned about future trends of climate change. Only through these measures can societies hope to have time to adjust to changes that may ultimately be necessary." [115]

The Report emphasizes that the quality of information available on climatic problems, as well as other global environmental problems, must be greatly improved, and the resources devoted to the study of such problems significantly increased, or "we may never be able to identify potential crises in enough time to avoid them and possibly to prevent irreversible global damage." [115a]

F. Hydroelectric Power Generation and the Environment

Conventional hydroelectric developments now have 15% of total generating capacity. By 1990, this share will fall to 7%, although increasing in absolute terms by nearly 60%. Pumped-storage developments now have only a 1% share of total capacity; by 1990, the FPC predicts this share will increase to 6% and the amount of pumped-storage capacity will increase by almost 20 times, reflecting much greater reliance on pumped-storage to supply peaking power.[115b] Conventional hydroelectric generation avoids the problems raised by use of fossil and atomic fuels, but, as might be expected, it has problems of its own. Damming of a waterway radically changes its characteristics by diminishing velocity and discharge and exchanging seasonal flow cycles for flow cycles related to power needs. The temperature and nutrient content of both released water and dammed water may be altered; evaporation of dammed water increases water loss, and silting behind dams will eventually cause a great decrease in the amount of water which can be impounded.[116] Pumped-storage projects share the problems of conventional hydroelectric projects and also introduce current changes and a daily draw-down of many feet of dammed water. All of these changes, plus the physical hazards of the dam and related machinery, can harm aquatic life.[117] In addition, since pumped-storage projects require the operation of conventional electric generating equipment to move water to the upper storage reservoir, they can cause the adverse environmental effects described above in the discussion of such conventional equipment.

Added to these factors are almost inevitable aesthetic controversies, since the very characteristics which make a dam or pumped-storage project site feasible from an engineering standpoint also contribute to the scenic beauty of the surrounding countryside.[118] Very real human problems are also created for those who must move from areas which are to be flooded.[119]

G. Power Transmission and the Environment

Last but not least in this catalog of environmental effects are the problems associated with electricity transmission. As stated above, the FPC predicts that 3 million acres will be needed for new transmission lines by 1990.[120] Undoubtedly routing of these lines, as well as the associated distribution lines and substations, will encounter opposition both from those who do not want a line on or visible from their property and from those who object to a particular corridor through wild or scenic areas on aesthetic grounds. Great differences of opinion can exist as to what areas are suitable for facilities, and what designs should be used even on acceptable sites. There is often a complete lack of concensus on the weight to be accorded aesthetics or on the degree of beauty particular equipment and locations possess.[120a] Poor construction and land management practices, including misuse of herbicides, can compound environmental difficulties.[121]

*   *   *

Two questions are raised by any discussion of the conflict between electricity and the environment. First, can the increasing demand for electricity be met, thus avoiding shortages and blackouts? Second, even

43

if demand is met, can we afford to pay the environmental costs involved? Supply problems and environmental problems have been identified, and efforts are being made to solve them; moreover, increased attention to various kinds of promising research projects will undoubtedly help minimize environmental harm. As of now, however, it must be admitted that neither of these two major questions has yet been satisfactorily or completely answered.

NOTES FOR CHAPTER III

1. *Federal Power Commission,* 1 *The 1970 National Power Survey* I–5–1, I–18–29 (1971); Testimony by J. N. Nassikas in *Hearings on H.R. 5277, H.R. 6970, H.R. 6971, H.R. 6972, H.R. 3838, H.R. 7045, H.R. 1079 and H.R. 1486 Before Subcomm. on Communications and Power, House Comm. on Interstate and Foreign Commerce,* 92d Cong., 1st Sess., ser. 92–31, 32, 33, pts. 1–3, Appendix A at I–4 (1971) [hereinafter cited as "Macdonald Hearings"]. The text of Chairman Nassikas' statement is in the printed hearings, but the appendices were not published and are in the files of the Subcommittee on Communications and Power.

2. Testimony by G. J. F. MacDonald in Macdonald Hearings at 306; *Council on Environmental Quality, the President's 1971 Environmental Program* 26 (1971).

3. *Office of Science and Technology, Energy Policy Staff, Electric Power and the Environment* 3 (1970).

4. *Id.;* Testimony by G. J. F. MacDonald in Macdonald Hearings at 306. Fossil-fueled power plants also contribute much smaller shares of substances other than sulfur oxides, nitrogen oxides and particulates, such as gaseous hydrocarbons and carbon monoxide. *National Academy of Engineering, Committee on Power Plant Siting, Engineering for Resolution of the Energy-Environment Dilemma* 39 (1972).

5. *Hearings on Environmental Effects of Producing Electric Power Before Joint Comm. on Atomic Energy,* 91st Cong., 1st Sess., pts. 1–2, at 812–13 (1969–70) [hereinafter cited as "JCAE Hearings"].

6. *Council on Environmental Quality, supra* note 2, at 26.

7. Paper by L. E. Niemeyer, R. A. McCormick, J. H. Ludwig, "Environmental Aspects of Power Plants," *Environmental Aspects of Nuclear Power Stations,* Proceedings of a Symposium held by the International Atomic Energy Agency, at 712 (1971) [hereinafter cited as "IAEA Symposium"].

8. *Id.*

8a. *Federal Power Commission, supra* note 1, at I–11–1.

8b. *National Tuberculosis and Respiratory Disease Association, Air Pollution Primer* 60–61 (1969).

8c. *Id.*

9. *Id.;* P. Goldstein, "Legal Control of Air and Water Pollution" 104 (unpublished).

9a. Respectively, 55% and 25%, and may be higher in some urban areas. See main text, *supra,* at notes 2, 4, and 5.

10. L. B. Lave and E. P. Seskin, "Air Pollution and Human Health," 169 *Science* 729 (Aug. 21, 1970).

11. *See* S. K. Mencher and H. M. Ellis, "Statement Regarding the Proposed National Ambient Air Quality Standards for Particulate Matter, Sulfur Dioxide and Nitrogen Dioxide" (Gordian Associates, Inc., New York, N. Y., 1971), for a review of certain studies which question, for example, the extent of the relationship between sulfur dioxide and bronchitis, asthma, heart disease and acute respiratory illness.

12. L. B. Lave and E. P. Seskin, *supra* note 10, at 729.

45

13. P. Goldstein, *supra* note 9, at 106–7; *National Tuberculosis and Respiratory Disease Association, supra* note 8b, at 65–72; L. B. Lave and E. P. Seskin, *supra* note 10, at 726–29; Paper by Y. Nishiwaki *et al.*, "Atmospheric Contamination of Industrial Areas Including Fossil-Fuel Power Stations, and a Method of Evaluating Possible Effects on Inhabitants," IAEA Symposium at 270.

14. *National Tuberculosis and Respiratory Disease Association, supra* note 8b, at 75; L. B. Lave and E. P. Seskin, *supra* note 10, at 727.

15. *National Tuberculosis and Respiratory Disease Association, supra* note 8b, at 76.

16. L. E. Niemeyer, R. A. McCormick, J. H. Ludwig, *supra* note 7, at 712; Y. Nishiwaki *et al.*, *supra* note 13, at 269.

17. Paper by M. Steinberg, "An Isotope-Ratio Method for Tracing Atmospheric Sulfur Pollutants," *Power Generation and Environment Change*, Proceedings of a Symposium held by the Committee on Environmental Alteration, American Association for the Advancement of Science, at 312–315 (1971) [hereinafter cited as "AAAS Symposium"]; W. H. Steigelmann, "Alternative Technologies for Discharging Waste Heat," AAAS Symposium at 405; P. Goldstein, *supra* note 9, at 99; *National Tuberculosis and Respiratory Disease Association, supra* note 8b, at 36; Y. Nishiwaki *et al.*, *supra* note 13, at 268; *National Air Pollution Control Administration, Air Quality Criteria for Sulfur Oxides* 10.3 (1969) [hereinafter cited as "Sulfur Oxides Criteria"].

18. M. Steinberg, *supra* note 17, at 302; P. Goldstein, *supra* note 9, at 106–7; *National Tuberculosis and Respiratory Disease Association, supra* note 8b, at 62, 75; Y. Nishiwaki *et al.*, *supra* note 13, at 263, 268, 270; Sulfur Oxides Criteria at 10.9–10.13.

19. M. Steinberg, *supra* note 17, at 302; P. Goldstein, *supra* note 9, at 109–10; *National Tuberculosis and Respiratory Disease Association, supra* note 8b, at 80, 83; L. E. Niemeyer, R. A. McCormick, J. H. Ludwig, *supra* note 7, at 715; Sulfur Oxides Criteria at 10.15–10.18.

20. P. Goldstein, *supra* note 9, at 110; *National Tuberculosis and Respiratory Disease Association, supra* note 8b, at 83.

21. L. E. Niemeyer, R. A. McCormick, J. H. Ludwig, *supra* note 7, at 715; W. W. Kellogg *et al.*, "The Sulfur Cycle," 175 *Science* 588 (Feb. 11, 1972).

22. P. Goldstein, *supra* note 9, at 100; *National Tuberculosis and Respiratory Disease Association, supra*, note 8b, at 84; Y. Nishiwaki *et al.*, *supra* note 13, at 271; *National Air Pollution Control Administration, Air Quality Criteria for Photochemical Oxidants* 10.1 (1970) [hereinafter cited as "Photochemical Oxidants Criteria"]; *Environmental Protection Agency, Air Quality Criteria for Nitrogen Oxides* 11.2 (1971) [hereinafter cited as "Nitrogen Oxides Criteria"].

23. Nitrogen Oxides Criteria at 11.8–11.9.

24. P. Goldstein, *supra* note 9, at 106; Y. Nishiwaki *et al.*, *supra* note 13, at 270; Nitrogen Oxides Criteria at 11.4–11.8.

25. Nitrogen Oxides Criteria at 11.8.

26. Photochemical Oxidants Criteria at 10.7–10.8.

27. Photochemical Oxidants Criteria at 10.5.

28. Photochemical Oxidants Criteria at 10.4–10.5; Nitrogen Oxides Criteria at 11.3–11.4.

29. *National Air Pollution Control Administration, Air Quality Criteria for Particulate Matter* 12.5 (1969) [hereinafter cited as "Particulate Matter Criteria"].

30. P. Goldstein, *supra* note 9, at 97 and 110; *National Tuberculosis and Respiratory Disease Association, supra* note 8b, at 33–34; Y. Nishiwaki *et al., supra* note 13, at 271; Particulate Matter Criteria at 12.5.

31. L. B. Lave and E. P. Seskin, *supra* note 10, at 728.

32. Particulate Matter Criteria at 12.11–12.15.

33. L. B. Lave and E. P. Seskin, *supra* note 10, at 730.

34. L. B. Lave and E. P. Seskin, *supra* note 10, at 732 n. 64.

35. Paper by G. J. F. MacDonald, "Energy and the Environment," at 11–12, Conference sponsored by Resources for the Future, Inc., Washington, D. C., April 21, 1971.

36. *Council on Environmental Quality, Second Annual Report* 106–07 (1971).

37. Paper by I. Michelson, "The Costs of Living in Polluted Air versus the Costs of Controlling Air Pollution," at 9, 11, U.S. Public Health Service Conference on Air Pollution Abatement in the New York—New Jersey Area, New York, Jan. 11, 1967.

38. Testimony by J. Tillinghast Before West Virginia Air Pollution Control Commission, Dec. 15, 1971, at 4.

39. *Id.* at 5; A. Squires, "Capturing Sulfur During Combustion," 74 *Technology Review* 52–59 (Dec. 1971); A. V. Slack and H. L. Falkenberry, "SO_2: More Questions than Answers," 176 *Electrical World* 50–54 (Dec. 15, 1971).

40. J. Tillinghast, *supra* note 38, at 5–7; A. Squires, *supra* note 39, at 52–59.

40a. *Federal Power Commission, supra* note 1, at I–1–3.

41. *Resources for the Future, Inc., Energy Research Needs* I–16 to I–17 (1971).

41a. *Federal Power Commission, supra* note 1, at I–4–14, I–4–17.

41b. *National Coal Association, Impact of Surface-Mined Bituminous Coal and Lignite on U.S. Energy Sector* (undated).

42. W. Kasper, "East Coast Supply and Demand for Low Sulfur Fuel," *New York State Public Service Commission, OER Report No. 1* 12 (1971); J. Branscome, "Appalachia—Like the Flayed Back of a Man," N.Y. Times, Dec. 15, 1971, § 6 (Magazine), at 30.

43. *National Coal Association, supra* note 41b.

44. *Council on Environmental Quality, supra* note 36, at 108.

45. Paper by H. Perry, "Environmental Aspects of Coal Mining," AAAS Symposium at 318; *Council on Environmental Quality, supra* note 36, at 108.

46. *Id.*; H. Perry, *supra* note 45, at 323.

47. *Id.*

48. *Id.* at 318.

49. *Id.* at 325.

50. *Id.*

51. Testimony by H. Perry in JCAE Hearings at 325.

47

52. J. E. Bryson, "Tanker Collisions, Spills, and Marine Traffic Regulation," *Natural Resources Defense Council Newsletter* ix (Summer 1971).

53. *Council on Environmental Quality, supra* note 2, at 220–21.

54. *Id.*

55. H. Perry and H. Berkson, "Must Fossil Fuels Pollute?" 74 *Technology Review* 40 (Dec. 1971).

56. Federal Power Commission, *supra* note 1, at I–18–29; J. N. Nassikas, *supra* note 1, Appendix A at I–4.

57. H. C. Hottel and J. B. Howard, "An Agenda for Energy," 74 *Technology Review* 40 (Jan. 1972).

58. Federal Power Commission, *supra* note 1, at I–6–1, I–18–29; J. N. Nassikas, *supra* note 1, Appendix A at I–4.

59. J. F. Hogerton, "Atomic Power Safety," *U.S. Atomic Energy Commission Division of Technical Information* 13–14 (1964); *Resources for the Future, Inc., supra* note 41, at VI–65 to VI–66.

60. H. R. Denton, "Summary of Statement on the Sources of Radioactive Material in Effluents from Light-Water-Cooled Nuclear Power Reactors and State of Technology of Waste Treatment Equipment to Minimize Releases," AEC News Release No. P–18 (Jan. 21, 1972).

61. Denver Post, Nov. 28, 1971, at 3, col. 1.

62. U.S. Public Health Service Report BRH/DBE 70–1, *Nuclear Safety* 457 n. 14 (Sept.-Oct. 1971).

63. *Compare* A. R. Tamplin, "Issues in the Radiation Controversy," 27 *Bulletin of the Atomic Scientists* 25–27 (Sept. 1971), *with* P. J. Lindop and J. Rotblat, "Radiation Pollution of the Environment," *Id.* at 17–24, *and* J. Lederberg, "Squaring an Infinite Circle: Radiobiology and the Value of Life," *Id.* at 43–45.

64. 35 Fed.Reg. 18385 (1970).

65. 36 Fed.Reg. 11114 (1971). *See also* "Reactor Emissions: AEC Guidelines Move Toward Critics' Position," 172 *Science* 1215–16 (June 18, 1971).

66. *Resources for the Future, Inc., supra* note 41, at VI–84 to VI–94; "Nuclear Reactor Safety: A Skeleton at the Feast?" 172 *Science* 918 (May 28, 1971).

67. "Nuclear Reactor Safety: A Skeleton at the Feast?" 172 *Science* 918 (May 28, 1971).

68. *Id.* at 919.

69. "Nuclear Reactor Safety: A New Dilemma for the AEC," 173 *Science* 128 (July 9, 1971); A. Ripley, "Safety Gear Untried at Power Plants," N.Y. Times, Dec. 11, 1971, at 1, col. 8.

70. *Resources for the Future, Inc., supra* note 41, at VI–94 n. 1; *see also* R. E. Lapp, "Thoughts on Nuclear Plumbing," N.Y. Times, Dec. 12, 1971, § 4, at 11, col. 3.

71. "Radioactive Cargoes: Record Good but the Problems Will Multiply," 172 *Science* 1318, 1320 (June 25, 1971); *see also Resources for the Future, Inc., supra* note 41, at VI–71 to VI–74.

72. *Resources for the Future, Inc., supra* note 41, at VI–46.

73. "Plutonium: Reactor Proliferation Threatens a Nuclear Black Market," 172 *Science* 143 (April 9, 1971) ; *M. Willrich, ed., Civilian Nuclear Power and International Security,* at 3–4 (1971).

74. *Resources for the Future, Inc., supra* note 41, at VI–47.

75. Paper by T. Taylor, "The Need for National and International Systems to Provide Physical Security for Fissionable Materials," Symposium of Committee on Environmental Alterations, American Association for the Advancement of Science, Philadelphia, Pennsylvania, Dec. 28, 1971.

76. "Plutonium: Reactor Proliferation Threatens a Nuclear Black Market," 172 *Science* 143 (April 9, 1971).

77. Paper by W. Hambleton, "Storage of High-Level Radioactive Waste," at 10, Symposium of Committee on Environmental Alterations, American Association for the Advancement of Science, Philadelphia, Pennsylvania, Dec. 28, 1971 ; *J. Holdren and P. Herrera, Energy* 62–63 (1971).

78. *Resources for the Future, Inc., supra* note 41, at VI–68, Table 1.

79. W. Hambleton, *supra* note 77. The AEC recently released the results of a study it had commissioned by the Kansas State Geological Survey, which found Rice County, Kansas, where the Lyons site is located, to be the worst choice of potential areas for waste storage in Kansas. *See* AEC News Release No. P–20 (Jan. 21, 1972).

79a. "AEC Announces Plans for Management of High-Level Radioactive Wastes," AEC News Release No. P–143 (May 18, 1972).

80. The AEC's role with respect to another form of radioactive waste, uranium mining tailings, has also been subject to criticism. *See* H. P. Metzger, "Dear Sir: Your House Is Built On Radioactive Uranium Waste," N.Y. Times, Oct. 30, 1971, § 6 (Magazine), at 14 ; A. Ripley, "Error Implied in Using Uranium Sands," N.Y. Times, Dec. 7, 1971, at 22, col. 1.

81. *Resources for the Future, Inc., supra* note 41, at I–24. Moreover, this figure represents a drop from the 33% average efficiency in 1968. H. Perry, *supra* note 51, at 324.

82. E. Cook, "The Flow of Energy in an Industrial Society," 224 *Scientific American* 144 (Sept. 1971) ; H. Perry and H. Berkson, *supra* note 55, at 43.

83. *Resources for the Future, Inc., supra* note 41, at VI–12.

84. Paper by S. E. Beall, Jr. and A. J. Miller, "The Use of Heat as Well as Electricity from Electricity Generating Systems," at 5, Symposium of Committee on Environmental Alterations, American Association for the Advancement of Science, Philadelphia, Pennsylvania, Dec. 29, 1971.

85. *Resources for the Future, Inc., supra* note 41, at VI–12.

86. *Resources for the Future, Inc., supra* note 41, at VI–12, VI–35.

87. F. L. Robson and A. J. Giramonti, "Increasing Gas Turbine Outputs for Combined Gas/Steam Systems," 74 *Technology Review* 60 (Dec. 1971).

88. Paper by R. E. Nakatani, D. Miller and J. V. Tokar, "Thermal Effects and Nuclear Power Stations in the U.S.A.," IAEA Symposium at 563.

89. Paper by S. F. Singer, "Environmental Quality and the Economics of Cooling," AAAS Symposium at 344.

90. E. Cook, *supra* note 82 at 142.

91. S. F. Singer, supra *note* 89, at 345.

92. *Id.*

93. *See e. g.*, Paper by D. Merriman, "Does Industrial Calefaction Jeopardize the Ecosystem of a Long Tidal River?," IAEA Symposium at 528–530; "The Effect of Temperature on Aquatic Life in the Ohio River" i-vi, 150–51 (WAPORA, Inc., Washington, D.C., 1971).

94. S. F. Singer, *supra* note 89, at 346.

95. S. F. Singer, *supra* note 89, at 346; Paper by C. A. Carlson, Jr., "The Impact of Waste Heat on Aquatic Ecology," AAAS Symposium at 355; Testimony by R. Johnson in JCAE Hearings at 341; Paper by W. L. Templeton and C. C. Coutant, "Studies on the Biological Effects of Thermal Discharges from Nuclear Reactors to the Columbia River at Hanford," IAEA Symposium at 591–92.

96. S. F. Singer, *supra* note 89, at 346; C. A. Carlson, Jr., *supra* note 95, at 356; R. Johnson, *supra* note 95, at 342; Paper by D. Mount, "Thermal Standards in the United States of America," IAEA Symposium at 197; W. L. Templeton and C. C. Coutant, *supra* note 95, at 591–92.

97. R. Johnson, *supra* note 95, at 348.

98. *Id.* at 341; D. Mount, *supra* note 96, at 197.

99. W. L. Templeton and C. C. Coutant, *supra* note 95, at 602.

99a. W. H. Stiegelmann, *supra* note 17, at 399–400.

99b. *Id.* at 400–01.

99c. Paper by W. G. Belter, "Thermal Effects—a Potential Problem in Perspective," AAAS Symposium at 370.

99d. *Id.* at 370–71.

99e. *Id.*

99f. *Id.*

99g. C. A. Carlson, Jr., *supra* note 95, at 358; W. H. Stiegelmann, *supra* note 17, at 401–05.

100. W. H. Steigelmann, *supra* note 17, at 404–05; R. Johnson, *supra* note 95, at 341, 343; W. L. Templeton and C. C. Coutant, *supra* note 95, at 602; G. J. F. MacDonald, *supra* note 4, at 306.

101. W. H. Steigelmann, *supra* note 17, at 404–05; R. Johnson, *supra* note 95, at 341.

102. *Id.* at 341.

103. *Id.* at 343.

104. Paper by G. J. F. MacDonald, "Climatic Consequences of Increased Carbon Dioxide in the Atmosphere," AAAS Symposium at 251–252.

105. Particulate Matter Criteria at 12.8.

106. C. Starr, "Energy and Power," 224 *Scientific American* 46 (Sept. 1971).

107. G. J. F. MacDonald, *supra* note 35, at 6.

108. Paper by R. T. Jaske, "Comments on the Use and Abuse of Energy in the American Economy," AAAS Symposium at 390–91.

109. G. J. F. MacDonald, *supra* note 35, at 6–7.

110. *Id.*; Particulate Matter Criteria at 12.8.

111. C. M. Summers, "The Conversion of Energy," 224 *Scientific American* 160 (Sept. 1971).

112. G. J. F. MacDonald, *supra* note 35, at 8.

113. *Id.*; G. J. F. MacDonald, *supra* note 104, at 247.

114. *Environmental Pollution Panel, President's Science Advisory Committee, Restoring the Quality of Our Environment* 9 (1965).

115. *Study of Critical Environmental Problems, Man's Impact on the Global Environment, Assessment and Recommendations for Action* 12 (1970).

115a. *Id.* at 4.

115b. *Federal Power Commission, supra* note 1, at I–7–1, I–18–29.

116. Paper by K. F. Lagler, "Ecological Effects of Hydroelectric Dams," AAAS Symposium at 136–147.

117. Paper by D. A. Berkowitz, "Pumped Storage Hydroelectric Projects," AAAS Symposium at 164–169.

118. *See* Scenic Hudson Preservation Conference v. FPC, 354 F.2d 608 (2d Cir. 1965), *cert. denied*, 384 U.S. 941 (1966).

119. *See* E. W. Kenworthy, " 'Pollution Dilution' Issue in Blue Ridge Power Plan," N. Y. Times, Nov. 7, 1971, § 1, at 50, col. 1.

120. *See* text, *supra*, at II–3, n. 7.

120a. On the difficulty of handling issues of aesthetics, *see* D. Sive, "Some Thoughts of an Environmental Lawyer in the Wilderness of Administrative Law," 70 *Col.L.R.* 612, 629 (1970).

121. *See Federal Power Commission, Electric Power Transmission and the Environment, Guidelines for the Protection of Natural, Historic, Scenic, and Recreational Values in the Design and Location of Rights-of-Way and Transmission Facilities.*

IV. AN OVERVIEW OF THE DECISION-MAKING PROCESS

A. The Issues

The preceding chapters have summarized the many, often conflicting, considerations involved in electric power and the environment. Seven issues usefully focus these considerations as a means to study the decision-making process. The seven issues are:

1. *Demand.* By what policies, if any, should the use of electricity be encouraged, discouraged, or limited? The issue of how much electricity society will use determines the very scope of the electricity/environment question and involves important value questions.

2. *Capacity and its Regional Allocation.* Given the answer to the demand question, how much capacity for generation and transmission is needed in each region and in what general parts of the region should it go? The resolution of the demand issue makes determining the needed generating capacity no more than a matter of computation since a plant itself does not encourage aggregate demand while not building a plant, whose output consumers would use, necessarily implies a decision to limit demand. But, deciding where to put plants affects the transmission capacity needed and involves allocating potential environmental risks among air and water sheds and populations of varying densities.

3. *Land Use.* Given the regional allocation of facilities, at which specific sites shall the plants and transmission lines be located? This issue requires consideration of compatiblity with adjoining uses, aesthetics, plant design, recreation, and historical preservation.

4. *Alternatives.* Which of the alternatives for producing power—atomic, hydro, fossil, and their subtypes—should a particular plant use? This issue requires choosing among various types

of ecological risk and its resolution will affect the land use choice.

5. *Research and Development.* How shall research funds be allocated? This issue will determine the alternatives available in future years and has implications for the attainable air, water, and safety standards.

6. *Air and Water Standards.* What standards for emissions to the air and water must the plant meet? This issue, like the safety issue, involves trade-offs between economic and environmental costs.

7. *Safety.* What safety standards must the plant meet? This issue relates mainly to atomic plants, but also to other types of plants and transmission lines. Like the air and water issue, safety standards will affect the land use decision.

Any such specification of issues is necessarily artificial because the resolution of one issue will affect the resolution of others, particularly where long run interactions are considered. Thus, higher air standards may induce more air pollution control research. Or, a slowed growth in the demand for electricity may ease pressures for tighter standards on thermal effluents.

B. THE PRIVATE SECTOR'S ROLE

Increasing government regulation has cut into the private sector's previously dominant role in resolving these issues, but still leaves utilities with, at least, the power of initiative in most areas.

1. *Demand.* Because utilities have historically provided all the electricity desired, users of electricity have chosen the amount of power used. Each corporation or individual decides how much electricity is wanted at the price. Since the price omits electricity's environmental costs that regulation has left unchecked, the demand issue is resolved without consideration of its remaining environmental impact. Utilities also carry out practices to affect usage, some of which are subject to regulatory review.

2. *Capacity and Regional Allocation.* Utilities and their regional organization initially determine the issue of capacity and regional allocation in the course of systems planning. Commissions have informal powers to review these plans, but have an actual veto power only as each facility comes up for review in the licensing process.

3. *Land Use.* Utilities study alternative sites and initiate applications to build at a particular site subject to regulatory veto. Utilities' initial choices are limited to some extent by zoning and other land use controls which rule out, from the outset, many types of areas. In addition, a few states such as New York have systems to purchase and inventory sites for power plants.

4. *Alternatives.* Utilities initiate the choice of production mode subject to regulatory veto.

5. *Research and Development.* Manufacturers of hardware and, to some extent, utilities financed and allocated research efforts without any major governmental involvement until the advent of the Atomic Energy Commission. The Commission now funds most nuclear power research. More recently, the federal government and some state governments have begun smaller research programs in such areas as coal gasification and siting respectively.

6. *Air and Water Standards.* Federal legislation now requires the setting of governmental standards. Utilities may decide whether or not their plants should emit less pollutants than the standards allow, subject to regulatory review.

7. *Safety.* While the utilities initiate the design of atomic plants, subject to regulatory review, the AEC has taken considerable initiative in developing the basic designs and safety standards.

C. THE PUBLIC SECTOR'S ROLE

The role of the public sector in electric power and the environment has grown in layers. From the outset, electric facilities were subject to police power regulation exercised by state and local government. Such regulation grew from the controls of public utility commissions and the laws generally applicable to any large industrial installation to include zoning, building codes, and increasingly comprehensive air and water pollution control schemes. As state and local regulation increased, the federal government made more systematic its jurisdiction over water power by creating the Federal Power Commission (FPC) in 1920. Then, after World War II, Congress created the Atomic Energy Commission (AEC) to develop atomic power and regulate its radiological safety. In the following years, Congress enacted a series of laws requiring the states to regulate air and water pollution more extensively and giving the federal government itself a larger role. Then, the National Environmental Policy Act of 1969 (NEPA) commanded federal agencies such as the FPC and the AEC to include environmental policy in their considerations and mandated procedures to that end. Most recently, an executive order has required the Army Corps of Engineers, in conjunction with the federal Environmental Protection Agency (EPA), to consider a wide range of environmental questions in determining whether to issue permits to emit water waste, as required under the 1899 Rivers and Harbors Act.

Thus, in general, government at all levels has responded to new concerns and new technologies by legislation which erected new structures more often than consolidating old ones. Therefore, the licensing of generating plants and transmission lines involves many layers of permits, licenses, and regulations.

Atomic plants and perhaps their attendant transmission lines require approval from the AEC acting under the Atomic Energy Act and NEPA. Also, permits to build structures and discharge waste in navigable waters are required from the Corps of Engineers. Neither the AEC or Corps approval may issue without a state certificate as to the impact on water quality (a section 21(b) certificate). In addition, the plant and transmission lines must receive a range of state and local permits which may involve any aspect of the facilities except radiological safety.

Hydroelectric plants, including pumped-storage plants, and their attendant transmission lines require approval from the FPC under the Federal Power Act. The FPC may not issue licenses without a section 21(b) certificate, but the FPC license largely preempts state and local regulation.

Fossil-fueled plants must usually receive permits from the Corps of Engineers under various sections of the Rivers and Harbors Act of 1899. NEPA probably requires broader consideration of environmental issues by the Corps in these cases because the Corps here has the lead role. A section 21(b) certificate is again required. Also, at the federal level, the plant must comply with EPA's regulations on air pollution for power plants. In addition, the plant must comply with state and local regulation.

Transmission lines attendant to no particular nuclear or hydro plant must comply with state and local law.

55

This thumbnail sketch gives little idea of the process's complexity but does show how laws at all levels of government modify the jurisdiction of the three lead federal agencies—the AEC, the FPC, and the Corps. Before summarizing their procedures, the report first outlines the framework in which they work. What follows then is a description of NEPA, which expressly reads environmental policies and procedures into their processes, and APA, which provides a charter of administrative practice. Thereafter, this section outlines the joint roles of federal and state agencies under the federal air and water pollution legislation as well as the complex of other state and local regulation. Then, the next section will trace the routes which atomic, hydro, and fossil plants must follow through the lead federal agencies working within this framework.

1. NATIONAL ENVIRONMENTAL POLICY ACT

The National Environmental Policy Act of 1969 (NEPA) [1] sets forth Congressional policy concerning environmental quality; it directs federal agencies to implement the policy through specific procedures; and it establishes the Council on Environmental Quality (CEQ). To clarify the Act, the CEQ has issued guidelines, pursuant to authorization by Executive Order [2] to assist agencies in fulfilling their NEPA obligations.

In its statement of policy, NEPA emphasizes the need for "man and nature [to] exist in productive harmony" [3] in a densely populated, highly technologicial society. Congress stated its desire that "each person should enjoy a healthful environment," [4] and that, as a nation, we should strive for "a balance between population and resource use which will permit high standards of living and a wide sharing of life's amenities." [5]

In order to implement these policies, the Act requires federal agencies to comply with certain procedural requirements, which have been called the "action-forcing" provisions of NEPA. By comparison to the directive that agencies "use all practicable means and measures" [6] to implement the policy statements, agencies are required to comply with procedural provisions "to the fullest extent possible." [7] The CEQ Guidelines interpret this to mean that agencies must comply "unless existing law applicable to the agency's operations expressly prohibits or makes compliance impossible." [8] Thus, agency procedural responsibilities under NEPA are mandatory.

Basically, the procedural requirements state that agencies must use "a systematic, interdisciplinary approach" [9] in their planning, recognize and appropriately consider environmental value in their decision-making, develop alternatives to proposals with environmental impact, support and assist international as well as state and local endeavors to maintain environmental quality, and issue "impact statements" on "major Federal actions significantly affecting the quality of the human environment." [10] This latter provision, requiring impact statements, makes the most specific demand on agencies and has been the most controversial.

The Act indicates that the statement should include information on the anticipated effect of the proposal on the environment, on possible adverse effects, on alternatives, on short-term uses of the environment compared with the fulfillment of long-term needs, and on the possible irrevocable loss of resources.[11] According to the Guidelines, the impact statement requirement applies to all federal agencies, except the Environmental Protection Agency in its "environmental protective regulatory activities." [12]

The Guidelines define "major Federal actions" to include legislative recommendations, contracts, grants, loans, subsidies, licenses, permits, regulations, and the like.[13] The Council advises that the phrase "significantly affecting the quality of the human environment" should be interpreted "with a view to the overall, cumulative impact of the action proposed." [14] In any event, controversial projects should be reported, and reports should be issued even if the agency believes that the proposed action will be beneficial in the long run.[15] The Office of Management and Budget (OMB) reserves the right to request statements from agencies when it feels they are necessary.[16]

The statute requires that the report be made by a "responsible Federal official"; [17] however, this phrase has not been further clarified by the Guidelines.

The precise stage in the development of a project at which a report must be issued is also unclear, but the Guidelines note that it should be prepared "as early as possible" [18] and "early enough in the agency review process before an action is taken in order to permit meaningful consideration of the environmental issues involved." [19]

While the Act mentions only "detailed statements," the Guidelines envision both "draft" and "final" environmental reports. Draft statements are to be circulated to other relevant federal agencies for comment and to state and local agencies and to the CEQ.[20] At the same time that draft statements are circulated for comment, the Guidelines indicate that they should be made available to the public, unless disclosure would increase procurement costs.[21] Public hearings should be held, "whenever appropriate"; [22] when held, draft statements should be made available to the public at least 15 days before the hearings.[23] Draft reports should be made public at least 90 days prior to administrative action; final statements, along with agency comments, must be publicly available 30 days before such action.[24] Legislative proposals should be publicized before Congressional hearings.[25]

Most agencies require that applicants for permits or licenses, contractors, grantees, and the like prepare draft impact statements. Agencies frequently have used these statements partly or wholly as the draft statement, but a recent judicial interpretation, now being appealed, holds that an agency must draft its own statement.[25a] Whether the draft report is written by the applicant or the agency's "responsible official," after it has been prepared, it is sent to various federal agencies, to interested state and local officials, and to the CEQ. Comments made by each "shall accompany the proposal through the existing agency review process," [26] and are to be reflected in the agency's final statement.

While most attention has been focused on the impact statement requirement of NEPA, agencies are also under an obligation to comply with several other statutory procedures concerning the approach taken to planning and decision-making. An obvious failure to "utilize a systematic, interdisciplinary approach," [27] for example, might render agency action void as arbitrary, capricious and an abuse of discretion. The procedural provisions of NEPA, like those of the Atomic Energy Act and the Federal Power Act, can be implemented through appropriate procedures under the Administrative Procedure Act.

The CEQ was established by NEPA to assist the President and federal agencies in their NEPA responsibilities. The Council consists of three members appointed by the President with the advice and consent of the Senate. By statute, the Council is empowered to employ officers and staff to enable it to fulfill its functions.[28] In 1971, the CEQ employed twenty-three professional and thirty-two administrative and clerical employees.[29] In addition, the Council is assisted by four advisory committees.[30]

58

The CEQ's responsibilities are to advise the President on environmental problems and national programs affecting the environment, to undertake research and accumulate data concerning environmental problems and progress, to report annually on the state of the environment, to consult with the Citizens' Advisory Committee and federal, state and local agencies, and to review and comment upon agency impact reports.[31] Beyond this, the CEQ has little power. It does not, for example, have authority to request an impact statement on a project which the lead agency does not consider a "major Federal action significantly affecting the quality of the human environment." As noted previously, OMB claims the authority to make such a request.

NEPA is silent as to enforcement of its provisions, but thus far citizens' groups have successfully enforced the Act through court actions based on the Administrative Procedure Act.

2. ADMINISTRATIVE PROCEDURE ACT

The Administrative Procedure Act (APA),[32] enacted in 1946, applies to most federal agencies, including all those concerned with electric power or the environment. The Act sets forth general administrative procedures to be followed unless expressly modified by the agency's organic statutes,[33] and outlines rights and obligations of both agencies and parties in agency proceedings. This subsection attempts only a quick review of some important concepts arising under the APA.

The typical administrative agency is delegated legislative powers by Congress; it is organized to carry out specific governmental tasks, and usually makes its own procedural rules within the framework of standards prescribed within its statute and the APA. The APA envisions two types of agency proceedings: rulemakings, which set procedural and substantive policies of broad application,[34] and adjudications, which decide specific controversies.[35] Because of the relaxed rules of procedure which agencies follow, these seemingly separate functions may be handled simultaneously. In any case, the APA requires in most instances that the publication of the time, place, and nature of agency proceedings appear in the Federal Register.[36]

The rulemaking procedure consists of publication of the proposed rule or of the subject of rulemaking, allowing an opportunity to interested parties to submit written comments.[37] After considering these comments, the agency publishes the final version at least 30 days prior to its effective date.[38] There is no right to present oral argument.[39]

Where, however, statutes require a determination on the record after an agency hearing, due process does require an adjudication in a trial-type hearing.[40] The issues must be decided on the hearing record. Hearing rights include calling of witnesses and cross-examination. Interested persons may intervene and become parties, where they are specifically granted this right by the agency statute, or where they have standing under constitutional principles governing judicial proceedings. The right to intervene is generally available when the interested person would in fact be adversely affected by contested governmental action.[41] Although a person who meets this requirement cannot ordinarily be denied intervention,[42] participation may be limited in some circumstances to the submission of a written statement.[43]

Agencies have also experimented with proceedings which are hybrids between adjudications and rulemakings. In these cases, parties may have some, but not all of the adjudicatory rights.

Agency decisions in adjudicatory hearings may be expressly made subject to judicial review by statute.[44] In any case, unless expressly precluded, a person legally wronged or "aggrieved by agency action within the meaning of a relevant statute, is entitled to judicial review thereof." [45] The scope of review includes questions of law.[46] Findings of fact are unreviewable unless they are not supported by substantial evidence, are in excess of statutory authority, or are arbitrary, capricious or an abuse of discretion.[47] Although a presumption of correctness favors the administrative body, courts are tending to take a close look at agency action.[48]

The APA does not provide parties with discovery rights, but agencies have discretion to adopt a discovery system. Most federal agencies have not done so,[49] but those most directly concerned with electric power and the environment have.

The APA has been amended by the Freedom of Information Act,[50] which deals with the availability to the public of government records. Written records must be disclosed to any person requesting them in accordance with agency rules.[51] Here again, the agency's organic statute may expressly exempt records from disclosure or allow the agency to exercise its discretion in deciding whether or not to disclose the information.[52] In addition, there is no disclosure requirement where an Executive Order has made such information secret in the interest of national defense or of foreign policy.[53]   Nor need the agency disclose "trade secrets and commercial or financial information obtained from a person and privileged or confidential," [54] or "inter-agency or intra-agency memorandums or letters" which would otherwise not be available.[55]   Also, inquiring parties must request *identifiable* records.[56]   That one may not know that a particular document exists or how to identify it, often presents a problem for members of the general public.

One final provision of the APA, dealing with electric utilities, deserves mention.   In general, the Act prohibits an agency employee from assuming the dual role of investigator/prosecutor and decision-maker.[57]   Excepted from the rule are hearings on applications for construction licenses and "proceedings involving the validity or application of rates, facilities, or practices of public utilities or carriers." [58]

3. AIR AND WATER STANDARDS

In the past five years, the federal government has taken an increasingly active role in controlling air and water pollution.   The passage of the Federal Water Pollution Control Act [59] and the Clean Air Act,[60] along with the creation of the Environmental Protection Agency (EPA) [61] as the federal department responsible for enforcement of the federal legislation, has further interjected the federal government into this area.   While standard-setting and supervisory powers are now vested in EPA, the states still retain responsibilities within the federal scheme for implementation of standards and for enforcement.

Air Standards.   The federal air amendments of 1970 give EPA power to set primary and secondary air pollution standards, to review state implementation plans, and to regulate major new stationary air pollution sources as well as the emission of "hazardous substances." Under the statutory scheme each state has primary responsibility for assuring air quality within that state; [62] each is to submit for the Administrator's approval an implementation plan specifying the manner in which national air quality standards will be achieved and maintained.[63]   Public hearings are required before the implementation plan is formulated and submitted,[64] and proposed plans must be publicized at least thirty days prior to the hearings.   State plans must consider not only emission standards, but also land use.   Every state plan must include prior review of the projected sites of new stationary sources of air pollution to determine whether the new operations will prevent the attainment of national standards within that area.[65]

States must adopt standards at least as stringent as the standards issued by EPA, and are encouraged to set more stringent emission standards than those promulgated by the Administrator.[66] If a state fails to submit a plan or to adopt suggested revisions, the Administrator has authority to establish an implementation plan for that state.[67] The Administrator may supplement state enforcement procedures by issuing cease and desist orders and by filing civil actions against violators of the Act.[68]

The national standards to be promulgated by EPA consist of two parts: primary ambient air quality standards are designed to protect the public health; [69] secondary ambient air quality standards are directed at protecting the public welfare "from any known or anticipated adverse effects." [70] This second category is rather broad, concerning itself with the effects on soils, water, crops, man-made materials, animals, wildlife, vegetation, climate, and property, "as well as effects on economic values and on personal comfort and well-being." [71]

The Administrator has issued primary national ambient air quality standards for six principal pollutants: sulfur oxides, particulates (soot and smoke), hydrocarbons, nitrogen oxides, carbon monoxide, and photochemical oxidants.[72] Within the next year, the Administrator is to publish air quality criteria and proposed national standards for other pollutants, and, after hearing comments of interested parties, he is to promulgate standards within ninety days.[73] The deadline for compliance by all sources with the primary national standards is three years from date of approval of the state's plan.[74] Secondary standards must be reached within "a reasonable time." [75]

Furthermore, as directed by the amendments, the Administrator has promulgated emission standards for new stationary sources, including power plants.[76] The cost of achieving low emissions is a factor to be considered in devising new source standards.[77]

Although states are mainly responsible for enforcing air standards, the Administrator also has power to issue compliance orders to violators. An additional tool for enforcement of the Act is the citizen suit provision, under which any individual may bring a civil suit against a violator or against the Administrator if he fails to fulfill his statutory obligations.[78]   Federal judges may award litigation costs, including attorneys' fees, to successful citizen plaintiffs.[79]

EPA's guidelines for state implementation plans were published on August 17, 1971,[80] and contain language which encourages states, in formulating plans, to consider the *costs* and *benefits* of alternate strategies.   They also encourage states to consider *social* and *economic* impact of their plans, including the availability of alternate fuels and energy sources.   Deadlines for compliance with secondary air quality standards are to depend on *reasonably available* technology, as well as social and economic impact.

Many environmentalists have denounced these changes as subverting the original intent of the amendments to achieve air quality favorable to the nation's health and welfare as soon as possible.   Additional criticism has been directed at the state implementation plans as failing to provide a comprehensive and long-range approach.[81]   At the same time, some utility industry members along with representatives of the FPC, the Commerce Department and Interior Department, believe EPA emission standards are unrealistically stringent.[82]   One company, Detroit Edison, has called the three-year deadlines unrealistic and unattainable.[83]   On January 25, 1972, four electric power companies filed a petition in the U.S. Court of Appeals for the District of Columbia for review of the standards of performance published by EPA.

Water Standards.   The Federal Water Pollution Control Act represents the primary statutory scheme for water pollution control. The Act derives from 1948 legislation [84] which was based on the concept of state responsibility for the establishment and enforcement of water quality standards.   The present legislation continues to rely on state action: the Act provides that "state and interstate" water pollution abatement action "shall be encouraged and shall not . . . be displaced by Federal enforcement action" [85] except pursuant to a highly restricted procedure.[86]   As of 1971, only one federal judicial proceeding had been commenced,[87] and that produced no judicial determination of issues.[88]   Thus, the basic scheme contemplates almost exclusively state-level enforcement.

The statute calls for the creation by the respective states of "water quality criteria applicable to interstate waters or portions thereof within [each] such state." [89]   The expression, "water quality criteria" has been uniformly construed to refer to "ambient" standards as opposed to "effluent" standards. That is to say, effluent standards have not been required. Accordingly, any implementation of the water quality criteria—whether in an abatement proceeding or in a regulatory proceeding—requires an *ad hoc* extrapolation from those ambient criteria to the particular discharge in question: how much does, or would, the particular discharge contribute to meeting or exceeding the general limits for the given body of water. Obviously, such an extrapolation is quite difficult when more than one source is discharging into the waterway.

In addition to the "water quality criteria," the Act requires that each state develop "a plan for the implementation and enforcement of the water quality criteria adopted." [90] EPA has promulgated guidelines for state plans and has the authority to review them. If the Environmental Protection Administrator "determines that such state criteria and plan are consistent" with purposes set forth in the Act,[91] then the criteria and plan shall apply, with the force of law, to the interstate waters in question.[92]

Although Congress promulgated the foregoing plan for interstate water quality standards in 1965, only a little more than half of the jurisdictions had fully approved standards by early 1971 [93] and, as of early 1972, eight were still not fully approved.[94]

Under § 21(b) of the Act Congress has attempted to obtain the cooperation of federal and state agencies in the control of water pollution.[95] That section requires, as a condition precedent to the granting of any federal license or permit for, *inter alia,* the construction or operation of facilities that discharge effluents into navigable waters, that the applicant for such license or permit obtain

> "a certification from the state in which the discharge originates . . . that there is reasonable assurance, as determined by the state . . . that such activity will . . . not violate applicable water quality standards." [96]

And, "no . . . permit shall be granted if certification has been denied by the state . . . ." [97]

§ 21(b), along with the Corps of Engineers' Refuse Act Permit Program which will be discussed below, provides an enforcement mechanism for the state standards. § 21(b) certification requirements would apply to all generating plants—including plants requiring Corps

64

of Engineers, FPC, and AEC licenses or permits—emitting effluents into navigable waters.

4. State and Local Regulation

While the states and localities share responsibilities with federal agencies for air and water pollution control, they have almost exclusive jurisdiction over land use, zoning, and building standards. In these respects, and because federal agencies frequently require information on compliance with state laws before licensing a power plant, state and local authorities play an essential role in power production regulation.

A variety of agencies participate in the licensing of power plants and transmission lines. In the past, the state authority most commonly involved was the state public utility or public service commission. In every state except Texas there is such an agency authorized to regulate utilities [98] but the scope of their jurisdiction varies from state to state. A single commission can have supervision over a great variety of public services.[99] In general, the function of the public utility commission is to assure adequate service at reasonable rates, however, most commissions have a broad range of responsibilities—they scrutinize utility standards and practices relating to safety and convenience, they require periodic reports on management and service, they supervise financial arrangements and business plans such as mergers and expansion or curtailment of service, they scrutinize discrimination among users, and the like.[100] Commission size ranges from 1 to 7 members, but the usual number is 3; most commissioners are appointed, and their terms range from 2 to 10 years.[101]

According to a 1970 study, 29 state public utilities commissions regulate construction of some or all power plants and 28 regulate the construction of some or all transmission lines.[102] Ordinarily, the utility in these states must secure a certificate of public convenience and necessity prior to the construction of any facilities. The state agency bases its decision largely on the "public interest," a standard which gives the agency considerable discretion.

Of the 29 states which do require certification at least for some plants, 14 require hearings while the other 15 either leave the holding of hearings to the discretion of the commission or to instances where requested by an intervenor.[103] Hearings have actually been held in 23 states.[104] In only 11 states does the commission staff present evidence at hearings, and only 19 state commissions consider environmental aspects in making their decisions.[105]   Thus, in only a minority of states does the public utility commission review the environmental implications of power plants in any colorably meaningful way.

The state regulation of air and water pollution required by federal legislation, discussed above, has encouraged states to develop agencies with some expertise in pollution control.   However, as of December, 1971, only 9 states had full-time environmental agencies; the rest had part-time citizens boards.[106]

The procedures of pollution control boards and their roles in the state regulatory process are evolving, since many are newly established. These agencies also vary widely in their regulatory capacities.   Some exist as advisory bodies only, others exercise stringent controls; some hold public hearings with a broad right of intervention, while others function *ex parte*.

Beyond the utility commission and the pollution control board, the states and localities exercise considerable regulatory control through zoning and building codes.   By and large, public utilities must abide by local zoning ordinances.   The municipality's power to zone derives, in most instances, from the state's police power through a general enabling act.[107]   Zoning is implemented by local zoning boards and boards of adjustment, which have appellate jurisdiction.   Variances generally can be granted only after public hearings.   In the past, zoning laws have been subject to no general state plan and have been developed solely by the localities, although a few state utility commissions have the authority to override local zoning laws where the commission determines that the facility would be beneficial for the region as a whole.[108] Some courts, as well, have decided that local zoning laws barring a proposed plant's construction were unjustified under the police power for failure to consider the region's need for the facility.[109]   Some states have established a type of inventory system in which certain vulnerable ecological areas are protected from damaging development.[110]   Under many of these schemes, the land is specifically classified by the state authority and is thus removed from the jurisdiction of the local zoning authority.   However, in most instances, local regulations control.

The same applies to local building codes.   Before construction, the utility must seek approval from the local building inspector, although in a very few instances a state agency is responsible for approving compliance with state building codes.[111]

Counties and major cities may also impose a myriad of licensing and approval requirements. The following chart indicates the possible range of requirements at each level:

State: Environmental Protection Agency (water resources commission, air quality board, etc.)

Department of Natural Resources

Department of Fish & Wildlife

Highway Commission

Public Utility Commission

Department of Public Health

State Police

Office of Parks & Recreation

State Planning Commission (wetlands agency, etc.)

Department of Transportation

Industrial Commission

County: Planning Board

Highway Board

Pollution Control Agency

Health Authority

Municipality: Fire Department

Department of Sanitation

Pollution Control Agency

Health Authority

Departments issuing miscellaneous permits for boiler operation, street changes, blasting, oil storage, etc.

D. THE REGULATORY PROCESS

The Administrative Procedure Act, NEPA, federal air and water legislation, and the complex of state and local laws constitute a general framework for the specific licensing schemes covering the different types of power facilities. The report now relates this framework to the licensing of nuclear plants under the Atomic Energy Act and the licensing of hydroelectric plants under the Federal Power Act. Thereafter, in less detail, we turn to the Corps of Engineers which also licenses aspects of atomic and hydroelectric plants, but takes on particular importance as the chief federal regulator of fossil-fueled plants. Finally, this section outlines the regulation of transmission lines and briefs certain other aspects of government activity in the field of electric power and the environment.

1. THE ATOMIC ENERGY COMMISSION

Statutes and Organization. The Atomic Energy Act of 1954 mandates the licensing scheme for nuclear power. The Act declares a policy of directing the development of atomic energy for peaceful purposes, subject to "paramount" defense objectives,[112] and finds that the public safety requires regulation of nuclear materials and that the possibilities of damage place atomic facilities in interstate commerce.[113] The Act's purposes include fostering research, disseminating information, controlling the use of atomic energy, and encouraging widespread participation in its development "to the maximum extent consistent with the common defense . . . and safety of the public." [114]

The Atomic Energy Commission, originally established in 1946, carries out the Act's purpose. The President appoints the five Commission members for five year terms, with the advice and consent of the Senate, and designates one of them to serve as Chairman at his pleasure. The Act, however, also gives a key role to the Joint Committee on Atomic Energy (JCAE), composed of nine members from each house.[115] The JCAE has powers, unique for Congressional Committees, to receive and classify information [116] and to use the facilities of the executive branch.[117] As such, the Committee has great "moral suasion" when it has taken a practically unanimous stand.[118]

The Commission appoints a General Manager, who is its "chief executive officer" [119] and administrates the AEC's operating staff. The operating staff acts in such areas as military applications, research and development, and the operation of the AEC's own nuclear material production facilities.

In 1961, the Commission removed its regulatory activities from the General Manager's jurisdiction and established a Director of Regulation to direct standard-setting, licensing, and enforcement. Thus, the AEC now has a "regulatory side" and an "operating side," both reporting directly to the Commission and both served by a General Counsel, but with headquarters in different Washington suburbs.

A license is required for activities in the production and use of nuclear fuels [120] as well as for activities in the construction and opera-

68

tion of production and utilization facilities such as power plants [121] and their operators.[122] The chief exemption relevant to civilian nuclear power is the operating side's own activities in research on new technologies, fuel enrichment, and waste disposal, which are subject to a distinct type of internal administrative review.[123]

In issuing licenses, the regulatory staff must follow the Administrative Procedure Act except in regard to classified information,[124] and follow the procedures and implement the policies of the National Environmental Policy Act.[125] The AEC licensing process also involves advice on antitrust matters from the Justice Department,[126] and on radiation health questions from the Environmental Protection Agency. As discussed below, atomic power plants are also subject to a wide variety of regulation and licenses from state, local, and other federal agencies.

Rulemaking. As contemplated by the Administrative Procedure Act, the licensing process at the AEC is composed of rulemakings and adjudications. The rules specify the procedures to be followed at rulemakings [127] and adjudications [128] as well as set policy and standards on substantive questions. The Commission may commence a rulemaking on its own motion, on the recommendation of another federal agency, or on petition of any interested person.[129] Notice of rulemaking, including either the proposed rule or a specification of the subject involved and a description of any public hearing, must issue at least 15 days before such public hearing.[130]

The Commission must afford interested parties, citizen groups as well as industry, an opportunity to submit information and comments and may hold informal hearings adopting the procedures for them thought appropriate.[131] Persons whose interest may be affected can demand at least an informal hearing and must be admitted as parties.[132] The Commission is experimenting with rulemaking hearings allowing participants unusually extensive rights to submit testimony, cross-examine, and argue.[133] While the Commission has apparently not issued any regulations on the subject to date, NEPA may well apply to such rulemakings.[134] The Commission's final decision on the rulemaking is reviewable in a Court of Appeals.[135]

The Division of Reactor Standards in the regulatory side is responsible on a staff level for proposing substantive rules for power plants. In cooperation with other divisions of the regulatory and operating sides, a variety of rules have issued on such topics relevant to power production as radiation standards, design, packaging and protection of special nuclear material, and site selection.[136]

The regulatory staff also issues safety guides which describe acceptable design solutions to some safety questions and information guides which describe information which should be in some parts of an application.[137] More guides as well as "codes, standards, and criteria" are planned. Such guides do not purport to have the force of regulations and rulemaking procedures are not followed in issuing them.[138]

Adjudications. The rules provide standards upon which license applications are judged and procedures to guide the process of adjudication. While the Commission has proposed some procedural modification, the following discussion deals with methods currently in use.[138a] The license process begins with a written application.[139] Recognizing that power plants and other civilian uses are subject to many AEC licenses, the Act provides for these licenses to be gained through a single application.[140] Given their relative importance, the following discussion will concentrate chiefly on the two most important licenses for civilian nuclear plants—the construction permit [141] and the operating license.[142]

Prior to the enactment of NEPA, the licensing process concentrated on safety, the AEC previously having had no jurisdiction over environmental effects other than radiological effects.[143] Under NEPA, the AEC must look into all environmental questions and has superimposed its new jurisdiction on the old structure designed to deal with radiological questions.[144] A summary of the treatment of safety and environment is followed by a description of the process for antitrust review.

The licensing of a nuclear reactor involves two stages.[145] Before the applicant can begin construction of the reactor, it must receive a "construction permit"; before its operation commences, it must receive an operating license. The application for a construction permit need not show a final design, but only the type of reactor proposed to be built, its chief safety characteristics, and the features of the proposed site.[146] In addition, the applicant must submit an environmental report covering the information required by a NEPA impact statement.[147] A construction permit may be granted, if, *inter alia,* it is found that

70

there is a "reasonable assurance that the . . . proposed facility *can be* constructed and operated at the proposed location without undue risk to the health and safety of the public" [148] and the requirements of NEPA are met.[149]

The Division of Reactor Licensing staff evaluates the application. Other federal agencies and outside consultants are asked to contribute within their respective areas of expertise.

The staff routinely finds the application lacks information or differs with the applicant in the safety evaluation. Through conferences and correspondence with the applicant, the staff presents the questions which it wishes to have answered. The responses to these questions generally take the form of amendments or supplements to the application. Then, informal private conferences between representatives of the applicant and the staff iron out the differences.

The staff then files its safety evaluation. This report includes analyses of the site, plant design, fuel handling and storage, waste disposal, the proposed research and development programs, the technical qualifications of the applicant, potential accidents, and the consequences of possible dispersions of radioactive material into the environment. It also includes the reports of any Government agencies and private consultants.

In addition to review by the staff, all applications for construction permits are required, under existing law, to be submitted to the Advisory Committee on Reactor Safeguards (ACRS).[150] The ACRS, originally established by the AEC *sua sponte,* became a statutory body in 1957.[151] Its fifteen members, serving on a part-time basis, represent the various disciplines involved in an evaluation of reactor safety. The ACRS reviews the application, consults with the applicant and the staff, and reports to the Commission its conclusion as to whether the proposed reactor may be operated "without undue risk to the public," but not environmental matters. The ACRS report ("the ACRS letter") is of public record,[152] but its meetings, conducted informally and without a transcript, are not open to the public. The report is conclusory in form although it may often specify areas of study which it believes must be looked into before operation. The staff takes the ACRS report into account in its own safety evaluation, but need not come to the same conclusion. In practice, the staff has disagreed with the ACRS only twice. In one case a construction permit was granted notwithstanding an adverse ACRS report; [153] in the other, a permit was denied although the ACRS letter was favorable. [154]

As the safety analysis proceeds, another group within the regulatory staff reviews the applicant's Environmental Report, which must contain a cost-benefit analysis which "to the fullest extent practicable" quantifies the various factors considered. [155] When the Environmental Report is filed, a notice is published in the Federal Register and a public announcement of its availability is made. [156] With help from the AEC's laboratories, the staff prepares a draft Detailed Statement on the project covering the same material as the Report. This draft and the Report are circulated for comment among interested government agencies at all levels inviting comment. [157] After receipt of the comments, a Final Detailed Statement is prepared. [158]

The Act requires that a public hearing be held before the grant of a construction permit, whether or not requested by any interested person and whether or not there are any *contested* issues. [159] The hearing is held before an Atomic Safety and Licensing Board (ASLB). By statute, the ASLB consists of two members with technical or other qualifications and one member "qualified in the conduct of administrative proceedings." [160] Most of the technical members are part time, but in a recent development, the majority of the lawyer members are now full time. In theory, the contest may be between the staff, urging denial of the application, and the applicant. In practice, no applicant has yet persisted in his application over the objection of the staff, [161] so that the opposition in contested hearings has been by members of the public who intervene to oppose the grant.

Under present rules, intervention can take place after a notice of hearing which must be issued at least thirty days prior to the hearing. [162] The notice will specify, *inter alia*, the issues to be heard. [163] "Any person whose interest may be affected" may file a petition to intervene setting forth the interest asserted and the contention to be made "in reasonably specific detail." [164] Any party may object within five days and, if the ASLB rules favorably to the intervenor, the petitioner becomes a party. [165] Provision is also made for limited participation of nonparties. [166]

The AEC's rules of practice provide for discovery, of particular importance to intervenors. Discovery provisions include depositions, written interrogatories, and production of documents, [167] on terms similar to those used in federal district courts for civil proceedings with the important difference that discovery can be made only upon motion. Motions for discovery are often dealt with at prehearing conferences, which also are used to clarify the issues and plan the hearings.[168] The AEC has also proposed new rules that would make some discovery possible without recourse to motions.[168a]

The hearings are public and are transcribed.[169] At the hearings, the safety analysis, environment impact statement, and other documents will be introduced. Much use is made of written testimony. Intervenors will mainly make their points by cross-examination on these documents and written direct testimony.

Controversy surrounds the scope of the hearings. Previously, the AEC's rules for implementation of NEPA had specified that a showing of compliance with the applicable regulation of other agencies was sufficient to meet the applicant's burden, but the case of *Calvert Cliffs' Coordinating Committee* v. *AEC* reversed this position.[170] Prior to *Calvert Cliffs,* water quality questions could not be considered on the theory that the issuance of a section 21(b) permit was conclusive and other environmental considerations were considered only if contested.[171] *Calvert Cliffs* held, however, that the ASLB had an affirmative duty to consider on the record all environmental effects including water quality and to weigh them in the balancing of costs and benefits required by NEPA.[172] It appears likely, however, that Congress will remove the obligation to hear evidence on water quality, but may still require that water quality be considered in the NEPA balancing.[173]

Another set of disputes surrounding the scope of the hearing concerns the extent to which the effects of the license beyond the plant itself will be considered. Intervenors have sought to raise such issues as the effects of waste disposal and the alternatives of purchasing the electricity elsewhere or using less electricity, but the relevance of such issues has not finally been resolved.[174]

After the close of the record, parties may file proposed findings,[175] and the ASLB may permit oral argument.[176] After hearing, the ASLB files an initial decision which becomes effective immediately in the case of a construction permit or operating license unless exceptions are filed.[177] Exceptions must be filed within twenty days of the initial decision along with a brief in support; all objections not made in the exceptions are waived.[178] Notwithstanding exceptions, the Director of Regulation must issue the permit or license within ten days.[179]

73

The Commission has delegated its authority to consider such exceptions to a three person Atomic Safety and Licensing Appeals Board.[180] The Commission will not consider petitions to review Appeals Board decisions. But, where issues of unusual importance are involved, upon the Commission's own motion or upon certificate of the Appeals Board, the Commission may act instead of the Appeals Board or review its decision.[181]

Antitrust considerations are treated in a separate process. The AEC must notify the Department of Justice of all construction permit applications.[182] The Attorney General must then notify the AEC within 180 days whether granting the permit would have adverse antitrust effects; if so, the AEC must usually hold an antitrust hearing.[183] The first such hearing was announced recently to be conducted by a board consisting of two lawyers and one economist.[184]

The final order of the Commission is then appealable under the Administrative Orders Review Act of 1950 to a U.S. Court of Appeals.[185] Appellant must be aggrieved by its outcome and may have had to be a party below.

After the issuance of a construction permit, the permittee may begin work on the site. In practice, the safety review will continue, however, because many design questions will have been left open due to the need for further engineering and applied research. Moreover, the AEC can order changes in design aspects already approved if economically justified.[186]

When the plant nears completion, the utility will apply for an operating license. The review process will essentially repeat itself except that a hearing is not mandatory unless requested [187] and the case need not be referred to the Department of Justice for antitrust review unless circumstances have changed.[188] Where the request for an operating license is pending in a contested case, the ASLB may authorize issuance of a license to test the facility at less than full power. After issuance of an operating license, AEC regulation will continue throughout the life of the plant.

Other Regulation. AEC licensing far from exhausts the regulation applicable to an atomic plant.[189] One exception is that Supreme Court has ruled that states may not regulate the amount of emissions of nuclear plants.[190] But, it is disputed whether states may forbid nuclear plants altogether or set ambient standards for radiation. As to regulation of non-radiological questions, the applicant must comply with the full range of state and local laws.[191] Moreover, the applicant must usually receive permits from the Corps of Engineers. The CEQ's guidelines indicate that the Corps need not repeat the AEC's NEPA analysis, but a recent district court decision has cast some doubt on this conclusion.[192] Both the Corps and the AEC cannot grant licenses if the state has denied a water quality certificate under section 21(b). The only relief from such non-AEC jurisdiction is for AEC-owned facilities.[193]

Temporary Operating Licenses. In June of 1972, a new § 192 was added to the Atomic Energy Act,[194] authorizing the AEC to issue temporary operating licenses pursuant to truncated procedures. Wherever, at the operating license stage, there is a contested hearing for the full-term license, § 192 allows the applicant to petition for a temporary operating license after filing of (1) the ACRS report, (2) the Staff safety evaluation, and (3) the Staff's detailed NEPA impact statement.[194a]

In cases where the application for the full-term operating license was filed on or before September 9, 1971, the petition may be filed prior to the completion of the final Staff NEPA statement, but

> "the Commission must satisfy the applicable requirements of the National Environmental Policy Act prior to issuing any temporary operating license . . . ." [194b]

The Joint Committee illustrated its construction of the term, "applicable requirements of the National Environmental Policy Act," as follows:

> "for example, the requirement for a limited environmental review, after the balancing of specified factors now provided for in the Commission's regulations in situations where the full NEPA review has not been completed." [194c]

The Commission "shall issue the temporary operating license upon finding" that the facility has been constructed and will operate in conformity with the terms of the construction permit, the Atomic Energy Act, and AEC safety rules and regulations,[194d] that the authorized operation "will provide adequate protection of the environment,"[194e] and that such operation

> "is essential toward insuring that the power generating capacity of a utility system or power pool is at, or is restored

to, the levels required to assure the adequacy and reliability of the power supply . . . ." [194f]

Factors bearing on adequacy and reliability include alternative sources, historical system reserve requirements, possible health and safety risks in event of power shortage, and government agency reliability data.[194g] Moreover, in aid of judicial review, the Commission "shall recite with specificity the reasons justifying the issuance" of the temporary license.[194h]

Section 192 requires, further, that each temporary license shall prohibit the licensee from retiring or dismantling "any of its existing generating capacity on the ground of availability of the capacity" thereby temporarily licensed.[194i]

The duration of temporary licenses may be determined by the Commission and may be extended from time to time,[194j] but the Commission's authority to issue such licenses expires on October 30, 1973.[194k] Temporary operating licenses issued prior to that date "could continue in effect thereafter if the requirements . . . [of § 192] are otherwise satisfied." [194l] On the other hand, § 192 directs the Commission to conclude the full-term operating license hearing "as promptly as practicable" and to vacate the temporary operating license in any case where it finds that the applicant has failed to prosecute the full-term license application "with due diligence." [194m]

Procedurally, the temporary license proceeding is commenced by the applicant's petition accompanied by mandatory affidavits "setting forth the facts upon which the petitioner relies." [194n] Any other party to the contested full-term operating license proceeding may file affidavits [194o] and the Commission "shall hold a hearing after ten days' notice and publication once in the Federal Register on any such petition and supporting material." [194p] The hearing, however, need not be trial-type,[194q] but must be conducted with such expedited procedures "as the Commission may by rule, regulation, or order decree appropriate for a full disclosure of material facts on all substantial issues . . . ." [194r] The Commission's decision "shall be subject to judicial review" under the Administrative Orders Review Act of 1950.[194s]

2. THE FEDERAL POWER COMMISSION

Statutes. The siting of hydroelectric plants on navigable waters is subject to the licensing authority of the Federal Power Commission,[195] whose five members are chosen in a similar manner to the

Atomic Energy Commission. The FPC was vested with this authority in 1920 when, in response to a widely supported effort of conservationists, Congress passed what is now called Part I of the Federal Power Act.[196] The purpose of Part I was to provide a comprehensive scheme of national regulation for hydroelectric plants, rather than proceeding by the piecemeal, *ad hoc* approach that characterized the old River and Harbor Acts.[197] In 1935, Congress enacted Parts II and III of the Federal Power Act giving the Commission authority in the areas of power planning and accounting respectively.[198]

In basic format, Part I of the Federal Power Act requires that hydroelectric projects constructed on "any of the navigable waters of the United States, or upon any part of the public lands or reservations of the United States," be licensed by the FPC.[199] The principal standards for granting such a license are, *first*, that the project is "desirable and justified in the public interest"; [200] and *second*, that the project, in the judgment of the FPC,

".   .   . will be best adapted to a comprehensive plan for improving or developing a waterway or waterways for the use or benefit of interstate or foreign commerce, for the improvement and utilization of water-power development, and for other beneficial public uses, *including recreational purposes.   .   . .*" [201]

Thus, the Federal Power Act mandates a comprehensive, planned approach to resource use including both power potential and "other beneficial public uses." In practice, however, and in major part because conflicts were not immediately present, the primary emphasis came to be placed on power development. Only in the 1950's, when the impact of dams on salmon and other anadromous fish became a serious problem, was the FPC asked to come to grips with conflicting resource questions. Then, in all but two relatively minor cases, the FPC decided to grant licenses, finding that the environmental risk was outweighed by the power potential.[202]

In 1965, the FPC's approach to licensing was severely criticized, and its broad statutory duties under the Power Act reemphasized, in *Scenic Hudson I.*[203] There, the Second Circuit held that, under FPA § 10(a),[204] the FPC had affirmative planning responsibilities which required it to weigh both the immediate and the long-range effects of a project, and that within this context, the FPC was duty-bound to consider environmental factors, such as the protection of river scenery

77

and fisheries resources, as well as possible alternative sources of generation which might substitute for the project itself. One year later, in *Udall* v. *FPC*,[205] the Supreme Court again underlined these obligations, holding that a project could only be licensed if it was in "the public interest," and that before any such conclusion could be reached, the FPC had to consider environmental as well as power factors, and to inquire into all available alternatives to the project.[206]

Prior to the *Scenic Hudson* and *Udall* decisions, the FPC had been in the practice of measuring project proposals against alternatives, but principally on a threshold economic basis. The thrust of the two decisions was to broaden the scope of the inquiries into alternatives and to thrust upon the Commission the additional responsibility of weighing the environmental impact of any project it was asked to license. Shortly thereafter, these mandates were, in effect, codified with the passage of the National Environmental Policy Act, applicable to the FPC and other federal agencies.[207]

So, the FPC is now required to operate within the overlapping contexts of the Federal Power Act and NEPA; the effectiveness of the measures to carry out this joint mandate is still uncertain.[208] Nonetheless, more, perhaps, than any other agency, the FPC has already been held by judicial interpretation to a comprehensive approach to the question of plant siting. Consequently, its procedures, summarized below, to develop pertinent data and arrive at its decisions are of major importance.

The License Application. The FPC's formal licensing process may be initiated in one of two ways—by the filing of an application for a preliminary permit under FPA § 4(f) [209] or the filing of an immediate licensing application under FPA § 4(e).[210] There is no requirement that a preliminary permit be obtained—and if such a permit is issued, it provides no authorization for construction, but only vests the applicant with priority against any other application while feasibility studies are made.[211] Thereafter, a full license application must be filed, as for any other case.

The contents of the license application are set forth in FPA § 9 [212] and, in much greater detail, in the Commission's rules and regulations.[213] The requisite information includes, among other things, technical data describing the proposed project and its economic feasibility, as well as exhibits setting forth the recreational facilities planned in conjunction with the project. In addition, pursuant to the

FPC's implementation of NEPA, applicants are also required to submit an environmental impact statement covering the questions enumerated in section 102(c) of the National Environmental Policy Act.[214]

Upon the filing of the license application—and in many instances, even before the filing—the FPC staff undertakes its review of the proposed project. This review generally includes meetings with the applicant, where changes may be suggested and other details ironed out. The applicant has no obligation to accept the suggestions of the staff, and in some circumstances it will not. Nonetheless, when the staff review is completed, there will, more likely than not, be general agreement that the project is feasible and, indeed, desirable, although certain details may remain in dispute.[215]

Under the FPC's initial regulations for the implementation of NEPA, the staff was not required to prepare an independent environmental impact statement, but only to review the applicant's statement and, if need be, issue a deficiency letter. The applicant's statement would then be subject to examination upon hearings if these were called. However, in *Greene County Planning Board* v. *FPC*,[216] the Second Circuit held this approach inadequate, finding that NEPA required an independent statement to be prepared by the staff at the outset. The FPC has indicated that it will seek certiorari to review the decision and has not, as yet, adopted new regulations to meet the *Greene County* mandate.[217] As a consequence, for the time being at least, the staff's role in assessing environmental impact is limited to its review, and deficiency comments on, the applicant's statement and whatever else it may contribute in the course of hearings.

Notice and Intervention. Upon the filing of a license application (or application for a preliminary permit), notice must be published once in the Federal Register and, in addition, "once each week for four weeks in a daily or weekly newspaper published in the county or counties in which the project or any part thereof . . . [is] situated."[218] The form of notice is generally concise; and this, as well as the relatively limited publication requirements, has sometimes meant that notice has been given "publicly" in the legal sense only, and not in a fashion that reaches citizens practically. Furthermore, in at least some cases, it appears that notice has not been given through publication in *each* county in which any part of the project works may be located, with the consequence that citizens in areas affected by project transmission lines may never have been officially informed of license application for the basic project.[219]

The official notice of filing will generally carry with it an invitation to interested parties to file for intervention if they wish. The notice will usually set forth a specific time period, of at least 30 days, in which petitions to intervene must be filed. This means that individuals and groups who may be interested or affected by a proposed project are given a relatively short period of time in which to organize themselves, become familiar with the pertinent facts, determine whether intervention is worthwhile, retain counsel and prepare and file the required petition. And these time limitations may be even more severe if, as is sometimes the case, the official notice constitutes the first public disclosure of the proposed project.

While the specified time limits can impose rather severe burdens on prospective intervenors, these burdens are sometimes mitigated by other circumstances. Thus, in recent years, an increasing number of utilities have announced their proposed plans well in advance of filing, and this has tended to facilitate the task of preparing for intervention. In addition, the FPC will usually provide a further opportunity for intervention whenever an amendment to an application is filed; and even when time limits have expired completely, the FPC will often permit intervention notwithstanding this fact.[220] Nonetheless, in statutory format, if not in practice, the time limitations and limited notice requirements can impose substantial difficulties on potential intervenors.[221]

The conditions to intervention, including the prescribed form of petition, are set forth in the FPC's rules and regulations.[222] Neither the Federal Power Act nor the rules and regulations mandate that intervention be permitted in practice. But, the FPC has granted intervention liberally, as long as some apparent interest is shown, subject to the proviso that the granting of the petition does not constitute a finding that the intervenor will be legally aggrieved by any final licensing order.[223]

The FPC rules governing the form and content of petitions to intervene, although concise, require a fair amount of detailed information, including the facts supporting the petitioner's claim of interest and the position of the petition

"so as fully and completely to advise the parties and the Commission as to the specific issues of fact and law to be raised or controverted, by admitting, denying or otherwise answering, specifically and in detail, each material allegation of fact or law asserted in the proceeding . . ." [224]

In many cases, intervenors cannot provide such detail, since they are unlikely to have at their command the details of the proposed design. Perhaps for this reason, the FPC has not insisted on strict compliance with its rules, usually accepting petitions with only general statements. On the other hand, under its regulations for the implementation of NEPA,[225] the FPC has now imposed on intervenors the further requirement of filing comments on the applicant's draft environmental statement, "specifying any differences with the applicant's detailed statement . . . and including therein a discussion of [their] position in the context of the factors enumerated in [Section 102(c) of NEPA]"; [226] while this requirement does not itself constitute an initial condition to intervention, it stands as a future obligation which may be difficult to fulfill before the hearings are well underway, particularly when the details of the proposed project are not fully disclosed, as is sometimes the case.[227]

Prehearing Discovery. Under the FPC's rules and regulations, discovery procedures are available only to "participants." As a consequence, intervention is a prerequisite to any kind of discovery. Furthermore, even where parties have intervened, discovery has been resisted in most instances. Thus, in the *Greene County* case, the intervenors had to seek judicial recourse under the Freedom of Information Act before they were able to obtain basic documents.[228] Similarly, while the FPC rules provide for the taking of depositions, the FPC has not encouraged such procedures and, as a consequence, they have seldom been used.[229]

It is to be hoped that, in the future, the FPC and the utilities alike may soften their stand on discovery, accepting expanded prehearing disclosure as a means of narrowing the issues for any subsequent hearing. In the meantime, however, the consequences of limited prehearing discovery are that intervenors must pursue discovery in the course of the actual hearings, through extended (and often unproductive) cross-examination.

The Hearing. There is no requirement in the Federal Power Act or the FPC's rules that hearings be held on any application. In general, however, when interventions have been filed in opposition to a project, the FPC will call for hearings once the staff has completed its review.[230] Such hearings are usually not conducted before the Commission or any of its members. Instead, the Commission will appoint a hearing examiner, whose responsibilities include the organization of the hearing, the taking of testimony and, ultimately, a recommended decision in the case.[231] The hearing examiner also rules on most motions submitted in the course of the hearing, the principal exception being motions that would bring the hearings to a standstill or premature end.[232]

Procedurally, the hearing will usually begin with a prehearing conference,[233] where the hearing examiner will make his rulings on preliminary motions, including discovery requests, and will work towards developing a schedule for the hearings. In recent years, the practice of requiring prefiled testimony has become more frequent; the examiner will fix dates for filing by each of the parties, including the staff. The applicant is always required to file its affirmative testimony first, followed by the intervenors and then the staff (although in some instances, the staff may be required to file before the intervenors).

The consequence of the above-described prefiling procedures is that the intervenors are often required to prepare their direct case before they have had an opportunity to cross-examine the applicant's witnesses and before they have had a chance to see the staff testimony (which may offer important technical data). Since it is likely that no opportunity for discovery will have been given, these procedures can result in proposed testimony that may require substantial revisions, at considerable expense, before it is finally presented. Indeed, in some cases at least, the order established for prefiling of testimony has meant that the intervenors' case is finally presented with precision only in the rebuttal phase of the proceeding, with the consequence that their investment in the initial direct testimony is largely wasted.[234] On the other hand, if the intervenors are unable to state their objections in reasonably detailed form, the applicant may labor under substantial hardships.

A substantial hiatus is likely to follow the prehearing conference while the parties prepare and exchange testimony and, in some instances, process appeals to the full Commission.[235] Ultimately, however, the actual hearings will commence. Particularly in cases of high controversy, the hearing examiner is likely to entertain at the outset unsworn statements by interested citizens, setting forth their positions on the proposal. These statements do not constitute evidence, serving instead to identify issues and air strong emotions.

Following the statements, the applicant will present its case. Where prefiled testimony has been used, witnesses will simply adopt that testimony (with corrections) and then submit themselves for cross-examination. The opposing intervenors are usually required to cross-examine first, followed by the supporting intervenors (if any) and then the staff. Where prehearing discovery has not been permitted or undertaken (which is the general rule), the intervenors' cross-examination is likely to be laborious and less for the purposes of undercutting the direct analysis, than to develop underlying data and, occasionally, to test assumptions. The staff's cross-examination, on the other hand, is usually more concise. However, conservationists often complain that the staff examination is often a form of redirect, less for the purpose of probing the issues than to bolster the applicant's case.[236]

In a complex hearing, the cross-examination of the applicant's witnesses may extend for days, with only an occasional break. Thereafter, the intervenors' witnesses are called and the same procedures re-invoked, although the cross-examination is likely to be less time-consuming. The staff witnesses will then follow the intervenors, after which all parties will repair to construct their rebuttal cases.

The rebuttal phase of the proceeding will generally parallel the format of the direct proceeding. However, with discovery largely completed and the issues narrowed, the rebuttal cases, including cross-examination, are usually carried forward more quickly. Upon their completion, the usual *pro forma* motions will be made, briefing schedules established and the record closed.[237]

The Decision. In most contested cases, the hearing examiner is called upon to make the initial decision.[238] In this connection, the FPC rules provide expressly for briefing by the parties—and since no length limitations are imposed, these are likely to be voluminous.[239] Following the receipt of the briefs, the examiner will review the record and sooner or later will issue his decision.[240] Under the FPC's regulations for the implementation of NEPA, the examiner's decision is now required to include an evaluation of the environmental factors enumerated in Section 102(c) of NEPA.

The examiner's decision will, in most instances, constitute the decision of the FPC unless one or more of the parties takes exception to it.[241] Exceptions are taken, and an appeal to the full Commission in effect perfected, by the filing of a "Brief on Exceptions" within 30 days after service of the examiner's decision.[242] The format of the Brief on Exceptions is spelled out in some detail in the FPC's rules, and the Briefs themselves will generally be accompanied by motions for oral argument before the full Commission.[243] Answering briefs, denominated "Briefs Opposing Exceptions," may be filed within 20 days, following which the FPC will (if it elects to do so) set the case down for oral argument.[244] Depending on the complexity of the issues, oral argument may be heard over a full day or even more. Thereafter, the FPC will undertake to prepare its opinion which, when eventually issued, will constitute the basic decisional document. The FPC's opinion is now required to include the final detailed environmental statement required by NEPA.[245]

Judicial Review. Any party "aggrieved" by an order of the FPC may obtain judicial review of the decision, but only if he first files with the Commission an application for rehearing pursuant to FPA § 313(a).[246] The application must be filed within 30 days after the order complained of is issued and must "set forth specifically the ground or grounds upon which . . . [it] is based." [247] Other than in exceptional circumstances, no grounds may be urged upon appeal that are not set forth specifically in the application for rehearing.[248] Consequently, considerable care must be taken to ensure that all objections are included in the application.[249]

Under the FPC's rules, an application for rehearing is deemed to have been denied if the Commission takes no action on it within 30 days [250]—and at that point judicial review may be sought. But this rule is not absolute, since by and large "interlocutory" orders may only be reviewed in conjunction with the FPC's final order denying or granting the license application.[251] An exception to this standard has, however, now been carved out in *Greene County*,[252] where the Second Circuit accepted an appeal before the final decision had been made on the grounds that the actions complained of would decisively affect the further conduct of the proceeding.

The appeal itself is perfected by filing a petition for review of the FPC's order with either the Court of Appeals for the District of Columbia or the Court of Appeals for the circuit in which the applicant has its principal place of business.[253] The petition must be filed within 60 days after the application for rehearing is denied.[254] Under the applicable Rules of Appellate Procedure, the petition need ask no more than that the order be reviewed; it is not necessary to set forth the grounds of appeal, such matters rather being reserved for the briefs.[255]

Once the petition is filed—and it should be noted that the right of review is absolute—the Court of Appeals has exclusive jurisdiction to review the order complained of, and to affirm, modify or set the order aside. In addition, the Court may direct the FPC to adduce such additional evidence "as to the Court may seem proper." [256] Proceeding within the Court itself, including the requirements for briefing, assembling the record and argument, are governed in all respects by the Federal Rules of Appellate Procedure.[257] The standards for review are basically those set forth in section 706 of the Administrative Procedure Act, including, with respect to findings of fact, the traditional substantial evidence test.[258] The judgment of the Court with respect to the orders is final, subject only to review by the Supreme Court if certiorari is granted.[259]

An order of the Commission may, of course, only be appealed by a party who has been legally aggrieved by that order. In this connection, however, the *Scenic Hudson I* decision substantially broadened the definition of aggrieved parties to take in (at least for the purposes of the Federal Power Act) parties with non-economic interests, including interests in the protection of scenic resources. While the Supreme Court's recent decision in the *Mineral King* case [260] raised some questions as to the exact scope of permissible interest, it can be said with substantial confidence that wherever, by use or otherwise, parties can connect themselves to specific resources, they will have standing to review decisions affecting those resources. Consequently, the courts will undoubtedly remain open for the review of FPC decisions on environmental grounds. The manner in which they will conduct that review, and their willingness and ability to enforce upon the FPC a meaningful concern for the environment, are quite different matters which are beyond the scope of the immediate discussion.[261]

Rulemaking. The preceding discussion has addressed itself primarily to the administrative process of the FPC in the context of adjudicatory licensing proceedings. Like other agencies, the FPC also acts in a rulemaking capacity. By and large, however, the FPC has restricted its rulemaking functions to procedural matters, including, for example, the development of rules governing uniform systems of ac-

85

counts. Unlike the AEC, it has not, as yet, attempted to deal with substantive issues on a generic basic through rulemaking. As a consequence, the conflicting problems of power development and environmental protection are continuing to be litigated on a case-by-case basis in connection with specific license applications.[262]

Other Regulation. An FPC license to build a hydroelectric plant overrides state and local law to a much greater extent that does an AEC license. While FPA § 9(b)[263] requires a demonstration of compliance with all revelant state and local law, the Supreme Court has held that this section does not mean that getting state permits is "in any sense a condition precedent or an administrative procedure that must be exhausted before securing a federal license." [264] Moreover, federal regulation overrides any "conflicting state controls." [265] But, the Act does not affect ownership of water rights under state law, nor does it exempt an applicant from compliance with state laws not relating to use of waterways.[266]

While the Federal Power Act does preempt much local regulation, Federal Water Pollution Control Act § 21(b) [267] has made a state water quality certificate a prerequisite to the grant of a license by the FPC. This legislation therefore has reintroduced what is, in effect, a state veto power over non-federal hydroelectric projects.

3. THE CORPS OF ENGINEERS

The Corps of Engineers is mainly a large construction organization doing both civil and military work under the aegis of the Department of the Army. But, a small part of the Corps is engaged in regulatory activity. As such, it issues two permits which most power plants must have. First, a construction permit under section 10 of the 1899 Rivers and Harbors Act is necessary to build any structure in navigable waters including in-flow and out-fall pipes, filling, and piers.[268] Second, a permit is needed to discharge refuse into certain waters under section 13 of the 1899 Rivers and Harbors Act, this section being also known as the Refuse Act.[269]

The authority of the Corps under these sections is not modified by that of the Atomic Energy Act, so that atomic plants still must procure Corps permits where applicable. But, the Corps is the most important federal agency for fossil plants. Since NEPA applies to the construction permit, and perhaps the refuse permit, the Corps is the "lead" federal agency for fossil plants in regard to drafting environmental

86

impact statements.[270] Therefore, the remainder of this part will focus on the licensing of fossil plants.

The construction permit program requires Corps approval of structures in navigable waters. Most large steam generating plants will require such structures. The original act was directed towards preventing obstructions to navigation. But, NEPA has been held to apply to this program [271] so that, according to the Corps, power plants must follow NEPA procedures to procure such a permit. The Corps has issued regulations on its NEPA statement requiring statements only when the Corps is the lead federal agency.[272] The regulations do not make clear whether the statement must analyze not only the structures in the waters themselves, but also stack emissions, and possibly even transmission lines, railroad sidings, and other facilities through which fuel is delivered. Depending on the scope of the statement, the construction permit program could involve a complete analysis at the federal level of fossil plants.

The second Corps program is for refuse permits. Section 13 of the 1899 law declares it unlawful to discharge "any refuse matter of any kind or description whatever" into "any navigable water of the United States," except liquid sewage.[273] Moreover, the same section applies the same prohibition to discharge into "any tributary of any navigable water." [274] Section 17 of the statute directs that "the Department of Justice shall conduct the legal proceedings necessary to enforce" section 13, and provides, further, that "it shall be the duty of district attorneys of the United States to vigorously prosecute all offenders   .   .   .   whenever requested to do so by the Secretary of War.   .   .   ." [275]

Section 13, however, contains the important proviso that whenever, in the judgment of the Chief of Engineers, "anchorage and navigation will not be injured," the Secretary

> "may permit the deposit of any material above mentioned in
> navigable waters, within limits to be defined and under con-
> ditions to be prescribed by him, provided application is made
> to him prior to depositing such material.   .   .   ." [276]

Over the years from 1899 through 1966, the Refuse Act had received little attention as anything but one of many statutes prescribing the regulatory jurisdiction of the Corps of Engineers to protect and enhance navigation.[277] In 1966, however, the Supreme Court, in *United*

States v. *Standard Oil Co.*,[278] transformed section 13 into an antipollution statute.

The narrow holding in *Standard Oil* was that commercially valuable aviation gasoline, which would not ordinarily be thrown away, was to be included within the prohibition of section 13 against the discharge into navigable waters of "any refuse matter of any kind or description." [279] More broadly, the Court concluded that the Congressional standard was "serious injury to our water courses" which might be "caused in part by obstacles that impeded navigation *and in part by pollution.* . . ." [280] The Court concluded that "the history of this provision . . . dealing with our free-flowing rivers 'forbids a narrow, cramped reading' of § 13," [281] and went on to observe:

> "This case comes to us at a time in the Nation's history when there is greater concern than ever over pollution—one of the main threats to our free-flowing rivers and to our lakes as well." [282]

The Supreme Court's mandate was followed by the lower federal courts, including *United States* v. *Interlake Steel Company*, which upheld a criminal information based on section 13 where the pollution in question was allegedy in compliance with water quality standards promulgated by Illinois and approved by the Secretary of the Interior under the Water Pollution Control Act.[283] The court ruled that the Water Pollution Control Act "cannot be held to supercede or emasculate the prohibitions of the Rivers and Harbors Act," [284] and held that

> "Discharge of matter prohibited by the Rivers and Harbors Act cannot be condoned under the standards set by a state agency pursuant to the [Water Pollution Control Act.]." [285]

Thus were the two Congressional schemes in competition.

Late in 1970, in an apparent attempt to accommodate the two systems, the President issued an Executive Order establishing a "Refuse Act permit program." [286]

Executive Order 11574 is brief, providing that the Secretary of the Army shall establish a permit program [287] under which he shall be responsible for passing Refuse Act permits.[288] But, in carrying out his responsibilities under section 13, the Secretary

> "shall accept findings, determinations and interpretations which the [EPA] Administrator shall make respecting ap-

plicable water quality standards and compliance with those standards in particular circumstances. . . ." [289]

The President's order provides, further, that the Secretary shall be bound by "the Administrator's review of . . . water quality certifications under section 21(b)" of the Water Pollution Control Act and that "a permit shall be denied" where such "certification . . . has been denied" or where issuance would be inconsistent with the view of EPA about "applicable water quality standards and considerations." [290]

In practice, this means that the Corps of Engineers receives applications, reviews them preliminarily, and bucks them to EPA where an intensive review is carried out.[291] But, the buck does not stop there. In keeping with section 21(b) of the Water Pollution Control Act,[292] applications for Refuse Act permits received by EPA are transmitted, after EPA review, to the appropriate agency of the state in which the facility is situated.

In addition to water quality review by EPA and state agencies, the regulations provide for the Corps to send the applications to other possibly concerned agencies.[293] For instance, the Department of Interior submits comments on the application's potential impact on wildlife. The Corps receives such comments and passes on the non-water-quality aspects of the application.[294]

The Corps took the position that NEPA does not apply to the Refuse Act program because it constituted an environmental regulatory activity, involving EPA, to which NEPA does not apply. But, in *Kalur* v. *Resor*, a District Court held that, under NEPA, the Secretary of the Army, first, cannot accept as conclusive EPA's determination of the water quality effects of a discharge and, second, is required to conduct a full NEPA review prior to issuance of a Refuse Act permit.[295] As in *Calvert Cliffs*,[296] it was held that the federal agency issuing a permit had to go beyond the state water quality criteria and consciously evaluate justification in the public interest for *any* discharge into a waterway. This decision is now under appeal.

Another possible dispute surrounding the Refuse Act is whether thermal effluent is refuse. Whether or not thermal discharge is classified as an effluent, many plants would still require permits because they add chemicals to their cooling water to protect pipes. But, thermal effluent is the water discharge from steam plants which has aroused the most environmental interest.

The Corps encourages a single application for both permits which goes to one of the Corps' thirty-six district offices. The staff of the District Engineer, who is a high ranking army officer, handles the liaison with other federal and state agencies. The permits would normally be issued at the local level, but may be bucked up to Division Headquarters or Washington.

APA applies to the Corps of Engineers.[297] But, the construction permit program provides for no hearing and the Refuse Act program allows for only an optional, non-adversary hearing except where a state challenges a permit or a permit is being revoked.[298] Under APA, the Corps' actions may be appealed.[299]

In addition to Corps permits, steam fossil plants must comply with the range of state and local permits as well as EPA's own regulations on air pollution from new power plants.[300]

4. LICENSING OF TRANSMISSION LINES

At the federal level, the only regulation of transmission lines grows out of the licensing of generating facilities. As to hydroelectric projects, section 4(c) of the Federal Power Act requires licensing of transmission lines attendant to hydroelectric projects within the Commission's jurisdiction. As to nuclear plants, the AEC does not license their transmission lines, but does consider the lines' consequences in its environmental evaluation under NEPA, although this practice may be challenged. The Corps of Engineers has not yet determined to what extent it will consider transmission lines attendant to fossil plants under any NEPA evaluation it performs. As to interconnections not specifically attendant to the construction of any particular plant, there appears to be neither federal licensing nor evaluation of the environmental impact under NEPA.

At the state level, about half of the jurisdictions license some or all transmission lines. According to a 1970 survey, 12 states license all transmission lines while 13 license some.[301]

But, aside from specific licensure of transmission lines, many state and local permits are required to build an interconnection. Many of the state and local regulations described in section C of this chapter apply, particularly those applicable to land use and the crossing of roads and other public property. But, instead of having to deal with one or two municipalities, as for a generating facility, the utility must seek permits from the myriad jurisdictions along the line's route.

New York has a licensing procedure which consolidates into one proceeding all questions relating to the location of major utility transmission facilities including their environmental impact.[302] Citizens of the affected localities may participate in the proceedings, but local law may be overridden if the state finds that local regulation is unreasonably strict.

5. OTHER GOVERNMENT ACTION

Government regulation of utilities goes beyond transmission lines and generating facilities. State commissions exercise plenary jurisdiction over public utilities, including the approval of their rates, a subject of some importance to the environment as described in Chapter VI. In addition, the FPC has jurisdiction over interstate sales of electricity at wholesale and dictates accounting procedures of utilities within its jurisdiction. The FPC, the Securities and Exchange Commission (SEC), and state commissions regulate financing practices of utilities. Finally, in addition to privately owned facilities, there are numerous types of direct government involvement in the construction of plants, the marketing of power, and the conduct of utility business itself including the TVA, the Bonneville Power Authority, the Rural Electrification Administration, the Bureau of Reclamation, and numerous municipal utilities.

In addition, government action in areas other than the utility business has bearing on the subject of electric power and the environment. A partial list includes mineral depletion allowances which reduce the price of fuels, oil import quotas which increase the price of oil and may reduce the quantity of low-sulfur fuel available, regulation of other energy forms and fuels, regulation of the costs of transporting fuels, building codes which can reduce the energy needs of buildings, the government's policies as to the use of electricity in its own buildings, and government mortgage programs whose regulations can include rules on insulation and other factors affecting electricity needs. Moreover, various government agencies carry out and fund research programs, the largest of which is that of the AEC's Division of Reactor Development and Technology.

Notes for Chapter IV

1. 42 U.S.C. §§ 4321 *et seq.* (1970).
2. Exec. Order 11514, 3 C.F.R. 531 (1971).
3. 42 U.S.C. § 4331(a) (1970).
4. *Id.* § 4331(c).
5. *Id.* § 4331(b) (5).
6. *Id.* § 4331(a).
7. *Id.* § 4332.
8. 36 Fed.Reg. 7724 (1971).
9. 42 U.S.C. § 4332(2) (A) (1970).
10. *Id.* § 4332(2) (C).
11. *Id.*
12. 36 Fed.Reg. 7725 (1971).
13. *Id.* at 7724.
14. *Id.*
15. *Id.* at 7725.
16. OMB Bulletin #71–3 in 1 Env.L.Rep. 46005 (1970).
17. 42 U.S.C. § 4332(2) (C) (v) (1970).
18. 36 Fed.Reg. 7724 (1971).
19. *Id.* at 7726.
20. *Id.* at 7724.
21. *Id.* at 7726.
22. *Id.*
23. *Id.*
24. *Id.*
25. *Id.*

25a. Greene County Planning Board v. FPC, 455 F.2d 412 (2d Cir. 1972), *petition for cert. filed,* 40 U.S.L.W. 3589 (June 8, 1972) (No. 71–1597).

26. 42 U.S.C. § 4332(2) (C) (v) (1970).
27. *Id.* § 4332(2) (A).
28. *Id.* § 4343.

29. *Council on Environmental Quality, Second Annual Report* 358–360 (1971).

30. The Citizens' Advisory Committee on Environmental Quality, The Advisory Committee on Advanced Automotive Power Systems, The Legal Advisory Committee, and The Tax Policy Advisory Committee.

31. 42 U.S.C. §§ 4332(2) (C) (v), 4344, and 4345 (1970).
32. 5 U.S.C. §§ 551 *et seq.* (1970).
33. *Id.* §§ 559 & 701.

34. *Id.* § 553.

35. *Id.* § 554.

36. *Id.* § 553(b).

37. *Id.* § 553(c).

38. *Id.* § 553(d).

39. *Id.* § 553(c).

40. *Id.* § 554.

41. S.Doc.No. 248, 79th Cong., 2d Sess. 212, 276 (1946).

42. 5 U.S.C. § 702 (1970).

43. *See* Association of Data Processing Service Organizations, Inc. v. Camp, 397 U.S. 150, 156 (1970).

44. 5 U.S.C. § 704.

45. *Id.* § 702.

46. *Id.* § 706; 4 *K. Davis, Administrative Law Treatise* § 29.01, at 116 (1958).

47. 5 U.S.C. § 706(2); *see Davis, supra* note 46.

48. *See, e. g.,* Scenic Hudson Preservation Conf. v. FPC, *infra* note 197, Calvert Cliffs Coordinating Comm. v. AEC, *infra* note 170, and Greene County Planning Board v. FPC, *supra* note 25a.

49. 1 K. Davis, *supra* note 46, § 8.15, at 391 (Supp.1970).

50. 5 U.S.C. § 552.

51. *Id.* § 552(a) (3).

52. *Id.* § 552(b) (3).

53. *Id.* § 552(b) (1).

54. *Id.* § 552(b) (4).

55. *Id.* § 552(b) (5).

56. *Id.* § 552(a) (3).

57. *Id.* § 554(d) (2).

58. *Id.* § 554(d) (2) (A) and (B).

59. 33 U.S.C. §§ 1151 *et seq.* (1970).

60. 42 U.S.C. §§ 1857 *et seq.* (1970).

61. Established by Reorganization Plan No. 3 of 1970, 35 Fed.Reg. 15623 (1970).

62. 42 U.S.C. § 1857c–2(a) (1970).

63. *Id.* § 1857c–5.

64. *Id.* § 1857c–5(a) (1).

65. *Id.* §§ 1857c–5(a) (2) (D) and 1857c–5(a) (4) (A).

66. *Id.* § 1857d–1.

67. *Id.* § 1857c–5(c).

68. *Id.* § 1857c–8(a) (1).

69. *Id.* § 1857c–4(b) (1).

70. *Id.* § 1857c–4(b) (2).

71. *Id.* § 1857h(h).

72. 36 Fed.Reg. 8186 (1971).

73. 42 U.S.C. § 1857c–4(a) (1) (1970).

74. *Id.* § 1857c–5(a) (2) (A) (i). Some extensions can be granted. *See* § 1857c–5(e).

75. *Id.* § 1857c–5(a) (2) (A) (ii).

76. 36 Fed.Reg. 15704 (1971).

77. 42 U.S.C. § 1857c–6(a) (1) (1970).

78. *Id.* § 1857h–2(a).

79. *Id.* § 1857h–2(d).

80. 36 Fed.Reg. 13486 (1971).

81. XXX Cong.Q.No. 10 at 500 (1972). *See* testimony of Mr. Richard Ayres, Director, Project on Clean Air, National Resources Defense Council, Inc., at Hearings on Implementation of the Clean Air Amendments of 1970 Before the Subcomm. on Air and Water Pollution, Senate Comm. on Public Works, Feb. 16, 1972.

82. Wall Street Journal, Jan. 10, 1972, at 22, col. 1.

83. 6 *Air and Water News* No. 9 at 4 (1972). Even EPA official Kenneth Johnson admitted that it will be very difficult for the states, specifically New York and New Jersey metropolitan areas, to meet primary standards for major pollutants by the deadline. *See* 2 Env.L.Rep. 1102 (1972).

84. 62 Stat. 1155 (1948).

85. 33 U.S.C. § 1160(b) (1970).

86. An insight into the past Congressional eagerness (or lack thereof) to attack water pollution may be obtained by examining this Federal abatement procedure. The EPA Administrator may begin action to abate pollution only after finding that the water quality of interstate waters has been reduced below the established standards, 33 U.S.C. § 460(c) (5), and is endangering the health or welfare of persons, 33 U.S.C. §§ 460(g) (1) and (2), but only after (1) notification to "the violators and other interested parties of the violation" and (2) the passage of 180 days, 33 U.S.C. § 1160(c) (5). Moreover, if the persons thus endangered are located "only in the state in which the discharge or discharges . . . originate," the Administrator must also first obtain the written consent of that state's governor, 33 U.S.C. § 1160(g) (2). In any event, the EPA Administrator "may request the Attorney General to bring a suit on behalf of the United States to secure abatement of the pollution," 33 U.S.C. §§ 1160(g) (1) and (2), but the statute omits to make Justice Department action mandatory upon such request. If the Attorney General exercises his discretion to bring an abatement suit, then a Federal Court shall have jurisdiction to abate the pollution in question, but only, *inter alia*, after having given "due consideration to the practicability and to the physical and economic feasibility of complying" with the standards sought to be enforced, 33 U.S.C. § 1160 (c) (5). It should be noted that the foregoing procedure is designed to cut short an even more elaborate "conference" procedure for abatement that truly defies rationality. For a description of the "conference" procedure, *see Barry, The Evolution of the Enforcement Provisions of the Federal Water Pollution Control Act: A Study of the Difficulty in Developing Effective Legislation* 68 Mich.L.Rev. 1103, at 1104–1110, 1116 (1970).

87. S.Rep.No. 92–414, 92d Cong., 1st Sess. 5 (1971).

88. It was brought against the City of St. Joseph, Missouri and was settled.

89. 33 U.S.C. § 1160(c) (1) (A) (1970).

90. *Id.* § 1160(c) (1) (B).

91. Those purposes set forth in 33 U.S.C. § 1160(c) (3), which reads as follows:

> "Standards of quality established pursuant to this subsection shall be such as to protect the public health or welfare, enhance the quality of water and serve the purposes of this Act. In establishing such standards the Secretary, the Hearing Board, or the appropriate State authority shall take into consideration their use and value for public water supplies, propagation of fish and wildlife, recreational purposes, and agricultural, industrial, and other legitimate uses. In establishing such standards the Secretary, the Hearing Board, or the appropriate State authority shall take into consideration their use and value for navigation."

92. *Id.* § 1160(c) (1). The statute goes on to provide for federally-established standards where any state fails to act, 33 U.S.C. § 1160(c) (2), but such Federal action had to be taken only in one case, Iowa.

93. The jurisdictions are the fifty states, the District of Columbia, Guam, Puerto Rico, and the Virgin Islands, of which only twenty-seven had fully-approved standards. S.Rep.No. 92–414, 92d Cong., 1st Sess. 4 (1971).

94. As of March 9, 1972, the states not fully approved were Alabama, Georgia, Illinois, Louisiana, Michigan, Mississippi, Ohio, and Tennessee. U.S. E.P.A., Division of Water Quality Standards, Washington, D.C., internal memorandum dated March 9, 1972.

95. 33 U.S.C. § 1171(b) (1970).

96. *Id.* § 1171(b) (1).

97. *Id.*

98. 1 *A. J. G. Priest, Principles of Public Utility Regulation* 2 (1969). In response to a questionnaire sent by the Committee, Texas' Railroad Commission reports no jurisdiction over electric utilities.

99. Commissions may regulate several or all of the following: rail, road, water and air carriers; warehousemen; stockyards; telephone and telegraph companies; electric, gas, water and heat utilities; and express companies. *Priest, supra* note 98, at 32.

100. *Id.* at 32.

101. *Id.* at 29–30.

102. *Office of Science and Technology, Electric Power and the Environment* 56 (1970).

103. *Id.*

104. *Id.*

105. *Id.* at 57.

106. Hill, "States Curtailing Polluters on Pollution Control Units," N.Y. Times, Dec. 19, 1971, § 1, at 1, col. 3.

107. 1 *Anderson, American Law of Zoning* 127 (1968).

108. *See* Council on Environmental Quality, *supra* note 29, at 60–67. Massachusetts, California, Arkansas, New York, Maryland, Florida and Delaware, among other states, have established an inventory system in which classified areas are protected from detrimental development by state override authority.

109. *See* 3 E. Yokley, *Zoning Law and Practice* § 28.72 (1967).

110. *See* note 108, *supra*.

111. *E. g.,* in Pennsylvania, the State Department of Labor and Industry oversees compliance with state building codes.

112. Atomic Energy Act of 1954 § 1, 42 U.S.C. § 2011 (1970) [hereinafter cited as "AEA"].

113. *Id.* § 2.

114. *Id.* § 3.

115. *Id.* § 201.

116. *Id.* §§ 205–206.

117. *Id.* § 205.

118. Statement by Senator Hickenlooper, 100 Cong.Rec. 10733–36, 83d Cong., 2d Sess. (July 16, 1954).

119. AEA § 24.

120. *Id.* §§ 53, 57.

121. *Id.* §§ 103, 104.

122. *Id.* § 107.

123. *Id.* § 110, 10 C.F.R. pt. 115 (1972).

124. *Id.* § 181. Parallel procedures have been established for restricted data. 10 C.F.R. §§ 2.900 *et seq.* (1972).

125. *See* IV(C) (1) *supra*.

126. AEA § 105.

127. 10 C.F.R. §§ 2.800–.807 (1972).

128. *Id.* pts. 10, 50.

129. *Id.* § 2.801.

130. *Id.* § 2.804.

131. *Id.* § 2.805.

132. AEA § 189(a) ; Siegel v. AEC, 400 F.2d 778 (D.C.Cir. 1968).

133. These experiments include the rulemakings on Emergency Core Cooling System (ECCS) and radiation standards.

134. 36 Fed.Reg. 7724 (1971).

135. AEA § 189(b).

136. 10 C.F.R. pts. 20, 50, 71, 73, 100 (1972).

137. 1 *CCH Atom.Eng.L.Rep.* ¶ 3951, 3971.

138. *Id.*

138a. The proposed changes are set forth in 37 Fed.Reg. 9331–47 (1972).

139. AEA § 182.

140. *Id.* § 161(h).

141. *Id.* § 185.

142. *Id.* § 103.

143. New Hampshire v. AEC, 406 F.2d 170 (1st Cir. 1969).

144. 10 C.F.R. pt. 50, App. D (1972).

145. The following description relies heavily upon Murphy, "Atomic Safety and Licensing Boards," 33 *Law & Contemp.Prob.* 566 (1968).

146. 10 C.F.R. § 50.34 (1972).

147. *Id.* pt. 50, App. D(A) (1972).

148. *Id.* § 50.35(a) (1972).

149. *See* generally 10 C.F.R. pt. 50, App. (D) (A) (11) (1972) for the basic rule of decision.

150. AEA § 182(b).

151. *Id.* § 29.

152. 10 C.F.R. §§ 50-58 (1972).

153. Power Reactor Dev. Co. v. Int'l Union of Elec. Workers, 367 U.S. 396 (1961).

154. The application of Pacific Gas & Electric to build a plant at Bodega Bay, California.

155. 10 C.F.R. pt. 50, App. D(A) (3) (1972).

156. *Id.* pt. 50, App. D(A) (6).

157. *Id.*

158. *Id.* pt. 50, App. D(A) (8).

159. AEA § 189.

160. AEA § 191.

161. While this is still true, there has recently been a contest between the staff and a licensee on an order to show cause why a license should not be suspended.

162. 10 C.F.R. §§ 2.104, 2.714.

163. *Id.* § 2.104.

164. *Id.* § 2.2714(a).

165. *Id.* § 2.714(b), (d).

166. *Id.* § 2.715.

167. *Id.* §§ 2.740–.744.

168. *Id.* § 2.752.

168a. 37 Fed.Reg. 9343 (1972).

169. *Id.* §§ 2.750–.751.

170. 449 F.2d 1109 (D.C.Cir. 1971) [hereinafter cited as "Calvert Cliffs"].

171. *Id.* at 1122.

172. *Id.* at 1125.

173. Water pollution control bills passed by both Houses of Congress contain identical sections stating that NEPA is satisfied "as to water quality considerations" if a state or federal Environmental Protection Agency permit

is received. S. 2770, 92d Cong., 2d Sess., § 511(d) (1971); H.R. 11896, 92d Cong., 2d Sess., § 511(d) (1972). According to Senator Howard Baker of Tennessee, the author of these sections,

"My amendment would make it clear that, for the purposes of making the kind of 'balancing judgment' required by NEPA, each individual Federal permitting and licensing agency would not be required to develop its own special expertise with respect to water quality considerations. My amendment should not in any way be construed to mean that water quality considerations do not play a role in such a 'balancing judgment.' On the contrary, where pertinent, water quality considerations must be considered by any agency when it decides, under the NEPA mandate, whether it is in the public interest to grant a license or permit and, if so, under what conditions and stipulations.

"However, my amendment would relieve any such permitting or licensing agency of the responsibility for determining on its own the standard of performance or effluent limitation that must be applied to the activity under consideration for a license or permit." 117 *Cong.Rec.* 17456 (daily ed. Nov. 2, 1971).

174. *A. W. Murphy, The National Environmental Policy Act and the Licensing Process* 13–17 (1st draft, 1972) (report to the Committee on Licenses and Authorizations of the Administrative Conference of the United States).

175. 10 C.F.R. § 2.754 (1972).

176. *Id.* § 2.755.

177. *Id.* §§ 2.760(a), 2.764(a).

178. *Id.* § 2.762.

179. *Id.* § 2.764(b).

180. *Id.* § 2.788.

181. *Id.* §§ 2.785, 2.786.

182. AEA § 105.

183. *Id.*

184. 13 *Nucleonics Week* No. 16, at 5 (April 30, 1972.)

185. AEA § 189(a).

186. 10 C.F.R. § 50.109 (1972).

187. AEA § 189(a).

188. *Id.* § 105.

189. *Id.* § 271.

190. Minnesota v. Northern States Power Co., 447 F.2d 1143 (8th Cir. 1971), *aff'd,* 40 U.S.L.W. 3483 (April 4, 1972).

191. AEA § 271.

192. *See* Kalur v. Resor, 335 F.Supp. 1 (D.D.C.1971).

193. AEA § 271.

194. P.L. 92–307 (June 2, 1972).

194a. AEA § 192(a).

194b. *Id.* § 192(a) (3).

194c. H.Rept.No.92–1027, 92d Cong., 2d Sess., April 27, 1972, at 8.

194d.   AEA § 192(b) (1) ; and *see* § 185.

194e.   *Id.* § 192(b) (2).

194f.   *Id.* § 192(b) (3).

194g.   *Id.*

194h.   *Id.* § 192(b).   *See* Citizens to Preserve Overton Park, Inc. v. Volpe, 401 U.S. 402 (1971).

194i.   AEA § 192(b).

194j.   *Id.*

194k.   *Id.* § 192(d), presumably including the authority to issue extensions.

194*l*.   *Id.* § 192(c).

194m.   H.Rept.No.92–1027, *supra* note 194c, at 10.

194n.   AEA § 192(a).

194o.   Within fourteen days after the filing of the petition or such additional time "not to exceed ten days" as the Commission may fix.   *Id.*

194p.   *Id.*

194q.   H.Rept.No.92–1027, *supra* note 194c, at 8.

194r.   AEA § 192(a).

194s.   *Id.* § 192(b).

195.   As set forth in Federal Power Act [hereinafter cited as "FPA"] § 23, 16 U.S.C. § 817 (1970), the licensing authority of the FPC extends to "any dam, water conduit, reservoir, power house, or other works incidental thereto across, along, or in any of the navigable waters of the United States . . . ," which facility is "for the purpose of developing electric power."   Under FPA § 3(11), 16 U.S.C. § 796(11) (1970), the FPC also has jurisdiction over the transmission lines carrying power from a project, but only to the point where such lines connect with the applicant's existing transmission or distribution system.

Historically, the FPC has interpreted its licensing authority to extend only to hydroelectric projects [including, initially, conventional hydro, and, more recently, pumped-storage hydro, *see* FPC v. Union Electric Co., 381 U.S. 90 (1965)].   The FPC has disclaimed jurisdiction over steam generating facilities, even though such plants draw water through "water conduits" for cooling purposes in connection with the production of power.   A suit is now pending seeking to force the FPC to take jurisdiction over steam plants—a suit which, if successful, would vastly change plant siting mechanisms across the country. *See* Chapter II, *supra*, text accompanying note 28.

196.   16 U.S.C. §§ 791a–823 (1970).

197.   The legislative history of the Federal Power Act (originally titled the Federal Water Power Act, Act of June 10, 1920, Ch. 285, § 30, 41 Stat. 1077), beginning with President Theodore Roosevelt's 1908 veto of legislation authorizing *ad hoc* construction of several dams, is summarized in First Iowa Hydroelectric Cooperative v. FPC, 328 U.S. 152, 180 *et seq.* (1946).   As stated by the Supreme Court there:

> "It [the Federal Power Act] was the outgrowth of a widely supported effort of the conservationists to secure enactment of a complete scheme of national regulation which would promote the comprehensive development of the water resources of the Nation . . . instead of the piecemeal, restrictive, negative approach of the River and Harbor Acts. . . . "

99

See also, Scenic Hudson Preservation Conf. v. FPC, 354 F.2d 608, 613 (2d Cir. 1965), *cert. denied,* 384 U.S. 941 (1966) [hereinafter cited as "Scenic Hudson I"].

198. 16 U.S.C. §§ 824–824h, 825–825r (1970).

199. FPA § 23, 16 U.S.C. § 817 (1970). The licensing authority of the FPC is applicable only to projects proposed for construction by applicants other than the United States. Projects to be constructed by the United States (for example, through the Bureau of Reclamation or the Corps of Engineers) are generally the subject of specific Congressional authorization. In certain instances, the licensing authority of the FPC may also extend to hydro projects on non-navigable waters. In this connection, *see* FPA § 23, 16 U.S.C. § 817 (1970) ; FPC v. Union Electric Co., *supra* note 195.

200. FPA § 4(e), 16 U.S.C. § 797(e) (1970). The "public interest" standard has been held by the Supreme Court to be the controlling test for any FPC license. Udall v. FPC, 387 U.S. 428, 450 (1967).

201. FPA § 10(a), 16 U.S.C. § 803(a) (1970) (emphasis added). As originally enacted, FPA § 10(a) required:

> "(a) that the project adopted . . . shall be such as in the judgment of the Commission will be best adapted to a comprehensive *scheme* of improvement and utilization for the purposes of navigation, of water-power development, and of other beneficial public uses. . . ."

The section was amended in 1935 to substitute the language of a "comprehensive plan" for "comprehensive scheme" and, at the same time, to add the specific language, "including recreational purposes." Act of Aug. 26, 1935, Ch. 687, § 206, 49 Stat. 842.

202. The two instances where the FPC denied licenses each involved small projects—the first on the Namekagon River in Wisconsin, Namekagon Hydro Co. v. FPC, 216 F.2d 509 (7th Cir. 1954), and the second on the Little Salmon River in Washington, Public Utility District No. 1 of Skamania County, Washington, Project No. 2199, 32 F.P.C. 444 (1964). In a 1966 letter to Representative Richard Ottinger, Lee White, then FPC Chairman, reported that since 1920 the FPC had granted 605 licenses for major projects, while denying licenses on resources grounds in only the two cases noted. Two license applications for a project at High Mountain Sheep were denied, but only in favor of a third application, which was granted. For cases of major dams licensed by the FPC in spite of serious or other resource problems, *see, e. g.:* State of Wash. Depart. of Game v. FPC, 207 F.2d 391 '(9th Cir. 1953), *cert. denied,* 347 U.S. 936 ; FPC v. Oregon, 349 U.S. 435 (1955) ; Udall v. FPC, *supra* note 200 ; Scenic Hudson I, *supra* note 197, relicensing upheld by Second Circuit.

203. The case, which involved the proposal of Consolidated Edison Company of New York to build a pumped-storage project at Storm King Mountain on the Hudson River, was remanded to the FPC for furthering hearings. The FPC relicensed the project in 1970, after the power-house had been placed underground. The FPC's determination was affirmed in a 2–to–1 decision of the Second Circuit in 1971, Scenic Hudson Preservation Conf. v. FPC, 453 F.2d 463 (2d Cir. 1971), *cert. denied,* 40 U.S.L.W. 3599 (June 19, 1972) [hereinafter cited as "Scenic Hudson II"].

204. 16 U.S.C. § 803(a) (1970).

205. *See* note 200, *supra.* The case, which involved several competing proposals to build a dam on the Snake River, was remanded to the Commission for further proceedings. The FPC Examiner subsequently recommended that a license again be granted, and the case is now pending before the full commission.

100

206. In discussing the FPC's responsibilities, Justice Douglas quoted Justice Holmes' earlier dictum that "a river is not an amenity, it is a treasure," and then went on to say that among other alternatives that had to be considered by the Commission was the alternative of no project at all. 387 U.S. at 439, 448.

207. *See* Judge Oakes' dissent in Scenic Hudson II where he noted that NEPA was in many respects the embodiment of the Second Circuit's Scenic Hudson I decision, 453 F.2d at 491–92.

208. *See, e. g.*, Greene County Planning Board v. FPC, *supra* note 25a, where the Second Circuit held that the FPC's implementation of NEPA was inadequate. In the same opinion, the Court also criticized the FPC for failing to carry out its planning mandates as interpreted in Scenic Hudson I and Udall v. FPC, *supra* note 200. It should also be noted that despite original setbacks, the FPC has again licensed the Storm King plant and is well advanced in the relicensing of the plant at issue in Udall v. FPC.

209. 16 U.S.C. § 797(f) (1970).

210. *Id.* § 797(e) (1970).

211. FPA § 5, 16 U.S.C. § 798 (1970). In one pending case, involving the proposal of New England Electric Co. to construct a pumped storage project at Canaan Mountain in northwestern Connecticut, the preliminary permit procedure is apparently being used less for the purpose of maintaining priority than to permit public scrutiny of, and reaction to, the proposal. Yet despite these salutary motives, conservationists have complained that the company has released very little pertinent information and has discouraged substantive discussions about the merits of the proposal.

212. 16 U.S.C. § 802 (1970).

213. 18 C.F.R. Ch. I.

214. *See* 18 C.F.R. §§ 2.80, 2.81, 4.40, 4.41.

215. Except in connection with competitive licensing proceedings, where one project may be opposed by the staff in favor of another, the instances where the staff carries its opposition to hearings have been extremely rare. This is not to say that the staff has not discouraged projects in the review stage and thereby caused applications to be withdrawn; however, there is no compiled record of these instances.

216. *See* note 25a, *supra*. An application for rehearing *en banc* has been denied.

217. *See* N.Y. Times, Mar. 8, 1972, at 16, col. 3.

218. FPA §§ 4(e), (f), 16 U.S.C. §§ 797(e), (f) (1970). Under section 4(e) of the Federal Power Act, it appears that publication of the filing of a license application is not required in county newspapers if publication has already been effected in those papers in respect of a preliminary permit. In practice, however, it is assumed that republication is required.

219. In Greene County, *supra* note 25a, for example, notice of filing for the project proper was given in 1968, but only in the county where the power house was to be located. No similar notice was given in several counties through which the transmission lines would pass. As a consequence, there was no organized opposition when the power house plans were reviewed and approved. It was only two years later, when the final route of one of the major transmission lines was announced, that many citizens came to realize the impact on them; and by then, the time for objecting to the plant in its entirety had expired.

It should also be noted that under FPA §§ 4(e) and (f), the county news-paper is required only for applications by private companies, and not in the case of applications by municipalities or public authorities. In practice, how-ever, it appears that similar notice is given in all cases.

220. In the Scenic Hudson case, petitions to intervene were granted in Feb-ruary 1964, despite the fact that the time for intervention had expired in Oc-tober 1963. However, when, after the close of the hearings, petitions to in-tervene and present newly discovered evidence were filed, they were all denied as untimely. The denials were subsequently criticized in Scenic Hudson I, and when, upon remand, the City of New York moved to intervene *two years* after the time for intervention had expired, the FPC granted the petition and reopened the proceeding for further hearings. *See also* Udall v. FPC, *supra* note 200.

221. *See* note 216, *supra*. It should also be noted that while contested pro-ceedings have become more frequent in recent years, the majority of FPC licenses are still granted without contest. It is unclear, of course, whether the lack of contest has been tied to the inadequacy of notice or restrictive time limitations in any of these cases.

222. 18 C.F.R. § 1.8.

223. In Scenic Hudson I, the FPC emphasized its "non-aggrievement" proviso in challenging the standing of the conservation group attacking its licensing order. The Court rejected the argument and, so far as is known, the FPC has not raised the contention in any subsequent case.

224. 18 C.F.R. § 1.8.

225. *Id.* §§ 2.80, 2.81.

226. *Id.* § 2.81(c).

227. The requirement is made even more compelling by the FPC's statement that "all interveners taking a position on environmental matters should offer evidence for the record in support of their environmental position. . . ." *Id.* § 2.81(d).

228. *See* note 25a, *supra*.

229. Following the remand in Scenic Hudson I, interrogatories were used, but were answered voluntarily rather than on compulsion of the FPC, which refused to exert its authority. Similarly, while depositions were taken in the course of the hearings, they were resisted initially by the FPC staff.

230. *See* 18 C.F.R. §§ 1.20, 3.103, 4.32. As noted in 18 C.F.R. § 3.103, "[w]here no hearing is held, the Commission acts on the basis of the material filed and the staff studies and recommendations thereon." Furthermore, "[w]hether or not a hearing has been held, an application may be made for rehearing under section 313(a) of the Federal Power Act," and judicial review may then be pursued in accordance with FPA § 313(b).

231. *See* 18 C.F.R. §§ 1.20(c), 1.27, 1.30. The hearing examiners are full-time employees of the FPC.

232. *Id.* §§ 1.12(c), (d), (e); § 1.28.

233. *See* 18 C.F.R. §§ 1.18, 3.103.

234. The expense of intervention is further compounded by the FPC's gen-eral filing requirements. Thus, under 18 C.F.R. § 1.15, an original plus 14 copies of all petitions, motions, prepared testimony and exhibits, briefs and other formal documents must be filed with the Commission itself. In addition, copies of all such documents must be served on all other parties, whether they

102

are participating actively or not. Under these circumstances, the costs of reproduction alone can be extremely heavy, particularly when there are multiple parties. To this, moreover, must be added the costs of obtaining transcripts. At rates ranging between $.35 a page for five-day delivery and in excess of $1.00 a page for same-night delivery (which is often imperative if effective cross-examination is to be pursued), the costs for transcripts in any extended proceeding can run to thousands of dollars. And all of the foregoing is exclusive of the fees for expert witnesses, much less for counsel.

235. While 18 C.F.R. § 1.28 limits the occasions where appeals may be taken from rulings of the hearing examiner, in practice motions can usually be made to the full commission under 18 C.F.R. § 1.12(e). However, this does not guarantee that the FPC will act promptly on such motions. *See* Greene County, *supra* note 25a.

236. The criticism voiced by conservationists reflects their belief that by the time the hearings are commenced (and, indeed, well before), the staff has already adjudged the proposed project worthwhile. Whether or not this criticism is fair, there can be no doubt that in almost every controversial case, the staff's testimony and cross-examination have been in support of the project. As noted previously, this does not mean that the staff has not sought in some cases to reduce the environmental harm caused by the project, but rather that it has seldom, if ever, argued against a project in its entirety.

237. Once the record is closed, it may nonetheless be reopened for good cause shown. The procedures for reopening are set forth in 18 C.F.R. § 1.33. Prior to Scenic Hudson I, the FPC took a restrictive approach to reopening. However, upon remand, the hearings in that case were twice reopened and in the last instance, more than 18 months after the record had first been closed.

238. 18 C.F.R. § 1.30.

239. *Id.* § 1.29.

240. On the Scenic Hudson I remand, the hearing examiner's initial decision was issued almost 15 months after the record closed. When, thereafter, the record was reopened, and again closed, some nine months elapsed before the examiner issued a supplemental decision.

241. 18 C.F.R. § 1.30(a).

242. *Id.* § 1.31. The Secretary of the FPC can and often does extend the time for filing Briefs on Exceptions.

243. *Id.* §§ 1.31(a), (b), (d).

244. *Id.* §§ 1.31(a), (d).

245. 18 C.F.R. § 2.81. Whether it is sufficient under NEPA for the FPC to include its final environmental impact statement in its final opinion and order is open to question, in view of the Council on Environmental Quality requirement that such statement be circulated for comments before any final action is taken by an agency. 36 Fed.Reg. 7724 (1971).

246. 16 U.S.C. § 825*l*(a) (1970).

247. *Id.*

248. FPA § 313(b), 16 U.S.C. § 825*l*(b) (1970).

249. *See also* 18 C.F.R. § 1.34.

250. *Id.* An application for rehearing may, of course, also be denied by specific order of the FPC within the 30-day period; indeed, this is generally the course that the FPC follows in important cases.

251. *See, e. g.*, Mid-America Pipeline Co. v. FPC, 299 F.2d 126 (D.C.Cir. 1962); Indiana & Michigan Elec. Co. v. FPC, 224 F.Supp. 166 (D.Ind.1963).

252. See note 25a, *supra*.

253. FPA § 313(b), 16 U.S.C. § 825*l*(b) (1970).

254. *Id.*

255. Federal Rules of Appellate Procedure, Rule 15; Form 3.

256. FPA § 313(b), 16 U.S.C. § 825*l*(b) (1970).

257. *See* note 255, *supra*. The cost of reproducing the record on appeal can be monumental. However, the courts will sometimes hear the appeal on the basis of the original record in which case the expense will be minimal.

258. 5 U.S.C. § 706 (1970). FPA § 313(b), 16 U.S.C. § 825*l*(b) (1970), also provides expressly that "[t]he finding of the Commission as to the facts, if supported by substantial evidence, shall be conclusive."

259. FPA § 313(b), 16 U.S.C. § 825*l*(b) (1970).

260. Sierra Club v. Morton, 40 U.S.L.W. 4397 (April 19, 1972).

261. The basic question now at issue is whether the courts, acting under NEPA as well as the Federal Power Act and other regulatory statutes, will hold the agencies to something more than procedural regularity and thereby enforce compliance with the substantive mandate of the statutes. In this connection, *see, e. g.*, Calvert Cliffs and Scenic Hudson II (including Judge Oakes' dissent).

262. In several instances, the FPC has used rulemaking to establish threshold environmental requirements made binding on all license applicants. 18 C.F.R. §§ 4.40, 4.41 require that applications include information regarding recreational facilities and wildlife protection, as well as a detailed environmental impact statement (*see* Exs. R, S and W). In addition, 18 C.F.R. § 2.81 prescribes requirements for implementing NEPA, and 18 C.F.R. § 2.7 imposes certain substantive requirements regarding public recreational facilities to accompany the construction of projects. *See also* 18 C.F.R. § 2.13 regarding the design of transmission facilities, and 18 C.F.R. §§ 8.1–8.11 regarding recreational facilities and public access thereto.

263. 16 U.S.C. § 802(b) (1970).

264. First Iowa Hydroelectric Cooperative v. FPC, 328 U.S. 152, 170 (1946).

265. *Id.* at 180–181.

266. FPC v. Niagara Mohawk Power Corp., 347 U.S. 239 (1954).

267. 33 U.S.C. § 1171(b) (1970).

268. *Id.* § 403.

269. *Id.* § 407.

270. 36 Fed.Reg. 7724 (1971).

271. Zabel v. Taub, 403 F.2d 199 (5th Cir. 1970), *cert. denied*, 401 U.S. 910 (1971).

272. 37 Fed.Reg. 2525, 2526 (1972).

273. River and Harbor Act of 1899 [hereinafter cited as 1899 Act] § 13, 33 U.S.C. § 407.

274. *Id.* § 13, 33 U.S.C. at § 407.

275. *Id.* § 17, 33 U.S.C. at § 413.

276. *Id.* § 17, 33 U.S.C. at § 413.

277. But *see* United States v. Ballard Oil Co., 195 F.2d 369 (2d Cir. 1952).

278. 384 U.S. 224 (1966).

279. *Id.* at 229–30.

280. *Id.* at 229 (emphasis supplied). The dissenters challenged that reading of the legislative history by the majority. *See* dissent of Mr. Justice Harlan, joined by Mr. Justice Black and Mr. Justice Stewart, 384 U.S. at 233–34.

281. 384 U.S. at 226.

282. 384 U.S. at 225.

283. 297 F.Supp. 912 (N.D.Ill.1969). *Accord,* United States v. Maplewood Poultry Co., 327 F.Supp. 686 (N.D.Maine 1971); United States v. U. S. Steel Corp., 328 F.Supp. 354 (N.D.Ind.1970).

284. United States v. Interlake Steel Corp., 297 F.Supp. 912, 916 (N.D.Ill. 1969).

285. *Id.*

286. Exec.Order 11574, 3 C.F.R. 556 (1971) [hereinafter cited as Exec. Order].

287. Exec.Order § 2(a) (1).

288. Exec.Order § 2(2) (2).

289. Exec.Order § 2(a) (2) (A).

290. Exec.Order § 2(a) (2) (A).

291. 33 C.F.R. § 209.131 (1971).

292. 33 U.S.C. § 1171(b) (1970).

293. *Id.*

294. *Id.*

295. *See* note 192, *supra.*

296. Calvert Cliffs, *supra* note 170.

297. Kalur v. Resor, *supra* note 192, at 6.

298. 33 C.F.R. § 209.131(k).

299. Kalur v. Resor, *supra* note 192, at 6.

300. 42 U.S.C. § 1857c–6(b) (1970).

301. *Office of Science and Technology, supra* note 102, at 56.

302. N.Y.Public Service Law, art. VII.

V. A CRITIQUE OF THE
DECISION-MAKING PROCESS

The process by which the issues in electric power and the environment are resolved has received much criticism. Often comments coming from divergent viewpoints voice similar complaints.

An initial problem is "gaps" in the process, issues for which government as now structured provides no forum in which to make a reasoned decision. The National Environmental Policy Act requires agencies to consider all the issues, but such consideration can cause unacceptable delay if done on a case-by-case basis. Rulemaking provides a way to resolve more questions generically, but not without first overcoming a number of legal and practical problems.

Just as the lack of rulemaking forces agencies to resolve the same issue in many license adjudications, multiple licensing requirements sometimes force the parties concerned with a single plant to relitigate the same issues in many forums. Such relitigation has caused part of the increased delays in the licensing process.

Another series of criticisms involves the interaction between the licensing process and the public. Complaints about the extent to which information is disclosed and the difficulties for the public in participating in the process have contributed to a growing sense of unease about the credibility and efficiency of the regulatory commissions.

This chapter investigates these criticisms.

A. GAPS IN THE PROCESS

Despite the complexity of the regulatory process, many of the most important issues receive no explicit attention. Instead, they are resolved only as an unconscious by-product of other actions because government is not structured to treat energy as a discrete area of decision-making. The relevant legislative committees, executive departments, and administrative agencies took shape in eras when fuel supplies seemed abundant, pollution irrelevant, and government's role limited to promoting private development and preventing monopolistic

106

practices. But, today, some energy sources seem exhaustable, pollution important, and government intervention in energy widespread.[1]

Given a decision-making process designed to cope with a different era, not surprisingly, no public entity has the mandate and power to make reasoned decisions on such important issues as the shaping of demand, the choice of alternate modes of generation, the allocation of research funds, the regional placement of facilities, and the relationship of power plant licensing to overall energy and land-use policy.

The National Environmental Policy Act has the commendable purpose of requiring agencies to consider all such issues. But, the current structure of commissions and their licensing processes may make it impossible for them to reconcile this full consideration with adequate speed in processing applications.[2]

1. DEMAND

The growth in demand for electricity is the most important issue because power requirements determine the scale of regulatory problems and the size of the potential environmental impact. Since utilities must try to supply all the electricity demanded by consumers,[3] who buy it at a price which fails to reflect those environmental costs of its production that regulation permits,[4] the demand issue is now resolved without balancing economic and environmental considerations.

Administrative agencies lack the power to take action directly aimed at affecting consumption. Rationing or a tax on electricity require legislation. State public utility commissions do have jurisdiction to set the electricity prices to which consumers respond, but the governing statutes prescribe rates based on costs.[5] Although commissions allegedly approve structures of rates which deviate from costs in ways that promote use of electricity [6] and one commission has taken account of environmental considerations in rate making,[7] the legislative standards do limit the extent to which new pricing policies can curb growth.

But, as a regulator of transportation, fuels, and the environment, government does indirectly influence consumers' electricity use through actions which affect utility costs. Also, as a consumer in its own right, government determines part of total demand, such as when it sets illumination and air conditioning standards in government build-

107

ings. But, generally, the agencies involved in such regulation and consumption believe they should not consider the impact of their actions on total demand for electricity and whether such impact is desirable.[8]

Even if agencies did seek to affect demand, directly or indirectly, they lack policy guidance as to whether and how much they should do so. The licensing process itself fails to provide an adequate forum in which to debate a policy on demand; the resolution of the demand issue requires a more visible setting than a hearing on one plant, particularly since the plant does not create the demand. But, because conflicting views on the issue of demand are so strongly held, the lack of a conscious policy stresses the licensing process.

Chapter VI of this report argues that it is Congress which should set policy on whether or not to curb electricity growth, but that the complicated nature of the facts will prevent a reasoned decision until an administrative agency helps the legislature to focus the issues and find the facts.

The Federal Power Commission would appear to have an obligation to lay this foundation for legislative action. The Supreme Court instructed the FPC in *Udall* v. *FPC* to weigh all alternatives, including the alternative of no construction at all, in fulfilling its licensing responsibility under Part I of the Federal Power Act.[9] Moreover, the FPC is directed to consider "conservation of natural resources" [10] in preparing power surveys under Part II of the Act.

But the FPC denies responsibility to consider power conservation. Planning for efficiency in power use is "not our job," according to FPC staff members.[11] According to one, the FPC's role is to remain "neutral" between growth and non-growth advocates.[12]

Whether or not a policy of neutrality might be appropriate for an agency charged with affirmatively representing the public interest,[13] the FPC is not always neutral. Chairman Nassikas told a House Appropriations Subcommittee last April:

> "If you do not increase electric power exponentially over the course of the next decade, I don't think that you are going to meet our national commitment to . . . improving our standard-of-living . . . [and] to the environment. . . . While we recognize that there has to be some destruction of the environment . . ., increased electric

power over the long run is going to be one of the solutions to our environmental problems." [14]

Yet, the FPC's 1970 Power Survey states:

"Recognizing that available energy resources are finite and that the ultimate per capita use of electric energy has an upper limit, it is inevitable that the rate of growth in electric energy consumption eventually will decrease." [15]

Presenting such possibly conflicting views might advance Congressional consideration if the FPC had based its statements on research on the range of questions necessary to make an informed judgment.[16]

An additional impediment to Congress' receiving the information and recommendations necessary to develop an energy policy is the lack of an administrative agency with jurisdiction over all forms of energy, a necessity given the possibilities for substitution between energy sources and the relationship between their prices.

2. ALTERNATIVES

The choice of alternative modes of generating electricity is of great importance because each production method involves a different mix of economic costs, including environmental costs. The utility's initial choice of production mode is partly predetermined by previous government actions affecting the price of fuel such as import controls, depletion allowances, regulated transport prices, and government-owned processing facilities. While contests over such actions are hard-fought, they are not noted for weighing the merits of alternate electrical generation methods.

Similarly, at the plant licensing stage, no convenient forum exists in which to debate the alternative which a particular plan should use. At the federal level, separate agencies control atomic, hydroelectric, and fossil-fuel generation.[17] So, even if the FPC decided a nuclear plant was preferable in a given case, it could only deny the application for a hydroelectric license, but not issue a license for the alternative.

3. RESEARCH AND DEVELOPMENT

While the decision among alternatives is important, of even greater importance are the research and development decisions which will determine the modes of generation available to ultilities a decade or two hence. Government structure for research allocation, however, prevents comparison of the various avenues available. Numerous agencies, executive departments, and Congressional committees have jurisdiction over the development of various forms of electrical production.

The problem is most clearly seen in the context of atomic energy, which has received the lion's share of government's electricity R&D money.[18] The Atomic Energy Commission is, of course, responsible for the promotion of atomic energy.[19] All legislation dealing primarily with atomic energy must go to one committee in Congress, the Joint Committee on Atomic Energy,[20] which has sought to help the Commission in its developmental mission.[21]

The AEC's budget request is reviewed by the Office of Management and Budget (OMB). In recent years, OMB has compared all agencies' energy R&D requests. But, a top OMB official concluded that the many agencies involved make it difficult for OMB to do more than work slowly towards a balanced research program.[22]

While OMB often recommends cutting back the AEC's requests, the Commission does at least receive sympathetic attention from this powerful office, charged with providing the President with objective opinions on budget requests and substantive policy recommendations. Recognizing its great power and the possibility of an examiner's becoming biased through working on one agency for many years, OMB has tended to try to shift examiners from agency to agency every three or four years.[23] The highly respected OMB Section Chief for atomic energy affairs has worked on the AEC since 1947.[24] In addition, the new AEC chairman was a former assistant director of OMB. A trade journal praised him in the following terms:

> "Outside his personal talents, the major assets that Schlesinger brings to the AEC is a real or implied understanding with the Office of Management and Budget that he will get the money he needs to do the job as he sees it." [25]

The White House parallels the Congress and OMB in lacking the means to balance alternatives in allocating research funds. An energy subcommittee of the Domestic Council is currently not operative. At the same time, the staff dealing with energy problems in the President's Office of Science and Technology is now down to one person.

110

The AEC itself could have a stronger mechanism to compare research possibilities in the nuclear field. To generate the information necessary to make such comparisons, the Commission recently created a central Office of Planning and Analysis.[26] But, in practice, the division charged with research on civilian nuclear power is exempted from having its various projects analyzed by this central office. Rather, this division has its own equally large staff of analysts, who do the cost/benefit studies with only general supervision from the central office.[27] Thus, in making its research budget decisions, the Commission must still rely in part on the project analyses prepared by the division that will receive the money if the analyses show the projects are worth funding.

4. REGIONAL ALLOCATION

No forum exists in which to debate the relative merits of various areas in which a needed plant and therefore its transmission lines should be constructed. Issues are involved beyond the power and interest of a town zoning board or state commission. Many potential sites are of scenic or historical importance to the nation. Ideally, sources of air pollution should be located away from high concentrations of population; sources of thermal pollution should be sited with regard to the capacities of various water systems to absorb heat.

But, population concentrations and watersheds do not observe state lines; the Federal Power Act, however, does. While environmental protection may require transmitting power from one state to another, the Federal Power Commission has no authority to order one state to build a plant necessary to provide power to another.[28]

While no government agency can ordinarily command the interstate provision of power, a utility can voluntarily decide to get its power from another state by buying the power or siting a plant, if the other state will agree. But, buying power is an alternative which must (and sometimes does) overcome a corporation's natural tendency to seize opportunities to grow and the difficulties of arranging secure contracts. And convincing one state to provide another's power needs appears to be increasingly difficult because environmental concern has arisen at the same time as economies of scale have made huge regional power complexes more economically attractive.

111

5. Relationship to Other Policy Areas

Electricity policy should ideally relate to overall energy and land use policy. But, present government structure makes such coordination difficult. There are many examples of fragmented authority.

Thus, state and federal agencies have promulgated air quality standards which will require substantially increased use of low-sulfur fossil fuels. Another agency, the Federal Power Commission, points out that there will not be a supply of low-sulfur fuels adequate to meet these environmental standards.[29] The FPC, in turn, lacks plenary jurisdiction to increase the supply of low-sulfur fuels.[30] This might have been done by changing the oil import quota system so as to allow the importation of more low-sulfur oil, by having placed earlier emphasis on efforts to create the technology necessary to gasify coal, or by having encouraged the petroleum industry to begin to install the capacity needed to remove sulfur from crude oil.

Another example is home heating. Gas is an attractive fuel both for residential heating and for producing electricity. But, it is in short supply. Due to the inefficiencies of converting energy into electricity, three times as much gas is needed if a home is heated by gas-generated electricity as is needed if the gas is used directly. But, simultaneously, various states order utilities to use gas or other low-sulfur fuels for generating electricity, allow them to promote electric heating, and, because gas is in short supply, limit the use of gas in some areas for space heating.

6. NEPA Fails to Fill Gaps in the Process

Thus, in key areas, policy emerges unconsciously from a series of unconnected actions rather than from reasoned decision-making. Such fragmentation can produce decisions which individually make sense but which together do not. NEPA was designed to combat this problem. As a Senate report stated:

> "Important decisions concerning the use and shape of man's future environment continue to be made in small but steady increments which perpetuate rather than avoid the recognized mistakes of previous decades. NEPA told agencies to consider the broad context and commanded individual agencies to inform it if their powers were not adequate." [31]

112

Federal agencies concerned with electricity responded that NEPA's implementation required no substantial increases in their authority. But, many factors make it difficult for them to fill the gaps in the process.

Thus, if an application is denied because another type of facility is preferable, the net result may be to build no facility, an eventuality which might be worse than granting the application. Moreover, agencies may not be able to handle the type of analysis required by NEPA in adjudications of reasonable length.[32] Non-environmental issues alone can lead to protracted delays and huge records. If the same adjudication also must deal with such questions as limiting the demand for electricity, the hearing could go on almost indefinitely. The agency cannot rule out issues because it lacks power to act on them.[33] Consideration of such questions as demand and national fuel policy, moreover, would tax the administrative process even if time were not a factor because they require at least initial legislative treatment.

Further, agencies are faced with demands by intervenors to deal with many such broad issues. Neither NEPA nor the Council on Environmental Quality Guidelines provide much information on the scope of issues to be considered. At least in AEC construction permit proceedings, the case law seems to require the agency to consider uncontested issues.[34]

Thus, to the extent that NEPA instructs agencies to fill the gaps in the process in their adjudications, the agency may have an unmanageable task. If NEPA is interpreted otherwise, gaps in the process will still remain. Thus, whatever the merits and demerits of NEPA, it cannot alone cure the fundamental problem of government's not being structured to handle many of the most important problems in the area of electric power and the environment.[35]

One possible way to reconcile the goals of NEPA with the objective of a hearing of manageable scope is to treat as many issues as possible generically through rulemakings, thereby attempting to eliminate them from the adjudicatory hearings. The following section concludes that rulemakings might be used more widely, but not without practical and legal problems.

B. LACK OF RULEMAKING

An agency will confront recurring issues in many of its license application cases. Through rulemaking, the agency can dispose of such issues generically and remove them from adjudication, thereby speeding the licensing process. All agencies have availed themselves of rule-making for procedural issues and, to varying degrees, for substantive questions.[36] The AEC has led the way at the federal level [37] and the New York State Public Service Commission has issued rules governing situations where transmission lines should be placed underground.[38]

But, even in the nuclear field, many possibilities exist for more extensive rulemaking, particularly in such areas as the design of reactor components and the permanent disposal of high-level nuclear wastes.[39] And, in the air pollution area, federal legislation requires federal stationary source emission standards and state plans, which are in effect rulemakings on emissions standards. This system could also extend to rulemaking on the efficacy of various types of emissions control equipment. In the water pollution area, federal legislation requires rule-makings on ambient standards, but not on emissions standards or mixing zones. Site selection and the related question of undergrounding transmission lines offer possibilities for treating land-use questions generically. Finally, many of the issues which are not decided because of gaps in the process should ultimately be treated generically.

1. THE PROBLEMS OF ADJUDICATION

Passing up opportunities for rulemaking creates a dilemma for an agency. If the agency treats all the potentially generic issues in its adjudication of each license application, the hearing can become a marathon, thereby lengthening the process and causing potential reliability problems. In turn, environmental groups must stretch their thin resources to cover many hearings, instead of one rulemaking where they could perhaps be most effective.[40]

If, however, the agency decides to omit some issues to save time, these issues become additional gaps in the process and intervenors will seek judicial reversal on the ground that the record is incomplete. Thus, intervenors in AEC license hearings have sought to raise questions about the nuclear fuel cycle outside of the plant itself such as the risks of high-level waste disposal. This issue is relevant to the balancing of a plant's overall costs and benefits, but a reasonably speedy adjudication

114

cannot hear evidence on all such questions.[41]   The logical remedy, whether or not legally sufficient under NEPA,[42] would be rulemakings prior to the issuance of licenses to resolve all generic questions including the overall costs and benefits of light-water reactors from one end of the fuel cycle to the other.

More rulemaking would also help utilities in system planning. Facilities must be designed and equipment ordered years before they are needed.   But, without standards, the industry must guess at what a regulatory agency will require by the time the equipment is to be installed.

The lack of rulemaking may have more subtle effects which could decrease the weight attached to environmental values.   According to a report prepared for the Administrative Conference, leaving policy decisions to lower visibility adjudications can have serious impacts on the accuracy of the administrative process and give undue influence to the best organized interests.[43]   The report states that dealing with interrelated technical questions in an adjudicatory context can dwarf the "soft variables," such as environmental values, and overemphasize past experience in gauging future risks,[44] effects which could be particularly important when a plant is necessary to prevent a blackout.

2.   Impediments to Rulemaking

While more rulemaking seems desirable, this course faces practical and legal problems.   One practical constraint is a lack of standardization.   The AEC regulatory staff points out that more features of nuclear plants could receive generic approval if manufacturers standardized components of their plants.[45]   Manufacturers, utilities, and architect-designers all blame each other for introducing new wrinkles in each plant design.[46]   Industry fears stifling innovation.   Intervenors argue that standardization has been impossible because atomic energy was put to widespread commercial application before the technology reached maturity.

Even without more standardization, however, the regulatory staff sees many opportunities for more generic treatment through regulations and guidelines.   But, the General Accounting Office (GAO) reports that the AEC staff has not used these recognized opportunities because much time of the group assigned to formulating generic criteria, the Division of Standards, was allocated to analyses of individual plants.[47]

115

The AEC has now agreed with GAO's recommendation to put some employees on the problem full time.[48]

Another practical problem is that some issues cannot be settled entirely by generic treatment. Appropriate air and water standards may vary so much from place to place, even in the same air shed or waterway, that a completely generic solution would be too complicated or costly. Practically, this problem might be solved by settling the main elements of a standard generically, but also allowing *ad hoc* consideration of variances upon a sufficient threshold showing.

The legal problems with rulemaking may also prove substantial. *Calvert Cliffs* forbade the AEC to rely upon the standards set by other agencies on the theory that NEPA requires the commission to consider the desirability of imposing more strict standards and because information on each aspect of the plant is necessary to the weighing of alternatives required by NEPA.[49] This holding may imply that the AEC must also adjudicate even those aspects of a plant covered by its own rules.[50] If so, rulemaking becomes pointless from the viewpoint of speeding licensing hearings. In its proposed procedural modifications, the AEC would allow no challenges to substantive rules except in petitions for waiver based upon affidavits making a prima facie case.[50a]

Yet, *Calvert Cliffs* is not necessarily inconsistent with the AEC's relying upon its own rules to remove issues from hearings. The problem of whether its rules are strict enough in a particular case could be handled by requiring a threshold showing before hearing evidence on stricter standards for a given plant. The problem of assessing the risks and benefits of the standard in the rulemaking might be solved if the rule's impact statement determined roughly the implications of the rule's observance in a typical plant and was incorporated by reference into the impact statement for the particular plant.

Yet, the AEC would run a risk if it relied upon such a speculative approach without legislative approval. Even riskier would be to apply this approach to the regulations of other agencies.[51]

The Administrative Procedure Act also could present obstacles to treating presently adjudicated issues through rulemakings. Many commentators have suggested an approach to rulemaking with more rights to parties than under the traditional rulemaking proceeding, but less than under adjudications, the specific mix of rights depending upon the nature of the issues to be covered.[52] Courts have responded favorably.[53] But, if an issue, to be treated in a rulemaking without full adjudicatory rights, had previously been adjudicated, a court could conceivably hold that excluding this issue from adjudication violates the Administrative Procedure Act.[54]

Given the consequences if the AEC or the FPC were to rely heavily upon rulemaking to take issues out of hearings and then were reversed by the courts, a preferable course would be for Congress to consider directly the role of new types of rulemaking under the APA and NEPA.

3. LEGISLATIVE STANDARDS

Congress would ease agencies' burdens under NEPA by itself filling some of the gaps in the process and by giving agencies better guidance in handling the issues already before them. In establishing administrative procedures, legislatures have the duty to make key value judgments, leaving to the agency the technological problems of implementation.[55] In the electricity/environment area, the questions posed to agencies are unusually value-laden. Agencies must balance nuclear safety against costs; they must weigh the benefits of inexpensive power against the problems of pollution.

The standards now imbedded in current legislation provide little guidance. How much of a risk of a nuclear disaster is an "undue risk" under the Atomic Energy Act?[56] What should the Corps of Engineers consider as relevant to "the public interest" in deciding whether to issue a construction permit?[57] By what standard should the FPC determine that a project is "best adapted to a comprehensive plan for improving or developing a waterway or waterways for the use or benefit of interstate or foreign commerce, for the improvement and utilization of water power development, and for other beneficial public uses, including recreational purposes?"[58] These different factors will almost always be in conflict, especially since "recreational purposes" are interpreted to include maintenance of the waterway in its natural state.[59]

Similarly, the FPC is instructed for various planning purposes to act "[f]or the purpose of assuring an abundant supply of electric energy throughout the United States with the greatest possible economy and with regard to the proper utilization and conservation of natural resources," [60] but without instruction on how to use and conserve such resources simultaneously.

117

Such open-ended statutory schemes vest considerable discretion in agencies and courts. The results of these broad delegations depend upon the quality of the agencies and courts which must make the value-judgments. Where, however, the agencies make little use of rule-makings, these judgments may never be made explicitly. Moreover, sparse use of rulemaking and general legislative standards, combined with unexpected legislation, impose on industry a considerable degree of uncertainty. Utilities have almost completed the licensing of a needed plant to find that new layers of proceedings are required.[61] They have installed the best air pollution control devices then available on existing plants to find that subsequent regulations require the devices be replaced with yet newer models. While utilities have no vested right to the continuation of existing laws and standards, changes do present serious problems for reliability and cost control.

More specific standards would minimize the number of necessary changes. To the extent allowed by the research done to date in pollution control, standards-setting agencies should try to calculate emission control needs with at least as great a lead time as is necessary for the utilities to plan according to the pollution standards which will be in effect when the facility becomes operational. Where new procedures and new standards are needed, however, legislatures and agencies should deal explicitly with problems of retroactivity.

C. Multiple Licensing

Given the number of licenses required for any power plant, the same issues must be raised again and again. This relitigation of issues stems from the absence of collateral estoppel among administrative proceedings. For example, the question of water quality for a proposed atomic energy plant must be raised before the AEC, the Corps of Engineers, EPA, and at least one state agency.[62] Since the most important delays have arisen at the lead federal agency this redundancy has been costly, but, thus far, generally not dilatory. But the potential for delay is obvious. Sometimes, delay results because permits cannot be obtained simultaneously, one agency requiring approval from another before it will consider an application.[63] Appeals could be especially time consuming with each decision being appealed separately.

Moreover, multiple licensing deprives agencies of their initiative to act and their power to consider alternatives. For example, if ten

118

agencies are involved in licensing a particular plant, the tenth agency cannot insist on a major change in plans without causing substantial delays. In effect, it can only approve or veto the project.

1. MULTIPLICITY AND FEDERALISM

Multiple licensing exists because so many different levels and agencies of government, each with a legitimate area of concern and expertise, have an interest in power production. The broad range of involvement, in turn, is related to the variety of issues involved in the licensing of a single plant. For example, just the siting of a nuclear facility involves consideration of safety, aesthetics, thermal water pollution, transmission lines, and more. Some of these issues are the particular province of one agency: the AEC is responsible for nuclear safety, the host community cares most about the plant's relationship to the landscape. However, in other instances, the issues are equally important at a number of government levels: a town, state and large region would be concerned about the effects of thermal pollution on a whole watershed.

The simultaneous regulation by so many agencies of the same *res*—one power plant—has resulted in clashes among regulatory bodies on the same and on different levels of government. One such case was *Orange County Air Pollution Control District* v. *Public Utilities Commission*.[64] There the District refused to grant a license for the proposed Huntington Beach Nuclear Facility on the ground that there was insufficient assurance that the plants would not violate California's Health and Safety Code. The Commission, however, not only granted a license but directed the utility to begin construction despite denial of the District's permit. The court held that the District, a statewide agency, held concurrent jurisdiction with the PUC, and that the utility must comply with both agencies' regulations before it could proceed with construction.

The possible conflicts presented by multiple licensing requirements also make settlements between applicants and intervenors more difficult. Difficulties may arise when many agencies are concerned with the resolution of a dispute, and one agency is left out of the negotiations. In one case, the utility settled a dispute with a citizens group that had intervened in AEC operating permit hearings. When the company approached the state public service commission to request that the cost of improvements—which the company had agreed to make to

119

satisfy the intervenor's demands—be included in the rate base, the commission balked, saying that the increased cost might not be included in the rate base because it was a result of a private agreement which the state had not sanctioned.

Also, conflicts between various levels of government agencies may frustrate planning. Often, it is difficult to structure decision-making so that the appropriate level of government has authority over a question which concerns it most without allowing that level to impinge on what would normally be thought to be the prerogative of another level. A proper allocation of responsibility would avoid the problems which now exist when agencies conflict with each other in the exercise of their authority.

One example of this type of conflict occurred recently when the Governor of Kansas voiced his opposition to AEC plans to construct a federal facility for the disposal of radioactive waste in that state; the state legislature is considering adopting legislation attempting to bar the proposed facility.[65] The ramifications of this difference of opinion are broad, since under the AEC plan, radioactive waste from all over the country would be handled by this disposal unit.

Similar conflicts occur on the local level. A wide variety of local regulation, including zoning, building codes, and control of local roadways, allows municipalities to control siting of generating facilities and transmission lines. Except in those cases where there is a state-level override, municipalities can then effectively veto a decision by a state agency. Yet an override could remove municipal control over aspects of siting questions of particular local concern.

As these examples illustrate, inter-governmental clashes result in a frustration of the planning objectives of each agency. Frictions arise, in large part, when the respective roles of the various agencies have not been determined. These tensions by themselves can be healthy. What is needed is a way of resolving the conflicts, so as to protect the interests of smaller groups without jeopardizing national or regional goals.

2. CALVERT CLIFFS, MULTIPLICITY, AND RELITIGATION

The Court of Appeals for the District of Columbia has recently added another dimension to the problems of multiple license requirements and relitigation of issues. In *Calvert Cliffs Coordinating Comm.,*

Inc. v. *AEC*,[66] the court held that NEPA requires the AEC to consider water quality in its impact statement and other procedures. The AEC had taken the position that, since the states had to review water pollution information under section 21(b) of the Federal Water Pollution Control Act, Congress intended that the AEC would not undertake a separate evaluation of that issue.[67] However, as the court noted section 21(b) requires only that the states enforce a minimum standard in their certifications, not balance alternatives as mandated by NEPA.[68]

Clearly, the state certifying agency is not often equipped to do the kind of balancing the AEC must do to fulfill its NEPA obligations, but the state agency, not the AEC, is responsible for the efficacy of the state water quality plan. So both a state agency and the AEC perform a distinct and essential task, but concerning the same factual questions. Neither could easily assume the responsibilities of the other.

Duplication of effort, delay, and increased costs result because the process demands the compilation of two separate, complete records on water quality (the count goes up to three if one includes the Corps' refuse permit program). The House and Senate have both considered this problem raised by *Calvert Cliffs* and have passed bills freeing federal agencies from building records on water quality.[69] While the conference committee has not yet acted, it seems likely that the AEC would still be responsible for a NEPA balancing which includes water quality.[70] But a question remains unanswered: where will the AEC get the information on which to include water quality in the balancing of alternatives?

D. DELAY

1. THE LENGTHENING LICENSING PROCESS

Environmental opposition had previously played little part in the licensing process and the past delays of plant construction but is becoming an increasingly important factor. Through the mid-sixties only rarely did an electric generating facility draw litigative opposition from environmental groups. While recently some cases have received wide attention,[71] the vast majority of power generating facilities still go unopposed. The staff of the Corps of Engineers can recall no past fossil fuel plant which created enough controversy to require handling by the Washington office.[72]

But, the sparse environmental opposition has had significant localized impacts. First, most opposition has centered on atomic plants. This has caused concern in the nuclear community and further burdened the overworked regulatory staff of the Atomic Energy Commission.[73] Second, delays in licensing a particular plant can have a significant impact on the availability of electricity in a particular locale. The Federal Power Commission has identified five areas where it believes that the lack of an AEC operating license may contribute to a power shortage.[74]

Whatever the past experience, licensing delays are on the increase from larger workloads, new statutory duties, court orders, and environmental interventions. At the AEC, the average time needed to get an initial decision on a construction permit increased from 265.3 days in 1966 to 607.6 days in 1970.[75] Moreover, the *Calvert Cliffs* decision has interpreted NEPA so as to substantially increase the AEC's duties [76] and make it more vulnerable to judicial reversal.[77]

At the FPC, regulatory delay has also increased. An application for the large Blue Ridge Project, filed in 1965, has still not been decided.[78] In addition, a Second Circuit decision, if upheld, will increase FPC staff duties and may require the reopening of a number of license proceedings.[79]

At the Corps of Engineers, until recently, the only permit required was for construction in navigable waters,[80] usually procured routinely by an engineer on the utility's staff.[81] Now, the application is a major legal campaign, taking at least a year if land fill is involved.[82] In addition, with refuse permits now needed and only 21 permits issued to date, the Corps has estimated a several years delay in cleaning up the backlog of 20,000 applications.[83] Since this estimate, a district court decision, now under appeal, has enjoined the issuance of any refuse permits until the Corps issues regulations requiring a NEPA impact statement for all refuse permits which are major federal actions.[84]

Although NEPA has increased the potential scope of hearings, some commentators believe that "the delays caused by intervenors to date have been exaggerated." [85] When Senator Howard Baker recently asked agencies to list all projects which, in the agencies' judgment, have been unreasonably delayed solely because of NEPA and where "the public interest would better have been served by something less than full compliance with NEPA," the AEC's letter in response could name only one such project.[86] That project, the Quad Cities 1 & 2 plants, was the subject of a court case which intervenors and the utility have agreed to settle.

While recent decisions have interpreted NEPA to require a more extensive environmental review than the federal agencies thought was required,[87] they also possibly foreshadow a trend towards increasing judicial reversals. In three cases, different courts expressed dismay at agencies' treatment of NEPA.[88] Judicial reversals can add years on top of the lengthening administrative process itself. An extreme example is Consolidated Edison's Storm King project which has been litigated for seven years. After the FPC issued a license subsequent to an initial judicial reversal, the Second Circuit affirmed 2-to-1, and denied a suggestion for rehearing *en banc* by a 4-to-4 vote. A petition for certiorari to the Supreme Court was denied.[89]

While many times more permits are required at the state and local level than at the federal, these opportunities for delay have not been used widely so far. But, the Storm King project also provides an example of the possibilities for delay at the state level. A state trial court has reversed a state commission's decision to grant a section 21(b) certificate necessary to finalize the FPC's license.[90] In addition, even without interventions, state and local officials may substantially delay or veto a plant.[91]

2. DELAY AND RELIABILITY

While the licensing process is lengthy, regulation has so far caused only a small portion of delays in plants and transmission lines coming into service. The FPC found that three quarters of the plants scheduled for completion from 1966–1970 were delayed more than a month, and one quarter for more than six months.[92] But, the vast majority of these delays came from non-regulatory causes. The FPC identified 124 different contributing causes for the delays of these steam plants. Fifty-two percent were labor related, and 37% were equipment related (due to late delivery, equipment failure, faulty installation or start-up problems). Just six percent of the delay factors were associated with licensing problems, including (but not limited to) environmental objections. In all, licensing problems delayed only 7 of the 114 plants, and they were, in no case, the sole factor causing the delay. Regulatory and environmental problems accounted for delays on 18% of the transmission lines behind schedule at June 30, 1970, the same amount as budget problems, and less significant than equipment problems (37%) and construction and design problems (22%).

Edison Electric Institute surveys of steam plants also demonstrate the comparative insignificance of environmental opposition in past delays.[93] In the 1966–1968 period, no delays were attributed to environmental objections and only four to regulatory slowness, while 80% of the delays were caused by labor problems, equipment failures and late deliveries.[94] Of the ten units which were scheduled for service in 1971 and had been delayed for over six months, environmental opposition was a factor in two cases and regulatory lag in three cases, again much less significant than equipment and labor problems.[95]

But, the FPC and the utility industry predict that delays from environmental causes are likely to become more frequent and lengthy in the future.[96] What the past experience shows, however, is that utilities are accustomed to working with some degree of uncertainty about when a new plant will come into operation. But, the recent licensing delays have caused concern because they added more uncertainty and came at a time of unexpectedly large delays from union and manufacturer problems—sources of delay which utilities better understood.

In the long run, then, the cure is to fashion a procedure which is not necessarily terse, but whose length and standards for decision are fairly predictable. To mandate a process which cuts off debate arbitrarily may result in judicial reversals, which are the worst sources of uncertainty because they are least unpredictable and can lead to the longest delays. If utilities could accurately anticipate the time needed in the licensing process and apply for all licenses well before they are needed, the problems posed by the length of the application process would largely be confined to extra legal costs. Thus, except for the AEC operating license, which must be applied for near the time of plant completion, it is the uncertainty of the process, not its length, which can lead to blackouts.

3. Delay's Impact on Utility Decision-Making

More extensive regulatory opposition and delay associated with atomic power plants has had an impact on utility decision making. Many companies have switched plans from atomic to fossil fuel even where they believe that atomic plants would be both more economic and advantageous to the environment. Because of environmental opposition, utilities have also made changes in plant design which they consider unwise. Thus, one utility agreed to install a cooling tower at an atomic facility at a cost of approximately $15 million, because gaining a contested operating license would take at least one year while the idle plant was costing over $1 million per month.[97]

Finally, in addition to delay, utilities have dropped plans for plants they would otherwise have built because of the possibility of environmental intervention. Since the building of a plant has no direct impact on the amount of electricity demanded and generated, these decisions mean either that the plant will be built at a place where environmental opposition is less likely, not necessarily where environmental detriment is smaller. It may also mean that older and more polluting plants must be kept in service.

4. WHAT CAUSES DELAY?

The word "delay" itself implies a particular viewpoint on the problem. Unless one believes that utilities alone should weigh electric power and the environment, the time needed for some regulatory consideration is time well spent if it improves the quality of the final decision. But, opinion varies widely as to the extent of appropriate review. Accordingly, there are as many ideas about the causes of delay as there are ideas about what form the licensing of power generating facilities should take.

Thus, for those utility executives who see environment as an emotional fad, the source of the delay is the environmental intervenors. For the environmentalist who sees the administrative process as a sham, the real delay is the period of time during which the utility and the regulatory staff keep the plans secret. Similarly, utility lawyers criticize allegedly foot-dragging commission staffs who in turn blame the poor applications submitted by the utilities. The commissioners themselves blame reversals by courts, while the courts castigate commissioners for begrudgingly administering laws designed to protect the environment.

Thus, an analysis of delay cannot simply be an accounting of the steps in the licensing process. Rather, on a fundamental level, the problem of delay is linked to the complete range of infirmities of the decision-making process, including the lack of rulemaking and the multiplicity of licenses.

Nonetheless, there are a number of more proximate causes for the increasing length of the regulatory process. The Atomic Energy Commission offers a good case study of both this problem and an agency attempting to grapple with it.

Applications. The regulatory staff of the Atomic Energy Commission complains that it has not yet received one complete license application.[98] Usually, the AEC staff must spend several months at the outset of the application process discovering what the application does not contain, requesting the missing information from the applicant, and then continued iterations of this process.[99] Applicants complain in turn that the staff has not provided them with adequate information on what must be contained in an application.[100] At the present time, the regulatory staff has begun issuance of comprehensive guidelines on the format of an application.[101] The Commission has also proposed new rules allowing the docketing of a tendered application only if it is complete.[101a]

A related problem is representations by applicants that a particular component of a plant is like a component of another plant which has been licensed and approved. Applicants, however, do not point out the dissimilarities between the components and therefore much time is consumed in tracking down the differences.[102]

Discovery. Much time at the outset of the hearing process is consumed in intervenor's discovery. In AEC proceedings, documents were usually not made available until the regulatory staff had internally approved the application, which took more than a year. In one case, intervenors asked for certain correspondence between the applicant and the commission in September, 1971, but were told that it would not be available until the case was set for hearing. When the prehearing conference was held in mid-December, an adjournment had to be taken because intervenors had not yet been provided with the correspondence nor given an opportunity to read it. The Commission has begun to cope with this problem by proposing that intervention be allowed considerably in advance of the hearing date, that intervenors receive a wide variety of information previously unavailable except through formal discovery devices, that an early prehearing conference be held to deal with discovery, and that discovery be completed before the final prehearing conference.[102a] These rules, however, allow no formal discovery before intervenors specify their issues, although it is not clear that intervenors have the information to do so before discovery.

Tactical Problems. In a number of cases, the applicant or the regulatory staff have made tactical decisions which ultimately delayed licensing. Such errors are understandable given the lack of specificity in much legislation.[103] For instance, having based NEPA procedure on the advice from the Council on Environmental Quality, the AEC regulatory staff decided to fight the issues raised in *Calvert Cliffs*.[104] Most commentators, however, now believe that the adverse decision was inevitable, except insofar as it related to water quality standards. Another example, on a smaller scale, arose in the *Vermont Yankee* case.[105] There, applicant advanced the need for electricity for the winter of 1971–72 as a reason to grant quickly a one percent testing license but resisted intervenor's request to cross-examine on this issue. At stake was perhaps an additional two or three days of hearings tacked on to the proceedings that did take place in the fall of 1971. Well into the winter, after several months of briefing and argument, the hearing board decided that the cross-examination must take place.[106]

Intervenors' lawyers point out that if the commission and applicants would follow a liberal policy on discovery and putting information on the record, it would be most difficult to get a reversal at the judicial level. On the other hand, if an issue is kept off the record or particular types of documents denied, intervenors in all other cases will raise the same point so that all litigated cases will go to judicial appeal with a long list of potential grounds for reversal, any one of which could undo many licenses. This presents a difficult problem for commissions, which must set some limits on relevance, and for a court, which may disagree with a commission ruling but is wary of upsetting many licenses.

Delaying Tactics. An intervenor insisting on a high level of proof may appear indistinguishable from an intervenor seeking delay for delay's sake. Both may behave similarly: seeking postponements, asking for broad rights of discovery, and cross-examining extensively. Parties in civil litigation use the same tactics in situations involving short notice and complicated facts largely known only to the opponent.

These circumstances can also provide cover to an intervenor who has faith in the hearing process only as an instrument of delay. But, according to Howard Shapar, Assistant General Counsel of the AEC for regulation, most intervenors are interested in litigation on the merits, not delay: "by and large, the intervenors are highly responsible . . . and are concerned about matters of safety or environment." [107] But, there are exceptions, intervenors who see litigation only as a bargaining tool and as a means to educate the public.[108]

Not unnaturally, industry has interpreted many well-motivated but tough litigation tactics as attempts at delay. Perhaps this is so because only recently have applicants had to face intervenors demanding substantial discovery and extensive cross examination. The first interrogatories were served in an AEC case in the spring of 1971.[109]

Delaying tactics are not unique to intervenors in licensing proceedings. Many lawyers see such use of process as obligatory when in the interests of one's client. Such tactics can be combatted with effective representation and rules of procedure which distinguish probative from dilatory behavior. Such rules have a better chance for success where the legitimate causes of delay—such as lack of information, witnesses, and adequate notice—are eliminated. The AEC's proposed rules seek to combat some of these underlying problems and arm the hearing examiner with power to prevent unproductive examination.[109a]

Staffing. Stresses on the overworked AEC regulatory staff have delayed the course of hearings themselves. Thus, in the *Indian Point II* case, all of the parties including intervenors agreed to expedite the hearings on the applicant's request for a 50 percent testing license.[110] An essential part of this arrangement was for the AEC regulatory staff to complete a NEPA statement on this subject by mid-October. On October 30, 1971, the attorney for the AEC stated that "this statement is expected to be completed in the near future." [111] On this basis, Consolidated Edison still hoped to have a 50 percent testing license by January 1, 1972. A hearing on the environmental issues, which intervenors had agreed not to contest, was to be held on December 14, 1971. But, the NEPA statement was not finally docketed until January 3, 1972.

More important, staffing problems delay the applications reaching the hearing stage.[112] A report to the Administrative Conference of the United States concluded that, from 1966 to 1970, the length of time from the date of application to the AEC until notice of hearing arose from 214 days to 461 days, the major cause of increased AEC licensing time.[113] GAO concluded that the AEC has neither had nor, until recently, requested a large enough staff to process applications on an expeditious basis.[114] The GAO also criticized the AEC for failing to analyze sources of delay at the staff level.[115] The director of the Regulatory staff has largely concurred in these conclusions and agreed to follow, in major part, GAO's recommendations.[116]

Other commissions have not, to our knowledge, been subject to similar analysis. But other failures to anticipate future work loads have become apparent. For example, even though a representative of the General Counsel's Office of the Corps of Engineers stated that they expected the ruling in *Kalur* v. *Resor*, the Corps had not formulated any plans for preparing impact statements for up to 20,000 refuse permit applications, even several weeks after the court's decision.[117]

5. The Need for Early Decisions

The AEC's reexamination of its rules and improvements in administrative procedure demonstrate the possibility of minimizing delay, without eliminating the opportunity for well-rounded litigation. One way in which to accommodate consideration of the issues and speed would be to require the filing of applications well before licenses are needed. A problem with this approach, however, is that applicants do not always have all of the information needed to make a complete application several years before the plant is to be built. But, some issues can be litigated early. Thus, the licensing process could consist of an initial approval of the site and general type of facility to be built and a subsequent approval of the design. Moreover, the acute problems arising from delays in applications for AEC's operating licenses might be relieved if all design questions were resolved at the construction permit stage. The operating license hearing would only consider whether the plant as built comports with the design. The hearing could be eliminated altogether without a threshold showing of such a deviation. Thus, provision for early resolution of many issues is another way of reducing delay without foreclosing consideration of any issue. More extensive rulemaking, as discussed above, is another such possibility.

These possibilities may make adequate speed in licensing possible without sweeping limitations on litigative rights. Moreover, such limitations fail to deal with the more fundamental causes of delay. As Judge Irving Kaufman wrote, "a major share of the blame for unnecessary delays and ineffectual public planning in the United States may be laid at the doorstep of fragmented government regulation of power development."[118] And, as Representative Melvin Price has warned:

"A piecemeal legislative solution to the existing problems should only be attempted as a last resort and in the long run would probably be counterproductive. What is needed is a cooperative effort by all concerned to help in the development of a sound framework and institutions implementing it." [119]

E. THE DISCLOSURE OF INFORMATION

1. THE PURPOSE OF DISCLOSURE

Disclosure of information about the public's business is a fundamental value which Congress has recognized in the Freedom of Information Act.[120] Information is particularly important in technical assessment. Commentators have argued that stimulating debate can reduce the gap between scientific breakthroughs and the full understanding of their implications.[121]

2. THE PRIVATE SECTOR'S ROLE

Before discussing the disclosure policies of relevant government agencies, it is useful to note the impact of the structure of the decision-making process on the flow of information. Where issues are resolved in public hearings, the considerations are spread upon the public record more automatically then if less formal processes are used. Many agencies, however, have created or presently participate in various kinds of industry-agency committees and advisory councils. The existence of such committees is, of course, public and some are described briefly below:

FPC Advisory Committees. The FPC has established and funded an Executive Advisory Committee and six Regional Advisory Committees, which assist the FPC in preparing growth projections and power surveys. All seven committees are chaired by utility executives and, except for a scattering of regulatory commission personnel, their membership consists exclusively of industry executives. The advisory committees are supported by Technical Advisory Committees, composed largely of utility and government employees.[122]

Reliability Councils. The nine regional reliability councils and the National Electric Reliability Council are groups of utilities, composed usually of investor-owned companies and large government-operated utilities. The councils help formulate the capacity estimates used by the utilities and government agencies. The councils take each utility's load forecast and combine all the estimates into unified projections.

Office of Management and Budget Advisory Committees. OMB has established three advisory committees dealing with public utilities.

They are composed of employees of regulated industries, their suppliers, consultants, and trade associations as well as OMB personnel.[123] Although other subjects appear to be discussed, these committees' responsibilities are to advise on information gathering techniques used by government agencies, an area over which OMB has great power.[124]

In general, these committees and others serve to provide agencies with the feedback they need and, in all cases mentioned, the relevant agencies still retain the right to make the final decision. If the committees did not exist, commission staffs would have to consume added time in interviewing individual utility executives or gathering the same information in formal proceedings. Formal proceedings would, however, put such information before the public and lessen the possibility that such committees improperly influence agency decisions.

Such doubts are bound to arise. For instance, according to the AEC's Director of Regulation, forty-six utility-commission committees exist to formulate codes and standards for the safety of nuclear facilities.[125] A manager in the AEC Division of Reactor Licensing can recall no case where the AEC regulatory staff overturned an aspect of an application founded on the recommendation of one of the councils.[126] One could conclude that the reason was either that the committees worked well in determining safety considerations and informing applicants of them, thereby preventing design mistakes needing wasteful corrections, or that agency participation made it difficult for the regulatory staff to reverse such committees. It is difficult for an outsider to judge.

Performing the information exchange functions of code and other committees in more formal proceedings would promote the flow of information to the public and reduce chances that commissions might rubber stamp industry positions, but would have attendant costs. The committees provide expert information to government without the payment of salaries or the expense of hearings. They allow for frank discussions and avoid the stagnation of formalism. In short, such committees allow society to harness the private sector's initiative and imagination.

Whether or not such considerations outweigh disclosure purposes in the case of any particular committee, steps could be taken to reconcile in part the conflicting objections. First, in the case of committees whose purpose is to help an agency to formulate a position (which is

131

apparently not the primary purpose of reliability councils), the committee might include members of the public identified with constituencies different from the agency or industry. With rare exceptions, such committees are now composed exclusively of regulators and the regulated. Second, the committees and councils could publish the results of their considerations. Thus, the FPC requires reliability councils to file their reports with relevant state commissions and the FPC, in whose Washington, D. C., document room they are available.[127] But, the FPC has assured the councils that they have no obligation to make the report available to the public in any other way,[128] although the cost of making such public reports more accessible to at least the most active environment groups in a region would be relatively minor compared to the importance of disclosure.

In contrast, the National Electric Reliability Council (NERC) recently completed a report warning of a "disastrous" power supply situation unless emergency legislation is passed.[129] The report was released, according to *Electric Week*, to "key Nixon aides and to a number of Congressional committee chairmen," but plans to release it to the public were postponed "indefinitely."[130] According to the trade journal:

> "Some industry officials felt that immediate objectives—getting legislation . . . or an executive directive . . .—could be better achieved by restricting circulation of the report to government channels for the time being . . .
> [An] industry source asked: 'What's to be gained? We already have it (the report) before the people who should be most able to help us.' "[131]

The report subsequently was put into the record of a Congressional hearing.[132]

Applicants also must resolve conflicting values in deciding what type of information to make available in licensing proceedings.[134] Their goal is to avoid stirring up unnecessary controversy. As the supervisor of environmental activities at one of the largest architect-designers of power generating facilities wrote, the AEC's requirement of providing information on alternative sites is:

> ". . . very difficult to handle. A utility may wish to keep its alternative sites confidential because it may wish to use those sites in the future. If the alternative sites are iden-

tified, unnecessary public concern may be aroused. At the
same time, discussion of the negative features of the alternate
sites may work to the disadvantage of the utility if the alternate sites are subsequently utilized." [135]

In any event, NEPA and the AEC's rules would seem to reconcile this
problem in favor of disclosing the alternatives' advantages and disadvantages and against allowing the applicant to determine what public
concerns are necessary or unnecessary.[136]

3. The Public Sector's Role

The adequacy of government disclosure policy has received much
attention. In addition to environmentalists' complaints, the Second
Circuit has criticized the FPC for forcing intervenors to seek judicial
enforcement of the Freedom of Information Act,[137] rather than disclosing data voluntarily. But, disputes about administrative response to
that Act are not unique to power regulation; complaints against agencies in other areas sound at least as serious.[138] On the other hand, the
Chairman of the Administrative Conference has generally praised the
Act as an improvement over past practices.[139]

We cannot deal with so general a topic as the Act's administration
here, but do point out its inevitable limitations. Such legislation fails
to help citizens get information when they do not know of its existence.
So, if information is to be disclosed, government must do more than
accede to requests. It must affirmatively inform.

Public hearings serve this purpose. The FPC and the Corps of
Engineers must hold hearings in many circumstances. Perhaps out of
recognition of the special place of nuclear power in the public mind,
Congress took the unusual step of requiring the AEC to hold hearings
on all construction permits for power plants.[140] The AEC also engages
in an extensive public information program.

Perhaps it is because of the AEC's efforts to inform, rather than
despite them, that there is a concern about nuclear policy which leads
to allegations of secrecy. *Forbes Magazine* stated:

"In the past three decades the AEC has spent $50 billion
with less public knowledge or scrutiny of its activities than
any other U. S. Government agency, excepting the far less
lavish Central Intelligence Agency. Operating in secrecy, it
could fend off the occasional critics of its nuclear power pro-

grams by referring cryptically to its military and national policy responsibilities. It has developed a dedicated group of supporters, lobbyists and vested interests both within and without the AEC, who yield little to the infamous Highway Lobby in their stubborn conviction that theirs is the only right way." [141]

That such charges are also echoed within the nuclear community may belie their accuracy. Some of the most active critics of AEC policy come from its laboratories. An executive of an AEC contractor charged that there is "inhibition of frank and free discussion" and censoring of reports by the AEC's Divison of Reactor Development and Technology.[142] When the head of that division, Milton Shaw, was asked about this charge during the ECCS hearings, he replied:

"Censoring? If you want to use this terminology in the sense that I think you are using it, yes, we are reviewing. We are attempting to get management there to review these reports better." [143]

In an interview, Mr. Shaw stated that when he reads statements by employees of AEC contractors and disagrees with their scientific results, he "cracks down" on the scientists' employers.[144]

These statements reveal the difficult problem of drawing the line between attempting to achieve accuracy and suppression of safety concerns which may or may not be sufficiently serious to warrant public discussion. That the bulk of experts in reactor technology either work for the AEC or for concerns with important business relations with the AEC aggravates the problem.

Congress sought to resolve this question by instructing the AEC to encourage and permit the dissemination of unrestricted information

"so as to provide that free interchange of ideas and criticism which is essential to .   .   .   progress and public understanding. .   .   ." [145]

The new chairman of the AEC has made clear that the AEC no longer intends to protect established technologies such as the light water reactor.[146] Moreover, after allegations of suppression were made, he explicitly asked scientists to testify freely on the ECCS and there was considerable testimony contrary to the AEC's position.[147] The net result was a tremendous quantity of information on all sides of the ECCS issue.

134

Given the possible implications of ECCS for electrical systems reliability in the summer of 1972, it would have been better for all concerned if the doubts expressed about ECCS had come to public attention and been resolved some time ago. Most committee members believe that, while there is little if any active suppression of dissent, a different institutional structure might bring issues like ECCS to public attention earlier.[148] Specifically, such a function might be performed by having some nuclear technology expertise in an agency whose primary orientation is the environment rather than energy production.

4. The Need to Provide Information

An open decision-making process requires information actually reaching the public. An agency may scrupulously follow the Freedom of Information Act, but the public may still receive little information. So long as the agency's public relations department publicizes only the favorable aspects of projects and treats controversial questions quietly, citizens may not know of the questions into which they should inquire. Two examples illustrate the problem.

In one case, the FPC received an application to license a large pumped-storage project on a site which conservationists felt had unique scenic value. The Commission followed the legal requirements to publish notice in a newspaper on successive weeks. But, it chose for this purpose only a local weekly paper of quite limited circulation. It neither published notices in any of the large regional dailies nor saw to it that any regional papers or broadcasters carried a story. Environmentalists learned of the application only because an undisclosed source alerted them.[149]

In another case, the President announced construction of two prototype fast breeder reactors in furtherance of the AEC's hope to have several hundred such reactors built by the century's end.[150] Among its features, the breeder produces much larger quantities of plutonium than today's reactors and requires this material's use in civilian plants.[151] Chapter II points out how a fraction of one shipment can make an atomic bomb. Some commentators believe the breeder program increases the chances of plutonium being hijacked or stolen.[152] None of the many government publications or speeches on the breeder which have come to the Committee's attention states that its fuel allows the making of bombs.[153] Two publications mention

135

explicitly the possibility of plutonium diversion, but do not elaborate why it may be a matter of concern.[154]

In neither case did the FPC or the AEC keep the issue secret. But, in both cases, the commissions had information available on request which would have been of public interest.[155] So, the issue concerns not secrecy, but the more subtle question of how far government should go to stimulate debate before it takes an important action. In his message vetoing the equal opportunity amendments of 1971, President Nixon provided one standard:

> "I also hold the conviction that such far reaching legislation should not, must not be enacted in the absence of a great national debate on its merit, and broad public acceptance of its principles." [156]

NEPA reinforces this view in the environmental area.[157] More specifically, as to atomic energy, Congress mandated an information policy to stimulate criticism, and many commissioners have expressed a policy of affirmatively bringing the issues to the public's attention.[158]

Similarly, a senior member of the AEC staff commented that the Commission feels it has an obligation to call important questions to the public's attention. While the Commission has not commented on this Report's description of its disclosure practices in the fast breeder case, the staff member continued that any failure to emphasize the diversion risks of the fast breeder is not a fair example of the lengths to which the AEC goes to highlight controversial issues. But, environmentalists say that the treatment of this issue typifies the Commission's low profile approach to difficult topics.

* * *

Disclosure policy affects the ability of the public to participate in decision-making, the next subject of this report.

F. Public Participation

Numerous courts and commentators have noted that intervenors can help government agencies be responsive to a broad range of interests and issues.[159] As Chief Justice (then Judge) Burger noted in *Office of Communications of the United Church of Christ* v. *Federal Communications Commission*, intervenors can bring out additional, otherwise unavailable information which the agency should consider in its decision.[160] Moreover, intervention places a discipline on the administrative process and can enhance confidence in agency proceedings by opening them to public scrutiny.[161]

This is not to indicate that intervention presents no problems. Partly due to such litigation, increasing delays have beset the licensing process. Some commentators argue that the adversary process, of which intervention is a part, is inappropriate to the resolution of complex technical issues because it shifts emphasis from accuracy to debate.[162] Others counter that technical issues usually also involve important value judgments beyond the mandate of experts and in need of broad public ventilation.[163]

In addition, it is charged that "public interest intervenors" fail to represent "the public interest." Few intervenors would disagree. They represent *an* interest important to the public, not "*the* public interest" which comes from balancing all such values. As such, intervenors do have a legitimate role, but not one that should allow them to determine a proceeding's result any more than other private parties. Thus, a process which gives intervenors the discretion to delay the licensing of a needed plant is no more satisfactory than a process which keeps them from making their arguments effectively and submitting them for decision to a body charged with protecting the public interest. Previous sections of this chapter have discussed ways to avoid delay; this section discusses ways to effect more meaningful public participation. Our recommendations suggest ways in which both goals can be attained.

1. OBSTACLES TO PUBLIC PARTICIPATION

The process sets up many preadjudication barriers to public participation. Some issues escape the public's notice. No forum exists in which to raise others. The lack of rulemaking and multiplicity of licenses troubles intervenors as well as industry, but the intervenors have less funds to pursue an issue in many proceedings. Finally, prehearing bargaining and the need to produce power quickly may foreclose full consideration of alternatives.[164] These, however, are only the threshold barriers to public participation. Additional obstacles exist at the hearing stage itself.

While statutes and courts have recognized the importance of public participation,[165] Professor Ernest Gellhorn's report to the Administrative Conference found a:

> ". . . frequency and sameness of agency and party hostility toward public interest intervention. There seems

almost a proprietary feeling that these intervenors are inter-meddlers more interested in the pursuit of publicity and psychic satisfaction than the 'public's interest.' The immediate concern often seems to be with how intervention could be curtailed. . . ." [166]

Such an attitude requires intervenors to build an independent case rather than one supplementing and supplemented by that of the Commission staff and other parties. This diverts attention from questions of policy to details of proof. Moreover, it aggravates intervenors' basic problem of inadequate resources—too little money to hire lawyers and expert witnesses, limited information, and short preparation time. In comparison to the utility, the intervenor is at a distinct disadvantage. The cost of intervention against a power plant application can exceed $100,000.[167] While intervenors must raise the funds necessary for litigation from contributions or foundation monies, the applicant recoups his litigation expenses through rates. In addition, the applicant is frequently aided by the regulatory staff, which, by the time the case comes to hearing, has often decided to support the application.

This inequality of litigative resources can have an unusually important effect in licensing cases. One argument noted is that:

"[P]roof of scientific fact through experts is such an immensely expensive proposition that if it is left completely to the parties, the contest will usually be won by well-financed interests which have a substantial monetary stake in the outcome of the proceedings." [168]

Some commentators believe that the relatively greater representational resources available to industry bias the commissions themselves. In a 1960 report to President-elect Kennedy, James Landis wrote:

"It is the daily machine-gun like impact on both agency and its staff of industry that makes for industry orientation on the part of many honest and capable members as well as agency staffs." [169]

Others argue that agencies in the power area bend over backwards to represent non-industry interests or that recent increases in the number of public interest environmental lawyers sufficiently balances the scales between industry and intervenors.

The former view has prompted suggestions for programs which would finance litigation on behalf of public interests. But, those who advocate additional public interest representation see some problems. Simon Lazarus and Joseph Onek, writing in the *Virginia Law Review*, conclude that government support of intervention is essential [170] and propose two possible methods: lawyers' fees for appointed counsel or a government public advocate office.[171] But, they note that counsel appointed by a commission may be too accommodating and that counsel appointed by a court may be inexpert in the particular subject matter.[172] A government advocate may be subject to political pressures and unaccountable to clients seeking representation.[173]

Since federal agencies may have the power to pay intervenors' counsel [174] and the Second Circuit has left open the question of whether it could order the FPC to do so in cases of "compelling need" [175] and has invited agency experiment,[176] more information may be available upon which to rest a conclusion in the future.

In the meantime, many ways exist to ease the burdens of litigation short of paying lawyers' fees. A number of factors unnecessarily increase the cost of intervention. First, counsel is usually required to be present at all stages of litigation, although contesting only a few issues.[177] Second, "daily" transcripts, helpful for cross-examination, run $1.38 per page in the case of AEC proceedings [178] while the transcript made available by the administrative agency comes a week or more later and cannot be copied, thereby reducing its usefulness. Agencies could restructure their contracts with private transcript companies to allow reproduction of more timely transcripts.[179] Third, agencies require many copies of filings.[180] Finally, the information that is made available to the public is frequently disorganized, although indices of file information could be expanded.[181]

Intervenors waste much effort in gathering information. The AEC appears to make documents available more readily than other agencies.[182] Agencies could also ease the burden by sharing the expertise of their staffs with intervenors as well as applicants. The Administrative Conference has recommended, and the Second Circuit seconded, that commissions make staff members available to intervenors to provide technical information.[183]

The commission might assign to their task staff members who personally oppose an application. It is unlikely that staff will always

139

have a unanimous view of applications, but they usually do present a single position. While a commission staff may have no obligation to point out dissent in its ranks, under NEPA, its documents should at least reflect viewpoints thought to have some threshold validity and the reasons for which they were rejected.[184] Some cases of unusual importance, however, may call for allowing a variety of staff positions to surface.

Certain procedures discourage intervention. Agency compliance with strict notice requirements may not adequately alert interested persons.[185] This results when the agency publishes notices in newspapers with a small circulation, or which fail to contain information about the issues to be considered at a hearing. The testimony at a Senate hearing of Richard Ayres, an environmental lawyer, contained examples of how public participation in the development of state air plans was hampered by failure to broadcast the time and places of hearings, by late notification, by lack of access to proposed plans so that adequate review was impossible, by prohibitive fees for copies of the proposed plans, by holding of hearings in remote parts of the states, by constant revision of proposals, and by last-minute changes in times and places of hearings.[186] One possible solution to the notice problem is:

". . . a permanent [agency] mailing list of individuals and organizations interested in licensing determinations. The [FPC] already has one, but its existence is not well known." [187]

Time problems further magnify the inequalities of resources and of information. The applicant has years to prepare its application and muster its case. Federal commissions have almost as long. But, intervenors usually have only three weeks, or at most three months, in which to decide to intervene, to raise the necessary funds, and to marshal a case—often with inadequate, volunteer technical resources.[188] Since cases usually arise when the need for more electricity is pressing, commissions may be justifiably reluctant to grant postponements to allow more time for preparation. The AEC has proposed rule changes which would allow earlier intervention.[189]

2. PARTICIPATION IN PLANNING

Allowing intervenors to participate in the planning process earlier than the administrative hearing would solve some of their problems. While public participation in the utility's own internal plan-

140

ning should remain at the utility's discretion, the public should play a role once substantive discussions begin between the commission's staff and the applicant. At this stage, whether or not an application has been filed, informal notice should issue through the press and through the mail to groups thought likely to be interested. Thereafter, all documents exchanged between applicant and staff, which would be susceptible to discovery, as well as memoranda of important decisions, should be put in a convenient public document room and mailed as available to members of the public actively participating. (When the number is large, the staff should have the authority to require that public participants agree upon a few individuals who will receive the information on behalf of all.) At the same time, members of the public should be able to comment in writing on such documents.

Since staff-applicant negotiation prior to formal application is a critical prelude to formal administrative proceeding, intervenor participation is necessary in these earlier stages if it is going to be meaningful at later stages. However, public participation in staff-applicant meetings does present problems which must be balanced against the possible gains in terms of credibility and accuracy from a more open prehearing process.

Since public interest groups lack the resources to intervene in the bulk of formal proceedings, they certainly cannot participate fully in most prehearing negotiations, some of which last for a year or more. Moreover, depending on the relevant issues and the parties involved, public interest groups may find that their time is better spent in litigation rather than negotiation. Accordingly, they will probably find it useful to negotiate in only some cases and then only as to some issues. Given their scarce resources and that the applicant has no obligation to compromise with intervenors, public interest groups should not be estopped from raising any issues in subsequent proceedings because they were not brought up in negotiation.

Similarly, the staff and applicant should have no obligation to invite public interest groups to all discussions. Some technical questions may be better handled in writing. Some members of the public will contribute more constructively than others. Since the staff has a duty to apportion its time usefully, it should have the authority to

141

decide what discussions should include citizens and to make citizens pick a reasonably sized group to attend.

The commission should help its staff exercise this discretion by defining, through regulations, the type of issues which can best be dealt with through open meetings. These might include technical disagreements which arise from using different assumptions and such value questions as trade-offs between environment or safety and cost. The regulations might also provide that, where staff decides to keep its discussions with the applicant bilateral, it should consider this factor in deciding how much time to spend with public interest groups in bilateral discussions with them.

Such a discretionary approach is open to several types of abuse. Accordingly, the commission and the legislature should exercise some review after a discretionary system has operated for a while.

G. AGENCY CREDIBILITY

These are hard times for administrative agencies, their efficiency and detachment being questioned widely. Some commentators see true prophecy in an 1894 statement by then Attorney General Richard Olney to worried railroads that the Interstate Commerce Commission:

". . . satisfies the public clamor for supervision of the railroads, at the same time that the supervision is almost entirely nominal. Moreover, the older the commission gets to be, the more likely it is to take a business or railroad view of things." [190]

The distrust applies no less to the administrative agencies charged with regulating the electric power business. The emerging concern about the growth of energy use has brought into question their very mission. Allegations of withholding information and resisting public participation compound the problem. Moreover, the commissions find themselves having to deal with complex scientific issues which:

". . . exacerbate the risk of partiality, because of the nebulous standards of decision, very limited role of *stare decisis* and potentially large numbers of interests affected— many of them possessed by non-parties, who may well be tempted to employ extra-record influence." [191]

The questioning of utility commission credibility has gone beyond public interest groups and intervenors. The Governor of Virginia stated recently:

"It is incredible that a public body should have confidence in
it as low as the corporation commission has today." [192]

Courts also have questioned agencies' good faith in enforcing environmental standards. In *Calvert Cliffs*, the District of Columbia Court of Appeals called "the commission's crabbed interpretation of NEPA . . . a mockery of the Act," [193] and its rules "a total abdication." [194] In *Kalur* v. *Resor*, the district court stated that the Corps of Engineers' interpretation of NEPA was "a total abdication of its responsibility." [195] In *Greene County*, the Second Circuit accused the FPC of "obstinate refusal to comply with NEPA" [196] noting that six years earlier it had warned the FPC that it could not act as an "umpire blandly calling balls and strikes for adversaries appearing before it." [197] The Court suggested that:

"The Federal Power Commission as well as other Federal
agencies must review their rules and rethink encrusted,
entrenched positions." [198]

Whether or not justified, such distrust is a reality with widespread implications. But, one should note that many sources of distrust, such as agency structure, are not of the agencies' own doing.

1. AGENCY STRUCTURE

As stated by a report to the Chairman of the Administrative Conference of the United States, "subtle forms of bias can result from agency structure." [199] The report goes on to point out that:

"[B]odies like the Army Corps of Engineers which are essentially 'construction agencies' may tend to favor structural
alternatives when confronted with a problem." [200]

The AEC has the conflicting jobs of promoting and regulating the use of atomic energy. As the new Chairman of the Atomic Energy Commission stated:

"Since I came into this job, I have been impressed on a
number of occasions by the failure in the industry and in-
house properly to distinguish between the role and responsibilities of the AEC. In the future I trust the distinctive
responsibilities of a government agency will become more
sharply etched in the minds of all of us." [201]

143

Almost since the AEC's inception it has been said that the regulatory and promotional aspects of the Atomic Energy Commission should be separated in the future. As Commissioner Ramey put it:

> "In several speeches over the last ten years I have indicated that further separation should be considered in five or ten years. Thus, I have introduced the concept of a rolling five or ten year period." [202]

The FPC has a similar, though perhaps less apparent problem. Its first *raison d'etre* was to oversee development of non-federal hydroelectric projects. With relatively few feasible conventional hydroelectric sites as yet undeveloped, the hydroelectric staff looks toward pumped-storage projects to provide most of its new licensing business in the years to come. If the FPC decided that pumped-storage plants were environmentally unsound, perhaps because of energy waste in the cycle, the workload would consist only of regulating and licensing already-built plants.

But, aside from the clash between promotional and regulatory missions, agencies have conflicting roles. They are called upon to help plan for reliability, counsel applicants, and then consider applications. Even in their regulatory capacity, agencies have diverse tasks. As Florida's Governor Askew stated in February, 1972:

> ". . . I submit that we have assigned too many different roles to the commission and its staff together. We have asked them to function not only as judge and jury, but as investigator, prosecutor, defense attorney, and enforcer as well. It is obvious that these roles are incompatible." [203]

Whether or not structure impairs the Commission's ability to advocate the public interest, the conflicts in missions and roles necessarily undermine public confidence.

2. STAFFING

The quantity and quality of staffing relates to both agencies' efficiency and credibility. Here, again, the legislature ultimately assigns the tasks and sets the budget, but with advice from the commission and others.

Corps of Engineers. The Corps of Engineers has assigned 174 people in its district offices to its regulatory program while 87 others

144

spend some of their time on regulation.[204]   These are almost all clerical personnel.   Decision-making at the local level is done by the district engineer who spends most of his time supervising construction projects.

In contrast, the Refuse Act program requires the Corps to assess water quality and wildlife, as well as navigation.   Its construction permit program involves considering the impact of the project on the water quality, biology, and structure of the river.   While the Environmental Protection Agency does relieve the Corps of responsibility in the water quality area,[205] it is difficult to see how the Corps at the local level has the capability to assess the other non-navigational considerations.   But, the Corps depends on a clerical and engineering staff to perform the interdisciplinary weighing of alternatives required by NEPA for its backlog of 20,000 Refuse Act applications (provided *Kalur* v. *Resor* is upheld).[206]   Staffing is no better at the Corps national level.   There, it has a staff of five engineers and three clerical persons which, however, reportedly relies upon scientists and engineers in other Corps departments.[207]

State Public Utility Commissions.   State public utility commissions must deal with many aspects of a wide variety of regulated industries. But, their small staffs, in most cases, allow little more than the shuffling of papers, and the compensation paid would appear to make it difficult to recruit personnel able to deal with the difficult problems involved.

Nine utility commissions have part-time commissioners.[208]   Of those states with full-time commissioners, only twenty-two pay their chairmen more than $20,000 annually.[209]   A 1967 survey indicated that forty-two state commissions paid their executive secretaries or staff directors $15,000 or less and all of the state commissions together had only seven geologists.[210]   Thirty-six state commissions had five or fewer engineers.[211]   While no information was available on the number of other technical people, it would seem likely that most would have far fewer environmental scientists than engineers.

State Pollution Agencies.   Only nine states have anti-pollution agencies with full-time staffing.[212]   The remainder of the states have air and water pollution boards composed of part-time, citizen members. Of these, thirty-two states have anti-pollution boards with members from those industries engaged in activities which are being regulated.[213]

Environmental Protection Administrator Ruckelshaus has concluded that:

> "I found in the past year that there is rampant mistrust of governmental institutions at every level. The only way to overcome that is to operate as openly as possible, and to eliminate any real or apparent conflict of interest, so that people can trust the decisions of these boards." [214]

3. Commission-Applicant Negotiations

While in theory the licensing process consists of an application, hearings, and a decision, in practice, commission-applicant bargaining precedes the hearings and even the filing of an application. Rarely does an application reach hearing without the applicant feeling fairly confident that the license will issue. While the reason for this predictability is much debated, its existence is clear. At the AEC, the commission has never denied an application for a construction permit or operating license after the case has reached the hearing stage. During the FPC's half century of operation, the commission has formally denied an application to construct a hydroelectric plant on environmental grounds twice.[215] At the Corps of Engineers, the staff can recall no case where it denied a construction permit for a power plant.[216] An informal survey of state utility commissions indicates that license denials have been quite rare.

There are many views on what causes this pattern. A report to the Administrative Conference argues that the negotiations prior to formal hearing create an inertia which is difficult to resist and an atmosphere which makes it discomforting for the commission to force an applicant to undo plans made jointly over long periods of time:

> "Agency projects gather momentum as time, effort and capital are invested in them—even if the only investment has been analytical time. . . . [T]here will be strong pressure to persist with the original plan if the superior plan later becomes apparent. Trial-type proceedings seem to provide little help in overcoming this kind of inertia, particularly where the evidentiary hearing is not held until a particular plan is substantially underway. In AEC nuclear reactor licensing, differences among the staff, the applicant, and the ACRS . . . are worked out in an extended pre-hearing . . . 'bargaining.' By the time that a trial-type hearing

is held on the issuance of a construction permit and public intervenors are allowed to participate, the parties to the negotiation are not likely to embrace alternatives which would mean substantial revision of the plans that they have worked so long to perfect. In this situation, it is not surprising to learn that intervenors often view the hearing as a 'stacked deck' and resort to 'no-win' delaying tactics rather than trying to make a useful contribution on the merits." [217]

This analysis, however, omits to mention the cases where the AEC has found a plant undesirable in mid-stream and asked the applicant to drop plans upon which millions of dollars have been spent.[218] It also omits to mention that the AEC routinely orders holders of construction permits to spend millions of dollars to redesign equipment already built in order to increase safety.

Thus, a view contrary to that of the Administrative Conference report is that the staff and commission will not hesitate to take any actions necessary to promote safety and environment. This argument certainly undercuts the view that costs will always override other considerations. In all likelihood money will still be a consideration in cases where a modification will result in marginal, although positive, improvement, since the amounts involved are large.[219] In one current case, a utility reported having spent $48 million before a hearing was had, $12 million of which was unrecoverable if a license were denied.[220] The AEC has alleviated this problem to a degree by forbidding site preparation before the issuance of a construction permit, but applicant can still make designs and order the plant hardware.[221] Moreover, it seems likely that, even if money were not a factor, staff members and applicant employees would approach safety and environmental criticisms with a different mind set after they had spent years working on a design together.[222] The degree of such inertia is difficult for an outsider to assess.

Yet, while such factors may militate against design changes, there are other countervailing considerations which militate towards greater concern for safety. The regulatory staff of the AEC with its great responsibility for safety has, as individuals, no personal reason not to make the applicant spend its money to improve safety, although the staff may be subject to bureaucratic pressures.[223] In turn, since no applicant would run the public relations risk of opposing the staff in

147

a full scale licensing hearing, the applicant must, in practice, follow the wishes of the staff, if it cannot be convinced to change its mind.

Thus, that the results of public hearing are predictable does not necessarily mean that they are without due regard for safety and environmental considerations. But, that one side always wins the confrontations which come into public view does create credibility problems. One of the primary benefits of litigation is the feeling that, after a hard fight, a fair decision was reached.

An easy, but not necessarily desirable, solution to this problem would be to eliminate commission-applicant negotiations. This, however, would create many new problems. Such negotiations are helpful in getting before the commission all of the information it needs. If the applicant could receive no feedback prior to the conclusion of a hearing, much design effort would be wasted on dead ends, although more rulemaking could potentially provide an alternative source of predictability. Finally, and perhaps most important, many commentators believe that to deal with complex technical questions entirely in an adversary context would harm, rather than help the cause of safety.[224] They see the hearing not as a decision *de novo* on plant design, but as a discipline on staff work.[225]

Assuming that commission-applicant negotiations should continue because they allegedly deal in greater depth with the more technical issues than a hearing would, the problems still remain of making the hearings an effective discipline on the staff, ventilating the value judgments made by the agency initially in the context of private negotiations, and dealing with the impact of predictable conclusions on public confidence. Moreover, if the hearings are no more than a discipline on private negotiations, the public cannot participate in the real decision-making. This dilemma underlines the importance of a number of reforms mentioned in this chapter and elaborated upon in Chapter VIII. First, if the hearing is to be a reasonable discipline on a process in which staff and applicant have reached agreement, the process must be structured so that intervenors in public hearings have an opportunity to make their points effectively against opponents with greater resources. Second, some public involvement in commission-applicant negotiations would decrease the need for discipline and increase real participation. Third, reducing the credibility problems of commissions that come from their structure and staffing would give the public more reason to trust the results of negotiations. Fourth, requiring applications to be filed well before a plant was needed and making the selection of site and method of generation a choice among alternatives instead of a yes-no decision would give the hearing process more practical possibilities among which to choose.

NOTES FOR CHAPTER V

1. Energy markets are altered through import quotas; fuels are rationed and prices set; environmental factors are controlled; major new technologies cannot be developed without major government support and protection, such as the Price Anderson Act; and the health of the industry is sometimes an explicit, relevant consideration in the regulatory action.

2. *See A. W. Murphy, The National Environmental Policy Act and the Licensing Process* 24–25 (1st draft Apr. 17, 1972) (report to the Committee on Licenses and Authorizations of the Administrative Conference of the United States).

3. 1 *A.J.G.Priest, Principles of Public Utility Reg.*, chs. 6, 10 (1969).

4. R. Nixon, "Energy Message" 9, June 4, 1971, Washington, D. C. ("One reason we use energy so lavishly today is that the price of energy does not include all of the social costs of producing it.")

5. 1 *Priest, supra* note 3, at ch. 3.

6. Such allegations are being pressed by suits in Washington, D. C. and New Haven, Connecticut.

7. Consolidated Edison Co. No. 26105, N.Y.Pub.Serv.Com. (Op. No. 72–6, Mar. 29, 1972).

8. *E. g. see*, speech by AEC Chairman Schlesinger, "Expectations and Responsibilities of the Nuclear Industry," in 2 *AEC News Releases*, No. 43, at 6, 9 (Oct. 27, 1971).

9. Udall v. FPC, 387 U.S. 428, 450 (1967).

10. Federal Power Act § 202, 16 U.S.C. § 824a (1970).

11. Interviews with FPC staff in Washington, D. C., Jan. 6, 1972.

12. *Id.*

13. Scenic Hudson Preservation Conf. v. FPC (Scenic Hudson I), 354 F.2d 608, 620 (2d Cir. 1965), *cert. denied*, 384 U.S. 941 (1966).

14. *Hearings on Public Works for Water and Power Dev. and AEC Appropriations Bill, before the Subcomm. on Public Works of the House Comm. on Appropriations*, 92d Cong., 1st Sess. pt. 3, at 1190 (1971).

15. *FPC, I The 1970 National Power Survey*, at 3–15 (1971).

16. Chapter VI, *infra*, points out some of these considerations, most of which are not discussed on the basis of data in *The 1970 National Power Survey, supra* note 15.

17. The AEC and the FPC deal with atomic and hydroelectric plants, while the Corps of Engineers regulates aspects of such plants as well as fossil plants.

18. *E. g.*, paper by David Rose, Nuclear Eng. Dep't, MIT, "Rational Development of Options" 19, AAAS Meeting, Philadelphia, Pa., Dec. 28–31, 1971; *Resources for the Future Staff Report, U. S. Energy Policies* 141 (1968).

19. Atomic Energy Act of 1954, §§ 1, 3, 42 U.S.C. §§ 2011, 2013 (1970).

20. *Id.* § 202, 42 U.S.C. § 2252.

21. *Nucleonics Week* reads recent developments as "being symptomatic of a new era in the Committee's life when it can no longer come to the aid of the

Commission like an indulgent father." 13 *Nucleonics Week* No. 17, at 2 (April 27, 1972).

22. Interview with Donald E. Crabill, Chief of National Resource Prog. Div., OMB, in Washington, D. C., Feb. 23, 1972.

23. Interview with William Carey, former Asst. Director of B.O.B., April 17, 1972.

24. *BOB, Professional Staff Roster* (June 1969).   According to Mr. Carey, *supra*, note 23, a former atomic energy section chief himself, BOB (OMB) acceded to the present section chief's desire to stay in his post despite his unusually long period of service in it, because of his widely acclaimed skill in atomic energy affairs.

25. 13 *Nucleonics Week* No. 1, at 6 (Jan. 6, 1972).

26. The office was created in the course of a major reorganization. *See* 12 *Nucleonics Week* No. 49, at 1 (Dec. 9, 1971).

27. Interview with AEC staff members in Washington, D. C., Feb. 22, 1972.

28. Federal Power Act § 202, 16 U.S.C. § 824(a) (1970).

29. *FPC, supra* note 15, at 1–20 to 1–21.

30. The FPC has authority over natural gas, but not coal and oil, which can be made into low-sulfur fuels and have varying sulfur contents in their natural states.

31. S.Rep.No.91–296, 91st Cong., 1st Sess. 5 (1969).

32. *See Murphy, supra*, note 2, at 24.

33. *Natural Resources Defense Council* v. *Morton*, 458 F.2d 827, 834 (D.C. Cir. 1972).

34. *Murphy, supra*, note 2, at 10–12.

35. As Judge Irving Kaufman put it: "We surely lack a federal agency with sufficient authority, power and purse to choose among the infinite patterns of potential development." "Power for the People—and by the People," 46 *N.Y.U.L.Rev.* 867, 872–73 (1971).

36. *See* IV(D) *supra*.

37. *Id.*

38. N.Y.P.S.C., case 25352.

39. *E. g. Comptroller General, Management Improvements Needed in the Review and Evaluation of Applications to Construct and Operate Nuclear Power Plants* 15, 22–23 (GAO B–127945, 1972).

40. *E. Gellhorn, Public Participation in Administrative Hearings* 13 (Oct. 29, 1971) (report to the Administrative Conference of the U. S.).

41. *Murphy, supra* note 2.

42. *Id.* at 10.

43. *B. Boyer, A Re-evaluation of Administrative Trial-Type Hearings for Resolving Complex Scientific and Economic Issues* 11, 23–30 (Dec. 1, 1971) (staff report to the Chairman of the Administrative Conference of the U. S.).

44. *Id.* at 26–27. *See* Tribe, "Trial By Mathematics," 84 *Harv.L.Rev.* 1329, 1361–62 (1971).

45. *Comptroller General, supra* note 39, at 16.

46. Interview with AEC staff, Washington, D. C., January 7, 1972.

47. *Comptroller General, supra* note 39, at 16.

48. *Id.* at 22–23.

49. 449 F.2d 1109, 1123 (D.C.Cir. 1971).

50. *A. W. Murphy, supra* note 2, at 10.

50a. 37 Fed.Reg. 9331 *et seq.* (1972).

51. Calvert Cliffs Coordinating Comm., Inc. v. AEC, *supra* note 49, 449 F.2d at 1123.

52. *E. g., A. W. Murphy, supra* note 2, at 42–50; *B. Boyer, supra* note 43, at 49–52.

53. *E. g.,* American Airlines v. CAB, 359 F.2d 624, 632–33 (D.C.Cir. en banc), *cert. denied* 385 U.S. 845 (1966).

54. *A. W. Murphy, supra* note 2, at 44–50.

55. *I K. Davis Administrative Law* § 2–03 (1958). But, delegations are often upheld even though broader than judicial language would seem to allow. *Id.* at § 2.04.

56. 10 C.F.R. § 50.35 (1972). Indeed, the statute seems to provide not even a rubric on safety-standards.

57. 33 U.S.C. § 403 (1970).

58. Federal Power Act § 10(a), 16 U.S.C. § 803(a) (1970).

59. Udall v. FPC, *supra* note 9, 387 U.S. at 443.

60. Federal Power Act § 202, 16 U.S.C. § 824a (1970).

61. *E. g.,* NEPA, 42 U.S.C. §§ 4321 *et seq.* (1970).

62. *See* IV(C), (D), *supra.*

63. *E. g.,* in Michigan, the Department of Public Health will not issue approval for construction of sewage treatment facilities until the Water Resources Commission has issued an Order of Determination on the proposed plant's compliance with water quality standards.

64. 4 Cal.3d 945, 95 Cal.Rpts. 17, 484 P.2d 1361 (1971).

65. 12 *Nucleonics Week* No. 49, at 5 (December 9, 1971).

66. *Supra* note 49.

67. 449 F.2d at 1122 (slip 25).

68. *Id.*

69. *See supra* note 173 of Chapter IV.

70. 117 *Cong.Rec.* 17,456 (daily ed. Nov. 2, 1972) (remarks of Senator Baker).

71. Scenic Hudson Preservation Conference v. FPC, *supra* note 13; Udall v. FPC, *supra* note 9; Calvert Cliffs Coordinating Comm. v. AEC, *supra* note 49.

72. Interview with Corps staff, in Washington, D. C., January 6, 1972. The staff, however, was anticipating dealing with Consolidated Edison's Astoria plant.

73. Thermal pollution relates to siting because the choice of location affects which part of the river or which river will be heated.

74. Letter from FPC Chairman Nassikas to AEC Chairman Schlesinger, November 15, 1971. In at least one of these five cases, Indian Point II, it now appears that construction difficulties will prevent operation during the peak of summer, 1972, even if an operating license were available—New York Post 3 (May 3, 1972). In another case, Quad Cities, the intervenors—environmental groups and state officials, have settled their dispute with the applicant, Commonwealth Edison.

75. *E. N. Ellis & J. H. Johnston, Licensing of Nuclear Power Plants* by the *Atomic Energy Commission* 21 (April 1, 1971) (staff report to the Chairman of the Administrative Conference, of the U. S.).

76. *Supra* note 75.

77. *See A. W. Murphy, supra* note 2, at 19.

78. The case is now pending decision by the Commission and appeals are likely.

79. Greene County Planning Board v. FPC, 455 F.2d 412 (2d Cir. 1972), *petition for cert. filed* 40 U.S.L.W. 3589 (June 8, 1972) (No. 71–1597).

80. *See* IV(D) (3) *supra.*

81. Interview with Corps staff, in Washington, D. C., January 6, 1972.

82. *Id.*

83. *Id.*

84. Kalur v. Resor, 335 F.Supp. 1 (D.D.C.1971).

85. A. W. Murphy, *supra* note 2, at 25.

86. Letter from L. Muntzing to R. Train, April 13, 1972.

87. Calvert Cliffs Coordinating Comm. v. AEC, *supra* note 49; Greene County Planning Board v. FPC, *supra* note 79; Kalur v. Resor, *supra* note 84.

88. Cases cited note 16, *supra.*

89. Scenic Hudson Preservation Conf. v. FPC, 453 F.2d 463 (2d Cir. 1972) *cert. denied* 40 U.S.L.W. 3599 (June 19, 1972) [hereinafter Scenic Hudson II].

90. DeRham v. Diamond, No. 9565 (N.Y.Sup.Ct. Mar. 31, 1972), appeal filed App.Div. No. 18798, Apr. 18, 1972).

91. *See* IV(C) (3), IV(C) (4), *supra.*

92. Statement by FPC Chairman J. N. Nassikas, *Hearings on H.R. 5277, H.R. 6970, H.R. 6971, H.R. 6972, H.R. 3838, H.R. 7045, H.R. 1079, H.R. 1486 Before Subcommittee on Communications and Power of the Comm. on Interstate and Foreign Commerce,* 92d Cong., 1st Sess., ser. 92–31, 32, 33, app. G. (1971) (hereinafter *Macdonald Hearing*). See also FPC, 1 *The 1970 National Power Survey* at 16–2 to 16–5 (1971) which paints the same picture in less detail.

93. Statement by J. E. Moss, *Macdonald Hearings* 375.

94. *Id.* at 375–76.

95. Statement by D. B. Mansfield, *Macdonald Hearings* 636, 639, 645–47, 649.

96. *FPC, I The 1970 National Power Survey* at 16–2 to 16–3 (1971); *National Electric Reliability Council, "Impact Of A 12-Month Delay Of New Nuclear And Fossil-Fired Steam Generating Units,"* (Feb. 1972).

97. Gendlin, "The Palisades Protest: A Pattern of Citizen Intervention," 27 *Science & Public Affairs* at 53 (Nov. 1971).

98. Speech by AEC Director of Regulation L. Manning "A Standard of Evaluation of Licensing Applications," 2 AEC News Releases No. 41, at 15–16. (November 24, 1971).

99. *Id. See also, Comptroller General, supra* note 39, at 16–20.

100. For a discussion of utilities' application problem, see *Comptroller General, supra* note, at 16–20.

101. *Id.* at 21–23.

101a. 37 Fed.Reg. 9331 *et seq.* (1972).

102. Speech by Muntzing, *supra* note 98, at 17.

102a. 37 Fed.Reg. 9331 *et seq.* (1972).

103. *E. g.*, NEPA, 42 U.S.C. §§ 4321 *et seq. See* also V(B) (3), *supra.*

104. *See* V(B) (3) *supra.*

105. 3 *CCH Atomic Energy L.Rept.* ¶ 11,267.

106. Order of ASLB, Vermont Yankee Nuclear Power Corp., AEC No. 50–271 (January 7, 1972).

107. Interview with Howard Shapar, in Washington, D. C., January 7, 1972.

108. Speech by Irving Like, "Multi-media Confrontation—The Environmentalists' Strategy for a 'No-win' Agency Proceeding," ALI-ABA Course, Washington, D. C.

109. Speech by Myron Cherry before ALI-ABA Conference, at 5, in Washington, D. C., November 12, 1971.

109a. 37 Fed.Reg. 9331 *et seq.* (1972).

110. Consolidated Edison Company (Indian Point II); AEC No. 50–247.

111. Answer of AEC Regulatory Staff, Consolidated Edison Company, *supra* note 110, (Oct. 30, 1971). At the November 16, 1971, hearings applicant's counsel castigated the staff for failing to complete the impact statement and the Chairman of the ASLB noted that the applicant had predicted "disasterous results" if there was delay, but that applicant's own testing schedule was well behind schedule.

112. *Comptroller General, supra* note 39.

113. *E. N. Ellis & J. H. Johnston, supra* note 75, at 21.

114. *Comptroller General, supra* note 39, at 4, 63.

115. *Id.* at 35–41.

116. *Id.* at 69–73.

117. Interview with Colonel Cousins, in Washington, D. C., January 6, 1972.

118. Kaufman, *supra* note 35, 46 N.Y.U.L.Rev. at 867.

119. 117 *Cong.Rec.* E11575–76, 92d Cong., 1st Sess. (Nov. 1, 1971).

120. *See* IV(C) (2), *supra.*

121. *B. Boyer, supra* note 43, at 48 ; *National Academy of Sciences, Technology: Processes of Assessment and Choice* 40 (July 1969).

122. Statement of FPC Chairman J. N. Nassikas, *Hearings on S. 3067 Before the Subcomm. on Intergovernment Relations of the Senate Comm. on Government Operations*, 91st Cong., 2d Sess., pt. 3, at 508 *et seq.* (1971).

123. *Hearings on S. 3067, supra* note 122, pt. 1, at 131–32.

124. Federal Reports Act of 1942, 44 U.S.C. §§ 3501 *et seq.* (1970).

125. Muntzing, *supra* note 98, at 16.

126. Interview, in Bethesda, Md., January 8, 1972. *See* also, Reinemer, "Budget Bureau: Do Advisory Panels have an Industry Bias" Science, July 3, 1970.

127. 18 C.F.R. § 2.11 (1971).

128. Reliability and Adequacy of Electric Service, Dkt. R–362, FPC, Order No. 383–2, at 7 (April 10, 1970).

129. *National Electric Reliability Council, supra* note 96.

130. *Electrical Week,* March 6, 1972, at 2.

131. *Id.*

132. Hearings on H.R. 13752, Before the Subcomm. on Fisheries & Wildlife Conserv., House Comm. on Merchant Marine & Fisheries, 92d Cong., 2d Sess. 131–148 (1972). While the full text of the report is in the Subcommittee's files, only parts are reproduced in the printed hearing.

133. Omitted.

134. Another problem is the extent to which utilities should go in pointing out objections to the application. One intervenor's lawyer frequently points to a memorandum summarizing a seminar held in 1970 to instruct employees on how to prepare documents and testify at AEC hearings. The memo states that:

> "When a witness is being cross-examined by an adverse party he must refrain from giving an answer beyond that required by the question, even though he is quite certain as to the point opposing counsel is trying to make." Memo, "Seminar on AEC Public Hearing, Gaithersburg, Md., December 1, 1970."

In addition, the memo implies that employees should refrain from committing any doubts about the safety of the plant to writing for fear of discovery bringing these doubts to intervenors' attention. Whether or not the memo correctly summarizes the seminar or the seminar is typical of industry practice, it does raise important issues. The instruction on cross examination may readily be read as a standard litigator's suggestion to avoid confusing the record with discursive answers. This is sound advice. The instruction about committing doubts to writing may be read in context as an admonition against casually or rhetorically recording doubts which may be misinterpreted after discovery. This too may be sound advice and shows that one of the costs of discovery is to dampen intra-industry safety discussion. But, such instructions could also be interpreted to suggest the suppression of hard facts relating to important safety and environmental problems. Any such ambiguity should be avoided.

135. Hartman, "Environmental Reports and New Power Plan Schedules," *Public Utilities Fortnightly* at 13, 20 (July 22, 1971).

136. 10 C.F.R. pt. 50, App.D (1972).

137. Greene County Planning Board v. FPC, *supra* note 79, 455 F.2d at 417 n. 12.

138. *E. g.,* Primack & Hippel, "Scientists, Politics and SST," 28 *Science and Public Affairs* No. 4, at 24 (April, 1972) (discussing how key technical reports were released "voluntarily" only after, in one case, extended litigation under the Freedom of Information Act and, in another case, threats by a Congressman to sue. *Id.* at 27).

139. "Information Act Scored as Futile," N.Y. Times, Mar. 15, 1972, at 19, col. 1.

140. Atomic Energy Act § 189(a), 42 U.S.C. § 2235 (1970).

141. "Atoms and Dollars," 108 *Forbes*, No. 7, at 24 (Oct. 1, 1971).

142. Testimony of Curtis Haire, manager of nuclear safety programs at Aerojet Nuclear Corp. at ECCS hearings, in 13 *Nucleonics Week*, No. 15, at 4. (April 13, 1972).

143. *Id.*

144. Interview with Milton Shaw, Germantown, Maryland January 6, 1972.

145. Atomic Energy Act § 141, 42 U.S.C. § 2161 (1970).

146. Schlesinger, *supra* note 8, at 7.

147. 13 *Nucleonics Week* No. 12, at 3 (March 23, 1972).

148. 13 *Nucleonics Week* No. 11, at 2 (March 16, 1972), states: "A new internal AEC memorandum—apparently suppressed by bureaucratic etiquette—has emerged in the AEC rulemaking hearing on emergency core cooling."

149. Comment, "Of Birds, Bees, and the FPC," 77 *Yale L.J.* 117, 31–32 (1967).

150. Message by R. Nixon, *supra* note 4; Speech by R. Nixon, Hanford, Wash., Sept. 26, 1971; Speech by AEC Commissioner William Doub, "The Future of the Breeder, Its Impact on the Environment, and Regulatory Aspect," in 2 *AEC News Releases* No. 50, at 7 (Dec. 15, 1971).

151. Currently used reactors do produce plutonium as a byproduct and may someday use it as a fuel. But, each fast breeder reactor "breeds" much larger quantities of plutonium and requires its shipment in forms which are easier for hijackers to convert into a bomb and its storage at civilian power and processing plants in forms easier for employees to steal in minute quantities. Interview with General Delmar Crowson, in Germantown, Md., Feb. 22, 1972.

152. *E. g.*, Shapley, "Plutonium: Reactor Proliferation Threatens a Nuclear Black Market," 172 *Science* 143 (Apr. 19, 1971).

As the Director of the Oak Ridge National Laboratory, Dr. Alvin Weinberg recently stated:

> "Diversion is a difficult problem. I do not have any simple answer but it is a price society will have to pay for cheap, clean electricity."

WNET-TV, 11 p. m., Dec. 27, 1971.

153. The following documents were reviewed:

a. *President Nixon's speeches*, cited *supra* note 150.

b. *The AEC's NEPA Statements*, AEC, Environmental Statement for LMFBR Demo. Plant 50–51 (draft 1971); Environmental Statement: LMFBR Demo. Plant 92–98 (Wash–1509, April 1972).

c. *The AEC's Chief Cost Benefit Study*, AEC, Cost-Benefit Analysis of the U. S. Breeder Reactor Program (Wash–1126, April 1969).

d. *Speeches by AEC Personnel*, All speeches printed in the AEC News Release since Oct., 1971 were checked as well as some earlier statements. One Commissioner noted the possible problems of plutonium use on two occasions. The statements explicitly mentioned neither the possibility of diversion nor the danger of bombs and appeared to be directed towards the problem of accidental release, not theft. Doub, *supra*, note 150, at 4, 8; speech by Comm. Doub, "Environmental and Regulatory Aspects of the Breeder Reactor," 2 *AEC News Releases* No. 45, at 4, 6.

e. *The AEC's Popular Education Series*, the following titles in the Understanding The Atom Series were checked: Nuclear Power and the En-

156

vironment; Breeder Reactors; Nuclear Power Plants; Plutonium; Atomic Power Safety.

154. See note 153(b), *supra*.

155. The FPC had the utility's application. The AEC has extensive literature on the dangers of diversion in general, but decided not to put it into the publications and speeches on the breeder.

156. Message by R. M. Nixon to the Senate, Dec. 9, 1971, at 4. *Compare* R. M. Nixon, *supra*, note 4, where he states "Well, don't ask me what a breeder reactor is; ask Dr. Schlesinger. But, tell him not to tell you, because unless you are one of those Ph.D.'s, you wouldn't understand it, either."

157. See IV(c) (1), *supra*.

158. Atomic Energy Act § 141, 42 U.S.C. § 2161 (1970). *E. g.*, speeches by Comm'r Doub, *supra*, notes 150, 153; speech by Comm'r Ramey, "The Energy Needs of the Nation and the Costs in Terms of Pollution," 2 *AEC News Releases* No. 47, at 10, 12 (Nov. 24, 1971).

159. See *Gellhorn, supra*, note 40, at 1.

160. 359 F.2d 994 (D.C.Cir.1966).

161. *Gellhorn, supra*, n. 40, at 1.

162. B. Boyer, *A Re-evaluation of Administrative Trial-Type Hearings for Resolving Complex Scientific & Economic Issues* (1971) (staff report to the Chairman of the Administrative Conference of the United States).

163. *Id.*

164. *Gellhorn, supra* note 40, at 1.

165. *See, e. g.*, Atomic Energy Act, 42 U.S.C. §§ 2021(e) and 2031; Scenic Hudson I, *supra*, n. 13.

166. *Gellhorn, supra*, n. 40, at 9.

167. Green, "The Risk Benefit Calculus in Nuclear Power Licensing," in *Nuclear Power & the Public* 134 (H. Foreman ed. 1970) ; *Gellhorn, supra*, n. 40, at 34.

168. *Boyer, supra*, n. 162, at 11.

169. J. Landis, *Report on Regulatory Agencies to the President-Elect* 18 (1960).

170. Lazarus & Onek, "The Regulators and the People," 57 *Va.L.Rev.* 1069 (1971).

171. *Id.* 1094–6.

172. *Id.* 1102–3.

173. *Id.* 1103–4.

174. *Id.* 1098–1102. *Cf.* Office of Communication of the Church of Christ v. FCC, No. 24,672, slip op. at 11–18 (D.C.Cir. March 28, 1972). Mills v. Electric AutoLite Co., 396 U.S. 393 (1970).

175. Greene County Planning Board v. FPC, *supra* note 79, 455 F.2d at 427.

176. *Id.*

177. Green, *supra* note 167, at 132.

178. *Id.* 133.

179. Gellhorn, *supra* note 40, at 32.

180. *Id.* 30.

181. *Id.* 33.

182. *E. g.*, Greene County Planning Board v. FPC, *supra* note 79, 412 F.2d at 417 n. 12, where the court stated:

> "Intervenors made several motions, either orally or in writing, which are not recounted here, since they were merely variations of the theme we already have presented.
>
> "Intervenors, however, unsuccessfully moved that they be provided copies of the transcript without charge, that their non-expert witnesses be allowed to testify orally without first filing written testimony, and that the hearings be held in Greene County. The Commission denied appeals from the Presiding Examiner's decisions, noting that it is within his discretion to determine procedural matters relating to the hearings. Although petitioners preserved their objections to the Presiding Examiner's decisions by petitioning for review of the Commission's orders, they have not raised these issues on appeal. Nevertheless, we are constrained to note that the Commission at nearly every turn had made it difficult procedurally for the intervenors. For example, intervenors were forced to go to court to compel disclosures under the Freedom of Information Act. *See Town of Durham* v. *Federal Power Commission*, 71 Civ. 3993 (S.D.N.Y. Oct. 26, 1971). We suggest that the Federal Power Commission, as well as other Federal Agencies, must review their rules and rethink encrusted, entrenched positions in light of the provision in NEPA that, 'to the fullest extent possible,' all regulations of the agencies must be interpreted and administered in accordance with the policies of the Act. NEPA § 102(1), 42 U.S.C.A. § 4332(1). We fully agree with the Council on Environmental Quality that compliance is required not only with the letter, but the spirit of the Act. Council on Environmental Quality, Guidelines § 1, 36 Fed.Reg. 7724 (April 23, 1971)."

183. Gellhorn, *supra* n. 40, at 33–34.

184. *See* 42 U.S.C. § 4332(2) (c) (1970).

185. *A. W. Murphy*, *supra* note 2, at 52.

186. Testimony by Richard Ayres, National Resources Defense Council, Hearings Before the Subcomm. on Air & Water Pollution of the Senate Comm. on Public Works, Washington, D. C., Feb. 16, 1972.

187. Comment, "Of Birds, Bees, and the FPC," 77 *Yale L.J.* 117, 132 (1967).

188. *E. g.*, Green, *supra* note 167, at 133.

189. The proposed new rules are set forth in 37 Fed.Reg. 9331–47 (1972).

190. Quoted widely in, *e. g.*, *B. Boyer*, *supra*, note 162, at 21; Lazarus & Onek, *supra* note 170, at 1069.

191. *B. Boyer*, *supra*, note 162, at 8.

192. Quoted in *Electrical Week*, April 10, 1972, at 5.

193. Calvert Cliffs Coordinating Comm. v. AEC, *supra*, note 49, 449 F.2d at 1117.

194. *Id.*

195. *Supra* note 84, 335 F.Supp. at 15.

196. Greene County Planning Board v. FPC, *supra* note 79, 455 F.2d at 424.

197. *Id.* at 419, quoting Scenic Hudson I, *supra* note 13, 354 F.2d at 620.

198. *Id.* at 417 n. 12.

199. *B. Boyer, supra,* note 162, at 8.

200. *Id.*

201. Speech by Chairman Schlesinger, *supra,* note 8 at 8.

202. Speech by Comm. Ramey, "Nuclear Power and Lawyers," in 2 AEC *News Releases* No. 48, at 7, 12 (Dec. 1, 1971).

203. Address by Governor Askew to the Florida Assembly, Feb. 1, 1972.

204. Interview with Corps staff, Jan. 6, 1972, Washington, D. C.

205. See IV(D) (3), *supra.*

206. *Supra,* note 84.

207. Interview with Corps staff, Jan. 6, 1972, Washington, D. C.

208. Chart received from Paul Rodgers, Nat. Assoc. of Reg. Comm'rs, Jan. 1, 1972.

209. *Id.*

210. Subcomm. on Intergovernmental Relations of the Senate Comm. on Government Operations, State Utility Commissions, Sen.Doc. No. 56, 90th Cong. 2d Session 7 (1967).

211. *Id.* at 9.

212. Hill, "States Curtailing Pollutors on Pollution Control Boards," N.Y. Times, Dec. 19, 1971, § 1, at 1, col. 3.

213. *Id.*

214. Letter to all Governors.

215. See IV(D) (2).

216. Interview with Corps staff in 1972, Washington, D. C. Jan. 6, 1972.

217. *B. Boyer, supra,* note 162 at 27–28. Similar analyses have been made of the Bureau of Reclamation and the FDA. *Id.* at 26 n. 107.

218. *E. g.,* Pacific Gas & Electric's Bodega Bay reactor.

219. Noll, the Economics and Politics of Regulation, 57 *U.Va.L.Rev.* 1016, 1022 (1971).

220. Mosby, "AEC Rates N-plant; Construction Sound," The Bay City Mich. Times, July 22, 1971, at 1.

221. 2 AEC *News Releases* No. 48 at 7 (Dec. 1, 1971).

222. *Accord,* A. Bower, "Descriptive Decision Theory from the administrative Viewpoint," in *R. Bauer and K. Gergen, The Study of Policy Formation* 124 (paper ed. 1971).

223. *See Boyer, supra* note 162, at 27. The GAO reports conflicts in AEC staff sentiment as to the impact of such pressures on the adequacy of the review process:

> "Specifically two of four project leaders that we interviewed concerning the extent of their review efforts informed us that at times the depths of their reviews had been influenced to meet applicants' desires for achieving their scheduled construction or operation dates. The other two project leaders informed us that their reviews had not been affected by such circumstances. The Director, DRL, advised us that scheduling, assignment of priorities, and decisions on depths of reviews were management functions and that, when decisions had been made to curtail the depths of reviews, such decisions did not imply any lack in the scopes or depths of reviews necessary to ensure safety."

159

"With respect to the adequacy of the site group's safety review and evaluations, the Assistant Director for Site and Radiological Safety informed us that, because of an increase in work load and because of staff limitations, his group was not reviewing certain assigned areas as extensively as he believed desirable. For example, he stated that his group was accepting the applicant's criteria and analyses for an unproven piece of equipment in the radioactive waste treatment system on the basis of discussions with the applicant rather than on the basis of a thorough review and evaluation of such equipment.

"In commenting on the statement by the Assistant Director for Site and Radiological Safety, the Director, DRL, in December 1971 stated:

'The areas referred to relate to rules which went into effect in January 1971, promulgating the Commission's policy of assuring that exposures to radiation and releases of radioactivity in effluents from power reactors are kept as low as practicable. Specific numerical guidance for achieving the "low as practicable" goal in further limiting radioactivity in effluents was issued in proposed form in June 1971, and was still pending adoption in the rule-making process. The increased workload in prospect due to the new requirements did not have to be accomplished immediately, and it is planned to obtain adequate staff in this area on a timely basis. Safety reviews performed to date have been fully adequate to assure that current requirements were being met.

'With regard to the acceptance of the applicant's analyses for equipment in the radioactive waste treatment system, the applicants' statements are under oath, and operational performance of the equipment is required to be within license-imposed limits.' "
Comptroller General, supra note 39, at 30–31.

The report also questions whether construction permits properly specified the R & D work needed to be done by AEC operating side:

"The above-described case indicates that AEC-supported R & D is related to the resolution of safety questions. We therefore asked AEC management officials why AEC's safety evaluations at the construction permit stage indicated that only the R & D programs of the reactor manufacturer were required to resolve safety questions but not those of AEC.

"The Deputy Director, DRL, informed us that AEC-supported research generally was not cited by AEC as being needed to resolve safety questions prior to the issuance of an operating license because AEC-supported research was related to safety questions of a general nature rather than to questions related to the design of specific reactors. He explained that these general questions had been considered by the regulatory staff in developing criteria for the construction and operation of nuclear power plants and that the criteria were sufficiently conservative to provide an adequate margin of safety, all of the various unknowns considered. He informed us, however, that no formal study had been made by the regulatory staff that would explain the rationale by which it had been concluded that not one of the safety questions discussed in the water reactor safety program plan was of sufficient significance to require resolution prior to the granting of an operating license." Id. at 56–57.

224. *See B. Boyer, supra* note 43, at 24.

225. Murphy, "The Atomic Licensing and Safety Boards: An Experiment in Administrative Decision Making on Safety Questions," 33 *Law & Contemp. Prob.* 566, 583 (1968).

VI. THE DEMAND FOR ELECTRICITY AND ENERGY

The demand for electricity grows each year. A debate has begun over whether this growth should be hastened, slowed, or reversed. Given the arithmetic of exponential growth, even seemingly small changes in the rate of growth can have a huge impact on the quantity of electricity consumed in the future. If electricity use continues to grow at 7% per year, power consumption will increase over sevenfold by the year 2000. A slower growth rate of 4% would increase consumption by the century's end three times to a level which is much larger than present usage but much smaller than what present trends would produce.

Given the magnitudes involved, accelerating or decelerating growth of electricity use involves consequences for the growth of the economy, the distribution of income, the protection of the environment, the sufficiency of natural resources, and the quality of life itself. Propondents and opponents of current policies disagree on whether each of these consequences would be good or bad.

Less consumption of electricity would reduce the need to produce power and, to the extent reductions took place at the time of system peaks, build plants. In turn, allowing fewer plants to be built means less electricity can be consumed and so will require a decision as to what uses or users will receive less electricity. In an emergency, use is reduced by blackouts, voltage reduction, or short-term measures to cut off specific users. If a reduction in supply is anticipated, many options might be able to obviate the need for emergency measures. Suggestions have included (1) taxes on electricity to discourage demand, (2) forbidding or limiting certain types of uses such as air conditioning or aluminum production or limiting the quantity available to business or individual users (such use or user limits are loosely termed "rationing"), or (3) regulations to require buildings and appliances to be designed to minimize their power consumption. There is widespread disagreement as to which of these possibilities would be most effective and desirable.

This Committee is not in a position to resolve these disputes or to recommend a growth policy. Our concern, rather, is with the governmental mechanisms that will chart the future. What branch of government at what level with what subject matter expertise should decide which aspect of the question? What are the legal and administrative consequences of different policy instruments such as taxes, rationing, or regulations? Should decisions about these possibilities be made at the federal or state level? By a body with jurisdiction over all forms of energy or only electricity?

But, even discussing the procedures through which government might formulate and implement a growth policy requires some common understanding about how electricity, energy, and the economy interrelate. After attempting to lay such a foundation, this chapter tries to isolate the various remaining factual and value disputes in preparation for discussing the procedures through which they might be resolved.

A. ENERGY, ELECTRICITY AND GROWTH

The economy uses labor and natural resources, including energy, to produce what we consume. How much goods and services can be produced with a given amount of labor and natural resources depends upon the technology available at the time. As technology develops, a larger gross national product (GNP) can be produced with the same inputs. But, over time, the relationship between energy and GNP has not been constant. In the late 19th and early 20th century, increasing amounts of energy were required to produce $1 of GNP.[1] Then, from 1920, increasingly smaller amounts of energy were used to produce a $1 of GNP until 1965 when larger amounts of energy per $1 of GNP began to be required.[2]

The energy-GNP ratio changes for two reasons. First, the product mix varies. Services such as medicine require less energy than that required to produce goods such as paper or plastic. Also, even some similar goods require more energy to produce or use than others, e. g. rayon vs. cotton, cars vs. mass transit. Second, different technologies can use different mixes of labor and natural resources to produce or operate the same goods. Thus, the technology exists today to build houses and office buildings which require much less energy to light, heat and cool. Or, engineers can design production processes which require different mixes of labor and natural resources.

What then would be the consequences of more or less energy being available for use? The answer depends on the time-frame in which the change in energy supply takes place. Today's technology is imbedded in past investments—production capacity installed, stores and office buildings constructed, household appliances bought. Such hardware and buildings are designed to use a given level of energy in particular forms such as electricity. A sudden increase in energy supplies would have little immediate use. A sudden decrease would shake the economy. A factory that received only half of the energy needed to run its machines would lay off part of its work force. An office building with only enough electricity to run its lighting would have to waste its investment in air-conditioning or perhaps close in the summer if its windows could not open for ventilation. So, a quick short-fall in energy supply would waste much existing capital and cause unemployment and economic dislocations.

But, a gradual slowing of the rate of energy growth would have far different consequences because capital structure and the underlying technology change over time. The result need not be a halt in technological progress, unemployment, and the return of the Middle Ages. Technological advances can be energy-saving as well as labor-saving, the heat-pump and advanced insulation being only two examples. Production equipment can give each worker the assistance of hundreds of horsepower instead of thousands. Consumption choices can emphasize services and less energy-intensive goods.

If energy growth were halved, but population grew at 1%, workers and consumers would have more energy to use each succeeding year.[3] Moreover, halving energy growth need not halve economic growth since technological progress would still allow more production from the same inputs.[4]

Thus, the consequences to the economy of a change in energy use depends on the timing. That the economy would suffer greater consequences from a given change implemented tomorrow than from the same change implemented over decades means that the arguments for a quick, large change in energy supply would have to be stronger than for a gradual change. This also means that, if energy use in the year 2000 ought not to grow to the level which would result from current patterns, changes in policy should begin now, rather than in the year 1995.

163

Should current growth patterns continue? To answer this question, one must assess the method by which the economy now chooses the amount of energy it uses.

B. ENERGY AND EFFICIENCY

The market place of sellers and buyers determines how much of every input the economy uses, including energy. In theory, a perfectly competitive economy would efficiently choose what products to make and with what inputs.[5] In such an economy, the "optimal" amount of such inputs as energy is determined by supply and demand. By assumption, the private cost of supplying energy reflects the social costs of its production and the private price of buying energy reflects the social benefits of its use. With increasing volumes of energy use, the cost of producing each unit rises [6] and the price each unit brings on the market declines. Equilibrium is reached where cost equals price. To consume one unit less would be to forgo the use of some energy whose cost is less than its price and so whose social benefits exceed its social costs. To consume one unit more would be to use some energy whose cost would be greater than its price and so whose social cost exceeds its social benefit. Thus, to use more or less energy would be inefficient although the total benefits of using energy might still exceed the total costs.

This free market model makes optimum decisions about production and consumption with elegant simplicity. But, the model differs from the real world in several important respects.[7] For one, the social costs of supplying energy are in addition to the private costs to corporations of its production.[8] Similarly, at the margin, the social benefits of using energy are less than the private benefits of its consumption.[9] One major reason [10] for these differences is that the pollution caused by the production and consumption of energy imposes real costs on the economy not reflected in private costs and benefits. Since the economy charges a zero price for using the biosphere to dispose of wastes, the resulting costs are external to the decisions which suppliers and users of energy make and thus are called "external costs."

Because of these external costs, the market place systematically underestimates the costs and overestimates the benefits of energy use. Thus, the level of energy use chosen is inefficiently high.[11] If the external costs were internalized—that is, if buyers and sellers were forced to pay for pollution—those energy uses where the gap between private benefit and private cost were less than the cost of pollution would cease while pollution would continue where the net private benefit outweighed its costs.

The inefficiency caused by external costs is mitigated only in part by environmental regulation. Regulation can stop pollution in cases where the social costs of pollution are both more or less than the social benefits and will thereby reduce external costs, but not eliminate them without stopping all pollution. But, to the extent that pollution continues under regulation, that pollution is still an external cost which energy users do not take into account in deciding how much energy to consume, although smaller than the external cost absent regulation.

While the external costs of energy use make the economy less efficient, it does not follow that internalizing the external costs of electric utilities alone would increase efficiency. The doctrine known to economists as the "theory of the second best" holds that dealing with only part of a set of interrelated external costs might make the situation worse, not better.[12] For example, if the external costs of using electricity were internalized, but not the external costs of other forms of energy, the economy would use more non-electricity forms of energy whose external costs may be even greater than those of the electricity which they replaced. Moreover, if the external costs of energy use in only one state were internalized, energy-intensive industries would then grow more quickly in other states where the external costs are perhaps even greater. Thus, if the inefficiency arising from the external costs of electricity use is to be corrected, the program should operate on all forms of energy on a national level.[13]

While charging for the pollution from all forms of energy would presumably help alleviate environmental problems, what would the impact be on the economy? In terms of employment, if the charges were implemented slowly, production patterns would change gradually to a mix which used more labor, more generating equipment with high conversion ratios, more anti-pollution devices, and less resources with difficult-to-control effluents. Since labor is non-polluting although sometimes unpleasant to the laborer, the work force, could be at full employment. As to productivity, less energy would be used and so fewer goods and services would be available. But, pollution would also decrease. Since government would presumably charge a dollar price for polluting equal to its real costs, pollution would be eliminated only in cases where its benefits were less than its costs. So, if GNP were redefined to subtract the dollar costs of pollution as so valued, GNP would be greater with pollution charges and the price paid for environmental protection would be "worth it" in the dollar terms of the market.

External costs are not the only possible reason for the market place to demand more energy than is efficient. Thus, in announcing an amendment to FHA regulations which requires the installation of better insulation in the construction of new homes, President Nixon stated that savings in heating costs would pay for the additional construction costs in one year.[14] Given the thirty-year or more useful life of a home, the savings achieved by such a regulation would amount to thousands of dollars over the life of the building. Apart from the environmental impact, a rational home buyer would insist upon such savings, it would seem. Why, then, was the government regulation needed to achieve the savings?

One possible reason why the market was not working efficiently is the lack of solid information upon which home buyers can judge the cost of heating and cooling their homes. If buyers have no information they trust, they will make their home purchase decision without regard to how well the home is insulated. This problem might be corrected by requiring that builders provide prospective buyers with the estimated annual cost of heating a home.

Limits on the amount of mortgage also reduce the importance of operating costs to builders and buyers. If it is difficult to build even a poorly insulated home or apartment within the limits imposed by FHA, then most buyers will not have the option of spending more for their house initially in order to save on operating costs eventually.

Thus, external costs and other imperfections in the market mean that the economy chooses to use inefficiently large quantities of energy. But, before continuing, it must be noted that a more efficient policy is not necessarily a more desirable policy. Efficiency means only that the impacts of a policy which can be measured in dollar terms add up to a net dollar gain.[15] The concept of efficiency says nothing about who gets the gain and who sustains the losses. It says nothing about the consequences of the policy which cannot be measured in dollar terms. These considerations necessarily involve hard value judgments which will be defined, but not resolved, in section D of this chapter.

166

But, before turning to this topic, it is useful to become more specific about the available techniques for possibly redirecting energy growth policy.

C. Techniques of Increasing the Efficiency of Energy Use

There are essentially three ways of producing more efficient energy use. First, government could ration energy or energy-using equipment such as appliances. Second, government could require buildings and equipment to be designed to minimize energy use. Third, government could internalize the external costs of energy use, not abated by direct regulation, by taxing energy or its pollutants. These methods are not mutually exclusive.

Rationing can take many forms. It could limit the amount of energy available to each user or it could limit the amount available to particular uses. It could be very broad gauge, dealing only with the biggest types of energy use, or it could regulate the manner and amount of use of a given household appliance. But, in all these forms, rationing has the common characteristic of substituting governmental decisions for the private decisions made by millions of individuals and firms. What is gained is perhaps a wider perspective about what uses of energy are most worthwhile; what is imposed is government intervention and decision-making which necessarily cannot take into account all the variables which a private decider might consider important.

Thus, while rationing can produce a conscious decision about the amount of energy used, there will be slippage in deciding how to use it and the enforcement of these decisions. Nonetheless, this and other countries have found rationing to be necessary from time to time. And, even today, rationing does apply to a number of important industries and situations, although not without problems. Some examples are the rationing of radio and TV licenses, of oil import quotas, and, in some cases, natural gas. On the individual level, the Selective Service System is also a form of rationing.

Rationing's chief virtue is that it can work quickly. Other policy instruments would take a decade or more to affect significantly the aggregate level of energy or electricity consumed. Given rationing's administrative difficulties, if other methods of controlling demand would eventually work, the chief reason for rationing would be a need to act quickly, a judgment this Committee is not in a position to make.

167

The second available technique would be regulations to require buildings and equipment, such as appliances, to be designed to use as little energy as possible. Such regulation could be applied to construction through building codes and government mortgage programs as well as to air conditioners, automobiles, packing equipment, and other hardware.

This type of regulation would appear to be easier to administer than rationing because government could choose to introduce regulation item by item. But, the piecemeal approach would tend to make this approach very slow moving. Moreover, even if applied widely, this method could solve only part of the problem of external costs. It could improve the choice of technology, but it would not affect the choice of products. Thus, goods would be somewhat less energy intensive, but there would be little market pressure to use services or the least energy intensive goods.

Finally, no less than rationing, regulation of the amount of energy required by buildings and equipment would involve government's second-guessing the choices of designers, engineers, architects, and consumers. But, to the extent that existing government programs for building standards and mortgage constrain the market to produce energy intensive buildings, changes in such regulations would be the only way to attack this problem. Similarly, to the extent that lack of an ability to judge a home or appliance's energy requirements keeps consumers from foreseeing what the operating costs of a home or appliance will be, the only ways to attack the problem would be requirement for the disclosure of predicted energy usage, if not direct regulation of design itself.

The taxation alternative has the chief attraction of involving no government intervention in corporate or personal decision-making. Rather, government expresses its policy through a tax system and allows the private sector to make the trade-offs. Such a system can reach efficient results and without the costs of administrating and enforcing a rationing or regulating system.

At its most accurate, the tax system would involve a tax on pollutants with the rate schedule reflecting the differing dollar costs of various pollutants in diverse air and water sheds. But, government now lacks the ecological and administrative sophistication to construct such a tax schedule.

A cruder system, but one which would work in the right direction, would be a tax on each root source of energy—e. g. coal, oil, gas. Given the existing lack of ability to define precisely the external costs of particular types of pollutants, Resources for the Future concluded that "the practical differences between imposing pollution charges and raising prices to curtail consumption may not be very large." [16] But, as knowledge develops, such a system could begin to build in incentives for using these energy forms in more non-polluting ways and in the places where they will do the least harm. In essence, such a tax would be a reverse mineral depletion allowance and be an analogue, on the energy side, of the income tax as a tax on labor.

If any significant change in energy growth is expected through a change in energy price levels, the change must be very slow. First, if unfairness to industry and consumers that already have invested in capital goods is to be avoided, the initial changes in price level must be small. Second, as relative prices change, gradually technologies will be developed which use less energy per dollar of GNP but their full effect must await a substantial turnover in the capital structure, which would take time, since the useful lives of appliances, automobiles, production equipment, and buildings range from a few years to 40 years or more.

How much effect an energy tax will have on the long-run growth in energy demand is far from certain. If a tax is set equal to the external costs of employing energy, how much less energy is demanded than otherwise would be depends on how many uses of energy would no longer be economically worthwhile at a price which reflects its full cost. Whether consumers eliminate or cut back many or few uses, efficiency will be promoted. But, the uncertain size of a tax's impact on demand is important in gauging the need for future energy supplies and in assessing the many non-efficiency aspects of energy use (discussed in part D of this chapter).

The uncertainty centers around the concept of "elasticity," which to economists is a measure of how readily demand or supply responds to market pressures. More precisely, the price elasticity of demand for a product is the percentage change in the product's demand induced by its price rising one per cent. If the percentage change in demand is more than 1, then it is called "elastic"; if less than 1, then it is called "inelastic." An elasticity of zero means the demand in question fails to respond to price. So, if 2000 widgets are being sold at $3.00 each and their elasticity is .5, then a $.03 or 1% price increase means a 10 widget or .5% decrease in unit sales.

Unfortunately, little is known about the elasticity of energy demand, despite energy's importance to the economy. Dr. Bruce C. Netschert, Vice President of National Economic Research Associates (NERA), a consulting firm which does work for electric utilities, has stated,

> "I venture to guess that we shall find energy demand to be generally inelastic over a price range extending to a 50 percent increase." [17]

This view is based upon the argument that many energy uses—such as the automobile, electrical appliances, and house heating—are unlikely to respond much to changes in the price of energy. But, this statement omits to mention that substantial price changes might well induce manufacturers in the long-run to design more energy-efficient equipment and structures because of consumer pressures and encourage consumers and citizens to shift their interest, for example, from automobiles to mass transportation or from air conditioning to better air circulation and fewer glass walls.

While little work has been done on the elasticity of energy, there has been some scattered work on the related question of the elasticity of demand for electricity. Its elasticity is likely to be greater than the elasticity of energy because users have more readily available substitutes for electricity in the form of non-electricity types of energy.

The price elasticity of electricity is probably near zero in the short run because, for instance, even a large price increase will not make most people use their electric toothbrushes faster. But, economists have noted that, for some goods, the effect of price on market behavior is quite gradual.[18] Electricity and energy are classic examples of this gradualism because they are usually only a small percent of most consumption or production which can be changed readily in the short run. Accordingly, most interest has focused on the long run elasticity of electricity. The following table describes the results of four recent efforts to estimate the long run elasticity of electricity using data based on variations in use over time and among different utilities' service areas with different prices.

	Residential	Commercial	Industrial
Wilson-1969 [19]	1.33	—	—
Chapman-Tyrrell-1972 [20]	1.76	1.88	1.90
Halvorsen-1972 [21]	1.20	—	—
Anderson (RAND)-1972 [22]	.91	—	—

Since Chapman and Tyrrell state that their estimates may be on the high side,[23] and since discrepancies necessarily arise from different data bases,[24] these four separate studies tend to have remarkably similar results.

An earlier study by Fisher and Kaysen found that six of the major industries surveyed had elasticities of one or greater with the highest being 2.6 for chemicals, one of the larger users.[25] But, they found low elasticities for the residential and commercial sectors except for such large uses as water heating.[26] A sixth commentator, Professor Richard Tybout, has concluded that Fisher and Kaysen's results probably tend to underestimate the price responsiveness of electricity demand.[27] So while a vote of the econometricians does not establish the truth, a consensus does appear to be emerging that electricity does react to price in the long run.

While a number of econometricians have reached similar results, their view is not without opposition, including that of NERA. NERA has taken the position that these direct measures of elasticity are too high because they use the average price of electricity instead of somewhat incorporating the full complexity of the rate schedules. It therefore places more credence on its empirical research on factors which intuitively would seem to affect elasticity.[28] But, one of NERA's econometric consultants, Dr. Damodar Gujarati, wrote that the preliminary results of a NERA study of electric space heating showed huge elasticities of from 5 to 8 [29] and that the high industrial elasticities found by Fisher and Kaysen "confirm the generally held impression that the industrial demand for electricity is more price elastic than residential-commercial demand." [30]

The Office of Economic Research of the New York Public Service Commission also based its findings of low elasticity for residential electricity demand on factors which would seem to determine elasticity rather than on direct econometric measurement.[31] Both the

171

PSC and NERA point to a number of plausible reasons why there would not be much price responsiveness: [32]

—consumers are often unaware of electricity price and, if they were, given that it is a small part of family budgets, would not usually change their behavior much without large price increases.

—studies of appliance sales do not show much response to electricity prices.

—many types of appliances require electricity.

—capital cost is probably a more important factor in building design than heating or cooling cost.

These factors appear to be more relevant to the short- or medium-run response to small price changes than to the long-range response to large price increases gradually introduced. Indeed, the PSC staff, after arguing against the notion of a significant *short-run* price response, then pointed out that "in the long run, the effect may be substantial" in certain circumstances and that sharply higher rates may dampen growth of big uses of power.[33]

More specifically, the PSC and NERA arguments are more attuned to shorter run responses for a number of reasons. First, since any slow-down in electricity growth rate is likely to come through a number of small, and gradual adjustments rather than some quick, big changes, and the intuitive approach may initially see only some small ripples, direct empirical study of elasticity might better aggregate the numerous ripples and predict the long range effects. Second, while electricity is a major factor in only a few household uses such as space and water heating and air conditioning, these uses are a big share of the residential market and an even bigger share of its projected growth. Similarly, while most industries use little energy, the few that use a lot dominate that sector's demand. Thus, in only four industries—paper, primary metals, machinery, and electrical equipment—do electricity and fuels count for more than 5% of value added, but these four industries consume 58.4% of manufacturing's energy.[34] Third, the intuitive analyses tend to neglect the possibility of price changes inducing energy-saving research. Moreover, the enactment of laws requiring disclosure of product's energy consumption would tend to increase price elasticity. Fourth, the intuitive analysis assumes that a large price increase is unthinkable. While a large increase applied quickly would produce great dislocations, the same increase applied over time would not have the same effects.

Returning now to an *energy* tax, a large tax is not unthinkable given that Dr. Gordon MacDonald of the President's Council on Environmental Quality estimates air pollution alone to cost $20 billion annually, growing to $41 billion annually by 1985.[35] Assume that Congress decided to impose a 50% tax on energy in increments of 2% over 25 years. Now, even if the price elasticity of energy was .5 over this price range, the long run effect would very roughly be a 1% reduction in use per year (.5 x 2% = 1%). Since energy use has grown at about 2½% over the past half century,[36] the net effect would roughly be to slow energy growth from 2½% to 1½%.

This example also illustrates a possible semantic confusion over the word "elasticity." A price elasticity of .5 is called "inelastic" by definition because it is less than 1. But, .5 is still larger than elasticity of zero which indicates no price response. As such, an elasticity of .5 can still produce significant results if combined with a large, although gradual, price increase.

Perhaps, however, further research will show that energy, unlike any other input, is totally unresponsive to price, that deep in the economy are forces at work which rigidly fix the mix between energy and other inputs. If so, much of the premises upon which present energy policy is based are false. The notion that energy use responds to price has bolstered promotional rates in the era when greater electricity use was thought to be an unambiguous blessing, prompted creation of agencies such as the TVA and the Bonneville Power Authority to provide cheap power as a spur to regional development, and was a factor in the decision to pursue atomic energy as an ultimate source of inexpensive power. If this notion is false, the burden of proof would appear to rest upon its original proponents. In any event, more thorough study of the elasticity of energy demand is long overdue.

D. Is a Limit on Energy Growth Desirable?

After discussing why the economy uses more energy than is efficient, this chapter pointed out some of the merits and demerits of possible ways to promote efficiency. But, efficiency alone is insufficient to justify any one of these possible programs to curb energy growth. Efficiency is a limited concept in many ways.[37] To say that

173

a policy is efficient means only that its dollar benefits outweigh its dollar costs; that is, a cost benefit study of the policy would produce positive results.[38] But, cost-benefit analysis neglects who gets the benefits and who gets the cost. It also neglects those other impacts of a policy upon which no dollar value can be put.

Such considerations differ from the question of efficiency, which should involve only a value-free prediction of market behavior. These other considerations only begin with such predictions, but then must necessarily go on to value judgments about the fairness of the income distribution effects and the desirability of those impacts which cannot be reduced to dollar terms. So, while an agency might conclude that a policy is efficient, legislative-type judgments are required to determine its desirability.

Such judgments are necessarily complicated in an area like energy policy which so widely affects society. As an example, it is useful to discuss briefly the considerations relevant to an energy tax to point out the variety of empirical information which a legislature ideally ought to have in determining the tax's desirability. The income distribution factors might include:

1.   Is the tax regressive or progressive?

2.   Will the tax work undue hardships?

3.   Is the tax fair as between consumers?

The impacts of the tax which could be considered to be impossible to reduce to dollar terms might include:

1.   What are the non-economic environmental effects, if any, of less energy use?

2.   What would be the impact of an energy tax on the maintenance of resources for the future?

3.   What would be the impact of an energy tax on life style?

This Committee can do no more than point out the complexity of these questions. If their answers amount to non-efficiency reasons for not implementing an energy tax, the legislature might conclude that no tax should be implemented or that the tax should be lower than what efficiency alone would dictate. If, on the other hand, the answer points to non-efficiency grounds for an energy tax, the legislature might decide on a tax greater than efficiency alone would dictate.

174

1. INCOME DISTRIBUTION EFFECTS

Is an energy tax progressive? Are progressive taxes better than regressive taxes? Determining whether or not an energy tax would be progressive involves assessing who ultimately pays the tax and who ultimately gets the benefits. It is difficult to say whether the poor or the rich would pay a larger proportion of their income towards an energy tax. The tax, being levied on energy resources, will initially fall on some of this country's richest institutions, mainly the large oil corporations which also own substantial shares of the gas, coal and uranium reserves. These corporations will try to pass the cost on to consumers, but determining the degree to which the incidence of the tax can be shifted requires empirical studies of market behavior. Consumers use energy directly and indirectly as inputs in the production of goods they buy. If, as seems likely, poor consumers spend a relatively larger proportion of their income on energy, directly or indirectly, they would spend relatively more of their incomes than richer consumers on the energy tax, but fewer dollars in absolute terms. Thus, the burden would fall more heavily on poor rather than rich consumers in relative terms, but the uncertainty as to the degree to which the cost would also fall on the rich energy companies makes it difficult to say whether the net impact could be called progressive or regressive.

Whether the incidence of an energy tax is progressive or regressive, it is unlikely to affect significantly the overall distribution of income. This is so, first, because the incidence of the tax will be shared to some significant degree and, second, because energy constitutes a relatively small portion of the gross national product. Although energy pervades the economy, it constitutes only about 5% of the value-added.[39] So, if the tax were gradually raised to be 50% of energy's current value, the tax would constitute a few percent of gross national product.

Determining who will get the benefits of an energy tax is as complicated as determining who will pay the cost. It is the inner city poor who are the most afflicted by pollution [40] and who can least avoid its effects by travel, air conditioning, and health care. But, many poor people may consider pollution to be of low priority in comparison to problems of food and shelter. So, while pollution may have a bigger physical impact on the lives of poor people, they may value environmental improvement at a lower per cent of their income than would the rich.

If the net income distribution effect of an energy tax is small but considered undesirable and if the impact on overall efficiency and environmental protection is large, it may be worthwhile to find ways to avoid the income distribution impact. Thus, if an energy tax were to be implemented instead of some tax with more undesirable income distribution effects, the total impact of the energy tax on income distribution would be considered good. Moreover, even if the energy tax were found to be undesirably regressive, its net impact could be made to be progressive by using the proceeds for purposes which largely benefit the poor.

A quite different income distribution impact of an energy tax arises from the possibility of economic dislocations resulting in undue hardship. Certain industries have grown rapidly in reliance upon cheap power. A drastic increase in the price of energy would have severe effects upon these industries such as primary metals and chemicals and their employees. Thus, while the long-run effect of an energy tax might be desirable, the short term dislocations might make the tax undesirable. But, if the energy tax were introduced gradually enough, adjustments could take place through attrition and the slower growth of such sectors instead of through unemployment and bankruptcies.

A third income distribution aspect of an energy tax is fairness as between consumers. Consumers with the same incomes use much different amounts of energy, particularly because of differing tastes for air conditioning and cars. Since the environmental impact of energy use is an external cost, those consumers who use a large amount of energy are getting a free ride. The energy tax could remedy this unfairness.

Critics of a policy to reduce growth in energy use say that this policy would be unfair to the poorer consumers who allegedly do not yet have many energy using appliances and use less energy. While valid against a government embargo on the purchase of color television sets, air conditioning and electric tooth brushes, this argument may cut the other way in regard to an energy tax since it applies to appliance use, not appliance purchase.

2. Non-Economic Effects

Some would argue that the wilderness, rivers, and air are irreplaceable natural resources which cannot be weighed in terms of money. Thus, they would conclude that there should be less energy used than efficiency alone dictates. Others counter that energy, rather than polluting the environment, is necessary to keep it clean.[41] They point to the environmental benefits of electrically run sewage treatment, recycling, and mass transportation. Others claim that such environmental protection activities use comparatively little energy relative to total demand and may result in net savings.[42] Assuming, however, that environmental protection activities will require increasingly large net amounts of energy, it does not follow that a tax on energy is undesirable. If the external costs of energy use are internalized for all types of energy uses, the economy would demand and use energy on consumption or environmental protection where the dollar social benefits exceed the social costs.

Another controversy centers around the possible exhaustion of resources. It is argued that, if current depletion of natural resources continues, certain critical resources will be exhausted in a matter of decades.[43] It is said that this generation has no right to deprive future generations of such resources. A response is that, if technology does not find replacement of these scarce resources, their prices will rise to reflect their scarcity.[44] According to this argument, our economic system contains built-in safeguards to assure resources for the future. But, the self-corrective mechanisms may not work adequately. Monopolies, the market's lack of perfect foresight, and government regulation make the economic system less than perfectly responsive.

Finally, whether energy use declines or multiplies two-fold or five-fold in the next half century can profoundly affect the quality of life. The impact may be larger than any aggregation of the effects on the economy, the air, and the water. Results may conceivably be felt in mechanization's impact on peoples' perception of nature, in automation's impact on workers' feelings about their jobs, or in the type of government required by an increasingly complex economy. Even the general outlines of such possibilities are difficult to predict and their desirability even more difficult for a diverse population to assess.

In sum, although an energy tax can produce greater efficiency, its implementation necessarily involves difficult predictions and value judgments about the shape of the future, which ultimately require the development of information and its evaluation in a legislative context.

E. A Process to Consider Demand Policy

The economics of energy lead to several important conclusions about the process by which government should consider whether and how to alter the current' growth in energy and electricity use. First, since the operation of the economy, not the construction of new plants, generates the demand, the issue of demand can be dealt with best in the context of considering the overall economy and ecology, not in the licensing of individual power plants. Second, since electricity demand interacts with total energy demand, government should preferably consider the question of energy usage, not just electricity usage. Third, since an energy policy which is efficient for the nation as a whole may not be efficient for a single state or locality,[45] a national policy should be established, but should not exclude experiments or complementary actions at the state level. Fourth, since current levels of energy usage and growth are inefficiently high as discussed in part B of this chapter, reasons exist for the federal government to address demand as an important question. Fifth, since energy demand affects far more than the efficiency of the economy, the federal government must make complicated value judgments based on equally complicated facts to determine if action is desirable. This implies a role both for an administrative agency to ascertain the facts and for Congress to make the value judgments. Chapter VIII discusses in detail the working relationship between such an agency or commission and Congress.

Finally, since a new energy policy could cause considerable dislocation if implemented rapidly, any such policy should begin to be introduced gradually as far in advance as possible of the time in which it might be needed. Given the increasing concern about growth, Congress should consider the problem actively and now. This implies taking steps to gather the necessary facts. The various Congressional energy studies are a good first step, but the empirical research needed exceeds the present capabilities of Congressional committees. Chapter VIII suggests an administrative structure, one of whose duties would be to provide such information to Congress. The need for active consideration also implies more than a decision by non-debate. Proposals on substantive action which are as realistic as possible should be drafted, debated, and put to vote on the floor.

This process requires much work. The time required will exceed the time limit by which many environmentalists believe action must be taken. But, possibilities exist whereby Congress could begin to take action, if it believes it advisable, but leave many important decisions to a later stage. One possibility, on which this Committee takes no position but puts forth for discussion purposes only, is the immediate imposition of a small energy tax on primary producers and importers of fuels, the proceeds of which could be used at least initially to fund energy research and development. Senator Magnuson has put forth a similar tax or levy, but applicable only to electricity.[46] An argument for such a step might include the following points. As a small tax on energy, this action would have an equivalently small impact on energy growth and energy users. As such, it would not require full-fledged consideration of the many efficiency, income distribution, and non-economic questions involved. But, the tax, besides funding research, would begin the debate and establish the principle that a policy instrument should exist in the energy area just as the interest rate and the budget exist as instruments to shape the economy as a whole.[47] Then, as Congress begins to deal with the various policy questions, it could eliminate, reduce, or increase the tax. By establishing the principle of the tax and working out its technical details, the nation could agree that energy policy is important, whether or not current growth patterns are desirable, and eliminate part of the advantage which a system of checks and balances necessarily gives to the opponents of any new action.

F. Promotional Practices

An energy tax would raise the overall level of energy prices or rates, but would not necessarily affect the rate structure. Rate structures allow different prices for different types and quantities of uses and so can potentially offer incentives for more or less energy use.

Electric utilities' rate structures generally provide for lower prices the more a customer consumes. At the margin, the marginal cost for small consumers is ten times or more than the cost to the largest industrial users. As the President's Office of Science and Technology commented:

> "At present, the rates for electricity (and all other forms of energy perhaps to a lesser extent) are designed to encourage consumption by providing for reductions in the unit price as the volume consumed by a particular customer increases. These rate schedules purport to reflect the lower unit costs of providing service to the higher volume consumer." [48]

If the decreasing rate schedules are justified by cost, they represent an efficient way of marketing electricity. If they are not justified by cost, then small users are paying a subsidy to large users whose net effect is to encourage greater use of electricity. Some have suggested that the rate structures be inverted to reflect higher unit costs as a customer uses more, either on the theory that present rates are not cost-justified or to protect the environment.[49] Others have sought to defend the rate schedules on the basis of cost, the encouraging of fuller use of capacity during hours of low demand, and other reasons.[50] Still others believe that large users are now subsidizing the administrative costs of servicing the very smallest customers.

1. The Theory of Rate Design

Rate design begins with the computation of the utility's total capital investment and total expected operating costs. The regulatory body will then calculate a total revenue for the utility which allows it to cover its operating costs and earn a reasonable return on capital. With total revenues fixed, the task then begins of deciding which customers shall pay how much of the total revenues.

While there are a number of theories of how costs should be allocated among customers, the most widely used is based upon a three-way conceptualization of expenses: customer cost, demand cost, and energy cost.[51] Customer cost is the expense of selling, hooking up, servicing, and billing customers; it varies with the number of customers and the type of administrative services which they require. Demand cost is the expense of building the generation, transmission, and distribution capacity needed to meet consumption need; it varies with the peak demand, usually reached only a few times a year. Finally, energy cost is the expense of running the facilities in terms of such operating costs as labor and fuels; it varies with the total number of kilowatt hours consumed over the year.

180

These three costs are then allocated among various classifications of customers and "blocks" of consumption. Customer classifications include residential, commercial, industrial and various special classes, particularly for large customers. Within each customer classification, different rates are charged for each block or level of consumption.

A utility usually first determines how much of the customer cost is attributable to each customer classification and then allocates it to the lower blocks in each classification on the theory that larger customers in a classification require little extra customer costs. Demand costs are allocated among classifications by determining how much each classification uses at the peak of demand. For residential and smaller commercial classifications, these costs are included more heavily in the lower blocks of consumption. For industrial and other large consumption classifications, a separate charge is made for demand costs. The utility generally determines what is the peak demand made by each customer and calculates a separate demand cost accordingly. Finally the energy cost or cost of producing each kilowatt is computed and added on to each block.

2. THE PRACTICE OF RATE DESIGN

Most state utility laws, as interpreted, require the state commission to insure that total revenues are calculated to produce a fair return and that these revenues are divided among customers without undue discrimination.[52] As a practical matter, however, much more regulatory attention is focused on the rate of return than on rate structure.[53] To what extent the results have allowed deviation from cost justification is unknown. At the same time, limitations in data give utilities difficulty in allocating costs for any given classification to particular blocks of consumption. As the director of one utility rate department recently testified:

> "There simply is no definable cost relationship among the blocks within any rate classification in [our ½] rate schedule. We make an effort to insure that the minimum block returns some reasonable percentage of the customer costs and that the terminal rate is compensatory; but beyond that about all any rate engineer can do is to spread the revenues he seeks to recover from the classification among the blocks in some reasonable way. Traditionally, he has done this on the basis of giving a greater discount for greater use." [54]

181

A 1971 Federal Power Commission report found that rates and other practices are widely used to promote greater consumption:

"Promotional rates and industrial allowances are the most frequently employed promotional practices; financial assistance and appliance allowances are the least frequently employed." [55]

According to the FPC survey:

"In most states the utilities have unrestricted freedom to initiate the promotional practices. . . . It is hard to detect any convergence among the state commissions toward a consistent and well documented set of standards for regulating utility promotional practices." [56]

3. Is Rate Structure Cost Justified?

If the substantially lower rates for higher volumes of consumption are not cost justified, rate design both encourages higher electricity demand and works unfairness on small residential consumers and small businessmen. If, on the other hand, utility commissions have given the small consumer a break because of political pressure, then present rate design has held back the growth in electricity consumption. Unfortunately, there is little empirical evidence on one side or the other. What may be true for one utility may not be true for another. In one rate case, Commissioner William Kenneth Jones of the New York State Public Service Commission concluded that Consolidated Edison had proposed a rate structure which would earn a 13.1% return on sales to small residential consumers and as low as 2.6% on sales to commercial and industrial concerns.[57]

We do not know whether Commissioner Jones was correct and, if so, how prevalent are such departures from cost justification. But, the Commissioner and others have raised a number of issues about rate design. First, the demand charge is usually placed most heavily in the lower blocks of consumption. But, it is the larger residential and office customers who must typically use air conditioning which often operates near the time of system peak. This would seem to imply that a cost-justified allocation of residential demand charges would require that they be spread at least evenly throughout the blocks of consumption.[58]

Second, utilities may have certain costs which do not vary with either the number of customers, peak demand, or total kilowatts consumed. These might include certain administrative expenses as well as low tension distribution facilities. These costs, however, are generally allocated to customer costs, along with metering and billing, for which small users pay the largest share.

Third, utilities have special schedules and enter into special contracts with extremely large users. In such contexts, the ability of the consumer to produce his own electricity is considered in addition to traditional cost factors.[59] Examples are large industrial plants and large housing developments which could use "total energy systems" which would both generate electricity and use the waste heat for space heating or industrial processes. It has been argued that departure from cost justification is helpful to the environment because the customer-owned plant would not meet the same environmental standard as the utility's plant.[60] But, the state commission could conceivably hold the customer-owned plant to the same standard or seek the jurisdiction to do so.

Fourth, utilities offer special arrangements to housing development builders who will build all-electric homes or apartments. If both electricity and its competitors, gas and oil, were priced to include their external costs, both efficiency and environmental protection might be best served by cost-justified pricing rather than such special incentives.

4. RATE CLASSIFICATIONS

Utilities could classify their customers in numerous ways. Some different types of classification and metering might improve results. Thus, separate classifications with lower prices for certain large customers are justified on the basis that they use less electricity at the peak than others. But, it is not known whether the reduction in price induces more on-peak or off-peak increases in consumption. On the other hand, no separate classification is made for residential and commercial consumers with heavy air conditioning loads, although their highest demand comes at the system's peak.

Metering also might be done differently. Large industrial consumers are metered and charge for their use at their point of highest demand, not the system's point of highest demand. By basing part of the bill for electricity on the level of peak use, an incentive is given to spread a customer's load, but, since some customers have individual peaks which are not at the system's peak, such customers may end up consuming more at the system's peak.

183

Defenders of the promotional rate system make a number of arguments. First, it has been suggested that rate structure only slightly affects patterns of consumption.[61] While this position seems inconsistent with utilities' former justifications for promotional rates during the era when greater electricity use was seen as unequivocally desirable, this argument may well have merit at least in the short run. But, in the long run, there is reason to believe that consumption patterns do respond to price.[62]

Second, it is argued that promotional rates are efficient because, by encouraging growth, they allow for economies of scale in the building of generating facilities. As the argument goes, larger facilities allow for better pollution control equipment. But, it does not necessarily follow that higher aggregate demand is essential to the construction of plants of the optimum size. If the best scale for new plants is 1500 megawatts, a utility or a power pool can build plants of this capacity whether its annual growth is 1000 megawatts or 10,000 megawatts.

Finally, it is argued that for less promotional rate structures "to discourage consumption in a manner that will reduce environmental pressures, they would have to discourage consumption *at the peak*." [63] This misses a big point. Reducing peak consumption will decrease the number of plants that must be built, it is true. Also, generation of a given number of kilowatts at the peak is generally more polluting because more marginal plants must be pressed into service and heat is dissipated more easily in cold weather. But, it is total electricity consumption—on-peak and off-peak—that determines largely how much fuel is burnt and how much the air is polluted.

5. CONCLUSION

Whether rates are cost justified or could be better designed, this Committee cannot say. But, enough questions have been raised to justify comprehensive study at the national level by the administrative structure proposed in Chapter VIII.

There are ways to reconcile local scrutiny of utility accounts and the national concern with rate structures. With rate regulation left at the state level, a national office could, on the basis of studies, issue instructions on methods of cost analysis and rate structuring, similar to the accounting rules now promulgated by the Federal Power Commission.[64] On the basis of such guidelines, it would be easier to judge whether local rate structures and promotional practices are cost justified. Federal legislation could then be enacted against certain types of promotional practices which are not cost justified, focusing with precision on the problem of fair price structures for regulated industries.

Notes for Chapter VI

1. *Resources for the Future, Energy Research Needs* at I–20 (1971) [hereinafter *Resources for the Future*].

2. *Id.* at I–22.

3. In the past half century, energy use has grown at 2½% annually, while population has grown in the range of from 1 to 2%. *Id.* at I–6.

4. Whether GNP growth slows more or less than energy growth depends upon whether technological change is more labor-saving or energy-saving. But, the change in energy policy would encourage more energy-saving technology thus minimizing the impact on the growth of GNP.

5. *E. g., I. M. D. Little, A Critique of Welfare Economics* (2d ed. 1957) [hereinafter *Little*]. Little's conclusions cited hereinafter have been widely adopted.

6. While costs at a single generating plant or mine fall until they reach capacity, the costs of producing more electricity or coal in the economy as a whole rise as the best sites are used up and less accessible coal veins must be tapped.

7. *E. g., Little* at 129–165.

8. This statement assumes that taxes and subsidies for the energy industry such as local real estate tax practices, mineral depletion allowances, intangible drilling expenses, and oil import quotas in comparison to taxes and subsidies for other sectors do not put the energy industry at a net disadvantage.

9. Except at the margin, the private benefits of using energy are higher than its private cost. But, in considering whether to encourage or discourage energy use, it is the marginal benefits and costs that are relevant. Many uses of energy also have social benefits in excess of the private benefits such as, perhaps, the electricity which runs the air conditioning used in hospitals. But, there are uses where the social benefits are less than the private benefits as, for example, where air conditioning office buildings makes the streets and sidewalks hotter.

10. Other possible reasons are subsidies for the production or consumption of energy such as oil depletion allowances and any unreimbursed government research.

11. External costs give rise to inefficiency. *E. g., Little* at 129–145.

12. *E. g., Little* at 163. "Second best" problems could also occur between energy and materials, but seem less likely because the degree of substitutability is smaller than between electricity and other forms of energy.

13. A program operating on a national level could be based on standards which vary among areas to take account of the differing costs of pollution in different areas.

14. *E. g.,* R. M. Nixon, "Energy Resources," President's Message to the Congress, June 4, 1971, in *Weekly Compilation of Presidential Documents* 855 (June 7, 1971).

15. *E. g., Little* at 87.

16. *Resources for the Future* at I–50 n. 1.

17. Address by Bruce Netschert, "How Much Power Do We Really Need?" at 13, Annual Conference of the Atomic Industrial Forum, Bal Harbour, Florida, Oct. 18, 1971.

18. Gujarti, "Demand for Electricity and Natural Gas," *Public Utilities Fortnightly* (Jan. 30, 1969).

19. Wilson, "Residential Demand for Electricity," 11 *The Quarterly Review of Economics and Business* 1 (1971). For convenience sake, all elasticities are expressed as positive numbers.

20. Paper by Chapman & Tyrrell, "Alternative Assumptions About Life Style, Population, and Income Growth" at 7, Sierra Club Conference on the Electric Power Industry, Johnson, Vermont, Jan. 14–15, 1972.

21. Paper by Halvorsen, "Residential Electricity: Demand & Supply" Sierra Club Conference, *supra* note 20.

22. K. P. *Anderson, Residential Demand for Electricity* 14, 17 (RAND, R-905-National Science Foundation 1972).

23. Chapman & Tyrrell, *supra* note 20, at 20 n. 7.

24. K. P. *Anderson, supra* note 22, at 16.

25. F. M. *Fisher* & C. *Kaysen, The Demand for Electricity in the United States* (1962).

26. *Id.*

27. Tybout, "Electric Power Rates and the Environment" at 12, Sierra Club Power Conference, *supra* note 20.

28. E. *g.*, Gerber, Energy, "Electric Energy, and the Environment," *Public Utilities Fortnightly* (Feb. 4, 1971); Testimony of Abraham Gerber, *In re* Consolidated Edison Company, New York PSC (No. 25343).

29. Gujarti, "Demand for Electricity and Natural Gas," *Public Utilities Fortnightly* (Jan. 30, 1969).

30. *Id.*

31. *Office of Economic Research, New York Department of Public Service, The Inverted Rate Structure—An Appraisal,* Part I at 11–18, 42–45 (1972) [hereinafter *The Inverted Rate Structure*].

32. *Id.*; NERA materials cited at note 28, *supra.*

33. *The Inverted Rate Structure* at 43, 45.

34. *NERA, Energy Consumption and GNP in the United States* at Table IX (March, 1971).

35. Address by Dr. Gordon MacDonald, "Energy and the Environment" at 11, Resources for the Future Conference, Washington, D. C., April 21, 1971.

36. *Resources for the Future* at I–6.

37. E. *g., Little* at 67–116.

38. *Id.* at 87.

39. *Resources for the Future* at I–5.

40. E. *g., EPA Task Force on Environmental Problems of the Inner City, Our Urban Environment* (Draft, Sept. 1971).

41. *FPC, Changed Underlying Factors Influencing Load Growth* (Task Force Report 1971).

42. Paper and Speech by Prof. Timothy Healy, "Electric Energy Requirements of Public Systems," Sierra Club Conference, *supra* note 20.

43. *E. g., D. H. Meadows et al., The Limits to Growth* (1972).

44. *E. g.,* Passell, Roberts & Ross, "The Limits to Growth," N.Y. Times, April 2, 1972, § 7, at 1, col. 1 (Review of Meadows, *supra* note 43).

45. This does not mean that there are not efficient and desirable actions that a single state could undertake or that the need for local experimentalism may not outweigh any undesired interstate impacts of a state or local energy policy.

46. Speech by Senator Warren Magnuson, "Power Plant Siting Act of 1971—Amendment," 117 *Cong.Rec.* S 12922 (daily ed. Aug. 3, 1971).

47. Employment Act of 1946, 15 USC 1021 *et seq.*

48. *The Energy Policy Staff, Office of Science and Technology, Electric Power and the Environment* 47 (1970).

49. *Id.*

50. *E. g., The Inverted Rate Structure.*

51. *J. Bonbright, Principles of Public Utility Rates* (1961).

52. *I A. J. G. Priest, Principles of Public Utility Regulation* 285–89 (1969).

53. There appears to be more cases on rate of return than rate structure. In addition, according to Priest, "initial rate design should be, and usually is, for management." *Id.* at 343.

54. Proposed rebuttal testimony of J. Monsees, Hearing Transcript, *In re* Consolidated Edison Co. at 3368 New York PSC (No. 26105).

55. *FPC, Promotional Practices of Public Utilities* 7 (1970).

56. *Id.*

57. Opinion, *In re* Consolidated Edison, NYPSC at 11–20 of Comm. Jones' concurrence (No. 25342, Aug. 12, 1970).

58. *Id.* at 16–17.

59. See, *e. g., The Inverted Rate Structure* at 45.

60. *Id.*

61. *Id.* at 42–45.

62. *Id.* For a fuller discussion see Part C of this chapter.

63. Stelzer, "Utility Pricing under Inflation, Competition, and Environmental Concerns." *Public Utilities Fortnightly* (Dec. 3, 1970).

64. 18 CFR subchapter C (1971).

VII. CURRENT LEGISLATIVE REFORM APPROACHES

A. REFORM PROPOSALS AND THEIR EVALUATION, GENERALLY

Consistent with the importance of the environmental and reliability problems of the electric industry and the complexity of the legal and political issues born of those problems, there is extant a large mass of ideas and proposals for solution. Some proposals appear to be directed toward overall national solutions and others, to various segments of the problem. Some take a national approach and others, a state or regional approach. At the state level, some proposals have been enacted into law during the last few years and others are pending. At the federal level a number of legislative proposals are pending. Moreover, with each week, it seems, additional analyses are published and more ideas enter the public domain.

This chapter attempts to identify the reform programs that appear to be most important, whether they have been enacted into law or are pending as legislative proposals, and to analyze those more important schemes in terms of the questions discussed and ideas presented elsewhere in this report.

Briefly stated, this Report advances the basic proposition that governmental structures and procedures ought to be designed to achieve the best possible balance between society's competing interests in obtaining a sufficient and reliable electric power supply, on the one hand, and, on the other, in obtaining and preserving a viable, healthy environment. Equally important is that those institutions and procedures achieve the stated ends efficiently and without undue delays in the process, and also in a democratic way, giving due regard to varying interests—national, regional, and local, as well as economic and social. Moreover, the governmental processes must be carried out in such a manner that the results will be widely credible to, and accepted by, the citizenry.

With those thoughts in mind, several standards emerge against which reform legislation should be measured. (The full conclusions and recommendations of this Report are set forth in Chapter VIII.)

First, reform legislation should in some way provide for a long-range national evaluation of the demand question. It should contemplate the development of an affirmative national policy on electric energy demand as a part of the overall electric reliability policy. A truly balanced policy cannot avoid a critical examination of demand factors as well as supply factors.

Second, a number of structural and procedural reforms seem paramount. They include an expansion of governmental regulatory jurisdiction to encompass all modes of electric generation; a merger of the subject matter jurisdictions of the Federal Power Commission and the Atomic Energy Commission; the functional separation into different agencies of promotion and development on the one hand and planning and regulation on the other; and a reallocation of regulatory authority within the federal system so as better to recognize (1) the national interests in energy, economics, and research and development questions generally, (2) the regionalization of the electric industry, and (3) state and local interests in land use control.

Additional essential elements of any legislative reform are the provision for long-range planning of electric power facilities, their construction, location, and operation; the provision for adequate public participation at all stages of planning and regulation; the maximum employment of the generic proceeding throughout the processes of planning and regulation; and the sufficient recognition of environmental and safety considerations within the overall balancing function—pollution standards for air and water; radiation standards; recreation, wilderness, aesthetic, and historic considerations; and national environmental policy.

With the preceding thoughts as a basis, this chapter examines the following categories of legislative reforms:

(1) The important electric facility siting legislation now pending in the Congress;

(2) The important land-use-control legislation pending in the Congress;

(3) The legislation, now pending in Congress, proposing a system for the encouragement of research and development; and

(4) Certain legislation in selected states, some enacted and some pending.

B. FEDERAL ELECTRIC FACILITY SITING LEGISLATION

As used here, the term "facility siting legislation" refers to legislation focusing on the planning, location, and construction of electric utility facilities and solution of the kinds of disputes that have arisen in recent years over such facility construction. More specifically, "facility-siting" refers to bulk facilities—the larger generating plants (*e. g.*, over 200 MW) and extra high voltage, long distance transmission lines. Siting legislation is to be distinguished, for example, from broad proposals for general environmental control or control of electric industry operation and from general land use control proposals.

At this writing, two major legislative packages devoted to utility facility siting have been lengthily considered by the Congress and several important related bills have been recently introduced. A subcommittee of the House Committee on Interstate and Foreign Commerce has held hearings [1] on, and the full Committee has before it, a proposal sponsored by Representative Torbert Macdonald [2] (hereinafter, the "Macdonald bill"). That bill would add a new "Part IV" to the Federal Power Act. The House Committee is considering also a bill presented by the Nixon Administration to create a new "Power Plant Siting Act of 1971" [3] (hereinafter, the "Administration bill"), and two recently introduced variations on the Administration bill, one sponsored by Representatives Bob Eckhardt and Henry Helstoski [3A] (hereinafter, the "Eckhardt-Helstoski bill"), and another by Representatives John Dingell and John Moss [3B] (hereinafter, the "Dingell-Moss bill").

The Senate Committee on Commerce has held hearings (not published at this writing) on the Administration bill [3C] and variations sponsored by Senator Magnuson [3D] and Senator Hart.[3E]

The following discussion first examines the Administration and Macdonald proposals, offers some commentary on them, and then considers the several variations on the Administration bill suggested by the Eckhardt-Helstoski, Dingell-Moss, Magnuson, and Hart bills.[4]

1. ADMINISTRATION AND MACDONALD PROPOSALS

The indicated general purposes of both the Administration and Macdonald bills include meeting society's needs for a reliable electric energy supply and for protecting the environment,[5] avoiding undue delays in decision-making,[6] and expanding the long-range planning for construction of bulk power facilities.[7]

Broadly, each bill would seek to achieve those ends, first, by calling on the fifty states to exercise more fully their regulatory jurisdiction over plant-siting questions not presently preempted by Congress and exercised by federal agencies, and, second, by calling on the electric utility industry to formalize, expand, and open up, in varying degrees, its long-range planning processes. Neither bill would enhance any national or regional *public* planning functions.

a. *Certification of Facility-Siting: the Single State Agency.* Both bills look to the establishment of a nationwide system of state agencies to decide state-level plant-siting issues [8] pursuant to some, but not necessarily very great, federal supervision. Each bill seeks to induce every state to vest a single plant-siting agency with final intrastate administrative authority,[9] thus aiming in the direction of the "one-step" licensing philosophy, at least at the state level.

The Administration bill would require a federal certification of each state's plan to determine its conformity to law, which certification, however, might later be revoked for cause.[10] If, within two years of the Administration bill's enactment, any state shall not have established a site-certification program, exclusive federal agency jurisdiction would fill the gap, as it would, also, in the event of revocation of federal approval.[11] The Macdonald bill, on the other hand, provides simply for a Governor's certification to federal authorities that his state's single agency fulfills the requirements of the federal law.[12]

Both bills bow to the ideal of regional solutions by approving, in advance, interstate compacts creating multi-state agencies to carry out the site-certification functions otherwise the responsibilities of the constituent states.[13] Neither bill, however, provides any incentives to the states to enter into such interstate arrangements. Any interstate-regional siting agencies would occupy, under either bill, exactly the same relationship as state siting agencies to federal law and federal agencies.

Each bill, also, would provide for some form of Federal overriding decision where power reliability may be endangered, and, in the case of the Administration bill, only in such a situation. Moreover, the Macdonald bill is much more limited in respect of override even where risk to electric reliability may be the issue. In the Administration bill,

192

federal override would be available where the utility might demonstrate urgency calling for construction of a particular electric facility and where it might demonstrate, further, that improper state agency action or inaction is impeding such construction.[14]   In the Macdonald bill, great deference would be given to the state plant-siting agency provided it is the state's *single* siting agency: only such an agency's inaction could lead to federal override,[15] and, in such a case the federal overriding decision apparently would not be conclusive of all state and local law questions.[15a]   Under the Administration bill, however, a federal overriding decision would be administratively conclusive of all matters of applicable state and local law.[16]   A noteworthy component of the Macdonald plan is that, uniquely, it would delegate such federal overriding jurisdiction (along with other significant powers discussed below) to a special *ad hoc* panel,[17] authorized to employ "any recognized formal or informal procedure" including "arbitration." [18]

b.   *New Federal Structures.*   Structurally, both bills ostensibly leave intact the present powers and responsibilities of the Environmental Protection Agency, the Atomic Energy Commission, and the Federal Power Commission.   But that is only the beginning.

The Administration bill would delegate almost all new federal responsibilities to a new "Federal certifying agency", which, it is expected, would be the new "Department of Natural Resources" proposed by the Administration elsewhere.[19]   The primary exception to the generality of those delegations is the assignment to the President of responsibility for establishing the federal guidelines for the state facility-siting programs.[20]   New federal functions delegated to the federal certifying agency would include reviewing and approving the several state facility-siting programs,[21] actually certifying facility siting for the federal operating utilities such as T. V. A.,[22] and similar actual certification of *all* facility-siting in any state not having established an approved program within two years of the bill's enactment.[23]   The new federal agency would also exercise the federal overriding authority to certify the siting of a facility wherever a utility can show

> "a failure of a State or regional certifying body or bodies to act upon a timely or conclusive basis with respect to any application   .   .   .   for   .   .   .   certification;   and that as a result thereof the public interest in an adequate and reliable regional bulk power supply imperatively and unavoidably requires a decision   .   .   .   ." [24]

In such a case, the new agency would refer the application for override to the Federal Power Commission for a determination whether power reliability will be materially impaired. If the FPC should find such material impairment, then the new federal certifying agency would take over jurisdiction in the case, to the exclusion of any state agencies.[25]

With one exception, present incidents of federal regulation would remain unchanged by the Administration bill. A condition precedent to the grant of any site certification (by the state siting agency or the new federal agency, as the case might be) would be that the granting agency "has ascertained that all applicable federal standards, permits, or licenses have been satisfied or obtained." [26] Moreover, the authority of the AEC and the FPC is expressly preserved [27] and facilities subject to FPC hydroelectric project licensing are specifically exempted from siting regulation under the Administration bill, although nuclear plants licensed by the AEC are not so exempted.[28]

The bill's one exception, however, is quite significant and relates to the NEPA § 102(2) (c) impact statement requirement. The Administration bill provides that where the site-certification agency "has followed a substantially comparable procedure," the NEPA impact statement requirement is waived.[29] Thus, it is contemplated that only the Federal Power Commission would remain subject absolutely to the NEPA requirement [30] and, in the typical case of a nuclear or fossil-fuel plant, the present NEPA responsibilities of the Atomic Energy Commission [31] and the Corps of Engineers [32] apparently would be transferred to the state facility-siting agency.[33] Moreover, the bill contains no provision establishing a standard by which a court might determine what "a substantially comparable procedure" is or whether a particular state procedure would comply. Nor does the bill direct that state agencies follow an impact statement procedure.[34]

The Macdonald bill, although technically an amendment to the Federal Power Act, would divide its newly created federal functions variously among the FPC, the Interior Department, and the *ad hoc* "Panels" mentioned above. Most importantly, the Macdonald bill would delegate to its *ad hoc* panels a whole series of powers to set aside, in particular cases, both state and federal formulas for electric power regulation and environmental protection. As indicated above, this bill provides for the establishment of a special panel to effectuate a limited federal "override" of state or local level interference with facility construction. But the bill does more. It establishes the panel as a body that may, under certain circumstances, override the permit, license, or certification actions of any federal agency "in connection with the construction or . . . operation" of bulk power facilities, except any action of the Atomic Energy Commission "in a matter relating to radiological safety." [35]

The "panel" proceeding would be commenced under the Macdonald bill by a utility's application to the Federal Power Commission. If the Commission should find that the applicant had complied with the required long-range planning provisions of the bill [36] and that the state or federal agency action or omission complained of "is likely to jeopardize meeting reasonable power needs," the Commission would request the Secretary of the Interior to assign the matter to a "panel." [37]

Panels would consist of three members each, one appointed by the Chairman of the Federal Power Commission, one appointed by the Chairman of the Council on Environmental Quality, and a third selected by the first two from a list submitted by the Chairman of the Administrative Conference of the United States, each of the three serving a two-year term.[38] The FPC appointee would be required to be a person "qualified by training and experience to evaluate reasonable power needs" and the CEQ appointee, a person similarly qualified to "evaluate reasonable environmental factors".[39] The persons listed by the Chairman of the Administrative Conference should be "neutral" on the foregoing issues and expert on legal procedure, and, in each case, shall serve as chairman of the panel.[40] It is not required that panel members work full-time although it is possible that they will do so. It is provided that the Secretary of the Interior may assign several cases at once to a given panel,[41] that panel members may be appointed and reappointed to different, successive panels,[42] that panels may request temporary staff from any federal agency,[43] and that the Secretary shall provide "administrative support services." [44] Thus, while such panels and their members might become regular fixtures of the bureaucratic scene, it is possible and more likely that they will in fact be *ad hoc* groups made up of persons who serve on a part-time and temporary basis, whose own individual skills and expertise, rather than collective, staff-assisted judgments, will be applied to their decision-making.

In any event, when the Secretary refers a case to a panel pursuant to the request of the Federal Power Commission, it would be the initial job of the panel to determine whether the utility and its plan have fulfilled the long-range planning requirements of the bill [45] and whether the utility has diligently presented its application to every federal or state agency whose action or inaction the utility seeks to have overridden by the panel.[46] If its findings on those questions are affirmative, then the panel is to review the utility's proposal and any alternatives

> "and shall select from such proposals the proposal which in its judgment achieves an acceptable balance between reasonable power needs and reasonable environmental factors." [47]

If it sees fit, the panel may impose upon the scheme it selects conditions designed to achieve the most acceptable balance.[48]

In examining a case assigned to it, a panel is quite free in its choice of procedure. It may employ, among others, "arbitration or mediation procedures" and may "utilize any information secured by it," but must keep minutes of its meetings and transcripts of any evidentiary hearings, all of which must be publicly available.[49] The panel's conclusion in any case should achieve "an acceptable balance between reasonable power needs and reasonable environmental factors." [50]

In a most important section, the Macdonald bill provides that, at such time as a panel decision "takes effect . . . no provision" [51] of "Federal law . . . other than provisions of the Atomic Energy Act which relate to radiological safety . . ." [52] "shall be applied so as to prevent the construction or commencement of operation of a bulk power facility in accordance with" the plan approved by the decision.[53] Although certain other language of the bill (relating to the powers of a reviewing court to stay the effectiveness of a panel decision) renders the matter less than crystal clear, the apparent intent of the bill is to authorize the panel generally to exempt any specific facility from all federal electric regulatory and environmental protection laws.[54] And that authority could be exercised in any case where (1) the utility has followed the planning and procedural steps required by the bill and (2) the FPC has found that failure to construct or commence operation of the facility "is likely to jeopardize meeting reasonable power needs." [55]

From the foregoing discussion, it may be seen that the Macdonald bill would establish the *ad hoc* panel as its key element for the relief of utilities from the constraints of federal law and proceedings, and particularly such environmental law and proceedings (except for radiation safety issues) as may be administered by the Environmental Protection Agency, the Atomic Energy Commission, and the Corps of Engineers.[56] On the other hand, vis-a-vis the states, it may be seen as only a prod to the creation of fifty single-agency state site-certification structures. It is a horrendous prod, to be sure, since three federally appointed, part-time, temporary bureaucrats would be empowered to decide *all* relevant issues under state and local law.[57] Nevertheless, it is a prod that the governor of each state may readily defuse. He may do so by certifying to the Secretary of the Interior that there exists in the state an efficient, adequately financed and staffed "single agency" with the authority to make "final administrative decisions" on all applicable issues of state and local law and to evaluate and give final approvals in respect of siting issues by balancing "reasonable power needs and reasonable environmental factors."[58] Once the governor has so certified, no federal override may be obtained except in a case where the single state agency totally fails to act.[59]

Thus, while effectively providing utilities with an avenue for release from *federal* non-radiological environmental constraints where "reasonable power needs"[60] may require, the Macdonald bill leaves entirely to the fifty separate state jurisdictions the responsibilities and final authority for determining all environmental questions and electric power questions not presently preempted to federal control. Moreover, except for its repetitious use or variation of the expression, "reasonable" or "acceptable balance between reasonable power needs and reasonable environmental factors,"[61] the Macdonald bill provides neither enforceable federal standards nor federal guidance concerning how such "balance" should be sought—either substantive or procedural.[62]

Finally, it should be noted again that neither the Administration bill nor the Macdonald bill establishes any procedure for federal override of the single state agency's decision on environmental grounds. The Macdonald bill contains provisions under which "any person" may seek a panel review of a proposal for facility construction.[63] But such a procedure is available only where, *inter alia*, "[n]one of the States in which the facility is proposed to be constructed or operated have [sic] a state siting agency."[64] The Administration bill is totally silent on this matter.

c. *Long-Range Planning.* The Administration and Macdonald bills both place great stress upon open long-term planning of facility construction by means of the formulation and regular annual publication of initial plans at least ten years ahead of construction.[65] Both, however, quite explicitly would leave the initiation of the planning function completely to the utility industry, through its presently existing regional councils [66] and each bill would allow the industry planning process to extend through several fundamentally important steps before providing any review and effective approval, disapproval, or modification by public agencies. Both bills call for the initiation of public agency review and decision on specific individual utility construction proposals not less than two years before planned commencement of construction—the facility-certification proceeding.[67] The Administration bill additionally requires separate public agency supervision and control over power plant site selections by individual utilities (but not transmission line routes) through proceedings to be initiated, in respect of each proposed site, not less than five years before contemplated construction.[68]

Under either bill, in almost every case, the public agency having jurisdiction would be a state agency.[69]

The bills thus contemplate very little controlling federal input in the long-range planning process and provide a meaningful regional dimension to the process only through the regional perspectives of the industry councils. [70]

In sum, then, both bills require long-range regional planning for bulk power facility construction, with planning to be undertaken by the industry through its regional councils, and with public-agency review and certification to be carried out predominantly by the fifty states in proceedings involving individual utility applicants for approvals of particular sites and construction. While such state regulatory control would be applied to planning for generating plants up to five years before expected construction under the Administration bill, it would be applied only two years before construction under the Macdonald bill. Under either bill, transmission line planning would not be subject to state control until two years before contemplated construction.

With the basic similarity between the stated long-range planning approaches of the two bills noted, their significant differences in implementation now must be examined.

The Administration bill declares it to be in the "national public interest" that "long-range planning be carried out through the electric reliability councils . . . and by participation of these councils in the work of the Federal Power Commission under section 202(a) of the

198

Federal Power Act." [71]   Although the regional reliability councils occupy the primary planning role under this bill, it says nothing further
about the councils' membership, structure, procedure, or operations.
Since present federal law and administrative regulation exercise little,
if any, actual control over those important qualities of the councils, it
is apparent that the Administration bill would continue the present federal "hands off" policy.

The Macdonald bill, on the other hand, addresses itself quite explictly and extensively to a number of important parameters of council
operation.   It provides that membership in each regional council shall
be open to all bulk power suppliers in the region; that representation,
voting, and cost-sharing shall be based upon "relevant factors such as
generating capacity and sales"; that there shall be "appropriate representation and participation" for the smaller utilities that are not bulk
power suppliers; that council members shall be free to express minority
views to public agencies; and that sufficient staff shall be employed to
allow each council to meet its responsibilities under the bill, "including
responsibilities respecting considerations of environmental factors." [72]
In addition, the bill would require each council to admit, and to allow
to "participate as nonvoting members" in its work, representatives who
"shall" be designated by the FPC and the EPA and "may" be designated by the states within the region.[73]   Finally, the FPC would have
the authority to review and approve or disapprove the regional council's
structure.[74]   When a regional council shall have been properly authorized under the provisions of the bill, the "antitrust laws shall not be
construed to prohibit any person from contributing" to its work.[75]

Although containing no such provisions limiting the regional
councils, the Administration bill specifies in somewhat more detail
than the Macdonald bill the long-range planning requirements applicable to the individual utilities and the state site-certification agencies.

To begin, the Administration bill directs every major utility (i. e.,
owner or operator of bulk power supply facilities), whether privately
or publicly owned, including federally owned utilities such as TVA,
to prepare and annually to revise its long-range plans for bulk power
supply facilities.[76]   The bill directs, further, that each such utility shall
"give initial public notice of" such plans by filing, annually, with the
FPC, the EPA and the state certifying agency a copy of those long-
range plans "together with its projections of demand for electricity

that the facilities would meet . . . ." [77] The same plans and projections shall also be filed with

> "such other affected Federal, State, regional, and local gov-
> ernmental authorities, and citizens' environmental protection
> and resource planning groups requesting such plans." [78]

The individual utility's long-range plans thus to be filed must
generally describe the "location, size, and type" of bulk facilities the
utility plans to begin constructing within the ensuing *ten* years [79] and
must specifically "identify the location of tentative sites" of major power plants and "the general location of" major transmission lines on
which construction is planned to commence within the ensuing *five*
years.[80] For the facilities to be constructed within five years, the utility
must also

> "indicate the relationship of the planned sites, routes, and
> facilities . . . to environmental values and describe how
> potential adverse effects on such values will be avoided or
> minimized." [81]

Moreover, those annual, published long-range plans would be required
to "reflect and describe" the utility's efforts at fitting both the ten-
year and five-year programs into "a coordinated regional plan for meeting the electric power needs of the region" [82] and its efforts

> "to involve environmental protection and land-use planning
> agencies in . . . [the] planning process so as to identify
> and minimize environmental problems at the earliest possible
> stage in the planning process . . . ." [83]

The foregoing requirements of the Administration bill are applied
only to the individual utility. This bill contains no parallel requirements applicable to the regional councils or to the procedural or substantive issues associated with the formulation or publication of the
concededly important regional plans. It should be noted, therefore,
that the role of the state agencies, next to be discussed, would be significantly limited. Each state agency would exercise only very indirect
authority over the regional planning process. It would be very indirect
because it would be exercised only (1) through its jurisdiction over the
operations of individual utilities (2) within its own state borders.

Upon the individual utilities' annual filing of their long-range
plans under the Administration bill, the fifty state certifying agencies [84]
would be "directed" to "review and comment on" each utility's annual

long-range plan and make the same "readily available to the general public and interested governmental agencies . . . ."[85] More specifically, each state site-certification agency is directed to "compile and publish each year" a summary document describing all the power plant sites and general locations of transmission lines within its jurisdiction as identified by the utilities' long-range plans.[86] That summary is required to identify each site within the state and the approximate year of expected construction, and such information also must be made

"readily available to the general public, to each newspaper of daily or weekly circulation within the area affected by the proposed site, and to other interested Federal, State, and local agencies . . . ."[87]

Respecting the site for each new power plant facility (as opposed to transmission facilities), the construction of which is to begin within five years, the state site certification agency[88] is directed "promptly"

"to conduct mandatory public hearings . . . and to decide whether or not any such sites should be approved for inclusion in the . . . [utility's] five-year inventory of sites."[89]

The basis for decision is to be whether construction of "any plant" at each identified site "would unduly impair important environmental values."[90]

Essentially, then, the Administration bill does three things to provide for long-range planning:

(1) It institutionalizes, but does not otherwise limit or control the electric utility industry's present regional council approach to long-range planning;

(2) It opens up the planning process by requiring the individual utilities annually to formulate and publish their ten-year plans for plants and lines and specifically identify sites for power plants planned for construction within five years, and by requiring both the utilities and the state site-certification agencies to publicize the information; and

(3) It injects the judgment of the public agency into the planning process through approval or disapproval of each proposed plant site for inclusion within a utility's "inventory of sites" after a public hearing approximately five years before planned construction.

201

The individual site-certification referred to above [91] takes place under the Administration bill when the utility proposes to construct a power plant on one of the sites previously approved for inclusion in its five-year inventory or to construct a transmission line in one of the corridors identified in its ten-year plan.[92] The utility is required to make application for the facility-site-certification not less than two years prior to the planned commencement of construction.[93]

By comparison, the Macdonald bill is much simpler and focuses more directly on the necessary regionality of long-range planning. Instead of each individual utility publishing separate, annual long-range plans for its expected future facility construction, the regional councils would bear that responsibility and the published plans would be regional plans.[94] Each individual utility would be required to prepare and annually file with its regional council, but not to publish, its long-range plan "giving proper consideration to reasonable power needs and to reasonable environmental factors." [95] Each such utility then would be required to work, within its council, for the coordination of all intraregional plans and the development of the annual regional plan [96] which the regional council would have to file with the FPC, Department of the Interior, EPA, and each state siting agency within the region [97] and publish and make "available for review by all interested persons." [98]

The annual regional plan would have to cover a ten-year period in advance of construction [99] and include a general inventory of plant and transmission line sites and the "specific location" of sites on which the construction of generating plants is expected to begin within five years.[100] The plan would be required to supply information about construction of lines and plans "sufficiently detailed . . . to permit public agencies and other interested parties to evaluate such proposals and to develop alternative proposals . . . ." [101] Specifically, the annual regional plan would be required also to:

(1) "[M]ake provision for meeting reasonable power needs in the region; " [102]

(2) Include a description of the alternative proposals considered by the council, a specification of "the grounds for a selecting or rejecting particular proposals . . . ," [103] and "a detailed statement of the environmental impact of the . . . plan (including any adverse environmental effects which cannot be avoided); " [104] and

(3) "[S]pecify the terms and conditions for making available to all electric utilities and their customers the benefits of a coordinated, adequate, reliable, and economical regional bulk power supply . . . ." [105]

The Macdonald bill, then, would require the publication and filing with public agencies of an impressive, annual *regional* long-range plan. Moreover, while the Macdonald bill omits to state with the clarity of the Administration bill the specific responsibilities of the individual utilities, it would do two things not contemplated by the Administration bill. First, it would expressly incorporate and apply to the regional plan substantial parts of the NEPA impact statement requirement, almost *in haec verba*. Second, by reason of its organizational requirements for the councils and its "benefits" statement requirement, last above quoted, it aims to provide some protection to smaller, frequently state, municipal, or cooperatively owned utilities in their perceived continuing competition with the larger, investor-owned utilities.

Nevertheless, the Macdonald bill contemplates no public agency action, no public regulatory control, until the very end of the process, where an individual utility applies to an individual state-siting agency for certification of construction of a particular facility, and that only two years before planned construction. [106] After each annual filing of a regional long-range plan, "the regional council shall determine whether such proposed plan should be revised" in light of comments or consultations with public agencies "and other interested parties," whereupon the council is required to publish a final plan. [107] This contrasts with the plan of the Administration bill which requires mandatory public hearings and state-agency approval for the site of any power plant but not transmission line five years before planned construction. [108]

Since, at the two-year construction-certification stage under the Macdonald bill an important element in the utility's petition for certification is that "the project is consistent with . . . [the] regional plan", [109] it may be seen that (1) the regional council's plan carries great legal weight at that point, but (2) its determinations of the centrally important question of generating plant location have not been previously presented to a public agency for approval. At the two-year construction certification stage, that state of affairs may be expected to put substantial pressure on the state-siting agency to go along with the long-range regional plan and approve the utility's proposed construction. Also, it may be expected to put any opponents of the utility proposal in the position of "creating" a power crisis by their opposition—the same position such opponents frequently are alleged to occupy today.

The same analysis may be applied to the treatment by both bills of transmission line cases. Only at the two-year construction-certification stage would a public forum be available for the testing of long-range plans for lines.

Clearly, such a time schedule puts a great premium on the individual utilities working out their differences with opponents prior to the construction-certification stage, if such other parties are to participate meaningfully in the process.

In respect of the two-year construction certification stage, one final point deserves mention. While both bills generally require a proposal for construction to be consistent with the applicable long-range plan,[110] each also contains a "grandfather clause." [111] The Administration bill goes further, however, containing two provisions for outright exception. In one, it requires that the utility shall have selected its power plant site from among the earlier approved five-year inventory or its transmission-line route from among those identified in its ten-year plan, "except for good cause shown." [112] Similarly, *any* element of the two-year construction-certification provision "may be waived by the certifying . . . agency . . . " within four years of the effective date of the Administration bill, "for good cause shown." [113] The expression, "except for good cause shown", is nowhere explained in the bill and so appears to provide a major loophole as against the whole long-range plan approach.

One major point emerges from the foregoing discussion of the two bills' treatment of long-range planning. Neither bill would allow for any effective role for publicly responsible officials at the actual planning stages. The Macdonald bill comes somewhat the closer, however, by requiring that FPC and EPA designees participate as nonvoting members in the industry's regional councils.[114]

The only application of public control under either plan would occur when an agency of one of the fifty states [115] reviews for approval the proposal of an individual utility. (The Administration bill is somewhat stronger here, since, under it, the individual utility would be made directly responsible for long-range planning and would be required to have an "inventory" of power plant sites approved five years before any planned construction.) Although both bills recognize the essential regionality of long-range planning by their reliance on the industry's regional councils, neither bill gives any public agency at any level of government the opportunity to review *and determine* the public issues involved in the councils' planning.

Under both bills, long-range planning is required, and it is "open planning" in the information sense. When it comes to creating a forum for responsible, public decision-making, however, there would be fifty forums, and, in each, Congress would establish a state agency to regulate an individual utility—but there would be no forum or agency competent to regulate the regional councils or to review the whole of a regional plan in the public interest.

d. *Public Participation and Judicial Review.* Neither the Administration bill nor the Macdonald bill goes very far toward expressly setting forth citizen rights of participation in the several planning and decision-making processes the bills contemplate. Only indirectly does either bill offer public intervenors any potential assistance, and neither bill addresses itself to any issues of public participation in the long-range planning process except through various requirements for publication of plans.

With respect to the availability of judicial review, the industry and the states appear to be generally better off than potential environmentalist intervenors under the Administration bill, but probably not under the Macdonald proposal.

Both bills would make long-range planning a foundation-stone of reform. Consistent with their policy in favor of leaving such planning to the utility industry, however, these bills would "open up" that process to the public only to the degree of requiring the various publications of planning data already discussed.[116] The bills contain no directions to either the regional councils or the individual utilities respecting consultation or coordination of planning with public groups. *A fortiori,* there arise no questions of judicial review in connection with the long-range planning process.

Similarly, although each state's single-agency facility-certification program is centrally important to both bills, neither bill sets forth any requirements for citizen participation in either the formulation of the plan by each state or, in the case of the Administration bill, the federal review process. Nevertheless, the Administration bill would provide a special review procedure for any *state* wishing to contest the federal certification agency's refusal to approve the state plan. The state would be authorized to obtain review in the local federal Court of Appeals (not the D.C. Circuit), whose decision might be reviewed by the United States Supreme Court by writ of *certiorari*.[117] No special mention is made of any intervenor rights.[118]

The Macdonald bill contains a general judicial review section [119] applicable also to review of each state governor's certification of his state's establishment of a single agency for facility certification.[120] Since it provides some general pressure favoring public participation in the administrative proceedings to which it applies, it is appropriate to explain it here. It provides that, subject to important exceptions,

"Any person who is aggrieved or adversely affected by agency action . . . may commence a civil action in the United States Court of Appeals for review of such agency action within sixty days . . . . ." [121]

An important exception is the exclusion from the group of persons to whom the foregoing right of review is extended of any

"person (A) who had adequate notice by publication (or other means) of the action and an opportunity to appear or present his views before the officer or agency which took such action and (B) who did not avail himself of such opportunity . . . . " [122]

In addition, the bill includes within the meaning of "agency action" the decisions of an *ad hoc* panel, the recommendation of the FPC or EPA with regard to the empanelling of an *ad hoc* panel, and the certification of the governor of the existence of an acceptable state agency.[123] The exact meaning of "adequate notice by publication (or other means)" is unclear, however. "Adequate notice by publication" of pending agency action is obviously something less than "actual notice," but its minimal requirements are uncertain, and the provision may well lead to litigation if the agencies seek to use this language as a loophole for denying public participation.

In the area of state agency action, public participation and judicial review are given somewhat greater consideration under the

Administration bill. Under the Macdonald bill, there would exist essentially only one incident of state regulatory authority—the individual utility's two-year application for certification of its plans to construct a generating plant or transmission line.[124] This bill provides only that, at that stage, the utility must "make public" its detailed construction plans as filed with the agency.[125] The bill contains no other procedural requirements relating to the public and the proceeding. Nor does it speak to the question of judicial review of the state agency's certification or denial thereof.[126] Since the Macdonald bill would establish no effective federal criteria for the state programs [127] and would provide only the most limited opportunity for federal administrative override of state single-agency decisions,[128] potential intervenors (as well as the utilities) apparently would be left to their devices in the fifty state capitols to obtain whatever procedural safeguards they might.

The Administration bill offers somewhat better prospects for procedural safeguards at the state agency level—for the utility industry and, possibly, for its potential adversaries. Although this bill provides generally that state agency orders and decisions should be subject to review "pursuant to applicable State law . . .," [129] the utilities might, under severe circumstances in two-year site-certification cases, obtain a federal administrative override of state agency action.[130] The interests of public intervenors in site-certification cases might be advanced, depending upon how the President should carry out his responsibilities to establish guidelines for the state programs. Among the requirements established by the Administration bill for those guidelines is that they "shall include":

> "procedures to insure full public participation in the certification procedures through public notice and opportunity for public hearings, consultation with appropriate citizens' groups, rights of intervention and appeal from decisions of the certifying body and other safeguards . . . ." [131]

Depending on the substance of the presidential response to the quoted directive, adequate public participation and opportunities for judicial review might come about under the Administration bill. Beyond that, the bill requires that public notice of such certification hearings must be published [132] and a "full public review" would be required.[133]

Significantly, however, the foregoing provisions apparently apply only to the two-year site and facility certification proceeding under the Administration bill and not to the earlier proceeding for approval of the five-year power-plan site inventories.[134]

It has been pointed out that another possible avenue to review of the state site-certification proceeding, at least under the Administration bill, would be through the federal override available under extreme circumstances to the utilities. Even though such proceedings may not be initiated by opposing intervenors, there remains a question about the rights of such parties once such proceedings may have been begun. The Administration bill requires that the federal certifying agency must provide public notice [135] and "assure full public review".[136] Beyond those directives, however, the federal certification agency procedure is subject to the same presidential guidelines as the state procedure. Thus, potential intervenors should benefit from the same procedural safeguards for public participation and appeal as in the state proceedings—again depending upon the substance of the presidential guidelines.[137] The Administration bill establishes no special public participation requirements, however, for the preliminary FPC determination of electric reliability impairment that would be a condition precedent to the federal override proceeding.[138]

While the final federal certification agency determination would be expressly subject to judicial review pursuant to 5 U.S.C. §§ 701–706,[139] the bill sets forth no special judicial review of either the preliminary FPC determination of electric reliability impairment [140] or the rulemaking proceeding through which that Commission is required to prescribe the facts necessary to constitute a basis for a federal override.[141]

Although the federal override procedure would be far less significant under the Macdonald than the Administration bill, the very same mechanism, the *ad hoc* panel, subject to one set of procedural requirements, is employed by the Macdonald bill for both the limited federal override of state agency actions and the much more important override of EPA, AEC, and Corps of Engineers formulations at the federal level.[142] That bill would impose explicitly virtually no special public participation requirements upon panel proceedings or the various preliminary administrative determinations established as conditions precedent to panel action.[143] The panel decision, however, and all but one of the administrative preliminaries, would be made subject to the general judicial review requirement, quoted above, which may tend to encourage administrative acceptance of public participation.[144] The

208

one exception is the decision of the Interior Secretary to refer a case to a panel. The bill contemplates that the Secretary would be requested to assign particular cases to panels [145] but nowhere would the bill make such a reference mandatory upon such requests. Nor does the bill contain any special provision for judicial review of the Secretary's exercise of that apparently discretionary function.

Finally, it should be recognized that both bills provide for many federal agency determinations for which judicial review is neither required or excluded.[145A] Each of these determinations may or may not be subject to judicial review, depending upon the applicability of 5 U.S.C. § 701 (Supp. V),[145B] but in any event the complexities of these agency determinations may lead to "delay" and litigation.

2. ADDITIONAL COMMENTS ON THE ADMINISTRATION AND MACDONALD BILLS

a. *The Demand Question.* Perhaps the most glaring omission from the Administration and Macdonald bills is their complete failure to address themselves to the demand question. That, of course, may be seen as a function of their focus on the construction and location of bulk power facilities. While each bill in its own way speaks of the need to achieve a proper balance as between the society's needs for reliable electric energy supply and for environmental preservation, they apparently assume that the measure of reliability can continue forever to be the constantly growing level of demand, unexamined by the Congress or any other publicly responsible agency. Ultimately, then, under these bills, only the environmental side of the balance would receive critical examination.

But that approach and its built-in assumption most likely would cause such legislative proposals to be self-defeating. The Administration bill talks grandly of the timely construction of bulk power facilities

"in a manner consonant with the preservation of important environmental values and wise comprehensive use of the Nation's air, land, and water resources for all beneficial purposes, public and private . . . ." [146]

It stresses also, and directs the President to publish criteria for "evaluating," *inter alia*, "the projected needs for electric power" [147] and the "effects of proposed sites and facilities on environmental values." [148]

209

Similarly, the Macdonald bill includes among its purposes meeting "reasonable power needs for the commercial life of the country and the general welfare of the people . . ." [149] and, in doing so, "reasonably to protect the environment, conserve natural resources and plan the proper use of available lands . . .," [150] and of achieving "a publicly acceptable balance of these competing objectives." [151]

To the extent that the demand question—the question whether additional capacity is broadly necessary, broadly consonant with the public interest—may creep into individual licensing proceedings, the issue is unmanageable. Yet the very proper language quoted above from the two bills would seem almost to guarantee that the Courts would require, under either bill, that the "balancing" include all relevant factors, all alternatives, including possible adjustments in demand. Without recognizing that issue and consciously transferring it to a forum wherein it can be addressed responsibly, there is great risk that it will sprout up case by case.

The same analysis may be applied to a closely-related question that has been referred to elsewhere in this paper as the "need question." Neither bill provides for either a national level forum or an effective set of regional forums [152] for the public allocation to particular regions or states of additional capacity that may be acknowledged to be part of a nationally needed increment. To that extent, it would seem to be proper to raise the question case-by-case in every siting proceeding. But the local forum and individual proceeding patently provide an inadequate setting for deciding whether capacity should be located at Storm King as opposed to the Vermont mountains or at Farmington, New Mexico as opposed to Los Angeles.[153]

b. *Restructuring of FPC and AEC.* As noted, both the Administration bill and Macdonald bill quite deliberately leave untouched the existing structure and jurisdiction of the Nation's two separate, primary national electric power agencies. Although the Macdonald bill would provide for an override by its special *ad hoc* panels—an override highly theoretical in the case of the FPC and significantly limited in the case of the AEC—the two Commissions would be allowed to continue their separate, overlapping functions. Also, the inherent development versus regulation conflict, existing within each agency but more pronounced in the case of the AEC, would persist.

210

The actual substantive problems, not to mention the credibility problem, spawned by such conflict of interest are discussed fully elsewhere in this report.[154] These bills totally ignore those issues.

c. *Allocation of National, Regional, and Local Power.* This report has proposed elsewhere,[155] that regulatory jurisdiction over the electric industry should be reallocated in such a way that the profoundly important reliability and environmental issues growing out of its operations might be decided each at a level of government where the greatest public interest lies and where the activities to be regulated may be most effectively controlled. It has been suggested that energy questions, economics, and most research and development questions are of national significance, that the actual functions of the industry have been, very substantially, regionalized, and that land-use questions seem to be matters predominantly of state and local interest.[156]

Both these bills completely ignore the relationship between electric power reliability and the broader questions growing out of the general energy crisis. To the extent that they avoid the demand question, they also turn away from any affirmative consideration of the role of energy, and electric energy, in the economy. As demonstrated above, the long-range planning contemplated by the Administration and Macdonald legislation would be neither public nor national.[157]

Also, the two bills almost completely omit consideration of the great current need for a national research and development program to assure that the United States can apply the best realistically possible technology to the balancing of power and environmental needs. (Other proposed legislation addressing itself to this matter is examined in Section D *infra*.)

It has been demonstrated above that these bills give only the faintest lip service to public regulation at the regional level.[158]

Finally, the bills give no express recognition to the relationship of electric facility-siting and land-use control generally. Although each bill would put the single state agency in a predominant position, neither specifies that siting or routing decisions should be coordinated with general land-use planning.

This Report elsewhere recommends that the land-use aspects of facility siting be separated from other considerations and treated in coordination with general land-use control systems to be created at

211

state and local levels.[159] Other proposed federal legislation, apparently well designed to fit such purposes, is examined below.

d. *The Generic Proceeding.* While these two bills establish a number of new proceedings, they make no attempt comprehensively to take advantage of the substantial recent thinking about the reform of administrative procedure and particularly the newly developed idea of the "generic proceeding" which would, technically, occupy a place somewhere between the traditional "rulemaking" and the traditional "adjudicatory" proceeding.[160] The Administration bill proceeding for approval of each utility's five-year inventory of generating plant sites might be a candidate for such treatment. But no procedural mechanisms have been spelled out.

In any event, the generic proceeding ought to be used throughout the electric power regulatory system, and, of course, these bills do not address themselves to that whole system.

e. *Recognition of Environmental and Safety Considerations within the Overall Balancing Function.* An important premise of this Report is that, while the recently emerging concerns for the environment may have put the administrative law system under great strain, the public interest in legislative reform calls for creative steps forward and not a retrogression that would attempt to sweep away the environmental issues that have proven so troublesome. Thus follows the conclusion that reform electric power legislation should not sweep aside existing standards for air and water pollution, radiation control, and recreation, wilderness, aesthetic, and historic considerations. Most importantly, reform legislation must not compromise the historic, comprehensive balancing function imposed on federal agencies by the Congress in the National Environmental Policy Act.

Institutional structures and procedures certainly should be revised to be made more efficient and more consonant with the public interest. Nevertheless, to the extent that any reform legislation displaces existing procedures, standards, or requirements of law directed toward environmental considerations, it is necessary to ask what replaces the superseded mechanisms.

Of the two bills here considered, the Macdonald bill is by far the worse in terms of the neglect of environmental values. It frequently repeats references to the balance between "reasonable electric power need" and "reasonable environmental factors." Nevertheless, this bill, as pointed out above, first would delegate a substantially unconstrained authority over that balancing function to state agencies, substantially without recourse to federal override,[161] and, second, would authorize its special *ad hoc* panels, which are not responsible public agencies, to override environmental and electric power rules and standards of other agencies (except for AEC radiological safety decisions) in the interest of best achieving that "balance" on a case-by-case basis.[162] With that one exception, the bill provides no firm substantive safeguards for national environmental policy or regulation.

The Administration bill would create no such sweeping breaches in existing environmental policy or control. It would, however, relieve the AEC and the Corps of Engineers (although not the Federal Power Commission) from the NEPA impact statement procedure while providing only the shakiest substitute in a "substantially similar" state agency procedure [163] the federal requirements for which would depend upon the President's establishment of "guidelines" for state agency operations.[164]

Enactment of either of these bills would represent a retrogression from present national environmental policy which is not necessary for the proper accommodation of the Nation's interest in an adequate electric energy supply.

3. Variations on the Administration Bill

The several House and Senate variations on the Administration bill [165] may be divided into two categories, both of which are directed primarily toward the Administration's failure to propose any mechanism for effective public-agency review of industry regional planning.

a. *Regional Councils as Federal Agencies*

In one category may be placed the Hart and Eckhardt-Helstoski bills. Each of these proposals would add to the structure of the Administration bill a statutory regional council replacing the existing industry councils upon which the Administration bill would rely for long-range planning.[166] In each variation, the statutory regional councils would include one representative each from the Federal Power Commission, the Department of Interior, the Environmental Protection Agency, and the Council on Environmental Quality.[167] The Hart bill would add to each regional council one appointee of the governor of each state within the power region.[168]

Every utility would be required to file its long-range plans with the council for its region, which, in turn, would prepare annually a long range plan for the region.[169] The regional plan would be required, among other things, to describe generally the location and type of facilities to be built by each utility in the region during the ensuing fifteen years,[170] identify the location of tentative plant sites and transmission line routes on which construction would be begun within five years,[171] describe generally any alternative facilities rejected in the development of the regional plan,[172] and describe the council's efforts to create a coordinated regional plan to meet identifiable electric power needs [173] and to minimize identifiable environmental problems.[174]

Under the Eckhardt-Helstoski proposal, utilities would be required to select each construction site from the five-year inventory developed by the appropriate regional council and to choose transmission-line routes identified in the council's long-range plans.[175] Under the Hart bill, each state certifying agency would be required to review the regional councils' long-range plans and designate areas within the state suitable and unsuitable for construction of plants and transmission lines.[176] Under the Hart bill, therefore, each utility would be required to choose construction sites from locations thus approved by the appropriate state certifying agency.[177]

Thus, the Eckhardt-Helstoski and Hart bills would make the regional councils into regional Federal agencies, with the Eckhardt-Helstoski councils acting as regulatory agencies, determining where plants may be built. Neither bill, however, would establish any process or public procedure for the councils; and the Hart bill would return the final approval authority of five-year site inventories to the fifty states.[178]

Like the Macdonald and Administration bills, they omit entirely consideration of the demand question, consideration of a unitary Federal agency for all modes of electric generation, consideration of the separation of R & D promotional functions from regulatory functions, and consideration of the generic proceeding and the corollary simplification of the traditional licensing proceeding. Also, they do not go far enough in recognizing the importance of early open, public participation throughout the planning and licensing process.[179]

214

b. *Federal Agency Review of Long-Range Planning*

The Dingell-Moss proposal is simplier structurally and procedurally than the Hart and Eckhardt-Helstoski proposals. Also, more clearly than any other pending bill, the Dingell-Moss proposal would establish a national focus for reform.

First and most important, this variation on the Administration bill would require the Secretary of the Interior to review annually every utility's long-range plans in cooperation with the Council on Environmental Quality and with the assistance of the Federal Power Commission "and other interested departments and agencies." [180]   On the basis of such review, the Secretary would be directed to prepare and publish a proposed national plan for bulk power facilities.[181]   Thereafter he may, in his discretion, consult with state or regional agencies and "any other persons or agencies" thereon and hold hearings.[182] Finally, the Secretary is directed to make such revisions as he deems necessary and promulgate an annual national plan.[183]   Thereafter, the Federal and State site-certifying agencies "shall comply with such plan" in discharging their certification functions.[184]

Additionally, the Dingell-Moss bill would make clearer than the Administration bill the limits upon the authority of the certifying agencies to determine conclusively any questions of compliance with federal law and standards [185] and would provide for federal court review of state certifying agency orders and decisions.[186]

The Interior Department–CEQ–FPC study and promulgation of a national plan would provide the opportunity for an open, public-agency review of the industry's regionalized planning. Any public hearings upon the proposed national plan would almost necessarily emerge in the "generic" form and ought to provide a substantial opportunity for meaningful public input. Unfortunately, the bill would allow the Secretary to determine, in his discretion, whether to hold such hearings and it is silent on related procedural questions. The opportunity, however, for direct federal court review of state certification agencies' orders and decisions would minimize any tendency toward parochialism in state implementation of the national plan.

Two provisions of the Dingell-Moss bill are quite significant. One would eliminate the NEPA impact statement exemption applicable in the Administration bill to proceedings wherein the certifying agency "has followed a substantially comparable procedure." [187] The other would add a specific supplementary balancing requirement on behalf of "the natural beauty of the countryside and public park and recreation lands, wildlife and waterfowl refuges, and historic sites." [188]

The Dingell-Moss bill thus goes much further than any other presently pending legislation toward the aims of the recommendations contained in this Report. That proposal, however, like the others, omits express consideration of the demand question, of a unitary federal agency for all modes of generation, or of separating research and development functions from existing regulatory functions. Finally, although setting the stage for possible generic treatment of planning questions, the Dingell-Moss bill fails actually to require public hearings at the national planning stage. Moreover, it omits the detailed procedure provisions that would be necessary to prevent with certainty the relitigation of issues in *ad hoc* certification proceedings and to guarantee adequate opportunities for active public participation in the planning process.

C. FEDERAL LAND–USE–PLANNING LEGISLATION

In its conclusions (contained in Chapter VIII), this Report recommends, generally, that utility facility siting decisions, by whomever made, should be integrated into the broader fabric of land-use planning. It would be unfair to the utility industry and contrary to the interests of environmental preservation to refuse permission to construct a generating facility at a given location on environmental grounds only to have some other industrial facility with similar environmental impact subsequently permitted at the same spot. Additionally, this Report adopts the view that land-use issues generally are matters of great state and local concern and therefore ought to be regulated primarily by means of state and local decision-making. Clearly, however, such regulatory control and the planning that underlies it must be comprehensive, and probably statewide. It is thought that, if some system of state and local decision-making were to zone for industrial parks (and perhaps even establish land banks) contemplating future construction of electric utility facilities along with other industrial needs, then the utility industry and any public agency in control of facility siting would have, at least in the first instance, a frame of reference for their own decision-making. More importantly, that frame of reference would already have incorporated decision-making on behalf of state and local interests.

Unfortunately, zoning authority, and particularly statewide zoning authority, is not uniformly or fully developed throughout the nation, as would be required by the foregoing scheme.

Two important bills presently pending in the Congress are directed toward developing comprehensive land-use control throughout the country, through the enhancement of state jurisdiction in every state. One bill has been sponsored by Senator Jackson (S. 632, 92d Cong. 1st Sess., hereinafter referred to as the "Jackson bill") and the other, by the Nixon Administration (S. 992, 92d Cong. 1st Sess., hereinafter referred to as the "Administration bill.")

Title III of the Jackson bill contains the meat of the land-use policy and program of assistance to the states. The purpose of the title is:

> "to establish a national policy to encourage and assist the several states to more effectively exercise their constitutional responsibilities for the planning, management, and administration of the Nation's land resources through the development and implementation of *comprehensive state-wide land use plans* and management programs designed to achieve an ecologically and environmentally sound use of the Nation's land resources . . . ." (emphasis added) [1]

The mechanism of Title III is to allow the newly created federal Land and Water Resources Council [2] to make land-use-planning grants (from an annual appropriation of not more than $100 million [3]) to state and interstate agencies that can conform to the standards articulated in section 305 of the bill. [4] The various agencies will be given grants for an initial five-year period in which they are to develop comprehensive land-use plans. [5] After the termination of that five-year period, no state will receive federal grants unless it has developed an approved land-use plan. [6] Perhaps the biggest incentive in this scheme is the provision that after the end of the initial five-year period a state which has not developed an acceptable "land use plan" will not be eligible for certain federal financial support. Federal funds earmarked for any new state-administered action "which may have a substantial adverse environmental impact" or which would "tend to irreversibly or irretrievably commit substantial land or water resources could not be given to such a nonconforming state." [7]

The central mechanism of the Administration bill is much like early federal legislation in the area of pollution in that it provides for federal financial assistance (from an appropriation of not more than $20 million annually [8]) to the *states* [9] upon compliance with certain federal standards.[10] The Administration bill allows three years for the development of the land-use program within each state.[11] Any state which does not have an acceptable land-use program by 1975 will be subject to the following sanction: Any federal agency intending to take action which will significantly affect non-federal lands must hold a public hearing and submit findings to the Secretary of the Interior and if appropriate to the Secretary of HUD.[12]

Both bills provide for a two-phased grants-in-aid program: the first for the development of the land-use program,[13] and the second for the management of an approved land-use program.[14] The magnitude of the grants, however, are dissimilar under the two bills. The Jackson bill would provide federal funding of 90 percent of the development costs for a five-year period,[15] whereas the Administration bill would supply federal grants for only 50 percent of the costs of developing a program over a three-year period.[16] During the second phase, the Jackson bill would limit grants to two-thirds of costs,[17] and the Administration bill would continue federal grants at the rate of 50 percent of costs.[18]

Although each bill provides standards which must be met in order to receive the grants, the Jackson bill specifically outlines the uses to which the land-use grants may be put.[19] Among those uses is the compilation and analysis of information and data related to the projected land-use requirements within the state or region for the "generation and transmission of energy." [20]

The standards which must be met apply to both development and management grants. Significant among the standards established by the Administration bill is the requirement of a system of controls and regulation pertaining to certain areas and developmental activities.[21] Those areas and activities are "areas of critical environmental concern," [22] "key facilities," [23] and "large scale development of more than local significance in its impact on the environment." [24] In comparison, the Jackson bill requires the state or interstate agency to develop, within the initial five-year period, a "statewide land use plan which . . . shall include all lands within the boundaries of the state" except land under the control of the federal government and, at the discretion of a state agency, lands within the boundaries of an incorporated city which has a population in excess of 250,000 or in excess of 20% of the state's total population.[25] Thus, the Jackson bill requires a specific land-use "plan," but the Administration bill speaks only of a land use "program."

The scope of the Jackson bill is considerably greater than that of S. 992, and it is therefore more likely to have an impact upon the siting of power plants. The Jackson bill, in fact, specifically contemplates control of the siting of power plant facilities.[26] The Administration bill, however, could only require the state regulation of power plant siting when such a facility meets one or more of the crucial definitions: "areas of critical environmental concern," "key facility," or "large scale development of more than local significance in its impact upon the environment." [27]

The Administration bill defines "key facilities" as those which "tend to induce development and urbanization of more than local impact" and it provides as examples (1) any major airport, (2) interchanges between the interstate highway system and other highways, and (3) major recreational lands and facilities.[28] In the hearings before the Senate Committee on Interior and Insular Affairs, a representative of the National Association of Electric Companies, made the following comment:

> "S. 992 has another advantage in our view in that it requires the State agency to select and regulate only those decisions which it considers to be of more than local importance. As we read the bill, investor-owned electric power facilities would not normally be classified as 'key facilities as defined in section 102(b). However, many power plants, because of their need for cooling water, would necessarily be located in 'areas of critical environmental concern,' as defined in section 102(a) . . . ." [29]

Thus, the Administration bill is not directed at comprehensive land-use control but, rather, at "spot" control.

Significantly, the Jackson bill includes substantive requirements for the availability of federal grants in its section 305. Illustrative is the requirement that the agency's authority "must include the power to prohibit, under state police powers, the use of any lands in a manner which is inconsistent with the provisions of the plan . . . ." [30] The

Administration bill, however, provides a framework around which both procedural and substantive methods of land-use control may be developed. Under that bill, the details of implementation and the substantive controls are to be determined by the various states.[31]

Of importance is the dissimilarity between the two bills in the sanctions imposed against a state which does not prepare an adequate land-use "program" (the Administration bill) or "plan" (the Jackson bill). Under the former, the absence of an acceptable state program merely requires federal agencies that intend to finance activities which affect land use within such a state to hold hearings.[32] The Jackson bill, however, disallows the expenditure of federal funds within a non-conforming state for any project which will have a substantial effect upon the environment.[33] The bill does provide a loophole: the President may temporarily allow the expenditure of federal funds if he deems the action is necessary for the public health, safety or welfare.[34]

It should be mentioned that Title II of the Jackson bill empowers the President to establish River Basin Commissions [35] whose authority will include the coordination of federal, state, interstate, local, and non-government plans for the development of *land* and water resources within the jurisdiction of each.[36] The jurisdictions of the River Basin Commissions will not, however, be likely to coincide with those of the utility industry's reliability councils. To that extent the Jackson bill's attempt to allow regional control may be unresponsive, or even harmful, to the problems of electricity and the environment.

It becomes obvious that Senator Jackson's bill is far more complete and ambitious than the Administration bill. Its use of specific standards to be met by the state land-use plans and the more pervasive control of the Land and Water Resources Council will make it far more likely to have a positive impact upon electric power plant siting. But the comprehensive requirements of the Jackson bill may make it hard to swallow, and indeed, the staff of the Senate Committee on Interior and Insular Affairs has, at the direction of its Chairman (Senator Jackson), prepared several "Committee prints" which incorporate many provisions of both bills. The third and last of these is (as of this writing) considered as strong as the land-use legislation can be and remain viable in Congress. Unfortunately, from the point of view of this

Report, Committee print number three adopts the Administration's approach of "spot" control instead of the comprehensive planning proposed by the Jackson bill. Additionally, the substantive economic, environmental, and social requirements of section 305 of the Jackson bill are replaced by the implementation and performance guidelines of the Administration bill. If this new version of the land-use bills is to become law, great care must be taken to insure coordination and substantive continuity between it and any power plant siting legislation. How this may be worked out is yet to be seen, but in general it may be asserted that any land-use plan must allow for the determination of power plant siting questions by a separate "utility regulating" authority, which, in turn, must observe the general land-use plan. There need be no requirement that the utility siting authority be on the same level of government as the land-use agency.

D. RESEARCH AND DEVELOPMENT LEGISLATION

This Report elsewhere suggests that substantial, national research and development efforts are required to enhance the technological potential for resolving electricity-and-environment issues that otherwise will require legal solutions. It is suggested, also, that no such R & D effort is now being pressed.

One important piece of pending legislation attempts to address itself to that issue. It is sponsored by Senator Magnuson as a proposed amendment to the Administration facility-siting legislation, discussed above.[1]

The Magnuson amendment would establish a "Federal Power Research and Development Trust Fund"[2] to consist of revenues from a newly created .15 mill per kilowatt hour surcharge, or tax, on electric energy,[3] expenditures from which would be made available, however, only through the Congressional appropriation process.[4] The .15 mill tax would be assessed against all purchasers of electricity for consumption and "every person generating more than 1,000,000 kilowatt hours per year . . . for his own consumption."[5]

The amendment would establish a Federal Power Research and Development Board,[6] exclusively authorized to make use of the revenue deposited in the fund[7] subject, as noted, to Congressional appropriation and directed to conduct an intensive research and development program.[8] The stated specific goals of the program include:

"(1) Increasing the efficiencies of energy generation, transmission, distribution and consumption processes;

"(2) decreasing the adverse environmental impact of present and future energy generation, transmission and distribution;

"(3) achieving . . . new means of reliably generating energy while protecting the environment;

"(4) making increased efficiencies and improved technology directly available to all electric utilities . . .;

"(5) other areas which the Board deems to be within the broad objectives of this title; and

"(6) [the allocation of at least 5% of the fund to projects that] search for adverse social environmental or economic effects of proposed or present technologies." [9]

The Board is also to report annually to Congress. The report must analyze presently funded projects; determine those areas most in need of future funding; analyze the import of energy technologies on electric energy supply and demand, the environment, and the economy; and evaluate the cooperation the Board has received from other governmental agencies and public and private institutions.[10]

Furthermore, the Board is directed to publish a bimonthly "newsletter" to inform all interested parties of current and future projects and proceedings.[11] The Board must give notice in the newsletter and the Federal Register to allow interested parties to "comment" on proposed grants of $5,000,000 or more.[12] In addition, the Board must conduct public hearings annually on its proposed budget for the following year.[13]

The Magnuson bill recognizes the inherent weaknesses and inequitable financial burden of the present purely voluntary research efforts of the industry, and it follows the thinking that a national program is essential to achieve an efficient, mandatory system of R & D funding and to pool research efforts. The establishment of a separate national program also reflects the urgency and priority that presently neglected technological solutions merit. Perhaps more importantly, the provisions requiring Board Members to have no interest in the industry [14] and requiring that all the results of funded projects be made freely available to the public [15] demonstrate an adherence to the policy that solutions to the environment-and-electricity problems are a matter of *public* concern.

Senator Magnuson estimates that the fund will receive about $300 million the first year.[16] Considering the immense effort needed to explore and perfect such new concepts as MHD and fusion, however, it is questionable whether this amount will be sufficient.

E. STATE LEGISLATION

1. INTRODUCTION

Underlying this Report, throughout, is the fundamental conclusion that a viable balancing of society's competing interests in a reliable electric power supply and in a decent, livable environment can be achieved only within a coherent, national framework of legal structure and procedure. This Report contemplates a framework better recognizing (1) the national interests in energy, economics, and research and development questions generally, (2) the regionalization of the electric industry, and (3) state and local interests in land-use control.

Consistent with that fundamental conclusion, the greater part of this Report and of this chapter has been directed toward federal law. Clearly, the several states, by reason of their geographically limited jurisdictions and their frequently competing interests, inherently lack the capacity to determine certain very important matters. First, they cannot achieve any solution to the basic question of demand because of the profoundly complex national economic and social elements of the problem. Similarly, they lack the capacity to promote the scale of research and development needed nationally, both because of the vast funding necessary and because the subject matter is predominantly national in scope, making it, among other things, unlikely that any one state would shoulder real responsibility even if it could do so financially. Finally, the states are incapable of applying a public interest standard to long-range planning sufficiently broad to meet the challenge of a thoroughly regionalized and interconnected electric system in which multi-state if not national considerations determine issues.

Nevertheless, in the absence of federal-level reform, there has arisen a quite understandable concern in state capitols around the land and many proposals for state-level action have been made in the last few years, some having become law. The scope of the states' legisla-

223

tive and administrative programs varies greatly. Some states have developed comprehensive land-use planning legislation; others have directed legislation specifically at the siting of power plants; and in others existing administrative bodies have stepped in and begun to regulate the location of power plants.

What follows is not an exhaustive discussion of the many state programs which affect electric utility siting but, rather, an analysis of some of those programs and attempt to present examples of the variety of ways in which the states have reacted. The purpose of this analysis is to highlight (1) interesting procedural mechanisms that may be useful at any level of government and (2) those land-use planning and control schemes that may merit replication in other states. Examples of the former include the fee imposed by New York law on license applicants to cover procedural costs of certain other parties in certification proceedings and the provision of the Washington statute requiring payment of a similar fee to finance independent scientific and engineering analysis of plant-siting questions. Examples of the latter would be the Maryland and New York land-bank statutes.

2. CALIFORNIA

On March 12, 1969, the Secretary for Resources issued the revised version of *State of California Policy on Thermal Power Plants*.[1] That document established, without specific statutory direction, a procedure through which all the California natural resources agencies participate in site selection and design for all thermal power plants. The resolution declares it to be the policy of the state

"to ensure that the location and operation of thermal power plants will enhance the public benefits and protect against or minimize adverse effects on the public . . . [and] on the ecology . . . ."[2]

Furthermore, the resolution recognizes that because the location of power plants has considerable impact upon the interests of the state, "plant owners should meet with the state's Secretary for Resources early in the planning stage to review and define proposed locations."[3] Thus, it is the state's interest "to seek courses of action which will balance the orderly processes of meeting the increasing demands for power plant location and operation with the broad interests of the public."[4]

To meet the enunciated goals, the resolution establishes the State Power Plant Siting Committee which consists of representatives of each major natural resource-related agency, most of which are elements of the Resource Agency and under the direction of the Secretary for Resources.[5] The various members of the Committee are responsible for reviewing proposed power plant sites, for identifying and working to resolve conflicts, and for communicating in writing the official position and comments of their agencies.[6] Upon the resolution of conflicts, the proponent and the Committee may enter into a formal agreement the effect of which is to pledge the support of the Resources Agency as consideration for the design modifications and restrictions to which the applicant has agreed. Because the Resource Agency is an important party in interest in construction permit hearings before the Public Utilities Commission [7] and the AEC,[8] such a formal agreement may well be a prerequisite to obtaining a construction permit.

The third section of the March 12, 1969 resolution outlines the specific considerations that the Committee must make in reaching a position with regard to the suitability of a proposed power plant location. It is recognized that the guides are to be followed flexibly.[9] Those guides require the state to consider, *inter alia*, the existing policies for air and water quality, the plans of local governments, the overall effect of the proposed plant on the environment, recreational and aesthetic policies, geologic and seismic conditions of the site, and the effect of the plant's use of cooling water.[10]

Thus, the Resource Agency exercises a considerable amount of control over the environmental impact of power generation, and the utilities are given a strong incentive to meet with representatives of the state's agencies and develop acceptable long range plans. The California scheme, however, does not provide for coordination between the PUC and other state agencies. In one case, the PUC, in granting a certificate of public convenience and necessity, attempted to "reverse" the refusal of an air pollution district to permit emissions from a fossil-fuel plant where that refusal effectively prohibited plant construction. At the suit of the air pollution district, the California Supreme Court held that the PUC had no plenary power, ruling that only the California courts could reverse the district's decision.[11]

Perhaps in an attempt to remedy the lack of coordination between agencies, California enacted the "Power Plant Coordination Act" in 1970.[12] That act requires the Resources Agency to develop a "plan indicating the optimum location for all electric power generating plants" expected to be constructed within 20 years and to submit the plan to the legislature by the beginning of the 1973 session.[13] The plan must "identify locations deemed suitable from an environmental standpoint," [14] and contain recommendations of the type of fuel to be used at each site "so that the least deleterious effect on the environment is achieved consistent with reasonable economy and efficiency of operation." [15]

The Resources Agency's control over the Power Plant Siting Committee and its duty to make a long-range inventory of acceptable sites may allow sufficient coordination of long-range planning and site certification merely because both functions are conducted under the same roof. Thus, as long as the Resources Agency is mindful of the public interest its considerable power will help the PUC and the AEC to properly balance the problems of environment and the need for electricity. The general public, however, is not able to enter the planning function, and is not allowed to voice its opinions until the licensing hearings commence.

At present, the greatest criticism of the California scheme may be its lack of an overriding legislatively created mechanism for resolving the issues of power and the environment. Certainly, there is no single state authority with power to make final decisions with regard to questions of land use or environmental quality. Thus, the present scheme is totally incompatible with any of the proposed federal power plant siting or land-use legislation.

3. MAINE

Maine has enacted a statewide land-use regulation mechanism,[16] the general scheme of which is to classify the state's land and to establish "land use guidance districts and standards," based on "sound land use planning and development guidance." [17] The purposes of the Act are carried out by the "Maine Land Use Regulation Commission," [18] and the provisions of the Act apply to all unorganized and "deorganized" areas of the state,[19] with the significant exception that:

> "Real estate used or to be used by a public service corporation may be wholly or partially exempted from regulation, when upon timely petition to the Public Utilities Commission and after a hearing, the said commission determines that such

226

exemption is necessary or desirable for the public welfare or convenience." [20]

Thus, it would appear that the Public Utilities Commission may have direct control of electric utility facility siting. But a 1970 amendment to the state's "Water and Air Environmental Improvement Commission" legislation has given that Commission broad powers to control the site location of "commercial and industrial developments." [21] It is this recent legislation that deals directly with the problems of electric power facility location and the environment. [22]

The Water and Air Environmental Improvement Commission consists of 10 members, appointed by the governor, two of whom "represent" each of the four following interests: manufacturing, municipalities, "the public generally," and conservation. The final two members of the Commission must be "knowledgeable in matters relating to air pollution." [23] Thus, the membership of the Commission is designed to allow it to balance the competing interests of environmental preservation and development. Among the responsibilities of the Commission is the "duty":

"to control, abate, and prevent the pollution of the air, waters, coastal flats and prevent diminution of the highest and best use of the natural environment of the State." [24]

In 1970, the Maine legislature found that the economic and social well-being of its citizens depended upon "the location of commercial and industrial developments with respect to the natural environment of the State .   .   ." [25] and that the location of developments that are capable of irreparably damaging the environment "is too important to be left only to the determination of the owners of such developments .   .   .   ." [26] Thus, the Commission was empowered to use the police power of the state to control the location of those developments so that they "will be located in a manner which will have a minimal adverse impact on the natural environment of their surroundings." [27]

The mechanism of control over the location of commercial and industrial developments is as follows: Before the construction of a facility may commence, the developer must give notice of its intention to the Commission, [28] and the Commission must (within 14 days) either approve the proposed location or schedule a public hearing on the matter. [29] The Commission must approve a development proposal if

227

it finds that (1) the applicant has the financial and technical ability to meet state pollution standards, (2) the development has made adequate provisions for traffic movement, (3) the development "will not adversely affect existing uses, scenic character, natural resources or property values . . .," and (4) the development will be upon "suitable" soil types.[30]

If a hearing is necessary, it must be held within 30 days of the Commission's decision not to approve the application, notice by publication must be given the public, a complete transcript must be made of the hearings, and the Commission must make its findings and give its order within 45 days of the adjournment of the hearing. The order of the Commission may grant or deny the application, and it may grant permission to construct "upon such terms and conditions as the Commission may deem advisable to protect and preserve the environment and the public's health, safety and general welfare." [31]

If a developer fails to notify the Commission [32] or if a developer fails to obey the order of the Commission,[33] the Attorney General must bring an appropriate civil action.[34] Indeed, if the developer had failed to give notice of its intention to construct to the Commission, the Commission may order the developer to restore the affected area to its condition prior to construction.[35]

Unfortunately, the legislation allows for judicial review only at the request of an applicant.[36] The review is limited to the record of the hearing and the court must decide whether the order of the Commission is supported by substantial evidence.[37]

The effect of the power of Maine's Water and Air Environmental Improvement Commission to control the location of electric power generating facilities and transmission lines may be significant. Certainly it will give the utilities strong incentive to consider environmental impact in their choice of location, and the mechanism provides for an efficient determination. There are, however, a number of aspects of the Maine scheme that do not meet the recommendations of this report.

Perhaps most important is that all planning functions are left to the utilities. The Water and Air Commission passively reacts to the proposals of the industry, and public impact is limited to those situations in which the Commission has determined that a utility's plan may substantially affect the environment. As a result, the Commission will doubtless be put in the position often of having to choose between

228

harming the environment and ordering a utility to undo complex and expensive planning, which may have been under way for decades. The pressure will be against requiring the utility to waste previously committed funds. Moreover, an intervenor who is displeased with such a decision by the Commission does not have standing under the legislation to obtain judicial review.

Another difficulty with Maine's control of utility facility location is the dispersal of authority among the state agencies. Although the interrelationships among the Maine Land Use Regulation Commission, the Public Utilities Commission, and the Water and Air Environmental Improvement Commission have been carefully spelled out,[38] their interactions may prove to be complex and wasteful. At any rate, the division of authority among these agencies clearly makes each ineligible for the "single state agency" requirements of pending federal power plant siting and land use legislation.

4. MARYLAND

The Maryland Power Plant Siting Law (Senate Bill No. 540) was passed in April 1971 and has been in effect since January 1, 1972. This elaborate legislative scheme amends many sections of the Annotated Code of Maryland and provides for coordinated action by the Public Service Commission, the Department of Natural Resources, and the Secretary of Health and Mental Hygiene. The law established two new mechanisms: (1) the "Environmental Trust Fund" which is to be managed by the Secretary of Natural Resources to provide for various research programs, long range power plant site evaluation, and power plant site acquisition,[39] and (2) expansion of the Public Service Commision's responsibility with regard to the issuance of certificates of public convenience and necessity to include the construction of all power plants and all transmission lines that may carry more than 69,000 volts.[40]

The Environment Trust Fund (hereinafter the "Fund") is to be independently funded by means of a "surcharge" on all electricity generated in the state, which is initially set at 0.1 mill per kilowatt-hour and which may be increased up to 0.3 mill per kilowatt-hour.[41] In addition, all revenue from the temporary use [42] or ultimate sale or lease to electric companies of property acquired by the Department of Natural Resources is to be deposited in the Fund.[43] Thus, the Fund is expected to be supplied with $4–6 million annually.[44] The primary function of the Fund is to finance the operation of the "Power Plant Environmental Research Program," which includes *inter alia*: the study of the biology and ecology of the state's waters, research on the environmental effect of electricity generation, the monitoring of the environmental effects of power facilities, the evaluation of the environmental impact of proposed electric power plant sites, the evaluation of the environmental effects of electric power technologies, the investigation of possible constructive uses for waste heat, and the analysis of the impact of power facility location on land use in the state.[45]

Additionally, the PSC and the Secretary of Natural Resources must work together with the state's electric companies to identify possible sites for the construction of new electric power plants. The utilities must submit annually their long-range (ten-year) plans "regarding generation needs and means for meeting those needs." [46] The PSC must assemble and evaluate those plans and annually forward a 10-year "plan of possible and proposed sites" to the Secretary of Natural Resources.[47] That department must then identify, on the basis of environmental considerations, acceptable locations,[48] and commence detailed investigations of those sites within "the plan." [49] The information developed in the Power Plant Environmental Research Program is to be utilized in the preparation of a detailed environmental statement on each site upon which construction is not to commence before July 1, 1974.[50] It is expected that the detailed statements will be published at least two years before construction is expected to commence.[51]

The Secretary of Natural Resources is charged with the duty of acquiring a number of desirable sites in the name of the state.[52] That number is to be determined upon "growth" information supplied by other agencies,[53] but the Secretary must hold at least four but not more than eight suitable sites at any one time.[54] The acquisition of such sites is financed by the Fund,[55] and revenue from the temporary or ultimate disposition of property so acquired is to be paid to the Fund.[56] Electric companies may, accordingly, purchase or lease such sites from the Fund, and the use of such sites cannot be impeded by any local law.[57] Even when leasing the property, however, the utilities must pay appropriate local property taxes.[58]

The second reform mechanism created by Senate Bill No. 540 prohibits the commencement of construction of a generating station or transmission line designed to carry more than 69,000 volts or the exercise of the right of eminent domain in connection therewith without having first obtained from the PSC "a certificate of public convenience and necessity" for the construction of the station or the line.[59] "Construction" is defined to include "any clearing of the land . . . or other action that would affect the natural environment . . . ."[60] After July 1, 1972 utilities must file an application for the certificate two years prior to the commencement of construction, but that two-year lead requirement may be waived by the PSC "for good cause shown."[61] The Secretary of Natural Resources is required to make an environmental investigation and recommendation with regard to each application.[62] The PSC must hold public hearings on all applications for a certificate, and it may take final action only after considering *inter alia* "the need to meet present and future demands for service . . . economics, esthetics, historic sites . . . and . . . the effect on air and water pollution."[63] The legislation takes pains to make the issuance of a certificate the exclusive state determination of both environmental and "need" questions.[64] Finally, any "party or person in interest" dissatisfied by the final determination of the PSC is entitled to judicial review, and the Secretary of Natural Resources is specifically given standing to seek judicial review.[65]

The site-certification procedure thus created is designed to allow input from the various agencies and the public to help the PSC determine the proper balance between environment and power needs. Typically, however, there is no requirement of public input prior to the application for a certificate. The elaborate provisions of the legislation with regard to the Fund and its long-range planning functions are nowhere directly connected to the site-certification process. Thus, the highly visible utility planning and environmental research called for by the legislation is not necessarily tied to the actual site-certification process. Presumably, the recommendation of the Secretary of Natural Resources[66] would take cognizance of the planning activities under his direction and the findings of the Fund's research programs, but nowhere are the two mechanisms directly coordinated.

Perhaps the legislature envisioned that the "land bank" program[67] would become the major vehicle for site selection. If that becomes the case, a detailed environmental impact statement[68] should be published before any particular site is chosen for construction. The exclusive use of sites upon which the Department of Natural Resources has published a detailed environmental statement would successfully coordinate the functions of the Fund and the PSC siting procedure, and, thus, allow

231

public planning well in advance of an electric company's application for site certification. That the legislature intended to make the environmental scrutiny of the Secretary of Natural Resources apply to sites owned by the utilities *and* those acquired by the state is apparent from the following provision:

> "[s]ites either owned or purchased in the future by electric companies shall be included in the inventory of possible and proposed sites." [69]

The phrase "possible and proposed" sites, however, clearly refers to sites which may later be determined unsuitable,[70] and, thus, utilities may ultimately attempt to gain certification for sites that the Secretary of Natural Resources has excluded from the land bank. Such a turn of events would put great pressures on the PSC, which could be avoided if the exclusive use of land bank sites were written into the statute.

Despite the uncertainty of the relationship between the two mechanisms created by Senate Bill No. 540 and some overly intricate division of functions between the PSC and the Secretary of Natural Resources, the Maryland legislation is ambitious and promising. It establishes well-funded programs of research, land acquisition, and long-range planning. The success of these programs and their coordination with the site-certification mechanism should be watched carefully.

5. NEW YORK

In New York, two statutory policies are worthy of note. The newer relates to the certification of electric utilities and the older to the "land bank" idea.

a. *Facility-Certification Legislation.* In 1970, New York had added Article VII to its Public Service Law requiring the Public Service Commission (PSC) to certify all major utility transmission facilities.[71] In 1972, major supplementary legislation was enacted providing for the licensing of generating facilities.[72] That new legislation presents a comprehensive, carefully coordinated plan for the certification of major steam electric generating facilities and long-range electric system planning.[73] The new mechanism is not unlike the plans developed in other states in that it prohibits the commencement of construction of a power plant without first obtaining a "certificate of environmental compatibility and public need" [74] from a newly created "state board on electric generation siting and the environment." [75] As in California, the Board consists of representatives of interested state agencies,[76] with the PSC Chairman serving as Chairman of the Board.[76A] In addition, it is required that the Governor shall appoint to the Board, for each certification proceeding, an *"ad hoc* member." The *ad hoc* member in each case "shall be a resident of the judicial district in which the facility as primarily proposed is to be located." [77] Typically, also, the Board must hold public hearings on every application; [78] it must issue a decision granting, denying, or conditionally granting a certificate; [79] and the decision is subject to judicial review limited by "substantial evidence rule." [80]

The new enactment, however, goes beyond the legislation of other states in several significant ways. Worthy of mention is the requirement that each application be accompanied by a fee of $25,000.[81] The fees are to be used to establish a fund a defray certain expenses of municipalities that are parties to application proceedings (except for any municipality which itself is the applicant). Covered expenses include the cost of transcripts, postage, service of documents, and the publication of notices. The legislation authorizes the PSC to provide such services for municipalities in lieu of payment from the fund. Thus, non-applicant municipalities will be afforded the opportunity to participate fully without financial restriction in both the certification hearings and any judicial review thereof. This innovation would be even more significant if the legislature extended such financial assistance to other non-applicant parties.

In addition, the new Article VIII includes a wide range of affected persons in its definitions of "party." Among those explicitly allowable as parties are: any municipality in which the power plant, or a portion thereof, is to be located; any individual residents of such a municipality; any non-profit organization formed to promote certification, the protection of the environment, personal health, the preservation of historical sites, consumer interests or the orderly development of the affected area; and any municipality or resident thereof located within a five-mile radius of the proposed facility.[82] These provisions clearly are intended to promote effective public participation in the site-certification procedure.

Although the statute requires neither public participation nor public agency approvals in the early stages of utility planning, it does require each utility annually to file with the Department of Public Service its long-range plans for future operation.[83] Moreover, in a certifica-

tion proceeding, the Board must find that a proposed power plant location "is consistent with long range planning objectives for electric
power supply in the state" or it cannot issue the certificate.[84]

The official element of a newly enacted program that merits comment is certain language covering coordination among the several levels
of government. Two sections of the statute speak to the relationship
between the Board and Federal agencies. The first excludes from the
purview of the legislation over which any agency or department of the
federal government "has exclusive jurisdiction, or has jurisdiction concurrence with that of the state and as exercised such jurisdiction, to
the exclusion of regulation of the facility by the state."[85] Although
this language is not a model of clarity, it is apparently intended that
any overlapping of state and federal site-certification processes should
be avoided. For example, the state would avoid concern with the radiological safety requirements for nuclear power plants.

The second provision for coordination between the state agencies
and the federal government specifically allows the Board to avoid re-
dundant hearings:

> "The Chairman of the Commission may enter into an agree-
> ment with any agency or department of the United States
> having concurrent jurisdiction over all or part of the location,
> construction, or operation of a major steam electric generating
> facility subject to this article with respect to providing for a
> joint hearing of common issues on a combined record pro-
> vided that such agreement shall not diminish the rights ac-
> corded to any party under this article." [86]

Thus, the statute makes specific provision to prevent needless duplication of scrutiny by both state and federal agencies. Unfortunately,
similar provisions are absent from most states' site-certification schemes.

The statute also includes provisions for the coordination of state
and local policies. One of the findings which the Board must make in
order to certify an application is that the proposal will comply with
state and local laws.[87] Thus to avoid conflicting local laws, the Board
is given the power to refuse to apply any otherwise applicable local
law or requirements that the Board determines to be "unreasonably
restricted" in view of "existing technology, or of factors of cost or
economics, or of the needs of consumers. . . ."[88] Additionally,
the statute includes an overriding provision that no state agency or

municipality may require any approval or license-type conditions for the construction or operation of a power plant except in accordance with otherwise applicable state laws for employee protection.[89] Thus, the legislation eliminates conflicts such as those that have arisen in California [90] and have expressly provided for "one-stop" certification at the state level. Carefully worded provisions for the avoidance of intrastate conflicts such as these should be included in any state site-certification legislation.

A major criticism of the new legislation is that it does not attempt to unite the certification of electric generation facilities and transmission lines under the same regulatory mechanism. These aspects of the utility industry's planning are closely interrelated and should be controlled by means of the same administrative procedure.

b. *Land Bank Legislation.* In New York, the advanced selection of sites for nuclear power plants and their inclusion in a "land bank" inventory is the responsibility of the state Atomic and Space Development Authority. The Authority is statutorily authorized to select, acquire, develop and furnish, through sale or lease arrangements with the State's utilities (including the State Power Authority) sites selected in a fashion intended to assure their suitability for the construction of nuclear power plants and related facilities.[90A]

The objective of the program is to identify and set aside appropriate sites before they become committed to other less vital land uses. Since the sites are sought well in advance of the need to install power plants, substantial time is provided for the Authority to perform environmental studies, engineering analysis, and land development planning in coordination with surrounding communities. Authority policy aims to assure also that use of sites for other compatible public purposes, such as conservation, recreation, sewage treatment, and water recycling, is explored to the maximum extent and made a part of the site's development plan.

In the selection of sites, the Authority is advised by a Nuclear Power Siting Committee which includes other state officials and utility industry representatives. The chairman of that Committee is the Deputy Commissioner of Environmental Management of the state Department of Environmental Conservation.

Authority policy calls for full participation by governmental agencies, industry, and the public prior to the selection of a site. Discus-

235

sions and consultations are held with local officials, planning boards, civic groups, and conservation groups. Local community meetings are held to accord the public-at-large an opportunity to become informed and express its views. In advance of any decision as to suitability of a site, a report is published containing extensive information with respect to such site and describing the manner in which it is planned to be developed.

The extensive site and environmental information developed by the Authority with respect to a selected location is intended to serve, later, in defining the design bases for proposed power generating facilities and by providing basic data needed in construction and operation license proceedings.

6. VERMONT

In April of 1969 Vermont enacted what must be the most concise power facility site-certification legislation in the nation.[91] In a single statutory section Vermont prohibits the preparation for or construction of an electric generating facility or transmission lines capable of carrying more than 48,000 volts without the prior approval of the public service board, requires a public hearing on each petition, and sets forth the findings which the public service board must make in order to issue its approval.[92] Before the public service board may approve a petition—by issuing a "certificate of public good"—it must find that the construction:

(1) will not unduly interfere with the orderly development of the region with due consideration having been given to the recommendations of the municipal and regional planning commissions and the municipal legislative bodies;

(2) is required to meet the need for present and future demand for service;

(3) will not adversely affect system stability and reliability and economic factors; and

(4) will not have an undue adverse effect on aesthetics, historic sites, air and water purity, the natural environment and the public health and safety.[93]

Despite the brevity of the statute it provides for procedure whereby the necessary balancing between environmental and power needs may be applied to every major power facility. Because of its brevity, however, the legislation omits a number of provisions which other states have deemed important aspects of their schemes. Absent is any provision to avoid redundancy between federal and state licensing proceedings; absent is a legislative resolution of possible intrastate conflicts; there is no provision for long-range planning by the utilities or the public; the discretion necessarily given the public service board with regard to applying the vague standards for certification may invite time-consuming litigation; and there is no indication of the scope or availability of judicial review.

7. WASHINGTON

The Washington State Thermal Power Plant Siting Act [94] has been in effect since February 23, 1970. The legislation and the regulations promulgated thereunder [95] have created a comprehensive and unique mechanism for the certification of major thermal power plants [96] and associated transmission lines.[97] Certification, or denial thereof, is made by the governor [98] upon the recommendation of a thermal power plant site evaluation council [hereinafter the Council]. The Council is composed of representatives of fifteen state agencies that have regulatory responsibilities over, or interest in, the location of power plants.[99] An additional member is appointed by each county legislature for deliberations on a site located within its jurisdiction.[100]

The Washington mechanism is premised on a typical prohibition of construction [101] of any facility for which there is no prior certification.[102] Not unlike the procedure in other states, an application for certification must be made to the Council,[103] but Washington requires each application to be accompanied by a fee of $25,000.[104] The fee is used to defray the cost of an "independent consultant study to measure the consequences of the proposed power plant on the environment," and the legislation requires the Council to commission such an independent study for each site application.[105] Thus, an environmental impact study, free from the control of the applying utility, will be made of every proposed site. This unique aspect of the Washington mechanism goes a long way to protect the public's interest in protecting the environment. But query whether $25,000 is sufficient to fund a thorough examination of the environmental impact? Moreover, the legislation requires the attorney general to

"appoint an assistant attorney general or a special assistant attorney general as a counsel for the environment   .   .   .

237

[who] shall represent the public and its interest in protecting the quality of the environment . . . until such time as the certification is issued or denied." [106]

The provision for a counsel for the environment does not prevent any person from being heard or being represented by counsel in any of the proceedings established by the legislation.[107] Those proceedings include: "informational" public hearings addressed to, among other things, the question of the compatibility of the proposal with local land use plans or zoning ordinances; [108] "formal," adjudicatory, public hearings at which "any person shall be entitled to be heard in support of or in opposition to the application for certification;" [109] a rehearing of the governor's final decision; [110] and judicial review of the governor's final decision.[111] The regulations allow any person whose interests may, as a practical matter, be impaired by the disposition of the site application to petition for intervention.[112] Intervenors are allowed to participate fully in all proceedings, and they are given, *inter alia*, the right to petition for a rehearing of the governor's final decision.[113] In sum, the Act and the regulations provide the public with opportunities meaningfully to participate at every stage of the certification procedure.

Perhaps the most unusual aspect of the Washington scheme is the lack of final decision-making power in the Council. Within 12 months of the date of receipt of an application, the Council must report its recommendation to the governor,[114] but it is the governor who must (within 60 days of the Council's report) approve or reject the application.[115] It should be noted that the Council's report must include, *inter alia*, "a statement indicating whether the application is in compliance with the council's topical guidelines . . . ." [116] The guidelines [117] require exhaustive studies on the environmental impact of a proposal to be furnished by the applicant and, furthermore, require the applicant to agree to provide such things as "a program and schedule to cover pre- and post-operational air quality monitoring . . . ." [118] and "replacement and/or compensation for any wildlife, fish and other aquatic life and eco-system damage or loss caused by project construction and operation.[119]

The decision of the governor may be made, apparently, notwithstanding the recommendation of the Council or the Council's statement with regard to the applicant's compliance with its topical guidelines. The final decision, however, is subject to judicial review.[120] The

238

mechanism, thus, allows an elected official to determine certification on the basis of his perception of the public interest.

If the governor's decision is in the affirmative, the Council must (within 30 days of the governor's decision) compose a certification agreement, containing any necessary conditions, for execution by the governor and the applicant.[121] The statute, accordingly, provides for enforcement of such an agreement by authorizing the courts to grant injunctive relief and civil penalties from $1,000 per day to $25,000 per day of construction or operation in material violation of the agreement.[122] Those penalties also apply to construction or operation without the required certification, and criminal sanctions are applicable to those who willfully violate the provisions of the statute.[123] These tough and explicit enforcement provisions are lacking in other states' certification statutes.

Finally, the Washington statute provides for intergovernmental coordination by making the Council-governor decision-making process the single requirement for power plant certification at the state level. The statute supersedes any other provision of state law or rule or regulation promulgated thereunder [124] and the "issuance of a certificate shall be in lieu of any permit   .   .   .   required by any department, agency, division, bureau, commission or board of this state." [125] Thus, any possible interagency conflict is removed. Furthermore, the statute bluntly declares that the state "hereby preempts the regulation and certification of thermal power plant sites and thermal power plants .   .   .   ." [126] Conflicts between the state and local governments are thereby obviated. Unfortunately, the legislation makes no provision for coordination between the state procedure and the federal government.

In sum the Washington thermal power plant siting legislation is a comprehensive and unusual approach to the problem. Despite the uncertainty of the effect of the delegation of final decision-making authority to the governor, the legislation should be noted for its many innovations: the financing of independent environmental research by a $25,000 application fee, the appointment of a "counsel for the environment," provision for intervention and public input at the various proceedings, the tough enforcement provisions, and the clear state-wide preemption of power plant regulation. Finally, the absence of any provision for long-range planning also sets this scheme apart from those of other states and may reflect the legislature's understanding of the regional nature of long-range planning problems. The statute contains no provisions for coordination with federal regulatory programs and therefore makes no attempt to ease the way for any later federal or federally regionalized approach.

8. PROPOSED MODEL STATE POWER FACILITY-SITING ACT

In a thoughtful law review article Mr. Henry E. Lippek has proposed a model power facility siting statute which combines and adds to many of the best provisions of the various state schemes.[127] The Model Act prohibits the construction of any non-hydroelectric power plant of 50 megawatts or more or transmission lines capable of carrying 200,000 volts or more without the approval of the "certifying agency."[128] The certifying agency may be either the "State Power Facility Siting Council" or an interstate/regional agency governed by the provisions of the Model Act.[129] Unlike the provisions of most states' statutes the Council is not composed of representatives of interested State agencies, rather the members are all appointed by the governor to equally represent environmental interests, development interests, and the public at large. No more than five of the nine members may be affiliated with the same political party.[130] Like the Maryland plan, the agency is empowered to "assess and collect a surcharge on all electricity generated in its jurisdiction sufficient to meet the agency's reasonable budget requirements."[131]

The Model Act [131A] requires the certifying agency to oversee interrelated long-range planning and site certification. There are two components of the act's long-range planning provisions: (1) The certifying agency must conduct independent studies to map those areas of its jurisdiction "where power facilities can be constructed and operated with the least adverse effect on the environment . . .," and thereafter the agency "shall require all electric utilities within its jurisdiction to locate power facilities only at these sites." [132] (2) Each electric utility must "individually or as part of a single regional plan" annually submit to the agency a plan indicating, *inter alia*, what power facilities will be constructed, altered, or retired within the next ten years and the specific location of any facility that will be constructed within the next five years.[133] Moreover, the Model Act makes all plans submitted to the certifying agency available for public inspection.[134]

In addition, the Model Act requires the certifying agency to obtain the participation of other state agencies in the planning process by sending each a copy of the long-range plans and inviting their comments. The agency must also send copies to and invite the comments of interested federal and local governmental units, citizen environmental protection groups, individuals who have requested copies, and the media.[135] Public participation in long-range planning is not, however, limited to the filing of written comments. The agency must hold informational hearings within 45 days of the receipt of the utilities' plans for the purpose of reviewing and commenting thereon.[136] Thus, the Model Act far exceeds the provisions of any state's statute with regard to public participation in long-range electric utility planning. By means of active solicitation of governmental and public comment on the utilities' long-range plans the certifying agency should be able to coordinate the location of power facilities so that, at the certification stage, utility applications for specific facilities should rarely invite public outrage and the reversal of utility plans.

The certification process is not dramatically different from that of the states earlier examined. The utilities must apply for certification two years in advance of anticipated construction, and the application must include, *inter alia,* a detailed environmental impact statement.[137] Of importance is the requirement that the application discloses that it is "in pursuance of the [long-range] plans publically [sic] filed or, if at variance, the reasons therefore . . . ."[138] The agency must conduct a public hearing on each application within approximately 90 days of receipt thereof.[139] Before the hearing, however, the agency must give eight weeks of public notice;[140] must transmit the application to all interested governmental agencies, citizen groups, and persons;[141] and must notify the Attorney General of the application, who, in turn, must "appoint a special counsel for the environment."[142] As under the Washington statute, the special counsel is to represent the public's interest in protecting the quality of the environment, and the appointment of the special counsel shall not prevent any person from being heard or represented by counsel in accordance with the provisions of the act.[143] The agency is delegated the power to prescribe the rules for the hearing, but it must "allow full participation by the public and other interested agencies of state and local government."[144]

In addition to holding a public hearing on each application, the certifying agency is required to consult with and obtain the comments of "local, state, regional and national planning, resource development, and environmental power [sic] and conservation groups."[145] Finally, the agency must conduct its own independent study of the environmental impact of the proposal financed by the application fee.[146]

In general, the environmental and design standards to be applied in deciding upon each application are to be developed by the agency,[147] but the statute sets forth few considerations and requirements. Although the agency may impose more stringent "pollution control, design and location standards . . .," [148] the agency is required, as a minimum, to incorporate in the certification all standards and requirements established by all local, state, and national "pollution control and land-use planning agencies." [149] The agency may waive unreasonable and arbitrary local regulations.[150] More generally, the agency must consider the balance between need and environmental impact, the extent of the applicant's R & D efforts, and "the measures the applicant has taken to conserve the use of power." [151] Specifically, the Model Act requires the agency to deny a certification of the proposal if it would use park land or other restricted property or violate pollution standards.[152] Additionally, the application must be denied if "interconnection and coordination with neighboring systems to reduce the need for new generating facilities and increased reliability has not been fully explored . . . . " [153]

The entire process of application, consultation, hearing, study, and decision is to take no longer than two years.[154] The decision of the certifying agency is to be final except that judicial review, on the substantial evidence rule, is made available.[155]

The Model Act provides that the certifying agency has exclusive jurisdiction over power facility siting and that "no other state or local agency may require additional permits or otherwise impede the certification received by the electric utility." [156] The effect of this broad language is, however, uncertain in light of other provisions of the act that require the electric utilities to comply with all state and local standards and requirements.[157]

Finally, the Model Act gives standing to the certifying agency to seek whatever injunctive relief or civil penalties are necessary to secure compliance with the provisions of the act or with the terms of a site certification.[158] Appropriate local or state officers and affected citizens may also bring civil or criminal actions to enforce the act or a certificate.[159]

In summary, a number of the most important features of Mr. Lippek's Model Act should be set forth. The most extensive innovation is the act's thorough application of this report's conclusion that long-range planning must involve the public from the beginning. The Model Act's requirements of governmental and citizen commentary and public hearings on the utilities' long-range plans, together with the certifying agency's active determination of the inventory of possible sites, provide for meaningful citizen participation and public decision-making in planning for power facilities.

Equally important is the Model Act's intended recognition of the regional nature of power facility siting problems. To that end the act allows the certifying agency (including the long-range planning functions) to be an interstate, regional body. Indeed, the bill authorizes and *encourages* the governor to enter into agreements with neighboring states for the purpose of establishing such an agency.[160] This authorization may allow a progressive state to establish its own power facility siting council and thereafter remove its functions and powers to an interstate agency. That flexibility would provide a vehicle for the development of regional control over the problems of electricity and the environment. But query: is there any assurance that regions formed by interstate agreement will conform to the realities of existing regionalization within the industry, and, moreover, how likely are the states to surrender their sovereignty to a regional agency?

The bill wisely borrows Maryland's independent funding approach by allowing the agency to assess and collect a surcharge on all electricity generated within its jurisdiction. Furthermore, it adopts the innovative environmental protection measures of the Washington statute: independent environmental studies funded by an application fee and special counsel for the environment. Omitted, however, is New York's proposed use of application fees to finance the clerical and administrative expenses of intervention by municipalities. But again we must ask if $25,000 is sufficient funding for the independent studies.

Finally only the Model Act attempts to deal with the demand problem. The Model Act requires the certifying agency to consider, in deciding upon each application, "the measures the applicant has taken to conserve the use of power," [161] and to deny certification to any utility that has not fully explored "interconnection and coordination with neighboring systems to reduce the need for new generating facilities." [162] Avoiding waste of energy and inefficient, overexpansion of generating capacity certainly is ameliorative. It must be recognized, however, that no single state—or even region—can provide fundamental solutions to a problem vitally affecting national economic development and national welfare.

NOTES FOR CHAPTER VII

(Part B)

1. *Hearings on H.R. 5277, H.R. 6970, H.R. 6971, H.R. 6972, H.R. 3838, H.R. 7045, H.R. 1079, and H.R. 1486 Before the Subcomm. on Communications and Power of the House Comm. on Interstate and Foreign Commerce*, 92d Cong., 1st Sess. (1971).

2. H.R. 11066, 92d Cong., 1st Sess. (1971) [hereinafter cited as *Macdonald*].

3. H.R. 5277, 92d Cong., 1st Sess. (1971) [hereinafter cited as *Administration*].

3A. H.R. 13966, 92d Cong., 2d Sess. (1972) [hereinafter cited as *Eckhardt-Helstoski*].

3B. H.R. 15199, 92d Cong., 2d Sess. (1972) [hereinafter cited as *Dingell-Moss*].

3C. S. 1684, 92d Cong., 1st Sess. (1971), introduced by Senators Magnuson and Cotton, by request.

3D. S. 1915, 92d Cong., 1st Sess. (1971) [hereinafter cited as *Magnuson-siting*].

3E. S. 3631, 92d Cong., 2d Sess. (1972) [hereinafter cited as *Hart*].

4. A number of other bills have been introduced in the Ninety-Second Congress. See, for example, the list contained in the title of the Macdonald Hearings, *supra* note 1. Since no such other proposals presently appear likely of passage, they are not included in this analysis.

5. *Administration* § 2; *Macdonald* §§ 401(1), 401(2).

6. *Administration* § 2(d); although not expressed as a "purpose" of the Macdonald bill, *see Macdonald* §§ 407 and 409 dealing, respectively, with the expediting of federal proceedings and the avoidance of serious obstacles to the construction of bulk power facilities.

7. *Administration* §§ 2(b), 2(f); *Macdonald* § 402.

8. *Administration* § 5; *Macdonald* § 405.

9. *Administration* § 7(a); *Macdonald* § 405(b) (1).

10. *Administration* § 5(b).

11. *Id.* § 5(c).

12. *Macdonald* § 405(b). Prior to the formation of such a single agency, the Macdonald bill would require only that the Governor coordinate the activities of such state and local agencies as might have some authority over plant siting.

13. *Administration* § 11; *Macdonald* § 406.

14. *Administration* § 6(d).

15. *Macdonald* § 409(a) (2); *See also* § 410 establishing a very limited federal override procedure to review environmental issues.

15A. *Macdonald* §§ 412(c) (1), 412(c) (2).

16. *Administration* §§ 6(d), 7(a).

244

17. *Macdonald* §§ 409, 411, 412 ; *see also Macdonald* § 410.

18. *Macdonald* § 412(a) (1) (A).

19. The "Federal certifying agency" is defined in § 3(d) of the Administration bill as "such Federal agency, agencies or department as may be designated by the President . . . ."

20. *Administration* § 9. In that section it is provided that those guidelines "shall include":

"(a) criteria for evaluating effects of proposed sites and facilities on environmental values ;

"(b) criteria for use in evaluating the relative environmental impacts of alternative sites ;

"(c) criteria for evaluating the projected needs for electric power ;

"(d) procedures to insure full public participation in the certification procedures through public notice and opportunity for public hearings, consultation with appropriate citizens' groups, rights of intervention and appeal from decisions of the certifying body and other safeguards ;

"(e) procedures with respect to the formation of regional certifying bodies ;

"(f) procedures to assure proper consideration of multistate impacts in certification proceedings ;

"(g) requirements with respect to staffing and technical and professional competence of State and regional certifying bodies."

21. *Administration* § 5(b).

22. *Id.* § 6(a).

23. *Id.* § 6(a).

24. *Id.* § 6(d).

25. *Id.* § 6(d).

26. *Id.* § 7(a).

27. *Id.* § 16(b).

28. *Id.* § 3(c). The omission to exempt nuclear plants appears to mark a return to the pre-1970 state of the law, wherein the AEC authority, although completely preemptive with respect to radiation protection matters, Minnesota v. Northern States Power Co., 447 F.2d 1143 (8th Cir. 1971), *aff'd*, 40 U.S.L.W. 3483 (April 4, 1972), does go beyond such consideration. *See* Calvert Cliffs' Coordinating, Inc. v. AEC, 449 F.2d 1109 (D.C.Cir., 1971) and New Hampshire v. AEC, 406 F.2d 170 (1st Cir. 1969).

29. *Administration* § 16(a).

30. Greene County Planning Board v. FPC, 455 F.2d 412 (2nd Cir. 1972). The FPC would not be exempted because facilities subject to that Commission's hydroelectric licensing jurisdiction would not be subject to certification under this bill.

31. Calvert Cliffs' Coordinating Comm., Inc. v. AEC, *supra* note 28, and Izaak Walton League v. Schlesinger, 337 F.Supp. 287 (D.D.C.1972).

32. Kalur v. Resor, 335 F.Supp. 1 (D.D.C.1971).

33. In the less typical cases where such plants might be approved by the new federal certification agency pursuant to § 6(a) or § 6(d) of the Administration bill, the NEPA impact statement procedure would be the responsibility of that agency, but still not of the AEC or the Corps.

34. *See, e. g., Administration* § 8 setting forth the several categories of action that every such certifying agency is "directed" to carry out, and § 9 directing the President to establish guidelines for the certification programs. The latter section, however, does require the President to include "criteria for use in evaluating the relative environmental impacts of alternative sites". *Id.* § 9(b).

35. *Macdonald* § 409(a).

36. *See* text at note 65 *infra*.

37. *Macdonald* § 409(a).

38. *Id.* § 411(a) (2).

39. *Id.*

40. *Id.*

41. *Id.* § 411(b) (3).

42. *Id.* § 411(b) (1) (B).

43. *Id.* § 411(c) (1).

44. *Id.* § 411(d).

45. *Macdonald* § 409(b) (1); *see* text at note 65 *infra*.

46. *Macdonald* § 409(b) (3).

47. *Id.* § 409(b).

48. *Id.*

49. *Id.* § 412(a) (1).

50. *Id.* § 412(a) (2).

51. *Id.* § 412(c) (1).

52. *Id.* § 412(c) (2) (A).

53. *Id.* § 412(c) (1) (A).

54. It is provided that a reviewing court may stay the effectiveness of a panel decision but only if "(A) the petitioners would suffer irreparable harm [absent such a stay] and (B) the court has reason to believe that the petitioners are likely to be successful on the merits." *Id.* § 412(c) (3). The bill fails to specify whether "the merits" upon which a petitioner might be successful include issues involving the panel's failure to observe federal law. In § 412(a) (2), the bill expressly authorizes the panel to nullify environmental standards for certain limited purposes and, in § 412(a) (3) expressly limits the panel's freedom to tread upon certain types of historic sites and public lands. Accordingly, there appears to be at least some ambiguity as to all other non-radiological federal law.

55. *Id.* §§ 409(b) (1) and 409(a), respectively. Another section, somewhat curiously worded, provides:

"If in seeking to achieve an acceptable balance among each of the elements which are included in reasonable environmental factors, the panel determines that the achievement of such balance requires authorizing modifications of standards or regulations which relate to environmental factors and which are prescribed under any Federal law (other than a provision of the Atomic Energy Act relating to radiological safety), in order to achieve the objectives of other Federal laws relating to environmental factors (but not in order to provide a more economical supply of electric power), the panel in selecting a proposal may authorize such modifications and in such case it shall so advise the agencies concerned with the administration of such laws." *Id.* § 412(a) (2).

That language probably relates only to the possibility of conflict between or among environmental standards. Nevertheless, its potential is not at all clear, especially considering (1) the loose procedural context in which such balancing is to be carried out by the panels, see text at notes 49 and 50 *supra*; and (2) the definition of "environmental factors" contained in § 415(2) of the bill:

> "The term 'environmental factors' means factors relating to environmental protection, including control of air and water pollution, waste disposal, conservation of natural resources, and *appropriate use of available land.*" (emphasis added).

56. It is to be presumed that the FPC, in deciding under § 409(a) of the Macdonald bill, whether a case involves the likelihood that reasonable power needs will be jeopardized, would not find its own Commission proceedings at fault in a hydroelectric project case. Accordingly, it seems unlikely that any pumped storage project cases would ever go to a panel.

57. *See* text at note 16 *supra*.

58. *Macdonald* § 405(b).

59. *Id.* § 409(a) (2).

60. *Id.* § 409(a).

61. *See, e. g.,* § 405(a) (2).

62. "In order to promote uniformity, insofar as practicable," § 408(a) of the Macdonald bill directs the Secretary of the Interior to publish "criteria which should be considered in making such evaluations."

63. *Id.* § 410.

64. *Id.* § 410(a) (3).

65. *Administration* §§ 2(f), 4, 8; *Macdonald* §§ 402, 403, 404.

66. *Administration* § 2(f); *Macdonald* § 402(a).

67. *Administration* § 6(b); *Macdonald* § 404(a).

68. *Administration* §§ 4(a) (2), 8(c).

69. The earlier discussion of the contemplated state siting agencies, text at note 8 *supra*, indicates that, under the Administration bill, wherever a federally approved state site-certification plan is in effect, the single state agency has jurisdiction in that state over all but federally owned utilities over which the federal certification agency would have jurisdiction. Under the Macdonald bill, it appears that, wherever a state's governor has certified the existence of a single state agency, that agency has jurisdiction, arguably over federally owned utilities as well. Under either bill, a federal instrumentality could take exclusive jurisdiction in states having no single-agency plan.

70. While both bills refer to the establishment of possible "regional" interstate compact agencies, the degree of realism involved in such references may be measured by the extent of their precatory tone. *See* text at note 65 *supra*.

71. *Administration* § 2(f).

72. *Macdonald* § 403(a).

73. *Id.* § 403(b).

74. *Id.* § 403(d).

75. *Id.* § 403(e). No *result* of such work, however, is exempted from the application of such laws.

76. *Administration* § 4(a).

77. *Id.* § 4(b).

78. *Id.*

79. *Id.* § 4(a) (1).

80. *Id.* § 4(a) (2).

81. *Id.*

82. *Id.* § 4(a) (3).

83. *Id.* § 4(a) (4).

84. Presumably the federal site-certifying agency is directed by § 8 of the Administration bill to carry out the enumerated functions only in respect of those utilities subject to its certifying authority, that is the federally owned utilities and those utilities operating within states not having established or effectively continued their own site-certification programs approved by the federal agency. The § 8 functions would, then, be carried out by state site-certification agencies for all other utilities.

85. *Administration* § 8(a).

86. *Id.* § 8(b).

87. *Id.*

88. *See* note 84 *supra.*

89. *Administration* § 8(c).

90. *Id.*

91. *See* text at notes 8–17 *supra.*

92. *Administration* §§ 6(a), 6(b).

93. *Id.* § 6(b).

94. *Macdonald* § 402.

95. *Id.* § 402(a).

96. *Id.*

97. *Id.* § 402(b).

98. *Id.* § 402(b) (8).

99. *Id.* § 402(b) (2).

100. *Id.* § 402(b) (3).

101. *Id.* § 402(b) (4).

102. *Id.* § 402(b) (1).

103. *Id.* § 402(b) (5).

104. *Id.* § 402(b) (6).

105. *Id.* § 402(b) (7).

106. *Id.* §§ 404(a), 405.

107. *Id.* § 402(c).

108. *See* text at note 89 *supra.*

109. *Macdonald* § 404(a).

110. *Administration* § 6(b) ; *Macdonald* § 404(a).

111. *Administration* § 6(a) ; *Macdonald* § 404(b).

112. *Administration* § 6(b).

113. *Id.* § 6(c).

114. *See* text at note 73 *supra.*

115. *See* note 84 *supra.*

116. *See* text at notes 87, 94 *supra.*

117. *Administration* § 5(e).

118. Query, however, whether the general provision of *Administration* § 15 would provide any basis for a public intervenor to obtain review of a federal approval at this stage:

> "The orders or decisions of the Federal certifying agency pursuant to this Act shall be subject to review pursuant to the provisions of sections 701–706 of title 5, United States Code." *Id.* § 15.

119. *Macdonald* § 413.

120. *Id.* § 413(d) (1) (C).

121. *Id.* § 413(a) (1).

122. *Id.*

123. *Id.* §§ 413(a) (1), 413(d) (1).   In the case of the formulation of state site-certification programs, it would seem to have the effect of putting the several Courts of Appeals into the reviewing role occupied by the federal certification agency under the Administration bill.

124. *Id.* § 404(a).

125. *Id.*

126. The general judicial review provision, *Macdonald* § 413, would not apply to such proceedings.

127. *See* text at note 61 *supra.*

128. *See* text at note 15 *supra.*

129. *Administration* § 15.

130. *Id.* § 6(d).

131. *Id.* § 9(d).

132. In each daily and weekly newspaper serving the affected area. *Id.* § 8(d).

133. *Id.* § 7(b).

134. The term, "site certification procedures" does not appear intended to apply to the "mandatory public hearings" which are "to decide whether or not any such sites should be approved for inclusion in the electric entity's five-year inventory of sites." *Id.* § 8(c). That proceeding is nowhere in the bill characterized as a "certification procedure."

135. *Id.* § 8(d). *See* note 132 *supra.*

136. *Administration* § 7(b).

137. *Id.* § 9(d).

138. *See Id.* § 6(d).

139. *Id.* § 15.

140. *Id.* § 6(d).

141. *Id.*

142. *Compare Macdonald* § 410 *with Id.* § 409.

143. *See Macdonald* §§ 409, 410.

144. *Id.* § 413. *See* text at notes 121 and 122 *supra.*

145. By the FPC under *Macdonald* § 409 or the EPA under § 410.

145A. See *e. g.*, the limited meaning of "agency action" in *Macdonald* § 413(d).

145B. *See Citizens to Preserve Overton Park, Inc.* v. *Volpe,* 401 U.S. 402, 409 (1971).

146. *Administration* § 2(a).

147. *Id.* § 9(c).

148. *Id.* § 9(a).

149. *Id.* § 401(1).

150. *Id.* § 401(2).

151. *Id.* § 401(3).

152. *See* text at note 13 *supra.*

153. *See* the opinion of Judge Kaufman in Greene County Planning Board v. FPC, 455 F.2d 412, 423 & n. 27 (2nd Cir., 1972) and the dissenting opinion of Judge Oakes in Scenic Hudson Preservation Conf. v. FPC, 453 F.2d 463, 482 (2nd Cir. 1971).

154. *See* discussion in Chs. IV, V *supra.*

155. *See* discussion in Ch. VIII *infra.*

156. *See* discussion in Ch. VIII *infra.*

157. *See* text at notes 114, 115.

158. *See* text at note 13.

159. *See* discussion Ch. VIII *infra.*

160. *See* discussion in Ch. VIII *infra.*

161. *See* text at note 15 *supra.*

162. *See* text at note 37 *supra.*

163. *See* text at note 29 *supra.*

164. *See* note 20 *supra.*

165. *See* text at notes 3A, 3B, 3D, and 3E *supra.* The Magnuson siting bill is so similar to the Administration bill in ways germane to this analysis that it is not included in the instant discussion.

166. *Eckhardt-Helstoski* § 3(a); *Hart* § 3(a): These bills would utilize the existing regions as defined and established by the Federal Power Commission.

167. *Eckhardt-Helstoski* § 3(a); *Hart* § 3(a).

168. *Hart* § 3(a).

169. *Eckhardt-Helstoski* § 4(a); *Hart* § 4(a).

250

170. *Eckhardt-Helstoski* § 4(a) (1) ; *Hart* § 4(a) (1).

171. *Eckhardt-Helstoski* § 4(a) (2) ; *Hart* § 4(a) (2).

172. *Eckhardt-Helstoski* § 4(a) (4) ; *Hart* § 4(a) (4).

173. *Eckhardt-Helstoski* § 4(a) (5) ; *Hart* § 4(a) (5).

174. *Eckhardt-Helstoski* § 4(a) (6) ; *Hart* § 4(a) (6).

175. *Eckhardt-Helstoski* § 6(b).

176. *Hart* §§ 8(a) and 8(b). The federal certifying agency would carry out the same function in respect of its jurisdiction and any interstate compact ("regional") agency would do the same.

177. *Hart* § 6(b).

178. The *Eckhardt-Helstoski* and *Hart* bills vary from the *Administration* bill, and from each other, in a number of additional ways not mentioned herein. For example, both bills attempt to clarify, in their respective versions of § 7(a), the limits on certification agency authority to determine conclusively questions of compliance with federal law and standards; the *Hart* bill employs language like that contained in the *Dingell-Moss* bill discussed, below, at note 183. Also, both bills eliminate from § 16(a) the Administration bill's exemption from the NEPA 102(2) (C) impact statement requirement discussed, below, in the context of *Dingell-Moss* at note 185; and the *Hart* bill employs in § 7(c) the supplementary balancing requirement discussed, below, in the same context at note 186. Other variations appear less important to the instant discussion.

179. Extensive provisions for publication of data on planning are all to the good, but not as effective as where joined with a decision-making process encompassing opportunities for public intervention. The *Hart* bill, in §§ 8(g) and (h), provides for an independent public consultant and independent public counsel to be appointed in the state certification proceedings, and, in § 16(d), provides for liberal judicial review of the state agency determinations obtainable by public interest groups. But such provisions do not take the place of an open planning proceeding.

180. *Dingell-Moss* § 4(c).

181. *Id.*

182. *Id.*

183. *Id.*

184. *Id.* Any interstate compact ("regional") site-certifying agencies would be similarly restricted.

185. *Id.* § 7(a).

186. *Id.* § 15.

187. *Id.* § 16(a) ; and see *Administration* § 16(a).

188. *Dingell-Moss* § 7(c), employing language from the Department of Transportation Act recently enforced by the Supreme Court in Citizens to Preserve Overton Park, Inc. v. Volpe, 401 U.S. 402 (1971).

NOTES FOR CHAPTER VII

(Part C)

1. S. 632, 92d Cong., 1st Sess. § 303(a) (1971) [hereinafter cited as *Jackson*].

2. *Id.* § 101.

3. *Id.* § 404.

4. *Id.* § 304(a).

5. *Id.* § 305(b).

6. *Id.* § 305(c).

7. *Id.* § 315(a).

8. S. 992, 92d Cong., 1st Sess. § 112(a) (1971) [hereinafter cited as *Administration Land Use*].

9. *Id.* §§ 103(a), 104.

10. *Id.* § 104.

11. *Id.* § 103(a).

12. *Id.* § 107.

13. *Administration Land Use* § 103; *Jackson* §§ 304, 305(b).

14. *Administration Land Use* § 104; *Jackson* §§ 304, 305(c).

15. *Jackson* § 310(a).

16. *Administration Land Use* § 103(a).

17. *Jackson* § 310(a).

18. *Administration Land Use* § 104.

19. *Jackson* § 304(b).

20. *Id.* § 304(b) (2) (F).

21. *Administration Land Use* § 104(a) (7).

22. *Id.* § 104(a) (1).

23. *Id.* § 104(a) (2).

24. *Id.* § 104(a) (6).

25. *Jackson* § 305(b) (1).

26. *Id.* §§ 301(b), 304(b) (2) (F).

27. *See* notes 22–24 *supra*.

28. *Administration Land Use* § 102(b).

29. *Hearings on S. 632 and S. 992 Before the Senate Comm. on Interior and Insular Affairs*, 92d Cong., 1st Sess., at 400 (1971).

30. *Jackson* § 305(c) (4).

31. *Compare Administration Land Use* § 104 *with Jackson* § 305.

32. *Administration Land Use* § 107.

33. *Jackson* § 315(a).

34. *Id.* § 315(b).

35. *Id.* § 201.

36. *Id.* § 201(b) (2).

NOTES FOR CHAPTER VII

(Part D)

1. Amend. No. 364 to S. 992, 92d Cong., 1st Sess. (1971). This Amendment would add a new § 18 to the Administration's "Power Plant Siting Act of 1971" and in turn add a new pt. IV to the Federal Power Act, consisting of §§ 401–410.

2. *Id.* § 403.

3. *Id.* § 402.

4. *Id.* § 403.

5. *Id.* § 402.

6. *Id.* § 401(a).

7. *Id.* § 403.

8. *Id.* § 404.

9. *Id.* § 404(a).

10. *Id.* § 406.

11. *Id.* § 407(a).

12. *Id.* § 407(b).

13. *Id.* § 408.

14. *Id.* § 401(a).

15. *Id.* § 409.

16. 117 *Cong.Rec.* S. 12923 (daily ed. Aug. 3, 1971).

NOTES FOR CHAPTER VII

(Part E)

1. New England River Basins Commission, *Power and the Environment Report No. 3* (Mar. 1972) [hereinafter *NERBC report No. 3*] appendix G–I.

2. *Id.* § I.

3. *Id.*

4. *Id.*

5. *NERBC report No. 3* at 89, appendix G–I § II.

6. *NERBC report No. 3*, appendix G–I § II.

7. The California PUC has adopted rules requiring the consideration of environmental issues in its proceedings with regard to the certification of generating stations over 50 MV. Case No. 9015 (Cal.Publ.Util.Comm'n. filed Jan. 27, 1970) 1 *Envir.Rep.* 148.

8. NEPA has been held to require the consideration of environmental issues in AEC licensing proceedings. *See* pt. B note 28 *supra*.

9. *NERBC report No. 3*, appendix G–I, § III.

10. *Id.*

11. *Orange Co.* v. *PUC,* 2 ERC 1602 (Cal.Sup.Ct., 1971). The decision suggests, however, that the standard of review may be quite liberal in such cases.

12. *Cal.Publ.Util.Code* §§ 2851–2855 (Supp.1971).

13. *Id.* § 2852.

14. *Id.* § 2853.

15. *Id.* § 2854.

16. Use Regulation, M.R.S.A. tit. 12, §§ 681–689 (Supp.1972).

17. *Id.* § 685–A.

18. *Id.* § 683.

19. *Id.* § 682, 1., § 681, § 683.

20. *Id.* § 685–A, 11.

21. Water Improvement Commission, Article 6: Site Location of Development, *M.R.S.A.* tit. 38, §§ 481–488 (Supp.1972).

22. H.P. 918 (Legislative Document 1264), enacted June 22, 1971, amended the Revised Statutes 38, § 488 to make the site location powers of the Water and Air Environmental Improvement Commission applicable to electricity transmission lines of 125 kilovolts or more. It also amended § 484 of that statute to make it clear that all power generating facilities and transmission lines carrying 125 kilovolts or more must be approved by both the Water and Air Environmental Improvement Agency and Public Utilities Commission. The scope of approval required of the latter was declared by the same Act of June 22, 1971 by adding § 13–A to Revised Statutes title 35 (Public Utilities and Carriers). That new section requires the PUC to make findings only with regard to "need" for proposed power generation facilities and transmission lines of 125 kilovolts or more.

23. Water Improvement Commission, Article 1. Organization and General Provisions, *M.R.S.A.* tit. 38, § 361 (Supp.1972).

24. *Id.*

25. Water Improvement Commission, *M.R.S.A.* tit. 38, § 481 (Supp.1972).

26. *Id.*

27. *Id.*

28. *Id.*

29. *Id.*

30. *Id.* § 484.

31. *Id.*

32. *Id.* § 485.

33. *Id.* § 486.

34. *Id.*

35. *Id.* § 485.

36. *Id.* § 487. This should be compared with the availability of judicial review to "any person aggrieved" by an order or decision of the Maine Land Use Regulation Commission. Use Regulation, *M.R.S.A.* tit. 12, § 689 (Supp. 1972).

37. Water Improvement Commission, *M.R.S.A.* tit. 38, § 487 (Supp.1972).

38. *M.R.S.A.* tit. 35, § 13–A (Supp.1972); *M.R.S.A.* tit. 38 § 484 (Supp.1972); *see* note 22 *supra*.

39. *Anno.Code of Md.* Art. 66C, §§ 766–771 (Supp.1971).

40. *Anno.Code of Md.* Art. 66C, § 5A; Art. 78, §§ 54A, 54B, 90 (Supp.1971).

41. *Anno.Code of Md.* Art. 66C, §§ 766(a), 766(b) (Supp.1971).

42. *Id.* § 769(a) (2).

43. *Id.* § 769(b).

44. Comments of the Dept. of Natural Resources on SB540: Fiscal Report (mimeo 1971).

45. *Anno.Code of Md.*, Art. 66C, § 767 (Supp.1971).

46. *Id.* § 768(a) (1).

47. *Id.*

48. *Id.* § 768(a) (2).

49. *Id.* § 768(a) (3).

50. *Id.*

51. *Id.*

52. *Id.* § 769(a) (2).

53. *Id.* §§ 768(a) (4), 769(a) (2).

54. *Id.* § 769(a) (2).

55. *Id.*

56. *Id.* § 769(b).

57. *Id.*

58. *Id.*

59. *Anno.Code of Md.* Art. 78, § 54A (Supp.1971).

60. *Id.*

61. *Id.* § 54B.

62. *Anno.Code of Md.* Art. 66C, § 5A (Supp.1971).

63. *Anno.Code of Md.* Art. 78, § 54A (Supp.1971).

64. *Anno.Code of Md.* Art. 43, § 706 (Supp.1971); *Id.* Art. 66C § 726; *Id.* Art. 96A, § 11; *Id.* Art. 78, § 54B(a).

65. *Anno.Code of Md.* Art. 78, § 90 (Supp.1971).

66. *See* note 62 *supra*, and accompanying text.

67. *Anno.Code of Md.* Art. 66C, § 769 (Supp.1971).

68. *See* note 49, *supra*, and accompanying text.

69. *Anno.Code of Md.* Art. 66C, § 769(a) (1).

70. *Id.* § 768(a).

71. *N.Y.Public Service Law* §§ 120–130 (McKinney Supp.1971).

72. Act of May 24, 1972, ch. 385, [1972] N.Y.Laws 195th Reg.Sess. [McKinney's Session Law News of New York, No. 6, at 823 (June 10, 1972)].

73. The new legislation adds a new Article VIII to the Public Service Law [hereinafter cited as "PSL Art. VIII], §§ 140–151.

74. *Id.* § 141.1.

75. *Id.* § 140.4.

76. *Id.* In New York, however, the Board is composed of the chairmen of the various agencies.

76A. *Id.*

77. *Id.*

78. *Id.* §§ 143–145.

79. *Id.* §§ 146–147.

80. *Id.* § 148.

81. *Id.* § 142.6.

82. *Id.* §§ 144.1(h), 144.1(i), 144.1(j), 144.1(k).

83. *Id.* § 149–b.

84. *Id.* § 146.2(e).

85. *Id.* § 141.4(c).

86. *Id.* § 145.4. The Chairman of the PSC serves as Chairman of the Board. *Id.* § 140.4.

87. *Id.* § 146.2(d).

88. *Id.*

89. *Id.* § 149–a.

90. *See* note 11 *supra*, and accompanying text.

90A. N.Y.Pub.Auth.Law § 1854. The description of the Authority's program is based upon the Authority's 1971 Annual Report, pp. 7–14.

91. *V.S.A.* tit. 30, § 248 (1970).

92. *Id.*

93. *Id.*

94. *R.C.W.A.* §§ 80.50.010–.900 (Supp.1971).

95. *Wash.Admin.Code* ch. 463–08; *Id.* ch. 463–12 (1970).

96. *R.C.W.A.* § 80.50.060(1) (Supp.1971).

97. *Id.* § 80.50.020(7).

98. *Id.* § 80.50.100(2).

99. *Id.* § 80.50.030(3).

100. *Id.* § 80.50.030(4).

101. "Construction" is defined in *R.C.W.A.* § 80.50.020(12) (Supp.1971).

102. *Id.* § 80.50.060(1).

103. *Id.* § 80.50.070(1).

104. *Id.*

105. *Id.* § 80.50.070(2).

106. *Id.* § 80.50.080.

107. *Id.*

108. *Id.* §§ 80.50.090(1), 80.50.090(2); *Wash.Admin.Code* § 463–08–035 (1970).

256

109. *R.C.W.A.* § 80.50.090(3) (Supp.1971); *Wash.Admin.Code* § 463–08–040 (1970).

110. *Wash.Admin.Code* § 463–08–055 (1970).

111. *R.C.W.A.* § 80.50.140 (Supp.1971).

112. *Wash.Admin.Code* § 463–08–025 (1970).

113. *Id.* § 463–08–030.

114. *R.C.W.A.* § 80.50.100(1) (Supp.1971).

115. *Id.* § 80.50.100(2).

116. *Id.* § 80.50.040(10) (a).

117. *Wash.Admin.Code* ch. 463–12 (1970).

118. *Id.* § 463–12–030(5).

119. *Id.* § 463–12–035(2) (c).

120. *R.C.W.A.* § 80.50.140(1) (Supp.1971).

121. *Id.* § 80.50.100(4).

122. *Id.* § 80.50.150(1).

123. *Id.* § 80.50.150(2).

124. *Id.* § 80.50.110(1).

125. *Id.* § 80.50.120(3).

126. *Id.* § 80.50.110(2).

127. Lippek, "Power and the Environment: A Statutory Approach to Electric Facility Siting," 47 *Wash.L.Rev.* 35 (1971) [hereinafter cited as *Lippek*].

128. *Lippek* at 64, "Proposed State Power Facility Siting Statute" [hereinafter cited as *Model Act*] § I(a). It is to be understood that this proposal is not a product of the Commissioners on Uniform State Laws.

129. *Lippek* at 65, *Model Act* § II.

130. *Lippek* at 65, *Model Act* § II(a).

131. *Lippek* at 65, *Model Act* § III(a).

131A. *See* note 128, *supra.*

132. *Lippek* at 67, *Model Act* § IV(a).

133. *Lippek* at 67, *Model Act* § IV(b).

134. *Lippek* at 67, *Model Act* § III(m).

135. *Lippek* at 68, *Model Act* § IV(c) (1).

136. *Lippek* at 68, *Model Act* § IV(c) (2).

137. *Lippek* at 68, *Model Act* § IV(e).

138. *Lippek* at 68, *Model Act* § IV(e) (1).

139. *Lippek* at 70, *Model Act* § IV(f) (7).

140. *Lippek* at 69, *Model Act* § IV(f) (1).

141. *Lippek* at 69–70, *Model Act* § IV(f) (1).

142. *Lippek* at 70, *Model Act* § IV(f) (3).

143. *Id.*

144. *Lippek* at 66, *Model Act* § III(g).
145. *Lippek* at 70, *Model Act* § IV(f) (4).
146. *Lippek* at 70, *Model Act* § IV(f) (2) ; *Lippek* at 65, *Model Act* § III(a).
147. *Lippek* at 66, *Model Act* §§ III(h), III(i).
148. *Lippek* at 70, *Model Act* § IV(f) (6).
149. *Lippek* at 70, *Model Act* § IV(f) (5).
150. *Id.*
151. *Lippek* at 71, *Model Act* § IV(f) (8).
152. *Lippek* at 71, *Model Act* § IV(f) (9).
153. *Lippek* at 71, *Model Act* § IV(f) (9) (iii).
154. *Lippek* at 71, *Model Act* § IV(f) (10).
155. *Lippek* at 71, *Model Act* § V(a).
156. *Lippek* at 71, *Model Act* § V(a).
157. *See* notes 149, 152 *supra*, and accompanying text.
158. *Lippek* at 72, *Model Act* § V(b).
159. *Lippek* at 72, *Model Act* § V(c).
160. *Lippek* at 65, *Model Act* § II(b).
161. *Lippek* at 71, *Model Act* § IV(f) (8) (i).
162. *Lippek* at 71, *Model Act* § IV(f) (9) (iii).

VIII. RECOMMENDATIONS

A. Introduction

As the preceding chapters have demonstrated, the new awareness of environmental problems, coupled with rising demands for power, has brought to the surface deep-seated flaws in the present system for regulating electricity and the environment. Among its its most critical defects, the present system

(1) fails to address itself to such key issues as the level of energy demand and the proper allocation of research funds;

(2) decides recurring issues on a piecemeal basis rather than generically;

(3) allows relitigation of once-decided issues due to multiple licensing requirements;

(4) takes more time than is necessary, in some cases, to reach decisions, thereby preventing timely construction of needed facilities;

(5) fails to provide for adequate public disclosure of important facts;

(6) presents unnecessary obstacles to public participation; and

(7) fails to inspire essential public trust in the objectivity of the results reached.

The Committee's recommendations attempt to deal with each of these criticisms.

1. The Failure to Address Key Issues

Initially, an institutional structure is proposed which can treat all relevant issues and which, through its jurisdiction over all energy forms, not just electricity, provides a means for considering questions of overall national energy policy. Separate institutions for developmental and regulatory duties at the federal level would end the mingling of these inconsistent functions. A single commission should handle the regulatory duties presently assigned to the Federal Power

259

Commission and the Atomic Energy Commission, as well as research into, and recommendations concerning, broader energy issues, and review of electric utility system planning. Also, a separate agency would consolidate developmental research on all energy forms and permit an allocation of funds based on a balanced overview of the alternatives available.

2. THE FAILURE TO DECIDE ISSUES GENERICALLY AND TO PREVENT RELITIGATION OF ISSUES

To remedy piecemeal treatment and possible relitigation of issues, certain issues should be treated apart from and in advance of the licensing proceeding: questions of proper demand policies (ultimately a legislative question), allocation of research efforts, the amount of new capacity needed, and proper safety, environmental and land use standards. Not all aspects of these issues can be settled generically in advance, but many can, and to the extent they can, relitigation during the licensing process proper should not be permitted.

3. THE FAILURE TO REACH TIMELY DECISIONS

The problem of failure to reach timely decisions, as well as the problem of failure to treat underlying questions adequately, is attacked by the Committee's recommendations for increased use of generic proceedings. Other proposals intended to reduce time needed for decision-making are those which recommend much more pre-hearing disclosure of information (aimed at shortening discovery and cross-examination during the hearing itself), and an earlier start for the entire planning-licensing process, to permit disputes to surface and be resolved well before new facilities are needed. As additional assurance that timely decisions will be reached, federal override of state licensing is proposed where states fail to provide sites for needed facilities within a specified time, and states are authorized to license facilities whether or not certain approvals (not including air, water and safety approvals) have been received.

4. THE FAILURE TO MAKE ENOUGH INFORMATION AVAILABLE

The need for full availability of information is recognized by the Committee's recommendation (mentioned above) for routine pre-hearing disclosure of agency information, whether or not favorable to pending or future applications. Other recommendations which seek to promote the flow of information include those for greater public participation in agency/applicant negotiations, greater public access to all government experts, separation of regulatory from developmental functions, and adequate funding for research on environmental shortcomings of existing and proposed technologies, within the Environmental Protection Agency.

5. THE FAILURE TO PERMIT SUFFICIENT PUBLIC PARTICIPATION
AND TO ENCOURAGE PUBLIC TRUST

The value of public participation in decision-making is recognized by the disclosure measures already discussed as well as the recommendations for the simplification of agency procedures which are needlessly burdensome to intervenors. All of the reforms which have been outlined so far should also increase public confidence in the planning and licensing process by dealing credibly with all relevant issues, eliminating conflicting regulatory and developmental duties within single agencies, increasing information available and making public participation simpler and more effective.

Few of these reforms are new. Rather, through selecting and combining proposals already made by representatives on all sides of the electricity/environment debate, the Committee has sought to provide a solution which will serve all interests, while requiring them to accept essential responsibility. First, the utilities will be provided an orderly framework within which to initiate and obtain timely review of their plans, while ultimate inclusion of other energy forms within this framework helps to ensure that the electric industry will not be unfairly overburdened with regulation. But, the utilities will have the duty of submitting the aternatives available for new facilities for public discussion and review at an early stage, when options are still open. Second, environmentalists will be afforded opportunities to raise all important issues for public debate in as simple and effective a manner as possible, and will be assured that their views will receive a fair hearing *before* key decisions are reached. But, by making it impossible to relitigate issues, the reforms will require environmentalists to argue effectively on the merits. Finally, the interests of the public will be served by giving its regulators the authority to consider options at an early stage and reach decisions in sufficient time to provide necessary electricity. But, regulators will have the responsibility to make choices explicit in highly visible generic proceedings and to seek affirmatively to provide the public with information. If the regulators fail to provide the public with information and to put both the *pros* and *cons* of alternatives on the record, then intervenors will have insufficient means to argue their viewpoint, and the system will lack the credibility which is a necessary precondition to a rational decision-making process, capable of producing decisions on a timely basis.

The process described is not "one-stop licensing," but it does serve the essential purposes of that concept while not pursuing "one-stop" to its extreme. A one-time regulatory review cannot deal with the realities of utility planning, which involves the gradual narrowing of options over many years. Nor can one level of government review deal with an industry which plans on local, state, and regional levels, and makes decisions of local, state, and national concern. The Committee has therefore attempted to pick out the key points in the utility planning process and expose them to review. While there is more than "one stop," each issue is required to be litigated only once and provision is made to ensure timely decisions.

These recommendations are long-range reforms of the decision-making process, and are not meant to be a response to possible short-range crises. This implies no conclusion as to whether or not there will be a near-term gap between supply and demand. Rather, the Committee decided to concentrate on the intermediate and long term partly because of the passage of new and untried emergency legislation, and partly because today's problems result from attempts to solve yesterday's problems by patches on the regulatory process instead of fundamental re-evaluation.

The next section summarizes the Committee's recommendations without argumentation. Succeeding sections detail and seek to justify recommendations concerning the treatment of the seven key issues. timing, administrative structure, generic proceedings, licensing, public participation and information, the workability of the system, and research and development.

B. Synopsis of Recommendations

The first step would be the creation of an Energy Commission and an Energy Agency. The Commission would be a regulatory body, consolidating the regulatory duties of the FPC, the AEC, and, preferably, those parts of the federal government which deal with energy forms other than electricity. The Agency would be a developmental body, consolidating the research activities of the AEC, the Office of Coal Research, and all other administrative and executive offices concerned with energy R & D. Federal legislation would also require the states to establish Siting Commissions, separate from either environmental or utility agencies, and would establish mandatory standards for facilities licensing at the state and local levels.

The legislation would provide an interim period during which plants would continue to be licensed under old procedures while the new structure developed its detailed procedures and generic standards and the industry could adjust its plans. This interim period would also allow for judicial review of the new legislation and the generic rules to be issued under it, so that the new system would only begin to function when its essential components had been tested and approved.

One of the federal Energy Commission's first duties would be to study the question of whether and how the demand for energy should be encouraged or discouraged. The Commission would present its studies and recommendations to Congress, which would actually vote on whether or not to take specific actions to affect demand for energy, such as taxes on energy or effluents, rationing of energy, or other measures. Absent Congressional authorization, the Commission would not seek to limit demand. But, the Commission would be authorized to participate as a party in proceedings of other agencies to introduce information about the energy implications of such matters as the FHA's building insulation requirements.

The Commission would also review the intermediate-range plans of utilities and the regional reliability councils. Each regional office of the Commission would receive plans from the reliability council in its region as to the amount of new capacity needed to come into operation ten years hence and its general location. States, localities, individual utilities, and citizen groups would have an opportunity to submit alternatives or otherwise participate in the proceeding. Based on the recommendations of its regional offices, the Commission would then conclude (1) how much new capacity would be needed to meet reliably all of the demand for power expected a decade hence, given all the factors affecting demand including any actions authorized by Congress, and (2) in what generalized locations such new generating stations and transmission lines should go to ensure reliability, minimize costs, and protect the environment. Absent a Congressional mandate, the Commission would be forbidden to affect demand by authorizing fewer facilities than required to satisfy expected consumption. The net result would be an order to each state in the region to license a given number of facilities in time to come into operation a decade hence. The Commission would be required to complete this proceeding in one year. These proceedings would repeat themselves annually, with each proceeding dealing with the capacity needed to come into operation ten years in the future.

Once the Energy Commission had issued its orders as to new capacity and its regional allocation, providing the exact sites for the facilities would be the responsibility of the states, with one class of exceptions. The Energy Commission would retain jurisdiction over types of facilities of national or major regional significance, such as off-shore nuclear plants, huge power parks, and conventional hydroelectric plants in navigable waters. The Commission would hold proceedings on such projects in time to decide whether part of the need for new capacity could and should be met by federally licensed instead of state licensed projects.

The basic contours of the licensing process would be shaped, as much as possible, by generic standards applicable to all plants. All plants would have to meet air and water emission standards established by the type of apparatus mandated in current federal air and water pollution legislation. Similarly, nuclear plants would have to meet safety standards to be set by the Energy Commission, just as the AEC now establishes safety standards. But the Commission would put high priority on developing more extensive safety standards. Finally, the state Siting Commissions would issue rules as to the land-use aspects of power plant and transmission line siting.

With the state Siting Commissions having received orders as to how much generating and transmission capacity must be licensed to come into operation nine years hence, the licensing process itself could begin. By this time, most of the troublesome issues now confronting licensing agencies would have been resolved.

The licensing process would center on one major state level proceeding where, following a hearing, all issues concerning the facility and its environmental impact, except its detailed design, would be settled. This proceeding would choose the actual site and the general type of plant to be built seven years before it would be needed, and issue a license specifying the chief characteristics of the facility, including limits on its emissions. A further proceeding, including a hearing, would be needed after the facility was designed in detail, but it would be limited to considering whether the design would meet the requirements of the preliminary license. The federal Energy Commission would hold one other proceeding, with a hearing, for nuclear plants, but it would be similarly limited to radiological safety issues.

The proceeding before the Siting Commission to choose a site and mode of generation or transmission would commence eight years before the facility was needed. The utility would submit basic information on the sites it was considering, along with its pre-design engineering for each site, and in addition, the Siting Commission staff, other utilities, and citizens groups would be free to submit proposals. Thus, the proceeding would not be limited to the application for a particular plant at a particular site, but rather would consider how best to fill the order of the federal Energy Commission to satisfy the need for additional capacity. The state Siting Commission would be required, within a specified period of time, perhaps a year or 18 months, to issue licenses to build the needed capacity, and this requirement would be backed up by granting the federal Energy Commission the right to license plants if the state Siting Commission failed to act within the time limit.

At this stage, approximately seven years before the plant was needed, the utility would begin to design the needed facilities. When the design took specific shape, it would be submitted to the state environmental agency and, in the case of nuclear plants, the federal Energy Commission. When the design had passed muster as to air, water and nuclear safety standards, construction could proceed.

This scheme would not prevent other state agencies and localities from imposing other requirements concerning power facilities, such as permits to cross public lands and highways, local zoning, and the like. But, if any such authority denied a permit application or did not act within six months, the utility could ask the Siting Commission to override such other requirements on the grounds that the design in fact met the local standards or the standards were unreasonable as applied in that instance.

Judicial review would be consolidated. Generic standards would be appealable when issued but not as a part of the licensing process. During the licensing process itself, the most likely subject of appeal

265

would be the state Siting Commission choice of site and mode as well as, in the case of nuclear stations, the federal Energy Commission safety approval. The number of appeals relating to state air and water review as well as the host of other state and local permits could be radically reduced by requiring all issues to be raised in single appeal from the final licensing order of the state Siting Commission.

After the design had been certified, construction could begin. No operating license would be required, but the relevant agencies would inspect the plant to ensure construction complied with the certifications, and would have discretion to require backfitting before or after operation began, where the improvement would be sufficiently worthwhile.

An essential part of the recommendations are the ways suggested to make the process as open as possible. The staffs of the respective Commissions would be required, for example, to present candid reports on the issues at the outset of the hearings. In particular, all generic proceedings would require the production of environmental statements, as would the state siting proceeding. On the other hand, no such statements would be required for the design reviews in regard to air, water and nuclear safety.

The public could also get information through the Environmental Protection Agency, which would have adequate funding to carry out environmental and safety research on energy matters, and through access to the staffs of the Energy Commission and state Siting Commissions, which would be mandated to provide the public with technical background information.

Equipped with this information, the public would have a right to participate in the process of pre-hearing negotiation involving applicants and regulatory staffs, as well as the right to early and complete discovery. Participation in the proceedings would be made simpler through elimination of unnecessary financial burdens on intervenors and reforms like improvement of notice of pending proceedings. Particular care would have to be taken to notify the public and facilitate its involvement in generic proceedings.

This chapter also contains recommendations concerning the funding of research and development and procedures to allow comparison between the various research possibilities.

C. THE SEVEN ISSUES

Electric power and the environment involve many types of issues. In constructing a system to resolve these issues, one must determine at the outset what level of government should decide each issue, whether the issue should receive generic or case-by-case treatment, and what the basic principles to guide that treatment should be.

This Committee believes that, in general, an issue should be treated at the lowest level of government which has jurisdiction over its important implications. Given the extended nature of electrical, economic, and environmental systems, many issues should thus be decided at the national or regional level. Yet, this precept would not involve any significant lessening of state government authority, since many of the issues which require national or regional treatment, such as the demand for energy, are not now dealt with at any level of government, as discussed in Chapter V(A). At the same time, parts of the federal administrative process, such as the AEC's licensing of nuclear plants, decide land-use issues with only a local impact.

On the question of generic or *ad hoc* treatment of issues, Chapter V pointed out the advantages of dealing with recurring issues on an across-the-board basis. These advantages include speeding the licensing process, higher visibility decision-making, and greater accuracy. But many issues are not susceptible to generic treatment, particularly where their proper resolution depends heavily on widely varying factual patterns. Thus, to decide which level of government should deal with issues and whether on an *ad hoc* or case-by-case basis, one must look separately at the seven key issues in electric power and the environment.

To summarize the discussion which follows, federal duties under the proposed treatment of the issues would include generic handling of demand, the question of the number of plants (and their regional location) needed to satisfy demand, research, and safety standards; the safety standards would be applied to particular plants in case-by-case proceedings. State duties would include generic handling of environmental and land-use standards and case-by-case application of these standards to particular plants and transmission lines, together with consideration of alternatives. The question of the need for new capacity might be handled generically at the regional level, with a number of

267

states grouping together by means of a compact, but federal authority to resolve disputes and mandate regional interconnections, as well as federal standards for any regional body, would be necessary.

Reference to generic or case-by-case treatment of issues does not necessarily carry any implication as to the type of procedures appropriate for carrying out such treatment. Generic treatment need not, that is, take the form of a rule making or legislative hearing, and case-by-case treatment need not be in the form of a trial-type adjudication. Appropriate procedures are discussed in a later section of this Chapter.

1. DEMAND

The most basic and difficult issue is demand, or the total amount of power society decides to consume. Chapter VI argued that the interdependence between electric and non-electric forms of energy requires that the demand for energy be treated as a unitary subject of decision-making. Moreover, since a single state's curbing energy use will have interstate impact, perhaps putting that state in fear of economic disadavantage, basic energy demand policy should originate at the federal level. But, individual states should be able to experiment with their own energy policies.

Given the important implications of energy demand policy, Congress must ultimately deal with the issue. But, the complexity of the questions involved requires that an administrative body provide the legislature with research on the types of questions raised in Chapter VI. Chapter V pointed out that the demand issue now receives no specific attention, particularly because no agency provides Congress with the requisite information. This would be one of the most important duties of the proposed federal Energy Commission. On the basis of such information, Congress might then impose an energy tax, limit energy use by empowering the Energy Commission to ration energy, require equipment and buildings to be designed to use less energy, favor land-use and transportation policies requiring less energy, and/or do nothing. In any event, the Energy Commission would not be permitted to limit demand, either directly through taxes or rationing, or indirectly through failing to authorize sufficient new capacity to meet projected consumption levels, without specific Congressional mandate. Energy demand must ultimately be a question for Congress, but a question which Congress has an obligation to decide explictly.

Since demand policy must take account of far-flung interrelationships and should not be changed lightly, it should be decided generically, and excluded from individual plant licensing proceedings.

2. CAPACITY AND REGIONAL ALLOCATION

Once demand policies have been set, forecasts of the levels of power consumption which will result from those policies must be made, and a process of selection followed to move from a generalized determination of need to a site for a particular facility. This narrowing process now has several stages: (1) utilities project the expected needs in their service areas, (2) they submit their estimates to regional reliability councils and power pools, which discuss needed new capacity in light of reliability and other considerations, with a view to picking the general location of new facilities, and (3) based on these discussions, utilities pick specific sites subject to regulatory review. This third stage of siting within states is dealt with separately below, leaving for consideration now the questions of how the forecast of a region's needs is to be made, and how the obligation to provide sites for required new capacity is to be divided among the states of the region.

Initially, it would seem clear that forecasts of need and their apportioning among states are generic questions, best decided apart from the question whether or not particular plants should be built and precisely where they should be sited. Next, the proper level of government for decision of allocation questions is regional. Utilities now plan and operate regionally for reasons of economics and reliability, and the size of newer facilities can only reinforce this tendency. Moreover, major states with congested urban areas are finding it difficult to satisfy their power needs within their own boundaries, a condition which seems certain to spread. These factors all point to the increasing necessity for some sort of federal or regional body to review utility plans and allocate the obligation to play host to generating plants and associated transmission lines, taking into account reliability criteria and relative environmental and economic impact. A new statutory scheme is thus called for, since Chapter V found that government had no means of reviewing the regional allocation of facilities and that, in practice, utilities are now deterred from deciding to place facilities outside their own state or even service area.

The allocation process should begin with utilities forecasting demand in their service areas, combining these forecasts with those of

269

other utilities in the same reliability region or power pool, and proposing in what general areas new plants and transmission lines should go. These plans would then be submitted to the regional office of the federal Energy Commission. It would determine whether or not the projected total new capacity was needed and sufficient to ensure reliability and recommend to the Commission in what general areas the new capacity should go. The Commission's final order would require each state to license the required capacity, with the state picking the exact sites.

In allocating new capacity, the federal Energy Commission would be required to service all the expected demand. The legislatively determined demand policy would be one of the factors determining how much power customers would consume. The Commission would have no authority to attempt to limit demand by authorizing less capacity than needed to satisfy customer desires. It has been argued that such a structure might tempt regulators to curb demand covertly by authorizing less capacity than needed to meet customer wants. But, since such action would not appreciably affect customer behavior, any such abuse of discretion would lead to power shortages, not a change in the fundamental demand for power. The remedy for such abuse would be a judicial appeal, which would be available nine years before the capacity was needed.

The system of regional allocation has important advantages over the present system. It allows for public review of the important question whether new capacity is sufficient for reliability or excessive, and therefore uneconomic. The industry now treats these questions regionally, but no public body with decisional authority now has the power to make final decisions in this area. More critical, the new system provides a mechanism to deal with the increasingly important but now neglected question of the regional placement of plants. Environmental questions may dictate that a city's needs be met by a plant in another state, perhaps despite the wishes of the utility concerned or the potential host state. As Chapter V points out, no mechanism now exists to make such a determination or to require a state to approve a site to meet another state's needs.

A variant of this proposal would assign the duties of the federal Energy Commission to allocate among states to regional bodies established by the states themselves through compact, subject to federal review of the terms of the compact and the area to be covered, to ensure that it would be reasonably self-sufficient. The compact should be limited in duration so that changes in the compact area could be made to reflect new developments in transmission technology or population patterns. Federal control over regional interconnections would be retained, and the amount of capacity each region would be required to site would remain fixed by federal forecasts. It should be noted, however, that even where encouraged by federal legislation, the states have not often used the compact device.

3. LAND USE

After the general locations of plants and transmission lines are determined, exact sites or corridors must be selected. There is much appeal in using a planning process based entirely on generic standards to pick sites, thereby setting aside certain areas where plants could be built without prior clearance. The history of land-use zoning in this country suggests, however, that total reliance on generic standards would be impossible. Zoning originally simply involved mapping districts, specifying areas where various types of land uses were and were not allowed. But, even for the relatively simpler task of preserving neighborhood-level amenities in suburban residential development, traditional zoning has been found to have severe limitations. Many important variables cannot be fitted into the classifications affixed to the maps. In response, localities now emphasize a more descriptive approach, using such devices as "conditional zones," "floating zones," and "planned unit developments" to set standards within which officials can exercise discretion in reviewing plans for development of specific sites.

With power facilities involving even more variables than residential development, it seems unlikely that all relevant aspects could be reduced to a traditional zoning map. But, the notion of mixing generic standards (expressed in terms of maps or performance formulae) with *ad hoc* determination of other issues, as used in residential development, is an attractive one.

While the Committee has not studied the various aspects of land use in detail, the following breakdown is suggestive of what might be done. Development of generic standards would take place in several stages, proceeding from the general to the specific. A first effort would be to identify areas where power was needed, and summarize the environmental and engineering constraints and opportunities in different areas. For a variety of reasons a number of areas would be

271

eliminated almost at once, because of nuclear safety standards, particular environmental value (parks, wilderness areas, historic sites, etc.), applicable air and water standards, susceptibility to natural catastrophe (flood, earthquake), topography (extreme slope or grade), compatibility with existing uses, and accessibility to cooling water, transportation, and fuel. The protection of parks, wilderness areas and historic sites cannot be compromised, but the relative importance of the other factors listed will vary depending on the type of plant (e. g., nuclear or fossil) and the type of equipment (e. g., cooling tower or once-through cooling) involved.

As the broadest generic standards become fixed, a number of more detailed factors would become relevant, such as the development of environmental standards to protect specific fish spawning grounds or airsheds, the meteorology of particular regions and its effect on population centers (or local roads and bridges if wet cooling towers are used), access to sufficient land for all projected needs, including waste disposal, and the aesthetics of particular areas as affected by the planned facilities. At both stages, a variety of possible trade-offs among the applicable factors would be possible, and the siting body would have the responsibility of defining situations or scenarios where various trade-offs would be acceptable. The less acceptable a particular site or region was, the greater the burden an applicant utility would bear in seeking to justify its choice of that site over alternatives.

Once the federal Energy Commission has picked the general location of the facility, siting is primarily a state and local concern, although in some situations, a federal proceeding may be required: for off-shore barge-mounted plants, for example, or hydroelectric developments blocking navigable rivers, or large power parks serving several states.[1] Since both state and local government cannot have the final say, the Committee has opted to place siting at the state level, in a state Siting Commission, because of the many municipalities potentially involved and because one town's decision to accept a plant will have implications for other towns in regard to transmission lines. But, once the state has decided to place a plant at a given site, the town will also have concerns of a purely local nature. To allow the town to express these concerns, it is suggested that facilities still be subject to local regulation, but with the proviso that the state Siting Commission have the power to override unreasonable local regulations.

272

4. GENERATION AND TRANSMISSION ALTERNATIVES

A fourth issue is what choice is to be made between alternative modes of generation and transmission. This decision must be made on an *ad hoc* basis, since for each facility the choices must be weighed, but it will be limited by what technologies research has provided, what fuels are available at competitive cost, and what the applicable environmental and safety standards are. The state or locality which must live with the facility should have primary say here, but the interests of those outside the state but still within the zone which will be affected by the facility must be protected as well, through consistent application of effective safety and environmental standards. National goals concerning resource use can also be protected through, for example, fuel pricing policies.

5. ENVIRONMENTAL STANDARDS

The fifth issue is that of environmental standards, primarily concerned with the limits on each plant's emissions, but also involving matters like noise and solid waste disposal. This is a mixed *ad hoc* and generic issue. There are minimum limits on emissions or noise which no plant anywhere should exceed, but once these limits are satisfied the characteristics of each site, airshed or water body should control in determining permissible effluents. Local, state, regional and national interests are all strong here, and there is competition within the various levels of government, e. g., between the environmental protection agency and the power agency, as well. Pressures exist at all levels which could result in too strict or too lenient regulation, and the overall system of air and water quality standards is still evolving. Perhaps the most satisfactory way to deal with these different conflicts is to follow the present statutory and regulatory scheme by leaving to the state air and water agencies, which can delegate authority to a locality, overall control of environmental standards for power plants, like those applicable to other pollution sources, with state standards subject to review by the federal Environmental Protection Agency to insure that they are not too lax. A state could raise its standards above federal minima if it desired, but if these standards prevented the state from licensing its share of plants within a specified time period, the federal government could be authorized either to modify prior determinations of need for those plants or to license them, with the applicable environmental standards being the lower federal ones, not the higher state ones. Exemption from state standards would be effective only for the federally licensed plants; the state standards would not be voided, but would remain in effect for other facilities.

6. SAFETY

A sixth issue is radiological safety, including both the development of standards and their implementation. Safety is a generic issue in that all nuclear plants should be equally safe, but *ad hoc* in that each plant must be inspected to insure that the uniform standards which are adopted are met in practice. Chapter V observed that there is now potentially greater scope for generic safety standards. The national importance of safe nuclear plants seems to require national control over the standards, as is presently the case, since the development of necessary expertise on any other level would be difficult and could cause unnecessary duplication of effort. All levels of government should, however, be consulted during the development of radiological safety standards. Safety standards for fossil plants could continue to be handled at the state level.

7. RESEARCH AND DEVELOPMENT

The development of alternative technologies for the future is of critical long-range importance, given the admitted environmental problems with all existing technologies for generation and transmission of power. There is a broad consensus on the need for increased research funding and improved mechanisms for allocating research efforts. This issue is generic, since solutions to research problems can usually be broadly applied, and the allocation of funds requires comparison between the different avenues of exploration. In addition, since improved methods will generally have extensive application, the cost of developing these new methods should likewise be shared by the entire country, thus requiring that funds for government research be raised at the federal level, although some provision for state research on problems unique to particular regions or localities should also be made.

Research and development in the electric power industry was in the past funded primarily through equipment manufacturers; the utilities themselves traditionally spent only an average of $1/4\%$ of gross revenues annually on research and development compared to an all-industry average of roughly 3% of gross annual revenues.[2] The R & D

Goals Task Force of the Electric Research Council, an industry organization, has summarized difficulties with prior handling of research as
follows:

> "Historically, our industry has relied heavily on manufacturers
> to do R & D and pass along the costs in the price of the ul-
> timate product. While this has led to many important ad-
> vances, it is not an altogether satisfactory arrangement. For
> example, it does not provide for comprehensive system orient-
> ed R & D. Manufacturers generally do not invest tremendous
> sums of money in projects that will not produce a marketable
> product and return of their R & D investment for many
> years. They try to remain competitive price-wise not only
> against other domestic manufacturers, but foreign manu-
> facturers as well. Much important R & D does not neces-
> sarily provide opportunity for mass production and profit.
> Thus the major efforts of manufacturers tend toward short-
> term R & D that will produce salable products and a profit
> within a relatively short time span—typically improvements
> in present technology. Long-range work on new methods
> does not get the attention from manufacturers that it needs.
> Some R & D projects are simply beyond the capability of a
> single manufacturer. Further, reliance on manufacturers
> does not give our industry the control over its own future
> that it needs to discharge its responsibilities to society. While
> we will continue to expect much from manufacturers, we can-
> not merely take what is given us to work with. We have an
> obligation to take the future more into our own hands." [3]

The magnitude of expenditures which will be required, the high
risks involved, the desirability of broad application of technological
advances, and the length of time which must be anticipated before heavy
funding produces tangible results, all make it difficult to rely in the
future solely on voluntary industry funding of R & D through either
the utilities or the equipment manufacturers. Government review
of industry efforts, and supplementing of those efforts, will be essential. Once the need for a government research program is recognized,
the relevant questions are: (1) How should funds for this program
be raised? (2) Who should decide on R & D goals and funding specific projects? (3) Should the R & D program cover all forms of
energy, or just electricity?

275

R & D Coverage. Since it is agreed that a national energy policy is needed, it would seem inappropriate to focus on developing the technological potential of one form of energy in isolation. This is especially so in view of the broad applicability of potential research advances: for example, a feasible coal gasification scheme could provide fuel for direct home use and for use in transportation as well as for use by a utility generating electricity; methods for cooling industrial heat discharges could be employed by fuel refineries as well as power plants; exhaust gas treatment systems for sulfur or nitrogen oxides could be applied to oil furnaces, automobiles or power plants. Given this substitutibility, a federal R & D program focused solely on electric power would lead to imbalances as serious as those which have been criticized in present government R & D spending on nuclear power as compared with fossil fuel technologies. Methods of funding and control should, therefore, be devised which permit attention to be given to energy research as a whole, not just to electric power research, coal research or nuclear research.

R & D Funding. There are many possible alternatives for raising the necessary funds for a government research program. Monies might be appropriated from general revenues, or a tax levied on energy consumed, as proposed in Senator Magnuson's "Federal Power Research and Development Act." [4] In any case, federal funding should not prevent or hinder continued industry spending on R & D; private research will still be very important in improving current technology and other smaller-scale projects. Indeed, federal programs might well be directed towards just those areas where risks are too high or expenditures too great to justify private efforts. Whatever form the federal program takes, private efforts should be encouraged by inclusion of R & D expenditures in a utility's rate base by the concerned regulatory agency. But private spending should not be allowed as a credit against industry obligations to the federal program. To do so would risk loss of a balanced and coordinated R & D program and pursuit of short-term goals at the expense of high-risk research for long-term payoffs.

Control over R & D. The federally funded energy R & D program outlined above should be directed by the proposed federal agency already described which has control of energy development. As provided by the Magnuson bill, a certain percentage of the total R & D spending could be required to be directed toward research on safety and the possible adverse effects of existing and new technologies.

276

Some of this research might be carried out through the federal Environmental Protection Agency.

For much the same reasons that a research expenditure credit is not recommended, the proposed R & D control structure should not use a joint industry-government board to supervise the program. Such a separate board might not permit adequate coordination with overall energy and electric power goals; if all energy industries were fairly represented, it would be so large as to be unwieldy; and an industry-government structure appears to exclude the public from decision-making without good reason. Control of research within the federal agency (similar to AEC control of nuclear research) would provide sufficient opportunities for industry expertise to be tapped without endangering the program's balance. Agency control might make possible kinds of research—on ways of using energy more efficiently, perhaps—which might not be undertaken were a joint industry-agency board to control the program.

D. TIMING

Having identified the issues which must be decided, it is necessary to specify the order in which these decisions are to be made. One of the chief problems with today's decision-making process is that issues are put forward for public review in an illogical order, and after the practical options are at least partly foreclosed.

Demand and the allocation of research and development funds are conceptually the first issues to be decided. This is because decisions on these issues are unlikely to have a significant effect on the production and consumption of power for many years hence. Chapter VI pointed out that gradual implementation of any demand policy will minimize the economic and social dislocation that such change may cause. At the same time, today's new research concepts must go through years or decades of development, prototypes, and other exploration before they become practical possibilities for the commercial production and transmission of power.

The establishment of generic standards for nuclear safety, air and water emissions and land use will be an on-going process. The initial versions of such standards should be in place before the new licensing process takes effect. Thereafter, new knowledge and new priorities will undoubtedly make desirable revisions in such standards. In any

277

event, standards should be subjected to periodic re-evaluation. But, facilities should be subject only to the standards in effect at the time that application is submitted unless there is some overriding reason for a new standard's retroactive imposition.

With the issues of demand, research and development and generic standards for nuclear safety, air, water and land use established, the stage is then set for determining the number, location, and design of facilities actually needed to produce power, both economically and with minimal environmental impact. The time of this process must comport with the realities of the systems planning. A typical timetable for systems planning is as follows. The planning department of the utility will assemble the information each year needed to make an intermediate-range or ten-year plan. This plan will include, first, estimates of the amount of power expected to be demanded by the system's customers a decade hence. Second, there will be estimates of new generating and transmission capacity needed to meet the increase in demand and retire older plants. Third, there will be specification of perhaps four or five general areas where the new facilities could go to meet the demand expected in ten years. At this ten-year stage, the utility will submit this type of intermediate-range plan to the power pool and/or regional reliability council to which the utility is attached. The reliability council or power pool will then discuss these plans of their members in the context of the overall characteristics of the region. At the end of this process, each utility will come away with a fairly precise idea of how much capacity it will need to build to meet future needs reliably, and have several alternate ideas of its general location.

The utility will then go into more detail as to the availability of specific sites and the types of plants suitable to the sites. Given the length of time needed to build a nuclear plant, and to get its license, the utility will have to opt for a nuclear plant at least eight years before it is needed. If this eight-year point goes by, the utility is committed by default to a fossil plant. From seven to five years before a fossil plant is needed, the utility will engage in pre-design engineering. With the range of specific potential sites narrowed to a few, its engineering staff will rough out the basic aspects of plants on the sites. This will include the means of generation, the size of the plant, the general location of boilers, generators, fuel storage areas, and cooling systems, and finally estimates of emissions expected to the air and water. At the same time, the utility will be getting a fairly precise idea of the availability and cost of fuel at the particular sites. Approximately five years before the plant is needed to come into operation, the utility will make a final choice of the site, begin to submit applications, order the necessary equipment, and enter into definite contracts for the supply of fuel.

Thus, at present, choices for nuclear plants must be made eight years before they are needed and choices for fossil plants five years before they are needed. But, part of this lead time is necessitated by the licensing process itself. In actual construction time, a nuclear plant takes only about four years to build, and a fossil plant about three years. Some equipment, such as reactor vessels and turbines, must be ordered before these times, but this equipment can usually be used at a variety of sites or sold to another utility.

It is the timing of today's decision-making process which creates many of its problems. Applications are usually not submitted until the actual design of the plant is fairly well advanced. At this time, the reliability council, power pool, and utility have been planning on the existence of this new plant for several years. By this time also, the utility will already have put out firm orders for equipment and arranged for fuel contracts. When an application for a fossil plant is submitted, time has foreclosed the possibility of the utility's needs being satisfied by a nuclear plant. Foreclosure of practical options is one cause of the decline in credibility in administrative agencies.

A better decision-making process would submit decisions for review at a time when as many options as possible are open. But, earlier review is not an unmitigated blessing. The longer the lead time in decision-making, the less information is available upon which to base a choice. For instance, one will have a more accurate notion of the demand for power in a particular year, the closer one is to that year. At the same time, if the utility is locked into a particular design far in advance of the time that it is actually needed, it will not be able to incorporate the latest advances in pollution control techniques or fuel efficiency. So in suggesting the timing of the decision-making process, we have sought to make the reviews take place before passage of time forecloses options, but also as late as practically possible.

The proposed sequence would go as follows. The federal Energy Commission's annual proceedings on the need for new capacity and its regional allocation will deal with the capacity needed to come into operation ten years from the time of the proceeding, similar to the time that utilities now discuss such questions within reliability councils. The federal Energy Commission would be required to issue its plan for capacity and regional allocation within one year. So, nine years before new facilities are needed, each state would receive orders as to the amount of capacity it must license to come into operation within nine years.

No later than eight years before the facilities are needed, the state Siting Commission could commence proceedings to choose the specific site and the mode of generation or transmission. The state Siting Commission would have to make its decision about the best site or sites and mode or modes within a fixed time, perhaps a year or 18 months, so that approximately seven years before the facilities are needed, an administrative decision would issue as to the specific site and the specific mode of generation or transmission. This is about two years before utilities now make final choices in regard to non-nuclear sites but a year after choices are made as to nuclear sites.

At this stage, the utility would convert its pre-design engineering into specific designs. No later than five years before the facility was needed, the utility would be required to submit its specific designs to the state Environmental Agency to review designs for compliance with air and water standards, and to the federal Energy Commission for safety review in the case of nuclear plants. During this design review period, the utility would also be submitting applications for the various secondary federal, state and local permits. As mentioned before, if any of these state or local permits were not forthcoming, the state Siting Commission would have the power to override other state or local agencies.

This process would repeat itself annually. In other words, each year the regional office of the federal Energy Commission would issue a plan for capacity and regional allocation for the facilities needed nine years hence. Each "class" of facilities would then go through the same countdown of site, mode, and design review.

This suggested timing sequence follows quite closely the timing of the decision-making process the utility industry uses today. But, there is a significant change in the point of first public review. Presently, public review takes place largely at the design stage, after a utility has made its own decision as to site and mode of generation. The suggested new procedure would change the chief public review to the more critical stage where the site is chosen and the mode of generation selected. It is at the site and mode stage where the environmental statement is required and environmental values weighed in. Subsequent design reviews are much more limited in scope, determining solely whether the facility as designed meets the generic standards and other prescriptions set forth in the license issued at the time that the site and mode are selected.

While this temporal sequence does not vary from the timing of the decision-making within the utility, it does require the utility to go public with its decisions at an earlier stage. To the extent that a utility now retains some flexibility of site selection between the seventh and fifth year before the plant is needed, the new approach does give the utility slightly less flexibility. This decrease in flexibility is more than worthwhile. First, it allows the public to become involved at an important decision-making stage while the options are more open. Second, it gives the utility a firm administrative decision on the basic outlines of its plant at an earlier stage, thereby reducing the possibility that the plant will not be licensed at all. Moreover, it allows the site to be approved before the utility invests substantial amounts of money in actual design.

After the facility is licensed and construction commences, the facility will not be subject to any further formal proceedings. The state Siting Commission, the state Environmental Agency, and, in the case of nuclear plants, the federal Energy Commission, will, however, inspect the plant before operation to make sure that it is constructed to comply with the permits issued. No hearing or license is required to go into operation.

E. STRUCTURE

Government agencies dealing with the electric utility industry must perform several functions: they must champion different and sometimes conflicting aspects of the public interest in regulating industry activities, serve as advisor to industry and promote its development, and finally act as a detached decision-maker concerning positions and applications which they initially helped formulate. As discussed in Chapter V, these often conflicting roles have in the past been a source of public and judicial distrust. Proposals have been made to improve the system by creating separate institutions for these separate roles.

Such separation has both advantages and disadvantages. If it were complete, that is, if there were one body charged with advocating the public interest, another charged with consulting with the industry and planning its development, and a third charged with passing on industry applications with no contacts with industry outside the quasi-judicial context, intra-agency conflicts of interest would be eliminated, the public and the courts would have the satisfaction of seeing disputes aired and resolved openly, and available information would be maximized. Efforts by private groups to represent the public interest, often hampered by lack of knowledge, expertise and funds, would be supplemented by the existence of a government-funded, institutionalized devil's advocate. Also, a separate advocate might provide an opportunity for experts to present valid criticisms of developmental or regulatory actions which they would be unwilling to make while employed in a developmental or regulatory agency.

On the other hand, such complete role separation might make impossible consultation between industry and the staff of the body passing on industry applications, which the Committee feels is essential to the development and review of sound proposals, and to the implementation of adequate nuclear safety standards in particular. If staff were institutionally separated from the final decision-making body, they might be discouraged from exerting full efforts in overseeing industry proposals because their work would be subject to *de novo* review by the decision-making body. Besides interfering with the quality of staff work, such separation might also make it difficult to recruit competent staff.

A separate government advocate might also be subject to abuse, opposing government or industry action for its own sake without responsibility for reaching any decision. A government advocate would also probably be less independent than outside groups or individual members of the public, although admittedly the resources of a governmental advocate would aid in assembling information and presenting the strongest possible case.

The Committee believes that the best balance of advantages and disadvantages would result from a separation of roles which is less than total. The Committee recommends the separation of developmental duties from regulatory duties, with the retention of present consultation between regulatory staff and industry in the preparation of proposals for facilities and implementation of standards. The advantages of such consultation would be retained, but the conflict of interest inherent in requiring a single body to both assist in development of an industry and regulate its own efforts would be removed. The risks entailed in such consultation between the regulated and the regulator could be minimized by allowing public participation in such prehearing negotiation as discussed more fully below. Even this limited separation of functions may have some adverse consequences. It may be difficult to recruit as competent personnel if their duties are solely regulatory; necessary communication between regulatory and developmental agencies may be difficult; and adequate funding for a solely regulatory agency may be difficult to assure.[5] The Committee believes, however, that these possible disadvantages are outweighed by the potential benefits of such a limited role separation.

Because of the difficulties which creation of a separate government advocate would entail, the Committee does not recommend institution of such a body, preferring instead to promote public participation in other ways, and to rely on existing governmental agencies to supplement the developmental and regulatory bodies as sources of information. In particular, the regulatory commissions should be obligated to provide the public with detailed technical information upon request and the federal Environmental Protection Agency should have the resources to carry out significant research and provide information on the environmental aspects of energy.

1. FEDERAL

In line with the preceding discussion, the basic federal structure dealing with power matters should be in two parts: an Energy Agency with developmental responsibilities, and an Energy Commission with regulatory responsibilities. The present separation according to generation mode between the AEC (nuclear), the FPC (hydro), and several different agencies (fossil)[6] lacks rational justification and should be ended.

There is good reason to combine the regulatory duties of the FPC and the AEC, even apart from the Energy Commission's duties in regard to demand and regional allocation. Consolidation would create a federal body responsible for making licensing work and in a position to foresee difficulties in the licensing of all types of facilities. Moreover, the Commission (like the Agency) could claim greater public trust because it would not be wed to one type of technology. Also, its plenary jurisdiction would allow it to deal with new technologies such as fuel cells and solar energy which are not now subject to existing

283

bodies whose jurisdictions are tied to particular technologies. Finally, a body with broad jurisdiction could better decide whether part of the capacity should be in the form of projects to be licensed solely at the federal level, such as barge-mounted nuclear plants and power parks, as well as override the state when it failed to grant a construction license in due time.

Moreover, this Agency/Commission structure would also provide a framework for inclusion of other energy forms, so that development of a coherent national energy policy would be possible. As it does not seem justifiable to treat different methods of generating power in different agencies, so separate treatment of different but often interchangeable energy forms seems also unjustifiable.

The Agency's duties would include conducting research, including research on demand. The Commission, with its staff, would formulate plans for allocating needed capacity to regions, develop safety standards, and issue certificates of compliance with those standards to particular plants. The Commission would also report annually to the Congress on major policy issues, including demand. It would also intervene in proceedings of other federal agencies when their actions had significant energy impacts.

The Environmental Protection Agency would continue, as at present, to develop minimum environmental standards and review state standards and implementation plans. Federal agencies with power-related or environmental responsibilities, such as EPA, should also be adequately funded to research environmental consequences of power generation and transmission, and should make available the results of their research to the Commission, in written reports or testimony by EPA or other agency witnesses in Commission proceedings, or in formal intervention in those proceedings.

Besides the power agencies and EPA, the other federal regulatory agencies concerned with power facilities are the FAA (review of structures near airports), the Coast Guard (approval of bridges over navigable waters), and the Corps of Engineers (approval of structures affecting navigation and the permit program for discharges into navigable waters). The FAA, Coast Guard and Corps navigational reviews serve the valid federal concern with commerce and have apparently not burdened the plant licensing process, so little reason to modify them appears. The Corps' permit program, on the other hand, seems to duplicate state water quality programs, which already regulate heated discharges from power plants. If federal legislation is enacted which would require state water quality programs to set emission standards, and if the states not only set emission standards but also establish effective mechanisms for their enforcement, power plants should be exempted from the Corps' permit program.

2. STATE

The states must develop environmental and land-use standards and apply them to particular facilities, while weighing alternative generation and transmission modes. Development and implementation of environmental standards are presently entrusted to state Environmental Protection Agencies; no change in this arrangement is warranted. Development and implementation of land-use standards should be the duty of a state Siting Commission, with (preferably) responsibility for all types of industrial facilities, not just power plants and transmission lines.[7] The Siting Commission would be charged with considering generation and transmission alternatives and the environmental impact of the proposed facility, and with issuing the license for the capacity which the federal Energy Commission mandates to be built. Traditional economic regulation duties with respect to utilities would be left with state public utility bodies, but they would be bound to accept the environmental protection costs imposed by the state Siting Commission as part of the rate base.

States desiring to force their neighbors to assume a disproportionate share of the burden of providing facilities might set environmental or land-use standards too high, or the state Siting Commission might try to block unwanted plants by simply refusing to act on a utility's application. This obstruction could be thwarted by granting to the federal Energy Commission the authority to license plants if (1) the utility had applied for a license from the state Commission, (2) the application was in proper order and had been diligently pursued, (3) the facility was within the state's need quota, and (4) a specified amount of time had passed (perhaps one year or 18 months) and the state Commission had not approved any site for the utility's facility. As is discussed above, such federal licenses would require observance of federal safety standards and minimum federal environmental and land-use [8] standards, but compliance with state environmental and land-use standards, as well as other requirements of state law, would not be compulsory.

At the state level, the Commission should be authorized to issue licenses without approvals (except for state Environmental Protection Agency approvals) required by state law if those approvals had not been received by a specified time after application, and the applications were in proper order and had been diligently pursued. This override would be based on a finding, following a hearing, either that the facility did meet standards for state and local approvals or that such standards were unreasonably strict.

3. STATUTORY CHANGES

Beyond the federal and state statutory changes which are implied in the discussion of the decision-making structure above, some significant additional changes should be mentioned. The Committee's recommendations assume, for example, an effective state system of water emission standards for power facilities, including an enforcement program, exemption of those facilities from the Corps of Engineers permit program, and a review of environmental effects and alternatives for power facilities which differs from that presently required under the National Environmental Policy Act.

NEPA now requires that before a federal agency licenses a power plant or transmission line, it must review the environmental impact of the facility and consider alternatives. But this process results in much frustration: to the utility, because the review is often lengthy, preventing costly facilities from going on line, and to the intervenor and regulator, because the fixed nature of utility designs and plans by the time licenses are sought makes significant changes in applications in response to environmental review difficult. It is in everyone's interest that environmental reviews be completed earlier in the process, and the Committee's recommendations achieve this result.

Under the proposed system, analyses of environmental impact would be made as a part of generic determinations, at the federal level where a federal body was making those determinations, and at the state level where a state body was involved. An analysis of environmental impact would also be made by the body weighing possible choices for facility sites. This analysis would be the only one made during the licensing process itself. As compared with the present system, when the design was certified for compliance with environmental and safety standards following site selection, no analysis of environmental impact would be required; rather, there would be reliance on the analyses already made during the development of the standards. Since there is no requirement of an operating license, there would also be no analysis of environmental impact before a completed plant began to operate.

This structure may result in a less than complete "maximization" because it would not require analysis of completed facility designs, but it has the advantage of forcing consideration of alternative policy choices early enough in the process that there is an opportunity for their adoption, and thus should be an immense improvement over the present situation. Early environmental impact analyses should also, of course, help speed the decision-making process considerably.

F. GENERIC PROCEEDINGS

Generic treatment is intended to serve two main purposes: to ensure more adequate and consistent treatment of generic issues, and to streamline the licensing process by making it possible to limit the scope of issues and avoid the relitigation of issues in that process. Innovative use of generic treatment could achieve both purposes simultaneously, as, for example, with an overall study of a river basin or airshed, to determine aggregate permissible discharges from all sources. On the basis of this generic proceeding, licenses could be issued to individual sources of effluent on a much simpler basis than at present.

No specific administrative proceedings with respect to the issues of research or demand policies would be needed, at least initially. The federal Agency and the federal Commission would be instructed to propose programs in these areas, and Congress would review these programs, providing through the legislative hearing process a forum for public participation in this review. The federal Commission would hold generic proceedings to set radiological safety standards and deal with such issues as radioactive waste disposal. It would also determine through generic proceedings the capacity needed in the various regions to satisfy expected usage. The state Siting Commission would hold generic proceedings to set land-use standards, and the state Environmental Protection Agency would hold generic proceedings to set environmental standards. As discussed above, an alternative to federal handling of the capacity question would be to treat this issue generically through regional bodies set up to meet federal standards.

Safety, environmental and land-use standards should be fixed through these generic proceedings for an indefinite period, subject to

287

reopening on a showing by any interested party, including utilities, governmental agencies, or public groups, that the standards were not operating as planned, that new information made different standards desirable, or that technological advances made higher standards possible. Review of utility planning for new capacity should be undertaken annually so that only a comparatively few facilities would have to be considered in each proceeding.

It is difficult to propose the exact administrative procedures which should govern the generic proceedings which are recommended, since we have as yet little experience with such proceedings. In any case, an attempt should be made to avoid strict use of the Administrative Procedure Act categories of rulemaking and adjudication. Procedures should be adopted which are appropriate to the nature of the proceeding; [9] because the plans and standards adopted will have *res judicata* effect and foreclose consideration of issues in later licensing proceedings, access to these generic proceedings should be easy and rights to present evidence, cross-examine witnesses and gain discovery broad. Judicial review of agency generic proceedings can be expedited to help avoid unnecessary delay. If it subsequently appears that a proceeding with such broad rights is unworkable, limitations can be imposed, but the importance of producing credible results in these unprecedented proceedings indicates that the initial grant of procedural rights should be liberal. Liberality also makes it more likely that the courts will give effect to generic determinations in later licensing proceedings. The success or failure of the present AEC experiments with generic proceedings should tell us much about how such proceedings should be structured for the future.

While the advantages of generic treatment of issues now appear clear, problems may arise in practice. It may not, for example, prove possible to make standards specific enough to limit open questions significantly in licensing proceedings concerning particular sites or particular equipment designs. Some commentators also have warned that it may be difficult to secure adequate participation by those who are to be affected by the plans and standards developed in these generic proceedings, since they will be held well in advance of the time the plans and standards are to be applied and probably in Washington or a state capital, not where new facilities are to be located.

"Where the effect of a decision will be on an industry, there ordinarily will be little difficulty in getting the people affected to focus on the issues. But notwithstanding the present high level of interest in environmental questions, it seems fair to assume that members of the public will not focus on issues until, at least, plans to build a power plant are announced. And even then they may be only dimly aware that a generic proceeding in Washington is foreclosing many aspects of the proposed plan from inquiry. To a large extent, this cannot be helped; effective public participation cannot mean that all decisions must wait until the average citizen wakes up to the problem. But it does suggest that special efforts must be made to give notice to environmental groups, state and local agencies, and individuals and groups in areas likely to be affected. It also suggests that special attention should be paid to the availability of opportunity to challenge the generic decision." [10]

The current AEC hearings on emergency core cooling systems seem to demonstrate that, where the issues involved are considered important by a large segment of the public, public participation will in fact be adequate. But the extreme significance of many possible generic determinations (for example, a determination that a state must find a site for a power plant it does not want) will require that every effort be made to ensure that such proceedings are open and fair.

G. THE LICENSING PROCESS

With generic determinations in effect, licensing of individual facilities would take place in two stages: the first, at which sites were selected and generation and transmission alternatives considered, and the second, at which certificates of compliance with environmental and safety standards were received.

At the initial stage of the licensing process, the state Siting Commission would consider land use, starting from its previously determined land-use criteria, and generation and transmission alternatives. Need would not be considered in this proceeding, if a generically determined need plan were in effect and the facility was within the state's quota. Comparative evaluation of different sites would be made, other agencies and the public could comment in addition to the utilities, and an analysis of environmental impact would be made. On a showing that characteristics of a particular site required it, the Commission could

289

raise environmental standards for that site, but would otherwise be bound by the state standards as minima, since in the present statutory scheme these standards represent the minimum controls necessary to achieve overall state environmental goals. If the standards were quite general, requiring, for example, use of "best available" control technology, it would also be necessary to consider the state of the art in this proceeding. It might in any case be wise to permit consideration of the state of the art on a showing of change since the standards were fixed, on the theory that generic proceedings could not be instituted after each technological advance. Land-use standards may well have to be more general than environmental or safety standards, and thus require more attention at this stage than the other standards, due to the difficulties of evaluating site characteristics in detail before specific construction proposals are advanced.

The result of Commission approval of a certain site or sites and generation mode would be a license. The utility would then design its facility and submit this design to the state Environmental Protection Agency, for checking against applicable environmental standards, and to the federal Commission (in the case of nuclear plants), for checking against federal safety standards. Hearings would be necessary here, but they would be limited to the question whether the designs met standards, and thus should be much simpler than at present. A joint hearing might be held at the state level if facility design had to be checked for compliance with other than environmental standards, such as non-nuclear safety standards or esthetic standards. In this case, each concerned agency could present material having to do with its area of responsibility, and then use the single record as the basis for its decision. Of primary importance, however, would be the environmental standards. No analyses of environmental impact would be made in these proceedings, and it might be possible to proceed largely on the basis of written testimony.

Once the safety and environmental certificates had been received, the utility could begin construction, unless a showing of changed circumstances requiring modification of the original conditions of approval were made. Provision for such a showing would be necessary if sites had been approved far in advance of their need for construction, but reopening of proceedings on such a showing could be made subject to a high threshold of proof.

290

When the facility to be constructed was of particular federal concern, such as an off-shore barge-mounted generating plant, a conventional hydroelectric facility or a major nuclear park, the state Commission could be bypassed entirely, with both initial and final approvals being given by the federal Commission. Applicable state environmental standards and land-use criteria would still have to be satisfied, however.

Following construction of the facility, it would have to be inspected prior to operation to ensure that the facility as constructed complied with the approved designs. The need for a mandatory public hearing before operation of the facility, however, is not clear. Concern has been expressed about the degree to which lengthy operating permit hearings have prevented completed nuclear facilities from going on line, at great cost to utilities.[11]

Licensing bodies of course possess the discretion to reopen licensing proceedings during construction or operation of a facility, and order it to cease or modify operation if the public interest requires. But this discretionary power should not be elevated into a requirement of a public hearing before clearance to operate a newly built plant is given. This conclusion should apply to nuclear plants in particular, which are now subject to operating license requirements. Instead, the applicant should specify the plant's design in detail in its application to the federal Commission. Then, the Commission's staff would inspect the facility during construction to ensure that it followed the licensed design.

The question of proper administrative procedures is not as difficult with licensing proceedings as with generic proceedings. Licensing proceedings have been particularly extended by late interventions and lengthy discovery and cross-examination.[12] These problems should be attacked by providing for early and thorough notice and routine prehearing discovery by all participants of documents and other evidence. Oral depositions of potential witnesses should be permitted, either as a matter of course, but subject to protective order, or on a showing of need. In any case, the aim of these practices should be to make all parties to the proceedings aware at an early stage of the issues and the supporting evidence, so that little time need be devoted during the hearing to either discovery or cross-examination, and the hearing will be focused and expedited. After such full discovery has provided the information, but not before, the parties should be required to define their positions by submitting a list of the issues to be covered during the hearing, thereby speeding the process.

In addition to procedural devices specifically mentioned, both generic and case-by-case proceedings should be made subject to the usual powers of a hearing examiner or other trial officer to shape the conduct of the proceeding to make it as efficient as possible. Schedules for the proceedings could be worked out, and testimony could be required to be submitted in written form instead of orally. If the number of companies, individuals or groups wishing to participate fully in the hearing, with rights of discovery and cross-examination, exceeds a figure which in the discretion of the hearing examiner would permit an orderly proceeding, he should be empowered to require parties with similar interests to act through a single attorney and otherwise consolidate their actions.[13]

Two questions are raised with respect to judicial review: who has the right to appeal and by what standard should an agency's actions be judged? Recent developments in the law have, of course, greatly broadened the right to seek judicial review. These developments reflect the view that such a broadened right can improve the decision-making process, as well as lead to greater public acceptance of agency actions. Without a strong case being made that too many court challenges to agency action are being mounted now and that the problem will not be greatly alleviated by other proposed reforms, no attempt should be made to limit the right to seek review: all those who are parties to an agency proceeding, that is, should be able to appeal the decision resulting from that proceeding. However, multiple court appeals should be prevented by requiring consolidation of all appeals from agency action during the licensing process at each level of government.

Similarly, the generally applicable "substantial evidence" standard for judicial review should not be limited or broadened without a showing that such a change will significantly improve matters. The history of the administrative process in this country seems to show that in general the courts will defer to agencies they trust, and reverse the actions of agencies they distrust, without according dispositive weight to the precise language of the review standard. If this is so, primary attention should be directed toward developing trustworthy agencies and not experimenting with the words governing judicial power to review those agencies.

292

H. PUBLIC PARTICIPATION

1. GENERAL CONSIDERATIONS

Public participation in the formulation of power policies and the siting of particular facilities serves two purposes: it can improve the quality of the decision which is reached, and it can increase public confidence in both the particular decision and the decision-making process. Increasing public trust is especially important now, when many people are questioning the impartiality of regulatory agencies, and concern over the environment is high. Certainly it cannot be assumed that all public groups will act responsibly, any more than it can be assumed that utilities will always choose the best site for a new plant. The challenge is to provide means for constructive public participation while guarding against abuses.

Increased public participation need not mean increased delay. The proposed reforms already discussed will shorten and simplify the decision-making process (by resolving generic issues generically, for example, and limiting the number of issues which need be resolved at various stages), thereby making the problem of "delay" from public participation itself less significant. Moreover, increased public participation may actually decrease delay: in the short run, by raising relevant issues for agency consideration and thus making judicial reversals less likely, and in the long run, by increasing public confidence and making resistance to agency actions and policies less frequent.

An agency which is receptive towards increased public participation need not permit itself to be victimized by any participant in a proceeding, private or public, who engages in dilatory tactics for their own sake. Adequate procedures for such protection can be devised (and are discussed elsewhere in the Report). But the overriding attitude should be one of favor toward public involvement, not only in occasional licensing proceedings, but also in the formulation of long-range plans, as advocated by some industry groups [14] and practiced by some utilities.[15] In other words, the public's role should be a continuing one, like that of industry.

Public involvement in utility planning before a utility brings its plans or applications before a governmental agency for review, however, must necessarily be limited. Initially, many tentative steps are considered by the utility and often rejected, and even when particular

293

sites are selected, the process by which their fitness is assessed is very complicated. Extensive geological tests must be undertaken, for example, including core borings, to determine whether the ground structure is adequate. If the plant is near a river or other body of water, comprehensive studies of heat diffusion into the water body must be made, including the building of model tanks. Plant structures and fish life in the water body must also be studied. To determine possible air pollution effects, meteorological conditions around the plant and the relationship of the plant to other plants and to populated areas must be considered. All of these are highly technical problems, determinable by research and analysis, and the contributions which laymen can make are limited.[16]

Furthermore, under our private corporate system, not only are corporate officers required by law to make decisions, they are also charged with financial responsibility for the corporation. They must raise the money for the construction of the plant and for making the enterprise viable. Any decision which is made with respect to a new plant is fundamental to the financial integrity of the corporation. It is appropriate and not in derogation of the public interest that these officers should make the corporate decisions relating to plant siting, within the framework, of course, of appropriate public decision-making.

Public review of corporate decisions is obviously essential, and once the plans are submitted to government agencies, or applications are filed for specific projects, no objection can be raised to full audit and disclosure. If the studies which have been carried out have been inappropriate or have given inadequate consideration to environmental and other public concerns, the public bodies which have jurisdiction should turn the plans or applications down or propose modifications or alternatives: the decisions made by the corporate officers have to withstand public scrutiny. Public opportunity to comment and voice both suggestions and objections prior to final planning decisions will help to relieve pressures when projects which conform to and implement such decisions come up for regulatory review.

When regulatory review of specific projects begins, full public participation is essential, if one of the prime causes of present frustration—the feeling that a hearing following lengthy industry-agency negotiations in private will reach a foregone conclusion—is to be remedied. Notice should be given when utility contacts with agency staff are initiated, and agencies should develop guidelines concerning free availability of documents and access to staff. Those interested should have the opportunity to critique utility and staff plans and discuss their comments with the staff. At the staff's discretion, public groups should also be permitted to participate in utility-staff negotiations. If an adequate degree of public involvement is not achieved through the discretionary approach, further legislative remedies will be required. Utility-staff negotiations are clearly very important in the development of agency positions; opening these negotiations up recognizes their importance and tends to balance resources of information and expertise among utility, staff, and public groups without requiring any overt public support.

2. INFORMATION

Improved access to information is essential if the "responsible" public participation in agency proceedings universally desired is to become a reality, since no one can make an adequate presentation in the complex electricity/environment area without access to the facts. Greater information availability is also necessary if the general level of debate on electricity/environment issues, apart from particular proceedings, is to be raised.

Agencies should be explicitly required by statute to make public favorable and unfavorable information relating to all aspects of their developmental and regulatory functions as a matter of routine. In addition to the participation in pre-hearing industry-applicant negotiations discussed above, public groups should have regularized access to agency staff experts, to discuss general questions as well as particular applications. In inviting outside contact with agency staff, commissioners should emphasize appearances before environmental and consumer groups no less than those before industry trade associations. Agency attitudes exemplified by the FPC's recent refusal to surrender files to intervenors in the *Greene County* litigation except when under court order to do so [17] should be replaced by a recognition of such groups as partners in the decision-making process along with industry.[18] Routine disclosure of information would not only make participation in agency proceedings simpler for public groups, but would also help speed such proceedings, since the need for lengthy cross-examination and discovery procedures (including litigation under the Freedom of Information Act, as in *Greene County*), would be greatly lessened.

As important as improved access to information should be the generation of more information, for use by Congress and the agencies themselves as well as the general public. The federal Energy Commission, freed from any developmental duties, should be able to determine better the costs and benefits of the technologies it is regulating, as well as developing information for use by Congress in fixing demand policies. In particular, the Commission should focus on ways electricity and energy can be used more efficiently, and make recommendations on how more efficient use can be achieved. The federal Energy Agency, charged with developing all energy forms, should be better able to weigh the values of projects involving these different forms against one another.

3. AGENCY OPERATING PROCEDURES

Many agency operating procedures could easily be reformed to make participation by public groups generally simpler and more effective. Initially, notice of impending proceedings could be vastly improved. Many agencies now do no more than satisfy bare legal minima with respect to notice. Procedures should instead be adopted which are designed to bring proceedings to the attention of both the general public and interested subgroups of the public, in the most effective way possible.

Mailing lists of interested individuals and groups could be maintained, possibly divided by state or region. When an action affecting that state or region is to be initiated, notices could be mailed to all those on the relevant lists; groups on the list could be counted on to send further notices to their members. Applicants for licenses might be required to submit with their application lists of organizations from their area to be notified; past proceedings might well have brought such groups to the applicants' attention. All legislators and local and state officials from the affected area should automatically receive notice by mail, as well.

In publicizing the proceedings, reliance on smaller newspapers published solely within the affected area should be supplemented with press releases to large newspapers of state-wide, regional or national circulation, wire services and (probably most important) radio and television stations covering the affected area.

296

Also, the notice should make clear exactly how interested groups could participate in the proceeding and exactly what issues were to be resolved, highlighting those most likely to be subject to dispute. Such expanded notice, when coupled with periodic release by agency and utility of long-range plans, should ensure that concerned groups and individuals have a full and fair opportunity to participate in agency proceedings in a timely and intelligent fashion. This kind of notice could also help to speed up agency proceedings by making late interventions much less likely or necessary.

Other procedural hurdles to intervenors' participation which serve only to increase the cost burden on public groups without benefiting the result, ought also to be eliminated or modified. Any procedure which tends to frustrate public involvement should be tested to make certain it serves a legitimate purpose, which could not be as well served by a less restrictive procedure. Professor Ernest Gellhorn of the University of Virginia School of Law, in a recent report to the Administrative Conference, made several specific suggestions: multiple copy filing and distribution requirements should be minimized, hearing transcripts made available free or at reduced cost, agency files systematized for easier public use, access opened to agency experts as advisors and witnesses.[19]

4. Costs of Participation

Some observers contend, however, that these procedural modifications, even when coupled with improved notice and broader access to agency information, may not be enough to ensure intelligent public participation in the decision-making process. In the report cited above, Professor Gellhorn notes that "major licensing contests in the FCC or FPC often generate fees in excess of $100,000." [20] The question is thus raised whether direct subsidization, through, for example, award of attorney fees or reimbursement of costs incurred, or appointment of special government attorneys for public groups, is appropriate Such direct support is unquestionably controversial, and will inevitably raise difficult problems of choice: if not enough funds are available to pay each of several intervenors, for example, what criteria should be used to decide which group gets paid? Should the substance of intervenors' positions, or the quality of their work, or their ultimate success, affect the decision whether or not to pay them? What guarantee is there that the right of such direct support will not be abused by those seeking merely to obstruct? (A counter-argument might well be made here: the fact that a group has money, and thus can afford to participate under the present system, does not ensure that its participation will be constructive.)

While noting these and other difficulties in this area, Professor Gellhorn recommends award of attorney fees and costs to public groups where they can make a showing to the agency involved that "their participation has made a contribution to the decision." [21] The Administrative Conference recently refused to adopt this recommendation,[22] and the Committee believes that the problems inherent in such an approach, including the need for some disciplinary control over groups receiving aid, make it highly desirable to avoid using it through other reforms designed to lessen burdens on intervenors. The other reforms proposed to encourage constructive public participation should, therefore, be implemented wholeheartedly in an effort to make consideration of direct support unnecessary.

I. Workability

Can this decision-making process actually produce decisions? While less baroque than present methods, any such proposal for major reform requires careful examination of its feasibility. Feasibility should be considered from the vantage point of the utility as the producer of power, the government as administrative body, and the public interested in participating to advance environment, consumer, or other interests.

1. The Utility's Perspective

Utilities must produce power and, in so doing, raise the necessary capital. These functions require a relatively high degree of certainty that definite decisions will be forthcoming in good time to meet consumer demands and to put funds invested to work. They do not require freedom from public regulation. So, the most important question from the utilities' perspective is, can the system proposed produce clear and timely regulatory decisions?

The Committee's recommendations do suggest a complex system, but one much less complex than the present system and with significant advantages in regard to producing seasonable decisions. First, the system removes many of the most troublesome issues from the licensing process altogether through generic proceedings. While these generic determinations may be appealed, the appeal can begin a decade or more before the plant is actually needed. Second, while there are two required stages in the licensing of fossil plants and three for nuclear plants, they each deal with separate issues, so that the system does not require relitigation of issues. Moreover, the controversial issues will be taken up at the earliest licensing stage, the preliminary license, which is issued seven years before the plant is needed and which is the only licensing step requiring an environmental statement. Third, the system eliminates the Corps of Engineers water quality approval and no NEPA statements are required at the federal level during the licensing process. Fourth, while the host of secondary state and local permits are not prohibited, the state Siting Commission's broad jurisdiction may encourage the relaxation of such requirements and safeguards are included to prevent these permits from frustrating the process. In particular, the Siting Commission will have power to override other state and local requirements. An exception is made for the air and water emission review, but this proceeding is limited to determining whether the equipment is likely to live up to the specifications of the preliminary license. Moreover, the granting of any permit other than the construction license can be attacked only by appealing the construction license. The Committee believes that it is better to provide for an override and consolidated appeal rather than eliminate secondary permits altogether, so that local government has some scope to express its concerns without having a veto. As a final safeguard, in case the state process breaks down, the Energy Commission may override the entire state and local process.

Thus, the Committee believes this system compares favorably to the present process where any one of dozens of administrative decisions can veto a plant at the last minute and any decision not to veto the plant can be appealed separately. While more likely to produce timely decisions, the new process does subject more utility decisions to review. But, the decisions picked for review are those where the interests of the utility and the public do not necessarily coincide. The Committee prefers to impose accountability in these areas rather than to ask utility executives to be both public and private officials at once. By spelling out as much as possible of the public's interest in advance through generic criteria, the system allows scope to the utility industry to serve its stockholders and customers imaginatively within the regulatory framework.

2. THE ADMINISTRATIVE PERSPECTIVE

The recommendations put considerably more responsibility on the states.   The federal government should accordingly provide the states with a major portion of the needed funds.   Too often, fine sounding regulatory schemes have failed for want of adequate budgets.

The biggest new challenge to the regulatory system will be promulgating generic standards.   The major problem will be at the outset where there will be a backlog.   Accordingly, our recommendations provide for a transition period.   There may be a continuing problem with the regional allocation determination.   The techniques for forecasting demand have been well established by the utility industry and the federal Commission's work here will be to verify the industry projections.   But, a regional allocation of facilities is a relatively new undertaking outside of the systems planning context.   Many extremely complex factors are conceivably relevant, including reliability, cost, ecological systems, economic development, and transportation of fuels. It would be best to simply recognize this difficulty and provide that the Energy Commission shall ensure reliability and look into other factors as much as possible given the time and techniques available. Even a rough and ready consideration is likely to be more beneficial than the present allocation, which is determined in part by factors outside the control of utilities and regulators, such as traditional service areas and state boundaries.

3. INTERVENORS

The recommendations give intervenors one shot at the major issues, but a shot which allows them to make their points more effectively.   In particular, forums are provided to contest regional allocation and such generic issues as the disposal of nuclear wastes.   Intervenors may present their views to the Energy Commission on the demand issue, and participate in Congressional hearings on the Commission's recommendations.   Finally, the issues of site and generation mode will be litigated earlier and intervenors may dispute the safety of nuclear design before the staff and applicant have reached agreement.

300

The most significant remaining problem for intervenors will be one of resources, monetary and technical. Generic proceedings may allow intervenors to concentrate their efforts, and better disclosure policies will allow a larger flow of information. Intervenors' need for witnesses may be lessened somewhat by the funding of EPA to do environmental and safety research. EPA may choose to have its witnesses testify at proceedings. Moreover, the recommendations would codify the obligation of the Commissions' staffs, at both the state and federal levels, to set forth risks and benefits in straightforward terms. If the staffs respond, then intervenors need only supplement staff work and thus act as check. If not, public concern will continue to outrun intervenors' ability to raise questions.

J. A Start Must Be Made On The Energy Crisis Now

The nation is confronted with a dilemma. Many industry officials, and various government agencies, including the Federal Power Commission and the Office of Emergency Preparedness,[23] tell us that unless certain plants are licensed, some areas will suffer power shortages. Other responsible voices tell us that we are in the midst of a general energy crisis that cannot any longer be avoided.[24] While debate and resolution of major energy policy questions will take time, the licensing process needs immediate reform.

So, one possibility is to reform the licensing process and deal with energy policy later. This alternative is unsatisfactory because it presents a real danger that the energy crisis will not be addressed until is becomes an energy disaster. As Senator Ted Stevens stated in arguing that a National Land Use bill should be passed instead of a Coastal Land Use bill,

> ". . . [O]ne of the best ways to get a bill national in scope is to make certain that you do not let the hot spots go first. . . ."[25]

With a legislative process which gives the advantage to the *status quo,* dealing with the energy crisis will have to overcome substantial obstacles involving huge financial interests. We cannot now afford this delay. The reserves of certain critical fuels can be measured in

301

decades. Each year that more of our fuel, air, and water resources are used at growing rates lessens our remaining flexibility. Even when a solution is enacted, it must begin to take effect only slowly since the effect of prices on market behavior in the energy area is slow and price changes must initially be small so as to avoid dislocations in particular areas or industries. If, however, the environmental crisis is as bad as some scientists say, even quicker action through rationing may be necessary.

Another alternative is to insist that licensing reform await the resolution of the coming debate over general energy policy. But, it will take years or decades to assemble the information needed to debate all of the energy issues. While the nation might get by the next few years without new siting legislation, without it, reliability problems will probably compound in the decade to come. Thus, easing licensing problems may not be able to await resolution of the energy crises.

A third alternative, which we recommend, is to link licensing reform to structural changes in the regulatory process which will help to ensure that the broad issues of energy policy come to light. Included within that scheme should be the federal institutions already discussed for all forms of energy. The Energy Commission should be given the authority to prepare an Annual Energy Report and recommend to Congress future policies concerning demand. Such a restructuring would focus attention on the issues of demand, research fund allocation, and the regional allocation of facilities; it assumes a Congressional commitment to vote up or down legislation seeking to regulate the rate of energy growth.

It might be argued that we will have serious power shortages before the year or two needed to debate even this smaller set of issues is over. If so, legislation reforming the licensing process alone, such as the Administration Siting Bill, will not help, because it speaks in terms of five- or ten-year planning periods.[26] Moreover, it takes much more than five years to build a plant. If there will be blackouts in the next few years, the solution must be more radical, involving emergency legislation to provide compulsory curbs on power consumption, mandated firm sales of power, or expedited licensing of already constructed facilities. This narrower approach would be more responsive to short-run problems than a siting bill of general application, which could well prevent society from eventually coming to grips with the total crisis of energy and the environment.

> SHELDON OLIENSIS, CHAIRMAN
> MAURICE AXELRAD
> DANA C. BACKUS
> ALBERT K. BUTZEL
> WILLIAM F. KENNEDY
> ROBERT LOWENSTEIN
> ARTHUR W. MURPHY
> SHELDON RAAB
> DAVID SIVE

Dissenting, in major part, in appended statements:

> THEODORE J. CARLSON
> JAMES B. HENRY

Additional individual views of Messrs. Kennedy, Lowenstein and Murphy, Messrs. Sive and Butzel, and Mr. Backus are appended.

It is noted that the Executive Director and the Staff Attorneys differ with the Report in certain respects.

Notes for Chapter VIII

1. These examples are not intended to be exhaustive; in each case, federal and state interests would have to be identified and weighed. A barge-mounted plant close to shore may require different treatment from a plant further out, and it might be appropriate to return to the states authority over pumped-storage hydroelectric projects in those instances where the effect of the project on the water body involved is no greater than that of a steam generating plant.

2. 117 *Cong.Rec.* S.12922 (daily ed. Aug. 3, 1971) (remarks of Senator Magnuson).

3. *R & D Goals Task Force, Electric Research Council, Electric Utilities Industry Research and Development Goals Through the Year 2000* 5 (1971).

4. Amend. No. 364 to S.992, 92d Cong., 1st Sess. (1971). *See* Chapter VII (D), *supra*.

5. These disadvantages are discussed in an address by J. T. Ramey, "Nuclear Power and Lawyers: What are the Alternatives?" ALI–ABA Course of Study on Atomic Energy Licensing and Regulation, Washington, D. C., Nov. 11, 1971.

6. The only federal licensing agency with authority over fossil plants is the Corps of Engineers, but several agencies deal with different aspects of fossil fuel research.

7. Federal legislation to encourage comprehensive state land-use planning has been introduced, and is discussed in Chapter VII, *supra*. The system which this Committee is proposing would benefit if such comprehensive planning were undertaken, since with a comprehensive land-use commission, utilities would receive equal treatment with other industries, and dominance of such a board by any particular industry would be difficult. Comprehensive state land-use planning is not, however, essential to the success of the Committee's recommendations, although it is important that the siting body not be the state public utility commission.

8. This proposal assumes the establishment of such minimum standards, possibly by the federal Commission.

9. For a discussion of what procedures may be appropriate and legal and other obstacles to their adoption, *see* A. W. Murphy, *The National Environmental Policy Act and the Licensing Process: Magna Carta or Coup de Grace?, A Report to the Committee on Licenses and Authorizations of the Administrative Conference of the United States* (First Draft, April 7, 1972).

10. *Id.* at 52–53.

11. *See* Testimony by W. F. Kennedy, in *Hearings Before the Senate on Public Works and Senate Comm. on Interior and Insular Affairs*, 92d Cong., 2d Sess. (unpublished, Mar. 8, 1972).

12. A. W. Murphy, *supra* note 9, at 39–40.

13. Four Committees of The Association of the Bar of the City of New York, while recommending such consolidation powers, caution:

"The Committees do not believe that it is either necessary or appropriate to force the attorneys for one party on other parties, whatever the similarities of their interests. In this connection, however, the

Committees . . . agree that appropriate procedures should be developed to ensure that hearings are not delayed by repetitive presentations and examination."

Committees on Administrative Law, on Atomic Energy, on Environmental Law and on Science and Law, Comments on Legislation to be Proposed Regarding Procedures to Regulate Siting of Major Public Utility Facilities, at 19 (undated).

14. *See, e. g., Western Systems Coordinating Council, Environment Committee, Environmental Guidelines* 3 (1971).

15. Northern States Power Company has experimented with such "open planning," and its experience is described in *National Academy of Engineering, Committee on Power Plant Siting, Engineering for Resolution of the Energy-Environment Dilemma* 307–309 (1972).

16. This is not to say that non-expert public participation in policy decisions, as opposed to technical ones, is not valuable and necessary. Problems in treating technical issues in an adversary context are discussed in *B. B. Boyer, A Re-evaluation of Administrative Trial-Type Hearings for Resolving Complex Scientific and Economic Issues, A Staff Report to the Chairman of the Administrative Conference of the United States* (1971).

17. The Second Circuit criticized the FPC in its decision for raising procedural roadblocks to intervenors "at nearly every turn." Greene County Planning Board v. FPC, 455 F.2d 412, 417 (2d Cir. 1972).

18. One government agency recently proposed changing its rules to open previously secret files to the public. "F.D.A. Acts to End Policy of Secrecy and Open Files," N.Y. Times, May 5, 1972, at 1, col. 1.

19. *See E. Gellhorn, Public Participation in Administrative Hearings, A Report to the Committee on Agency Organization and Procedure of the Administrative Conference of the United States* 29–34 (1971).

20. *Id.* at 34.

21. *Id.* at 35.

22. Greene County Planning Board v. FPC, *supra* note 12, at 427.

23. *See* "F.P.C. Chief Warns 5 Regions Face Summer Power Shortages," N. Y. Times, Mar. 28, 1972, at 53, col. 1, "Power Shortages This Summer Are Feared by Administration," N. Y. Times, April 12, 1972, at 14, col. 1.

24. *See, e. g.,* J. D. Emerson, "Outlook for Energy in the United States," 27 *Bulletin of the Atomic Scientists* 18 (Oct. 1971).

25. *Hearings on S.582, S.632, S.638 and S.992 Before the Subcomm. on Oceans and Atmosphere of the Senate Comm. on Commerce,* 92d Cong., 1st Sess., ser. 92–15, at 264 (1971).

26. *See* the discussion of proposed legislation in Chapter VII, *supra.*

*

SUPPLEMENT A
INDIVIDUAL VIEWS OF
COMMITTEE MEMBERS

*

INDIVIDUAL VIEWS OF MESSRS. KENNEDY AND LOWENSTEIN AND PROFESSOR MURPHY

In separately stating our own views on the Report, we think it important to distinguish between (i) its basic recommendations in which we generally concur, with the qualifications noted below, and (ii) some of the rhetoric employed both to justify the conclusions and to characterize the present situation. We would have much preferred to have avoided retrospective characterizations of a long and complicated history and particularly of the roles of Federal and state agencies, industry and environmental organizations. However, to review point by point our numerous differences with the language and tone and specific statements in the Report, would divert discussion to secondary issues and would not contribute to an understanding of the policy choices to be faced in the next few years.

With this preliminary note, we would like to make some specific observations on the *recommendations* in the Report.

I.

The main value of these recommendations is that they can provide in the aftermath of the National Environmental Policy Act ("NEPA"),[1] a new starting point for reappraisal and reform of regulatory structures and procedures directed to electric power and the environment. Each of us joining in this statement has elsewhere expressed the view that NEPA has had a positive effect in requiring a disciplined analysis of environmental issues associated with expansion of electric generating and transmission capacity, but that it can also have negative effects when this analysis is attempted to be carried out in the context of a trial-type proceeding directed to whether a specific plant should be allowed to be built or whether a completed plant should be allowed to go on the line.

---

1. Pub.L. No. 91–190, Jan. 1, 1970, 83 Stat. 852, 42 U.S.C. § 4321 *et seq.* (1970).

The principal contribution of the Report is to recognize that the range of issues required to be considered in a NEPA review must be handled in a manner different from that contemplated under presently applicable statutes, notably as interpreted in *Calvert Cliffs*.[2]

1. Specifically we endorse the position in the Report that basic choices as to whether there should be constraints on demand for, or use of, electric energy cannot be effectively considered in the context of a review of a specific facility, and instead should be examined on a broad basis by the Congress. This view is predicated on a series of propositions, namely,

> (i) the effect of any conceivable restraints on our way of life and on the economy are so great that decisions should be made by officials directly accountable to the electorate,
>
> (ii) for the reasons suggested in the Report, these issues have to be considered at the national level rather than state-by-state,
>
> (iii) any restraints would probably have to be imposed very carefully and with considerable lead time, and
>
> (iv) in any event, it is wholly irrational to attempt to impose restraints indirectly by denying authorization for particular facilities.

We do not share the concern expressed in some industry comments about this aspect of the Report, basically because we are subscribing to it on the premise that what it calls for is Congressional examination and public debate, without prejudgment as to what the outcome should be. Certainly we have no prejudgment ourselves. We think the examination and debate are an essential corollary of taking the question out of individual plant reviews, that they are in any event inescapable, and that they will have a healthy effect in bringing before the general public the real questions and the hard choices. Without forecasting the outcome, we are prepared to abide it when it flows from this kind of political process.

However, although we endorse in the main the basic approach of the Report to constraints on demand and use, we would note two substantial qualifications:

2. *Calvert Cliffs Coordinating Committee* v. *Atomic Energy Commission*, 449 F.2d 1109 (D.C.Cir. 1971).

First, we do not mean to endorse by implication the idea of an energy tax which is given extended consideration in Chapter VI of the Report. We wish we had the professional economic competence to appraise this idea, but we do not, and at this stage we can only observe that the concept, or variants of it, may be worth some further discussion and debate.

Second, we note our disagreement with the cumbersome requirements for federal determinations with respect to demand. Questions as to whether generating capacity can be increased without serious prejudice to the environment do not require consideration annually; if such reviews are to be meaningful, they should be conducted as long-range studies at perhaps five-to-ten-year intervals by specially constituted fact finding panels comprised of members with outstanding credentials, rather than as a routine exercise by some federal agency.

2. Another major contribution of the Report to our mind is the recognition that supplying electric power needs of metropolitan areas such as New York or Los Angeles may require installation of generating and transmission capacity in other states and that a federal mechanism may be required to deal with this problem. The capacity allocation device suggested in the Report could serve this purpose. Not that preparing projections of capacity requirements as such should be all that intricate—although experience indicates that there can be errors in either direction; however, it is desirable to anticipate growing interstate conflicts of interest of the kind exemplified at Four Corners and the Report suggests a means for dealing with them which seems to us worth consideration. Also, it should be clear that the allocation device is not proposed as a back-door mechanism for limiting capacity.

In this area too, however, the Report proposes too much of a good thing. The whole concept of a federal determination of need is useful only where there is a potential for interstate conflict. Absent this potential, the need-projection, capacity-allocation procedure could be an unnecessary exercise. Broadly we think it desirable wherever possible to preserve utility company initiative and responsibility for planning and constructing new generating and transmission capacity.

3. Again, we think the Report makes a contribution in recognizing that issues such as land use and alternatives can more properly be considered at the state rather than the federal level. The incongruity of asking the Atomic Energy Commission, or possibly the Corps

of Engineers, to resolve these questions under the mandate of NEPA, hardly requires elaboration.

4. We strongly endorse the recommendation that wherever feasible issues be considered and resolved generically rather than case-by-case.

5. We support most emphatically the proposition that regulatory reviews with respect to such matters as siting and plant design should be completed prior to start of construction. The whole notion that basic environmental policy questions can be effectively considered after the plant has been built and prior to operation seems to us untenable.

6. We have three varying individual views on the specific changes in Federal Government structure proposed in the Report * but the three of us are in accord on some key propositions. First, we believe there should be a careful Congressional reexamination of federal organizational structure and consideration of a variety of detailed solutions. Second, we think it essential that major regulatory policies be set directly by officials appointed by the President and confirmed by the Senate, and not delegated. Third, we believe a strong case can be made for an integrated single agency approach to federally-supported research and development on energy/environment programs. In this connection, we are not persuaded that the Environmental Protection Agency is a logical vehicle for even the environmentally-oriented research and development called for in the Report. Fourth, we believe that regulatory matters common to both fossil-fuel plants and nuclear power plants should be administered by a single agency.

II.

This brings us to some specific points of difference with the Report.

1. We believe that the pros and cons of various forms of regulatory organization at the state level require further analysis. For example, careful consideration will have to be given to how to integrate general state land-use planning with specific planning for location of generating and transmission facilities. Also, the observa-

---

* Professor Murphy does not believe that the case has been made for separation of the regulatory and developmental functions of the Atomic Energy Commission. On the other hand, he concedes that separation may be a cliche whose time has come.

tion has been properly made in industry comments that a state body oriented to land-use planning is not necessarily the best equipped body to consider questions of alternatives—the choice, for example, between a fossil and nuclear station.

Again, we believe some further detailed consideration should be given to how best to integrate, both at state and federal level, the reviews of non-radiological discharges to air and water with other reviews.

2. The Report fails to deal plainly with the interrelationship between its recommendations for reform, and the requirements of NEPA. It seems to us that clear thinking in this area would be promoted by an explicit recognition that the regime proposed by the Report is a substitute for the system presently effective under NEPA as interpreted by *Calvert Cliffs* and other decisions.

For example, in the evaluation by a state of a proposed site for a generating facility what issues would be considered in an impact statement if demand, alternatives, and specific environmental effects are all considered elsewhere and are not subject to relitigation? Again in a proceeding to set standards for thermal discharges what issues would be considered in the impact statement different from those called for by the general legal requirement to make appropriate findings?

We submit that the whole theory of the case underlying the recommendations of the Report, namely, to consider defined issues (i) at separate stages, (ii) in different levels of government, (iii) generically whenever possible, and (iv) without relitigation—is inconsistent with the current procedures thought to be mandated by *Calvert Cliffs*, and that it is important to say this unequivocally.

3. Another thorny question requiring further work is the character of the procedure to be employed in each of the various reviews called for in the recommended new decision process. Those of us subscribing to this statement have varying views as to the value of trial-type procedure, and specifically about the role of cross-examination, but we would broadly propose the following:

First, the limited procedural rights traditionally associated with rule-making under the Administrative Procedure Act—namely, right to notice of the proposed action and opportunity for written comment—

313

seem to us inadequate.[3] In general, we would favor broad opportunity for discovery of private documents, liberal administration of the Freedom of Information Act with respect to government documents, and public hearings with provisions for direct testimony and rebuttal testimony (although much of this could be required to be in writing) and opportunity for briefs and oral argument.

Second, we doubt that other elements of trial-type process—notably a requirement for a decision based on substantial evidence on the record, and an opportunity for cross-examination—are suitable for arriving at many of the policy or value judgments involved in energy/environment tradeoffs. For example, any hearings designed to develop, for Congressional consideration, data and recommendations on the demand issue, should properly be of the traditional legislative-type rather than trial-type.

Third, we believe as a minimum that hearing officers should have and should exercise broad discretion in controlling cross-examination and that such cross-examination should be rigorously confined within the scope of issues previously specified after opportunity for full discovery.

4. Finally, we would note some differences with the views expressed in the Report on funding and management of research and development. Broadly we believe that there will be a continuing need for privately-financed work by manufacturers and others, and that on the other end of the spectrum there should be an expansion of federally-supported research and development financed out of general tax revenues. The currently relevant debate arises with respect to an intermediate approach under which additional research and development would be financed out of revenues derived directly from sales of electric energy. The question is whether these revenues should be raised by way of a Federal tax or by way of a rate surcharge collected by the utilities with regulatory commission approval; the related issue is

3. *American Airlines* v. *CAB*, 359 F.2d 624 (D.C.Cir. 1966), *cert. denied*, 385 U.S. 843 (1966); *Walter Holm & Co.* v. *Hardin*, 449 F.2d 1009 (D.C.Cir. 1971); Boyer, A *Re-evaluation of Administrative Trial-Type Hearings for Resolving Complex Scientific and Economic Issues*, a Staff Report to the Chairman of the Administrative Conference, December 1, 1971; Murphy, *The National Environmental Policy Act and the Licensing Process: Magna Carta or Coup De Grace?*, April 7, 1972, prepared for the Administrative Conference; Kennedy, *Nuclear Electric Power and the Environment—New Regulatory Structures and Procedures*, American Law Institute—American Bar Association Course on Atomic Energy Regulation, November 13, 1971.

how the research and development supported by these funds will be managed—by a federal agency with industry consultation, or by an industry-managed entity with close federal government collaboration. These seem to us practical questions negotiable among reasonable people rather than broad issues of principle.

July 7, 1972

INDIVIDUAL VIEWS OF MESSRS. SIVE AND BUTZEL

We endorse and support the principal recommendations of the Report. Out of an initial disparity, there has, in our view, been fashioned a substantial consensus—and it is a consensus with which we agree.

At the same time, we would be remiss if we failed to note certain reservations that attend our general approval. These reservations stem largely from our belief that the ethic of constantly increasing power usage is no longer a matter of merely academic concern, but poses for our society—*today and not tomorrow*—the fundamental question of whether we can afford it from the standpoint of our environment. In this regard, the Report, in its initial chapters, indicates some of the problems which may ensue if growth in electrical usage continues unchecked. Yet, in its final recommendations the Report leaves the usage issue to uncertain congressional action in the future, and then only in the context of the "possible" as distinguished from the "essential".

The consequences of the foregoing, as we see it, are to reendorse indirectly the validity of constantly increasing power usage and, at the same time, to continue to relegate to a subordinate status questions of environmental protection. For as long as increasing demand is to be met without question, new plants and new transmission lines will have to be built regardless of the environmental consequences. In our view, these consequences are already far too serious to justify the perpetuation of the historical approach; and projections for the future being what they are, we believe it essential that the validity of the historical ethic be faced now.

In short, we believe that what has been characterized as the "demand issue" cannot be left to some abstract consideration in the indefinite future, but must be opened to resolution beginning today. And in this regard, as indicated, our view is that the Report falls short. Furthermore, because the failure to stress the need for immediate action on the demand issue perpetuates the assumption that all demand *must* be met, there is an inevitable downgrading of environmental prob-

316

lems—as if these are not really so serious as to require immediate attention.

We do not suggest that there can be an instant resolution, on a
comprehensive basis, of the conflicts inherent in the demand for more
power and the increasingly critical need to safeguard our environment before it is too late. But in our view, a beginning must be made
now—and within a context which, at the very least, recognizes an
equality between meeting power demands and protecting the environment, rather than perpetuating by inaction the priority of the former. In
this last connection, we note that in adopting its recently enacted Power
Plant Siting Bill, the State of New York has already moved in this
direction, providing in the Preamble to that Bill as follows:

> "The legislature hereby finds and declares that there is at
> present and may continue to be a growing need for electric
> power and for the construction of new major steam electric
> generating facilities. At the same time it is recognized
> that such facilities cannot be built without in some way af-
> fecting the physical environment where such facilities are
> located, and in some cases the adverse effects may be serious.
> The legislature further finds that it is essential in the public
> interest that the factors of meeting power demands and pro-
> tecting the environment be regarded as equally important and
> that neither be subordinated to the other in any evaluation
> of the proposed construction of major steam electric gener-
> ating facilities. Without limiting the generality of the fore-
> going, the legislature finds and declares that under certain
> circumstances power demands may be regarded as controlling
> even though the adverse environmental impact may be sub-
> stantial, but that under other circumstances, given the nature
> of the resource involved and the public interest in preserving
> and enhancing the quality of life, the protection of the en-
> vironment may be regarded as controlling even though this
> might result in restrictions on the availability of public utility
> services."

We had hoped that the Special Committee's recommendations
would deal more directly with this basic question of resolving priorities and face more frontally the serious environmental consequences that have followed, and will undoubtedly continue to follow,
from the assumption that all demand must be met. Unfortunately,

317

by relegating the issue to the indefinite future, we do not believe that the recommendations have done so. Whether, as a consequence, the resolution of the question should now be carried forward on a case-by-case basis or rather be dealt with in generic-type proceedings remains to us an open issue. But of one thing we are convinced: we simply cannot afford a resolution by default over the next 10 or 20 years, since the damage once done can never be repaired.

We also hold some limited reservations over the administrative process that is suggested by the Report. In this regard, we have no quarrels with, and, indeed, affirmatively support, the administrative structure that has been proposed and the allocation of decision-making responsibilities at both the Federal and state level. Our reservations rather arise from our doubt that, however well intentioned, administrative agencies will be able to free themselves of the biases that have often resulted in regulators becoming promoters.

The answer to this recurring problem is not, as we see it, to dispense with the administrative process. On the contrary, we would view this as a serious mistake. Rather, we believe that the decision-making process must be tempered in another way—and in this regard, we believe the role of the courts to be the key.

The Report would retain a narrow role for the courts in their review of administrative action. With this, we disagree. However, by this disagreement, we do not suggest a role of *de novo* review for the courts, or a broadscale disregard for agency expertise. Rather, what we believe essential is that courts be given the freedom to deal with essential value judgments, in the context of changing times and in a manner which does not restrict them to merely procedural matters. The courts, in short, should have the authority to cross the substantive threshold where the balancing of competing values, rather than technical expertise, is the real issue. Without at this point going into any extended discussion of the scope of judicial review of administrative environmental determinations, we believe that such a balancing function can be exercised by the courts under the Administrative Procedure Act, other statutes, and the generally accepted statements of the scope of such review.

INDIVIDUAL VIEWS OF
MR. BACKUS

First I wish to pay tribute to the diligence of Committee members and Staff members in setting out the manifold problems and some solutions in the energy area.

Emergency Licensing. A system which must rely on Congress to pass special legislation to avoid in meritorious cases the delays of the procedures generally applicable is not carrying out its full functions. The idea of having an already existing agency of the government so empowered has merit to take care of special situations. Indeed as to atomic plants, an interim authority in this area has already been given to the Atomic Energy Commission under recent legislation (June 2, 1972 PL 92–307; 37 Fed.Reg. 11871 of June 15, 1972). It is just human nature for individuals who face losses in the short term not to appreciate the long term merit of environmental standards. A safety valve for reasonable exceptions under the circumstances could be most useful to all concerned.

The Proposal of a New Separate Agency for Research and Development has been made by the Committee. This would be separate from the proposed new Commission which would act as the licensing and regulatory body with authority over hydro and atomic plants to which would be added new authority over fossil fuel plants.

Lawyers naturally think of separating rule making and licensing from R and D. Under a strong Commission with a clear mandate, there are those who think the lawyers' views are not essential in this type of situation. Be that as it may, it is important to preserve expertise of the Atomic Energy Commission and not to ignore its long record of progress in the field. It is therefore suggested, that the Atomic Energy Commission continue and have its research directive expanded also to cover fossil fuel research and hydro plant research as well as solar batteries and more unusual power sources. In addition to its role in the atomic power field, a clear mandate could give it valuable authority to be an all-inclusive research energy commission for scientific progress.

319

Reliance upon Construction License. Once the various standards have been met to justify a construction license, the Committee voted that the utility should be able to rely on the construction license. Indeed given the requirement for going to the public for investment funds and relying on the customers to come forward for the use of the new facility, no other course is economically feasible. Of course the construction should meet the terms of the license. Modifications in the license to allow improvements in the state of art should not be considered a new license.

General. Of course in an effort as ambitious as that of the Committee, it is inevitable that some individual members will not subscribe to all portions of the Report. Nevertheless, it must be remembered that the Report is an intelligent and sincere effort to find a balance between the limitations which environmental good health places on man's activity and the human desire to use power and energy for economic goals.

SUPPLEMENT B
DISSENTING STATEMENTS
OF COMMITTEE MEMBERS

*

DISSENTING VIEWS OF MR. CARLSON

The Report represents a major effort to deal with fundamental problems related to society and its energy use. It is the result of a great deal of hard work and study and contains many useful and provocative ideas. I believe that its basic recommendations are rational and based upon a thoroughly considered understanding of the issues as seen from many points of view. Its recognition of the essentiality of both environmental requirements and the need for electricity is progressive. Its emphasis upon generic attention to decision making is encouraging.

I am disappointed, however, that the Committee, having a broad portfolio to study legal institutions, could not have found a new approach which did not follow the old format of administrative proceedings. Regulatory mechanisms always appear so attractive on paper, but in practice tend to become frustrating. The regulatory process recommended by the Report, logical and reasonable as it might appear, could be so burdensome as to significantly affect the ability of the industry to operate. The well-being of the industry is too easily taken for granted; and just as the well-being of the railroad industry at an earlier date was taken for granted, it is assumed that the electric industry can continue no matter what system of regulation is imposed on it. The industry literally could be killed by regulatory "featherbedding." It is already overjudicialized, and is rapidly becoming more unattractive to investors and also to capable people of the younger generation as an industry in which to seek employment. It would be refreshing for a change to see some suggestions for a deregulation of the industry, all consistent with a concern for the public interest, and a recognition that governmental agencies, even when operated efficiently with the best of personnel, do not have, by virtue of their being governmental, a peculiar and special insight as to what the public interest is.

The Report accepts the common tendency to suggest that solutions to industrial problems will be obtained by transferring the major decision making functions to governmental officials. The ultimate consequence of this tendency in the utility industry will be to provide for electric supply by and through public authorities. Under such a system, the role of a conservationist, among others, may be far more difficult than it now is.

In contrast, I would have hoped that a recognition could have been made that corporate officers, as duly constituted representatives of state chartered bodies corporate and subject to liabilities and to disclosure requirements, are public officers and are responsive to the community will *when that will is clearly expressed.* Mechanisms for increasing the responsibility of public corporations in the general directions suggested in the many writings of the late Professor A. A. Berle and recently by Professor Phillip I. Blumberg should be explored; and ways for increasing community inter-associational activity should be considered. We should be looking for more vibrant, ebullient institutions than those which are based upon the often tedious processes of regulation.

Furthermore, I have three additional concerns:

1. The Report gives little or no recognition to economic factors and the needs of a very extensive industry to raise large amounts of capital in a competitive market. Ramifications of the economic questions show up in many ways, including the need for the maintenance of an institutional framework for decision making by the entity which has the function of amassing the capital necessary for construction. The responsibility for initiating decisions which relate to the need for obtaining money must remain with those entities which are accountable therefor. This means that the private utility must have a considerable degree of flexibility in its operations and an assurance of success in its endeavors.

2. The Report fails to recognize the contemporary development of effective clean air and clean water standards and the vast steps which the industry has undertaken in the last few years in pollution control. In fact, with reference to fossil fuel plants, major environmental problems are already being dealt with; for, if to the present stringent clean air and clean water controls there could be added land use regulations, it seems to me that environmental concerns would be satisfied. A state system, somewhat akin to zoning, could be devised which would clearly indicate areas which would be forbidden to industry and other areas which would be clearly in society's interest to be used for industrial purposes. If a fossil-fueled utility plan then were

proposed to be built in any of those areas, i. e., those set aside for industrial use, and the plant satisfied stringent clean air and clean water standards, the plant could presumptively be constructed with only minimal review. The presumption could be negated by demonstration of special circumstances, but in most instances prompt and economical construction could be undertaken with complete environmental assurances.

3. While I know that the Report does not suggest the precise mechanisms for dealing with the question of demand, to the extent that the Report suggests implicity or explicitly that a federal or regional governmental agency or even Congress might at some point restrict demand by regulatory or legislative measures or try to allocate the installation of capacity among regions, the Report, I believe, is moving literally in an impossible area. Any such suggestion is without precedent; and in the areas in which regulation remotely similar has been tried, the process has been complicated, difficult and unsatisfactory with results which can only be characterized as dubious. The intended goals, I believe, are literally beyond the capacity of the administrative process to achieve. Even the existence of a possible power to allocate the installation of capacity would create incomparable political pressures as well as economic ones and its exercise will produce an incalculable effect upon the economic ecology. This does not mean that conservation efforts, such as building codes requiring construction procedures which will diminish the use of electricity, codes requiring efficient devices and other mechanisms should not be pursued, but any direct restrictions on the demand for electricity may require even broader societal controls. Any such proposals will necessarily involve broad economic planning, which, it is hard to believe, would be acceptable to the American people.

In somewhat the same vein, although he did not deal with the question of restraining demand, Chairman Swidler indicated at the public hearing of the Committee his view that the imposition of power allowables and the allocation of such allowables to states and regions was wrong in principle and would be impractical except as part of a completely planned society.

This conclusion seems inescapable to me.

Notwithstanding these comments, I believe the Report provides a basic and long-range view of social problems which must be faced and it has been a great pleasure to participate in the dialogue through which the Report was prepared.

DISSENTING VIEWS OF
MR. HENRY

The Report, "Electricity and the Environment," is the product of a great deal of hard and conscientious work and contains many useful ideas and much valuable information. I agree with many of its conclusions, such as the desirability of dealing with as many issues as possible in generic proceedings rather than in licensing proceedings for individual plants.

Unfortunately there are also recommendations with which I do not agree, and certain of these go to the heart of the Report—namely, the concept that a new federal agency structure should be created to deal with aspects of the licensing of all power plants. I think that this proposal can be justified only if all three of the following express or tacit positions taken in the Report are valid: (1) that the generation of electric power by any method in the amounts which can be now projected is in the long run inconsistent with adequate preservation of the environment; (2) that a solution of this problem can be furthered by creation of yet another federal scheme to regulate certain aspects of the electric power industry; and, (3) that an important contribution can be made to such a solution by the unlimited participation as parties in agency proceedings of self-appointed special interest groups, such as those which often designate themselves as "public interest" groups or as groups representing "the public."

1. *The environment-electricity "dilemma".*

The recommendations of the Report are designed to deal not with short-term problems of electric power supply but rather with the long-term* reconciliation of the supply of power in adequate amounts with the environmental impact of producing and delivering such power.

The statement of this proposition illustrates its difficulties when the field being dealt with is both new and rapidly changing. The decision-maker must assume the mantle of a prophet. It is not pertinent, for example, to point to the "energy crisis" which may or may

* Report VIII–J and elsewhere.

326

not occur during the next few years. If there are energy shortages in certain regions of the country they will be the product of short-term causes, such as (1) unanticipated delays in delivery of equipment, (2) unanticipated work stoppages in erection of generating stations, (3) unanticipated difficulties in putting into service new types and sizes of generators, and, above all, (4) unanticipated delays created by intervention of self-styled "public interest" groups.

The plan proposed by the Report does not purport to deal with the first three of these causes, nor could it; and it could only exacerbate the fourth. The plan can work only for an industry geared to a lead time of ten years or more, as is apparent from the discussion of timing in Chapter VIII, Part D of the Report. I doubt that any proponent of it would suggest that the first power plant built under the legislative scheme advocated by the Report could possibly go into service before, say, 1982. Since the lead time for a major generating station at present runs about eight years for a nuclear and five years for a fossil-fuel plant, after one takes into account the time for enacting the legislation and conducting licensing proceedings under the new regulatory scheme 1982 seems optimistic.

But if that analysis is correct, the discussion of the environmental aspects of power generation in Chapter III of the Report is entirely academic. What is the relevance, in developing a regulatory scheme, of such statements as those in Chapter III, Part A, "Sulfur emissions from power plants may in 2000 even exceed natural sulfur emission," and "An individual large power plant can emit 1000 tons of sulfur oxides a day" and ". . . studies have also associated sulfur oxides statistically with respiratory and cardiac disease, and rises in death rates." Even if taken at face value, these statements tell us nothing about 1982. The Environmental Protection Agency has issued regulations, 37 Fed.Reg. 5767 (March 21, 1972), requiring all new power plants to limit production of sulfur dioxide, beginning in 1975, to a nominal amount; and many states are propounding regulations requiring backfitting of emission control equipment on existing plants. The fact that at present there is no commercially proven technology for controlling sulfur dioxide emissions does not mean that by 1982 there will not be such technology, in view of the commitment made by the members of Edison Electric Institute on June 6, 1972 to expend annually upward of $150,000,000 on research and development, and other commitments of the industry to expend additional significant amounts for such purposes, a substantial part of which will undoubtedly go into developing sulfur emission controls, and in view of the many projects already devoted to this subject.

Sulfur dioxide is the product of fossil-fuel generation which has been most widely regarded as having undesirable health consequences. The facts that properly designed tall stacks disperse sulfur dioxide emissions over an area so wide that the increment at any particular point at ground level is often not measureable *, and that the effects, if any, of sulfur dioxide on health in the concentrations which power plants can produce are not well documented **, facts not adequately covered in the Report, illustrate that conclusions on environmental issues are often based on speculation rather than facts.

But even if sulfur dioxide would truly become a menace if unchecked, the fact that the industry and existing agencies are already committed to bringing it under control eliminates it as a reason for creation of a new agency. Precisely the same is true of other power plant emissions, such as particulates, nitrogen oxides, radioactive wastes and thermal discharges. After all, the whole environmental concern in its present activist phase is hardly more than four years old, and to call for radical solutions when the problem has not been formulated is not a responsible course.

Thus the creation of another federal regulatory scheme cannot at present be justified on environmental grounds. But if it is not to protect the environment from pollution, a field already occupied, such a scheme can have only one of two principal purposes: (1) it can be a vehicle for dealing with the "demand question"; or (2) it can assist electric utilities in obtaining plant sites or permits when obstacles have arisen which threaten to bring about inadequate power supply if plant sites or permits are not obtained expeditiously.

a. *The "demand question."*

There has arisen, together with the pure environmental issue, what I can only characterize as a mystique that the time has come to

---

* "The Tall Stack for Air Pollution Control on Large Fossil-Fueled Plants", a collection of recent papers with an introduction by Phillip Sporn (1967); "Tall Stacks—How Effective Are They?", Clarke, Lucas and Ross, Second International Clean Air Conference (1970).

** What Sulfur Dioxide Problems?" Ross, Combustion, August, 1971 Vol. 43, No. 2; "Air Pollution Study is Industry's Largest Health Related Research Project," EEI Bulletin, March–April, 1972, P. 78.

retrench consumption of power, or "to limit demand", as this concept is often stated. I suppose this could be called a quasi-environmental issue. The Report expressly, and correctly, leaves the implementation of such a limitation of consumption to Congress. However, one cannot escape the impression that a primary assumption upon which the regulatory framework proposed in the Report is erected is that Congress will find a necessity to limit demand. As discussed above, this conclusion cannot at present be based validly on pollution problems. There appear to remain only two other bases for "limiting demand" (1) conservation of fuel, and (2) unwillingness to assign land for power plant sites. Are these considerations sufficiently weighty to call for limiting demand, with all the obviously undesirable consequences of such a step, including degradation of our standard of living and in many ways of the environment. (After all air-conditioning is part of our environment, and lack of it has an impact on health.)

Conservation of fuel is without question a desirable thing, but in itself conservation of existing fuels can never be a long range solution to the energy problems with which society must deal. No one can doubt that fossil fuels will one day be exhausted. On the other hand, there can be no doubt that there are adequate supplies of coal to meet any anticipated demand for power for substantially more than one hundred years from now, that uranium exists in sufficient quantities to produce power for many thousands of years if breeder reactor technology is perfected, and that chances are excellent that within the next fifty years other power sources, such as fusion, will prove to be practicable.

Accordingly, the problem of conserving fuel is too long range to be dealt with today by new administrative mechanisms. There is no reason, assuming we have remaining a fossil-fuel supply of one hundred and fifty years, to try to stretch it to three hundred years. That problem can be and will be solved by other methods.

b. *Plant siting.*

There remains one possible reason for creation of a new agency structure, and that is plant siting. Obviously any generating station will have an environmental impact upon the land on which it sits and the surrounding neighborhood from which it can be seen. However, assuming it creates no significant pollution, I suggest an effort to prevent construction of a power plant just because it will exist—*i. e.*, to

329

"limit demand" for this reason—is trivial. The question is not whether it will be built but where it will be built.

Is this problem sufficiently grave to require a new federal agency structure? Perhaps it is, because of the rising activism among those who want the power plant if it is built in someone else's back yard. However, as discussed below, experience teaches that federal agencies are not good vehicles for solving such problems, and indeed Report VIII–B–5 largely leaves this type of problem to state and local authorities.

2. *The shortcomings of federal agencies.*

The purpose of the foregoing discussion was to show an absence of need for a new federal regulatory scheme to deal with the electric utility industry's impact on the environment. However, assuming that it has failed in that purpose and that it is believed that the industry's impact on the environment is not already sufficiently regulated, the question remains as to what contribution a new federal scheme superimposed on the Federal Power Commission, the Atomic Energy Commission, the Environmental Protection Agency, etc. can make.

I submit that the only contribution a federal agency could make would be to expedite the securing of a plant site acceptable to all those substantially affected. However, under present practice in administrative proceedings, it is doubtful that a federal agency can do this. In fact, injecting a federal agency into plant siting would in all likelihood produce quite the reverse result.

It is precisely because there is at present no federal agency with jurisdiction over construction of new fossil-fuel generating plants that this country has not already been the victim of severe power shortages. The minor power shortages of the past few years are in part directly attributable to the inability of the Atomic Energy Commission and the Federal Power Commission, and the courts which review their decisions, to deal adequately with the delays created by intervenors who purport to represent "the public" on environmental issues in the licensing of atomic and hydroelectric generation projects. A federal agency designed to deal with the necessity of eliminating delays in getting generation and transmission facilities in service may ultimately be required in view of the increasing amount of regulation which is now coming into existence at state and local levels. But the emphasis for such an agency should be to eliminate roadblocks, not to encourage them.

Unfortunately the administrative process as it has developed in this country appears in many instances to be incapable of dealing with an adversary proceeding. The fault lies primarily with hearing examiners, who have in general shown themselves unable or unwilling to control introduction of immaterial "evidence" and endless cross-examination in proceedings before them, even when the obvious purpose was delay.

Accordingly, if an agency is created to control plant siting, it should be made clear in the Act that creates it that special interest groups, while free to appear and present their views in the proceedings, will not be regarded as parties with the right to cross-examine or appeal. Otherwise the agency will be worse than useless.

There is a further point about such an agency. A natural question is why the electric power industry should be singled out for environmental regulation in view of the fact that many other industries, such as steel, aluminum and chemicals, also produce pollutants. If, however, there is deemed to be justification for special controls for the electric power industry, as distinguished from other manufacturing industries and other energy industries, then all the responsibility should be lodged in a single agency, including the setting of environmental standards. The Environmental Protection Agency has already demonstrated through standards ordered by it, and particularly its sulfur dioxide emission standards premised upon a presently nonexistent technology, that it does not understand the power industry. If a new agency structure is to be created to regulate the electric power industry, that structure should prescribe environmental standards and be clearly responsible for power shortages which may flow from unrealistic standards.

3. *The role of special interest groups.*

The position in the Report with which I most strongly disagree is that with respect to what is characterized as "public participation" in part VIII–H of the Report and elsewhere. "The public" does not participate in administrative proceedings. Various groups with particular points of view may intervene in order to try to prevent a project from being licensed or to impose conditions for the licensing. Such groups have in recent years won great victories in procedural law, such

331

as being accorded standing to sue and right to appeal. In general, however, most such groups would be hard put to show any achievements of substance, other than success through delay and attrition which are in the long run likely to be contrary to the public interest.

The Report discusses the proposition that such special interest groups might somehow be subsidized and, while not adopting this view, refers at some length to the suggestions of Professor Ernest Gellhorn along these lines. I dissent vigorously from any type of public support of special interest groups.

The fact that such groups have difficulty in raising funds is a concrete demonstration of the fact that they do not represent the public. If any substantial segment of the public cared about the particular hobby-horses that such groups may ride in a given situation, funds would be made available by the public for such purposes.

The protector of the public interest is, of course, the agency which licenses the activity in question. The sort of participatory democracy contemplated in the Report can create nothing but chaos, as has been amply demonstrated in recent licensing proceedings before the Atomic Energy Commission.

The one issue requiring legislative action today is the development of a method of giving all members of the public, and of the special interest groups, an adequate opportunity to present their views to decision-making bodies, while withdrawing the power to enforce particular prejudices through delay. Various measures could produce this result—limiting the right of cross-examination, limiting the right of appeal, requiring the posting of a bond in appropriate cases, requiring intervenors to respond in damages for unjustified delay. Some or all of these measures may be presently available in appropriate cases. But my principal objection to the Report is that it fails to grasp this nettle and suggest a plan for controlling special interest groups while allowing full freedom for all to express their views in a useful and noncoercive manner.

END OF VOLUME